Vampire Game

JUDAL

Translator - Ikoi Hiroe
English Adaptation - Jason Deitrich
Associate Editor - Tim Beedle
Retouch and Lettering - Abelardo Bigting
Cover Layout - Anna Kernbaum

Editor - Nora Wong
Digital Imaging Manager - Chris Buford
Pre-Press Manager - Antonio DePietro
Production Managers - Jennifer Miller, Mutsumi Miyazaki
Art Director - Matt Alford
Managing Editor - Jill Freshney
VP of Production - Ron Klamert
President & C.O.O. - John Parker
Publisher & C.E.O. - Stuart Levy

E-mail: info@TOKYOPOP.com

Come visit us online at www.TOKYOPOP.com

A  Manga

TOKYOPOP Inc.
5900 Wilshire Blvd. Suite 2000
Los Angeles, CA 90036

Vampire Game Vol. 6

ISBN: 1-59182-558-X

First TOKYOPOP printing: May 2004

10 9 8 7 6 5 4 3 2

Printed in the USA

VAMPIRE GAME

Volume 6

by

JUDAL

Los Angeles • Tokyo • London

VAMPIRE GAME
The Story Thus Far...

This is the tale of the Vampire King Duzell and his quest for revenge against the good King Phelios, a valiant warrior who slew the vampire a century ago. Now Duzell has returned, reincarnated as a feline foe to deliver woe to... well, that's the problem. Who is the reincarnation of King Phelios?

Duzell and the Princess Ishtar have journeyed to Ci Xeneth to investigate two of Ishtar's relations: her uncle Jened and his daughter Falan. Pretending to be twin siblings named, well, Du and Ishta, Duzell and Ishtar have infiltrated the palace and befriended Illsaide, the Captain of the Guard. Especially Duzell. Mistakenly believing the Vampire King to be of the fairer sex, Illsaide has asked Duzell to be his fiancée, an offer that Duzell has begrudgingly accepted, knowing that it will allow him to get closer to Jened and Falan. Surprisingly, the plan seems to be working. Sneaking a quick taste of Falan's blood, Duzell is able to rule her out as the reincarnated Phelios.

Ishtar, meanwhile, has been doing what she does best—getting into trouble. Wandering into Jened's basement, she's surprised to find a collection of creatures even uglier than her uncle. Diaage, Jened's High Sorcerer, explains that the creatures are used to create Ruelles, magical objects of great power. As the weight of this lesson sinks in, Ishtar's uncertain what she finds more disturbing, the discovery that her uncle is willing to sacrifice living beings to feed his freaky fetish...or the realization that Sidia, the magic sword she's come to depend on, is powered by the souls of Duzell's fallen comrades.

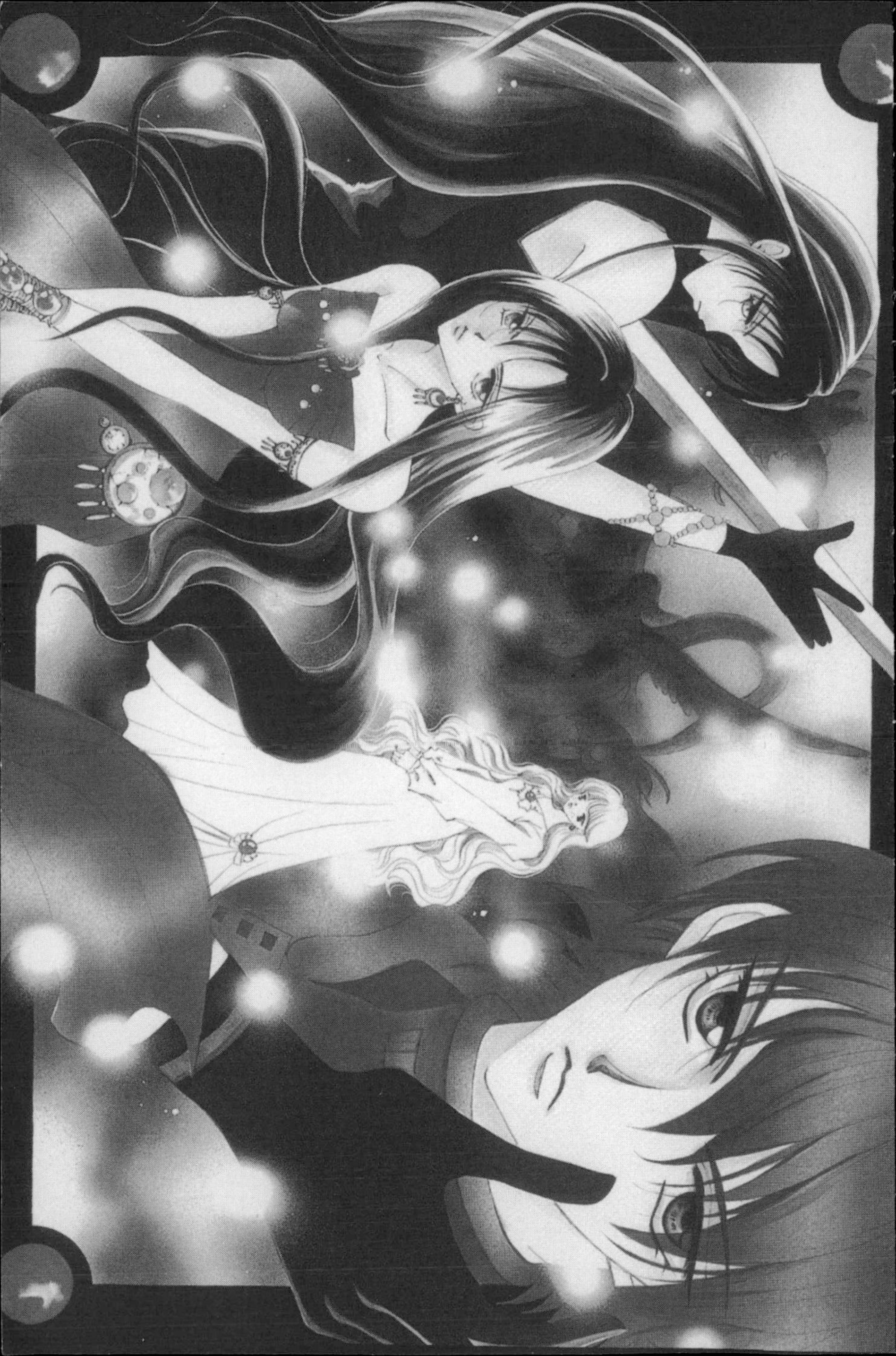

Table of Contents

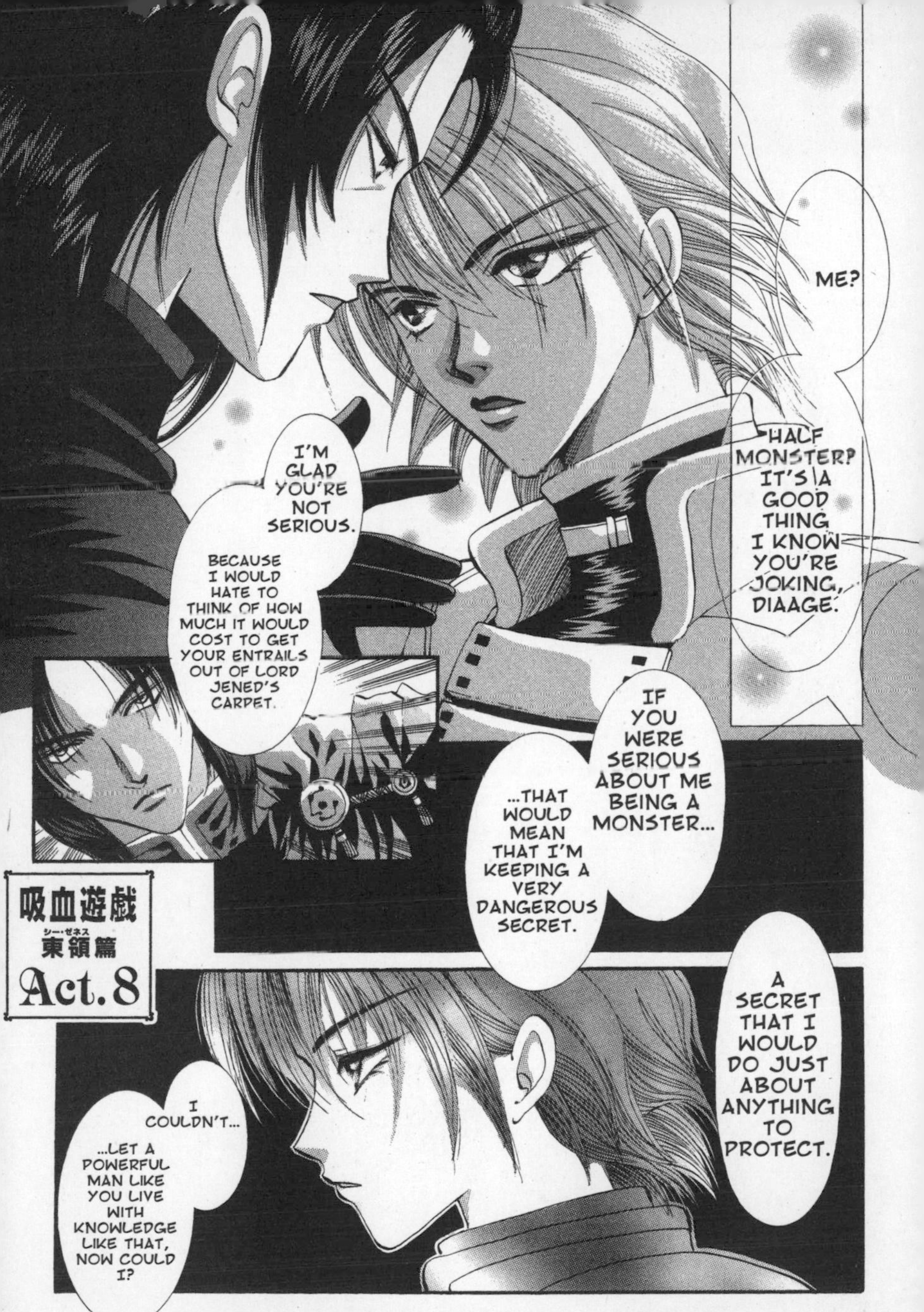
ME?
HALF MONSTER? IT'S A GOOD THING I KNOW YOU'RE JOKING, DIAAGE.
I'M GLAD YOU'RE NOT SERIOUS.
BECAUSE I WOULD HATE TO THINK OF HOW MUCH IT WOULD COST TO GET YOUR ENTRAILS OUT OF LORD JENED'S CARPET.
IF YOU WERE SERIOUS ABOUT ME BEING A MONSTER...
...THAT WOULD MEAN THAT I'M KEEPING A VERY DANGEROUS SECRET.
吸血遊戯
東領篇
Act. 8
A SECRET THAT I WOULD DO JUST ABOUT ANYTHING TO PROTECT.
I COULDN'T...
...LET A POWERFUL MAN LIKE YOU LIVE WITH KNOWLEDGE LIKE THAT, NOW COULD I?

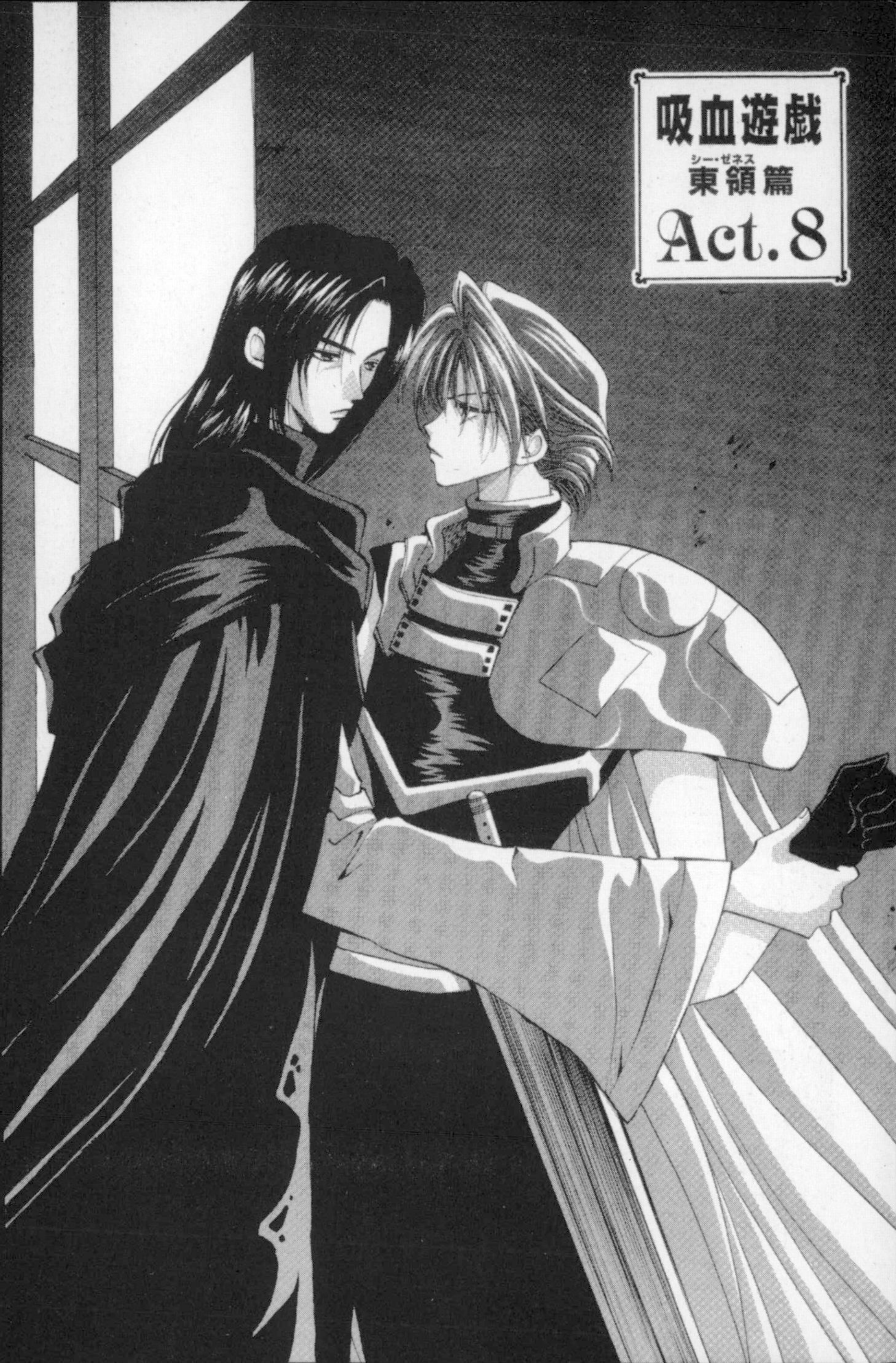
吸血遊戯
シー・ゼネス
東領篇
Act. 8

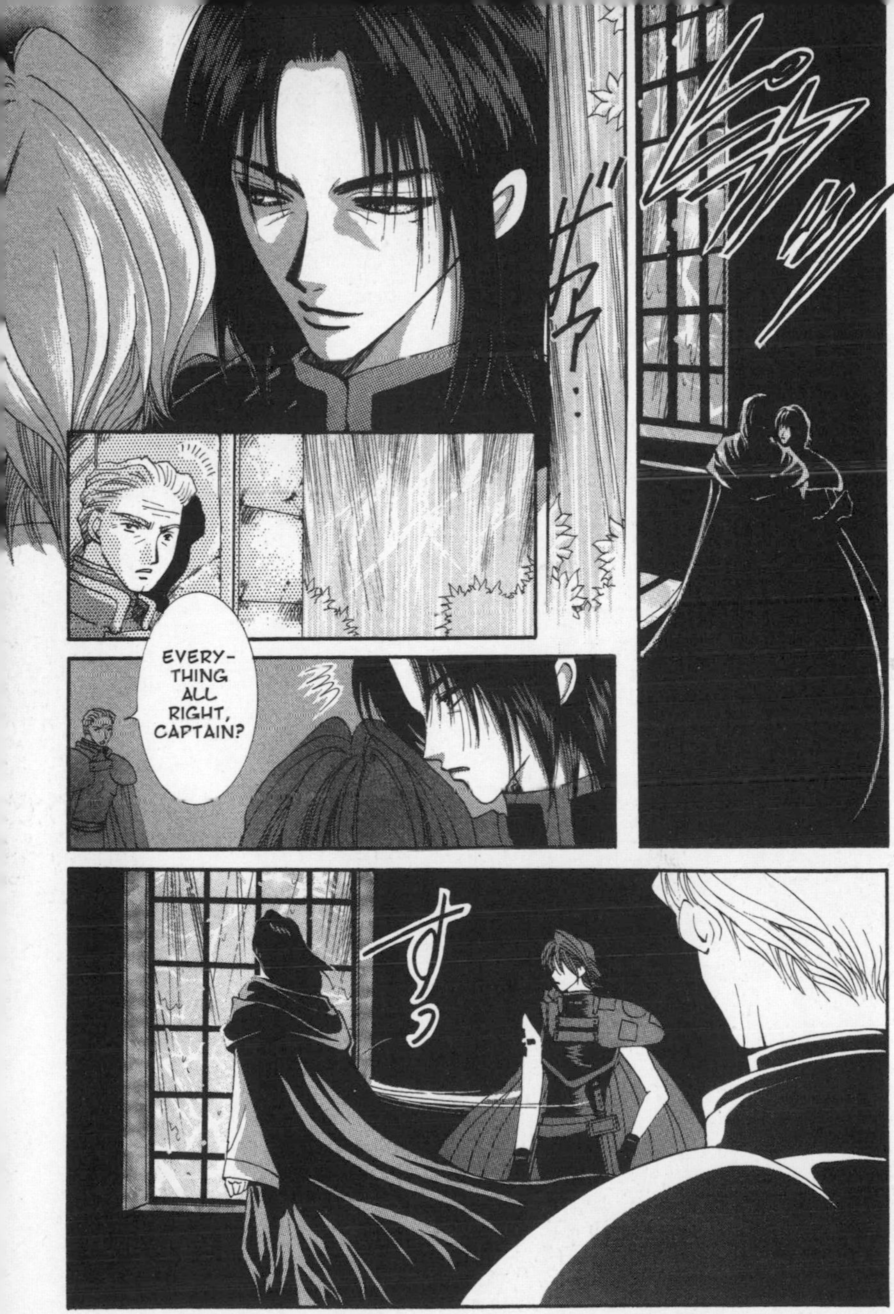
EVERY-
THING
ALL
RIGHT,
CAPTAIN?
すっ

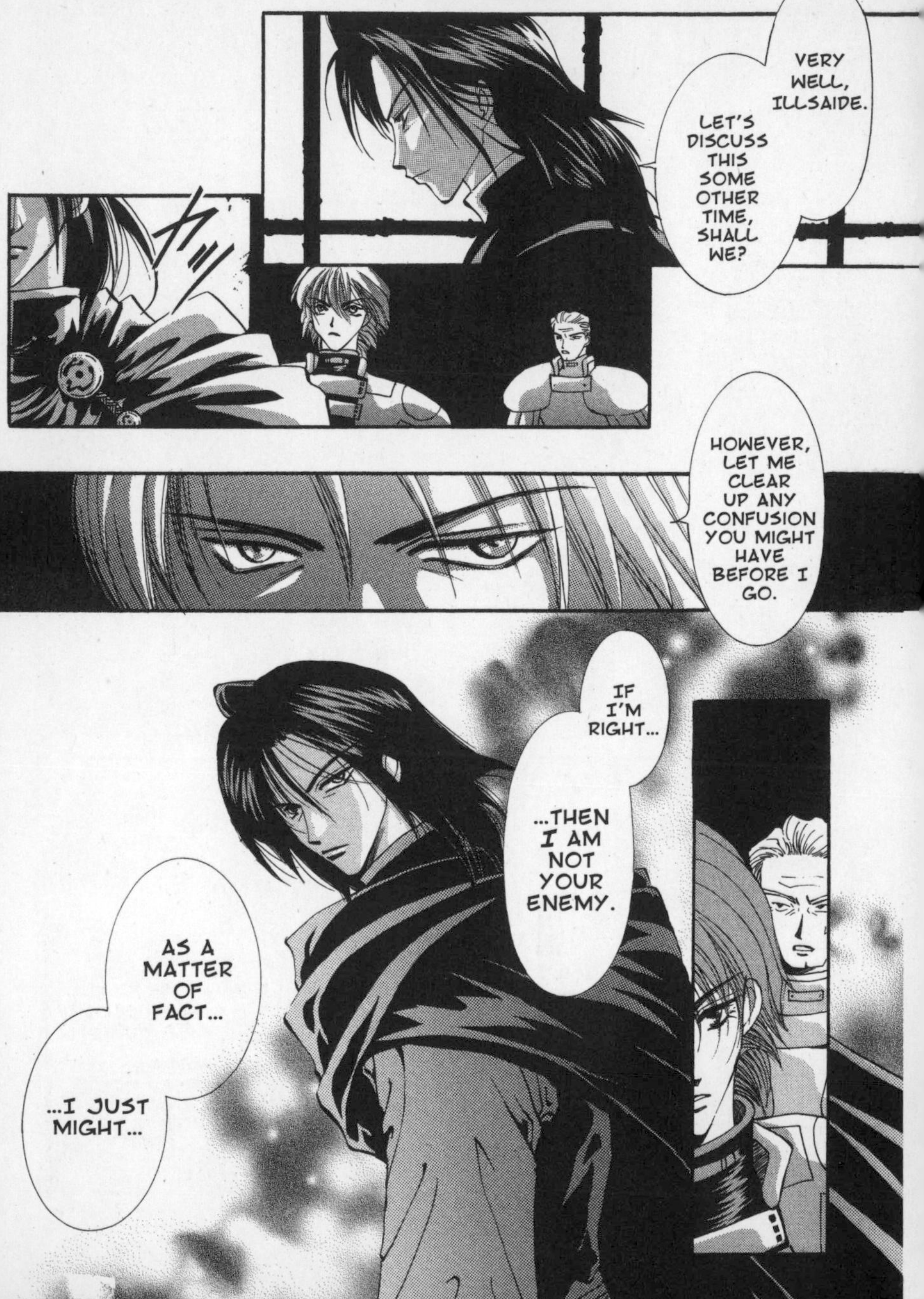
VERY WELL, ILLSAIDE.
LET'S DISCUSS THIS SOME OTHER TIME, SHALL WE?
カッ
HOWEVER, LET ME CLEAR UP ANY CONFUSION YOU MIGHT HAVE BEFORE I GO.
IF I'M RIGHT...
...THEN I AM NOT YOUR ENEMY.
AS A MATTER OF FACT...
...I JUST MIGHT...

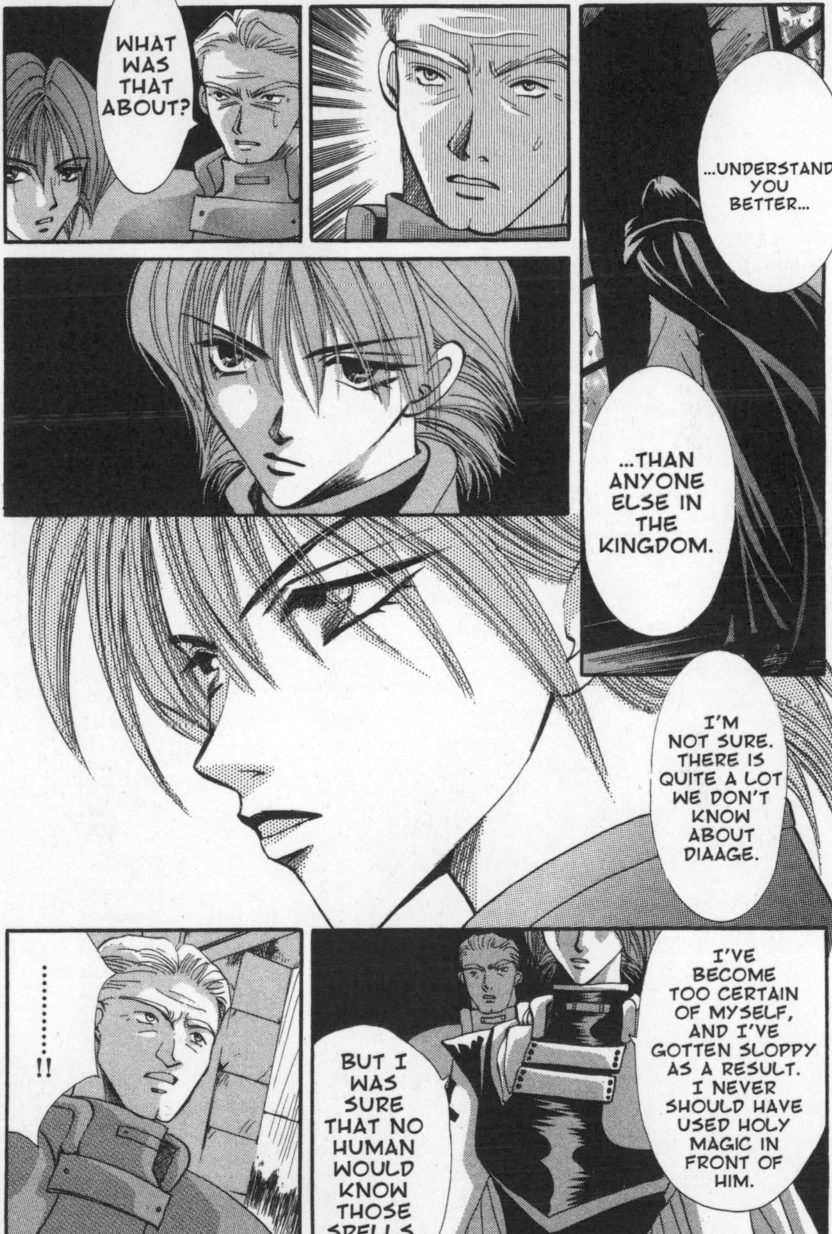
...UNDERSTAND YOU BETTER...
...THAN ANYONE ELSE IN THE KINGDOM.
WHAT WAS THAT ABOUT?
I'M NOT SURE. THERE IS QUITE A LOT WE DON'T KNOW ABOUT DIAAGE.
I'VE BECOME TOO CERTAIN OF MYSELF, AND I'VE GOTTEN SLOPPY AS A RESULT. I NEVER SHOULD HAVE USED HOLY MAGIC IN FRONT OF HIM.
BUT I WAS SURE THAT NO HUMAN WOULD KNOW THOSE SPELLS.
......!!

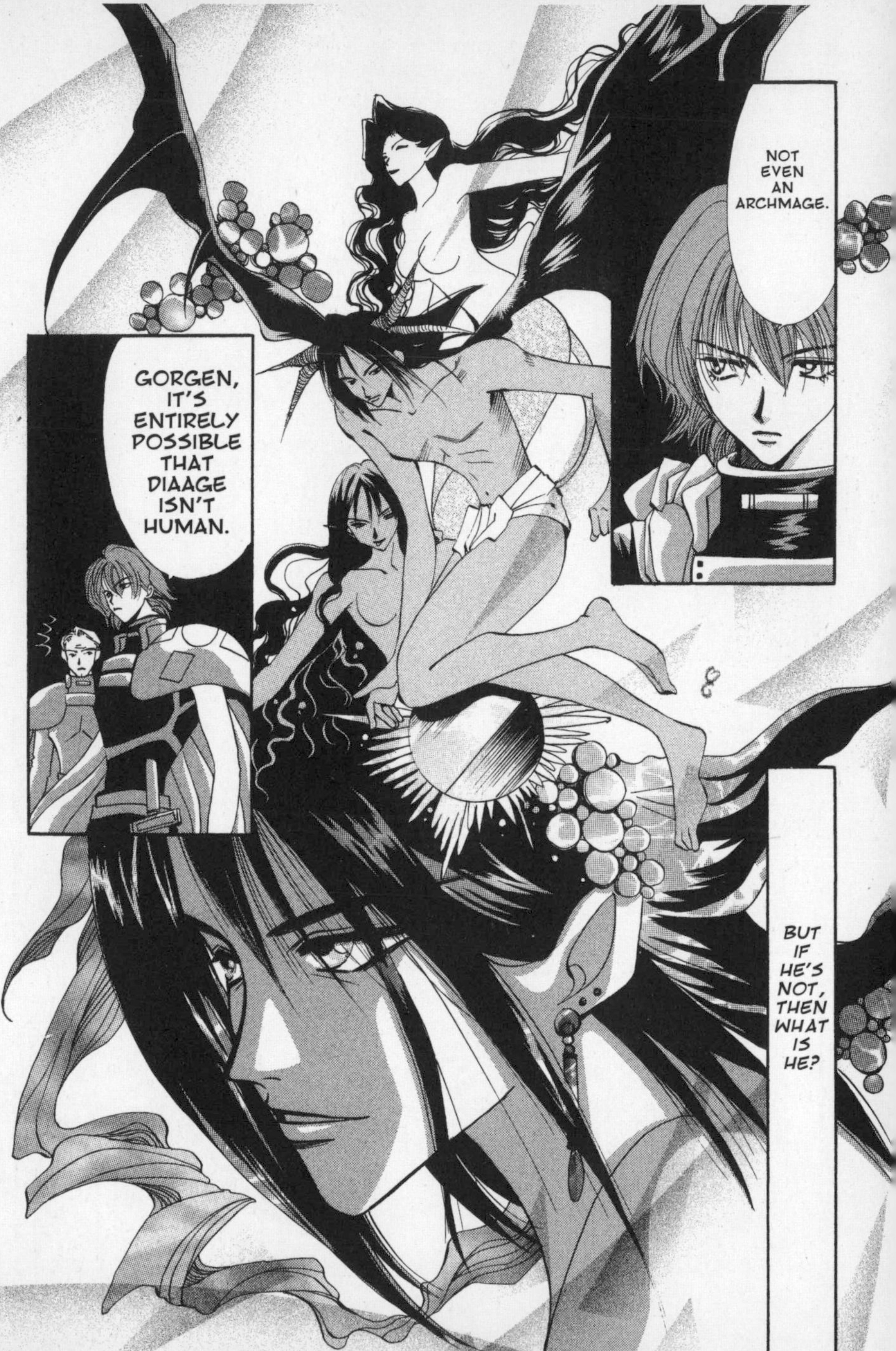

NOT EVEN AN ARCHMAGE.
GORGEN, IT'S ENTIRELY POSSIBLE THAT DIAAGE ISN'T HUMAN.
BUT IF HE'S NOT, THEN WHAT IS HE?

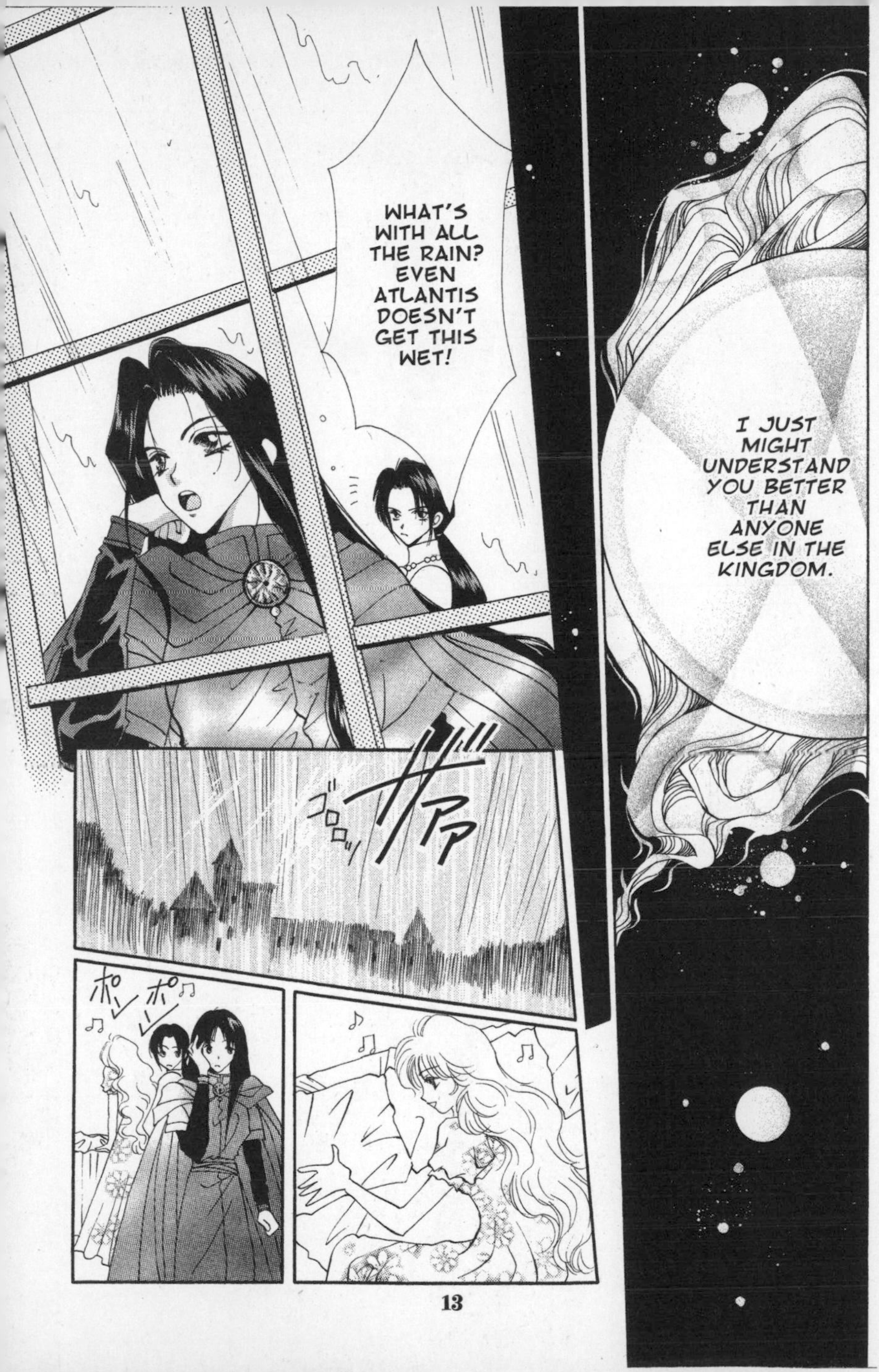
I JUST MIGHT UNDERSTAND YOU BETTER THAN ANYONE ELSE IN THE KINGDOM.
WHAT'S WITH ALL THE RAIN? EVEN ATLANTIS DOESN'T GET THIS WET!
ザァァ
ゴロロッ
ポンポン

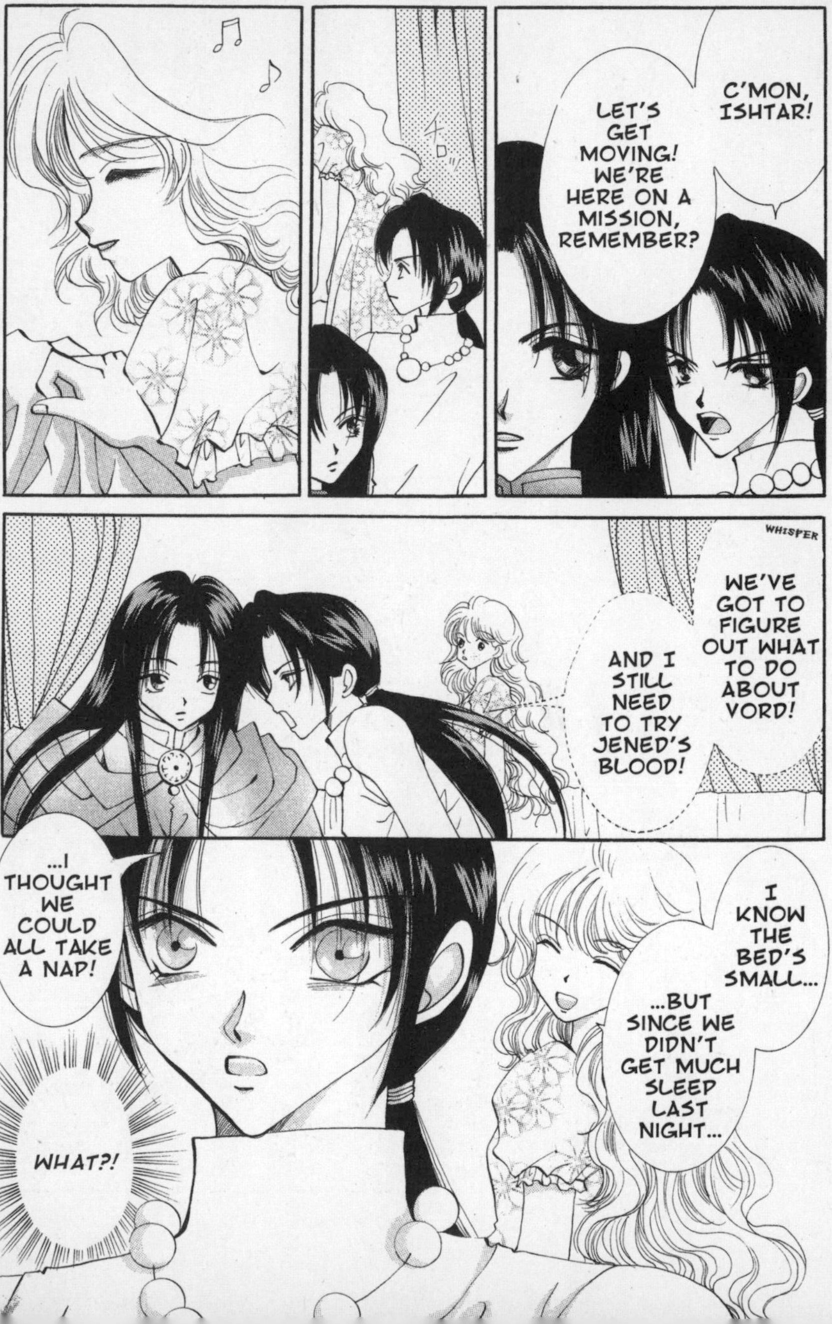
C'MON, ISHTAR!
LET'S GET MOVING! WE'RE HERE ON A MISSION, REMEMBER?
WHISPER
WE'VE GOT TO FIGURE OUT WHAT TO DO ABOUT VORD!
AND I STILL NEED TO TRY JENED'S BLOOD!
I KNOW THE BED'S SMALL...
...BUT SINCE WE DIDN'T GET MUCH SLEEP LAST NIGHT...
...I THOUGHT WE COULD ALL TAKE A NAP!
WHAT?!

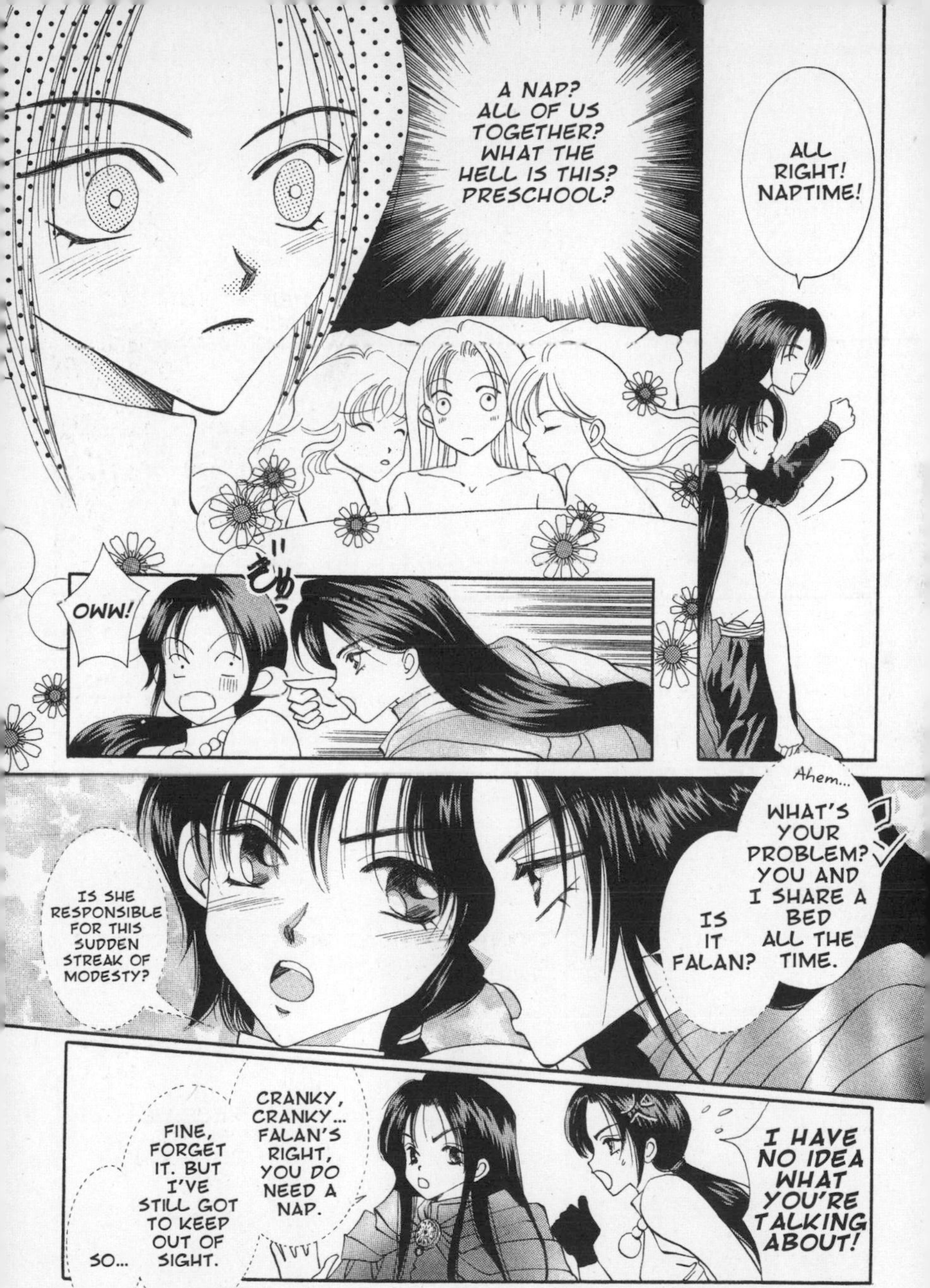
ALL RIGHT! NAPTIME!
A NAP? ALL OF US TOGETHER? WHAT THE HELL IS THIS? PRESCHOOL?
OWW!
Ahem...
WHAT'S YOUR PROBLEM? YOU AND I SHARE A BED ALL THE TIME.
IS IT FALAN?
IS SHE RESPONSIBLE FOR THIS SUDDEN STREAK OF MODESTY?
I HAVE NO IDEA WHAT YOU'RE TALKING ABOUT!
CRANKY, CRANKY... FALAN'S RIGHT, YOU DO NEED A NAP.
FINE, FORGET IT. BUT I'VE STILL GOT TO KEEP OUT OF SIGHT.
SO...

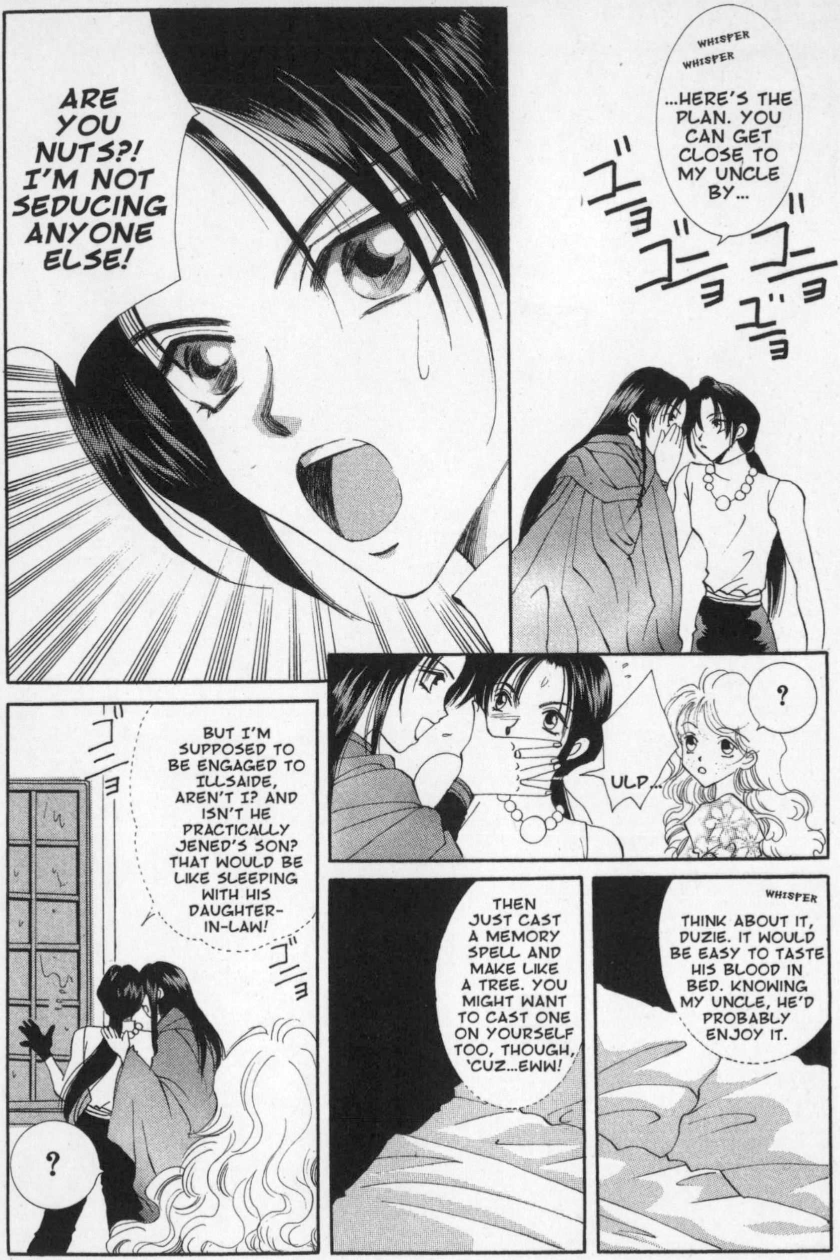
WHISPER
WHISPER
...HERE'S THE PLAN. YOU CAN GET CLOSE TO MY UNCLE BY...
ゴョゴョゴョゴョゴョゴョゴョゴョ
ARE YOU NUTS?! I'M NOT SEDUCING ANYONE ELSE!
ULP...
?
WHISPER
THINK ABOUT IT, DUZIE. IT WOULD BE EASY TO TASTE HIS BLOOD IN BED. KNOWING MY UNCLE, HE'D PROBABLY ENJOY IT.
THEN JUST CAST A MEMORY SPELL AND MAKE LIKE A TREE. YOU MIGHT WANT TO CAST ONE ON YOURSELF TOO, THOUGH, 'CUZ...EWW!
ゴョゴョ
BUT I'M SUPPOSED TO BE ENGAGED TO ILLSAIDE, AREN'T I? AND ISN'T HE PRACTICALLY JENED'S SON? THAT WOULD BE LIKE SLEEPING WITH HIS DAUGHTER-IN-LAW!
?

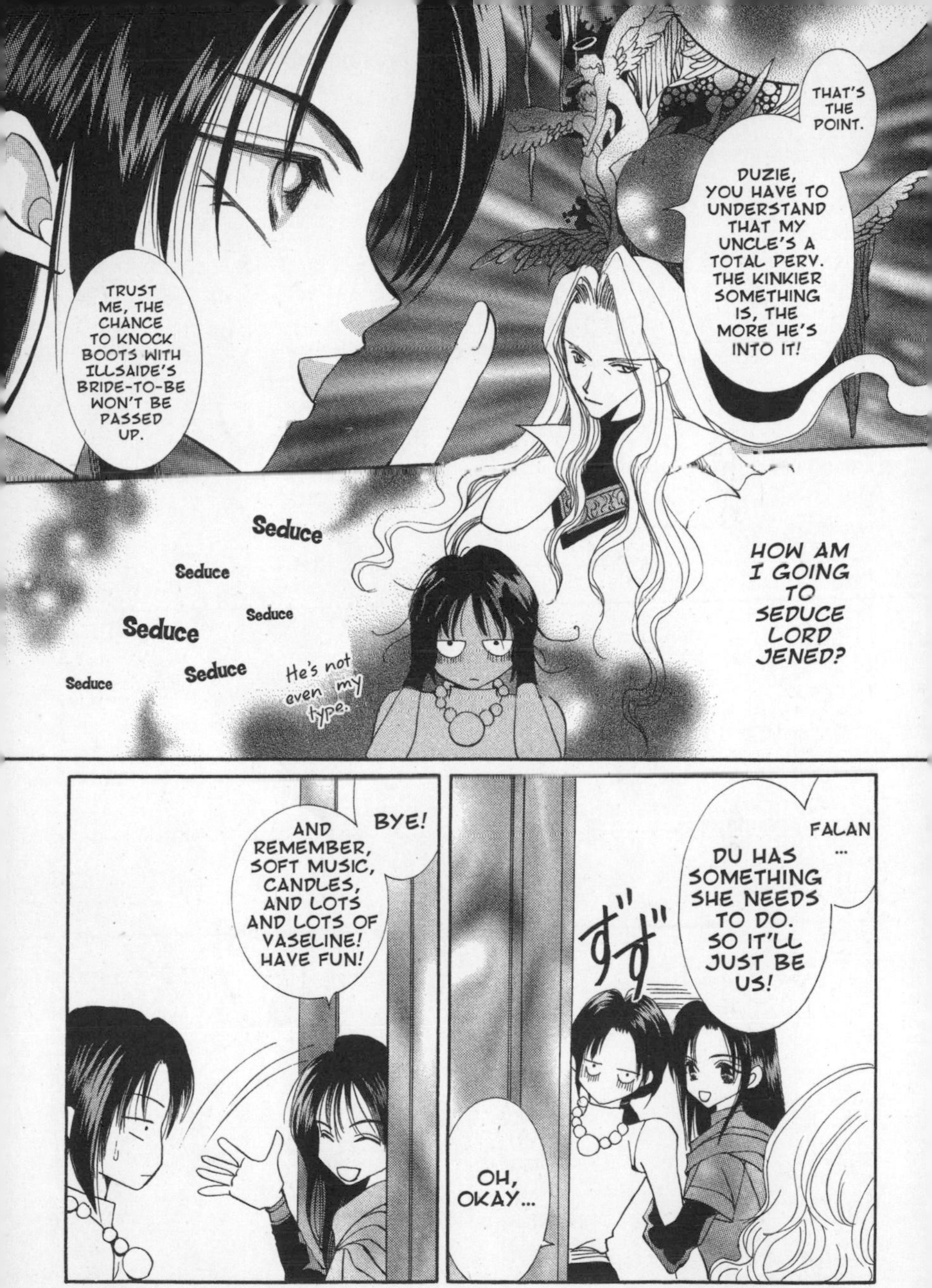
THAT'S THE POINT.
DUZIE, YOU HAVE TO UNDERSTAND THAT MY UNCLE'S A TOTAL PERV. THE KINKIER SOMETHING IS, THE MORE HE'S INTO IT!
TRUST ME, THE CHANCE TO KNOCK BOOTS WITH ILLSAIDE'S BRIDE-TO-BE WON'T BE PASSED UP.
HOW AM I GOING TO SEDUCE LORD JENED?
Seduce
Seduce
Seduce
Seduce
Seduce
Seduce
He's not even my type.
FALAN...
DU HAS SOMETHING SHE NEEDS TO DO. SO IT'LL JUST BE US!
ずず
OH, OKAY...
BYE!
AND REMEMBER, SOFT MUSIC, CANDLES, AND LOTS AND LOTS OF VASELINE! HAVE FUN!

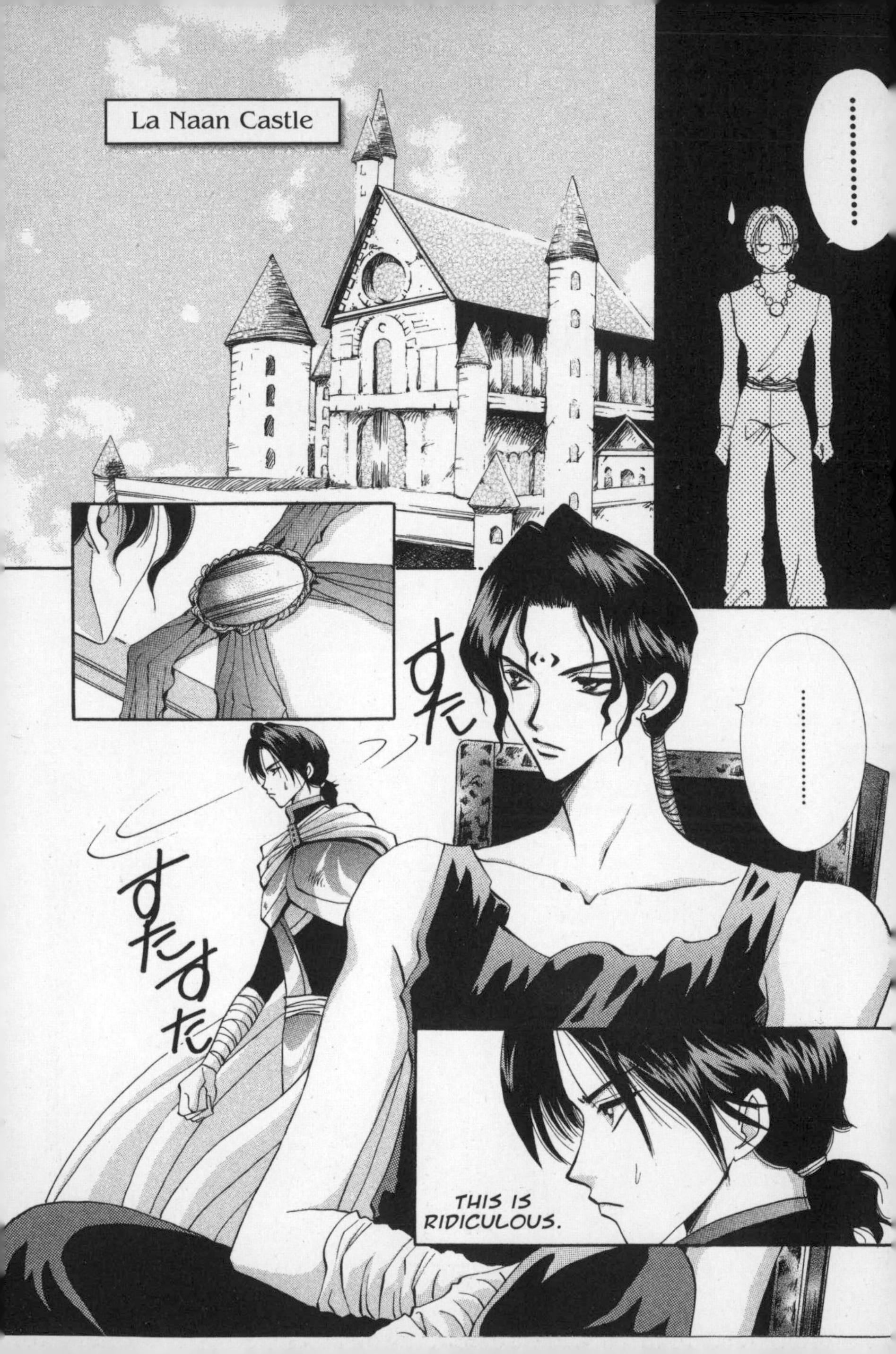

......
La Naan Castle
......
すた
すたすた
THIS IS RIDICULOUS.

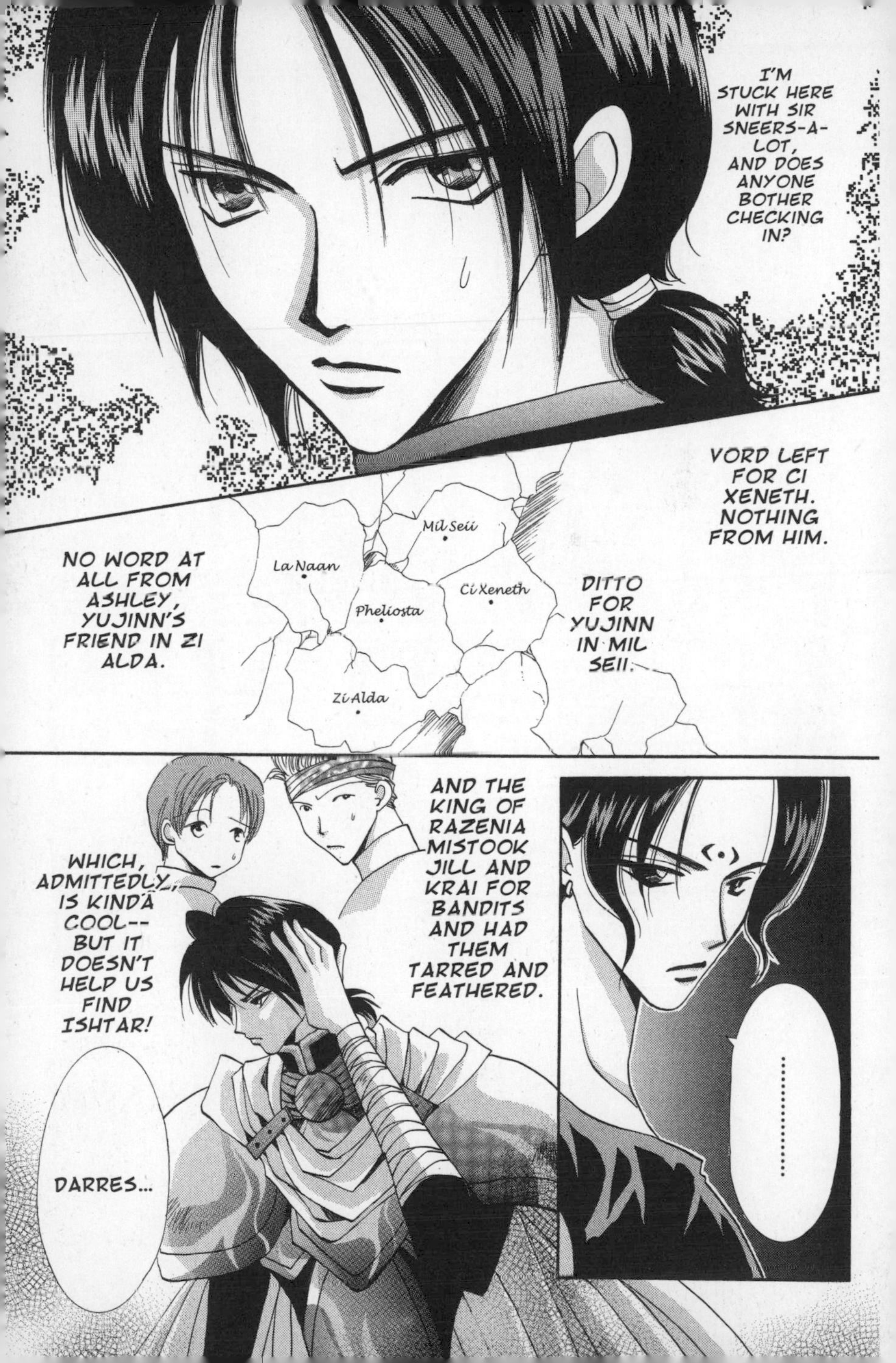
I'M STUCK HERE WITH SIR SNEERS-A-LOT, AND DOES ANYONE BOTHER CHECKING IN?
VORD LEFT FOR CI XENETH. NOTHING FROM HIM.
DITTO FOR YUJINN IN MIL SEII.
Mil Seii
Ci Xeneth
La Naan
Pheliosta
Zi Alda
NO WORD AT ALL FROM ASHLEY, YUJINN'S FRIEND IN ZI ALDA.
......
AND THE KING OF RAZENIA MISTOOK JILL AND KRAI FOR BANDITS AND HAD THEM TARRED AND FEATHERED.
WHICH, ADMITTEDLY, IS KIND'A COOL--BUT IT DOESN'T HELP US FIND ISHTAR!
DARRES...

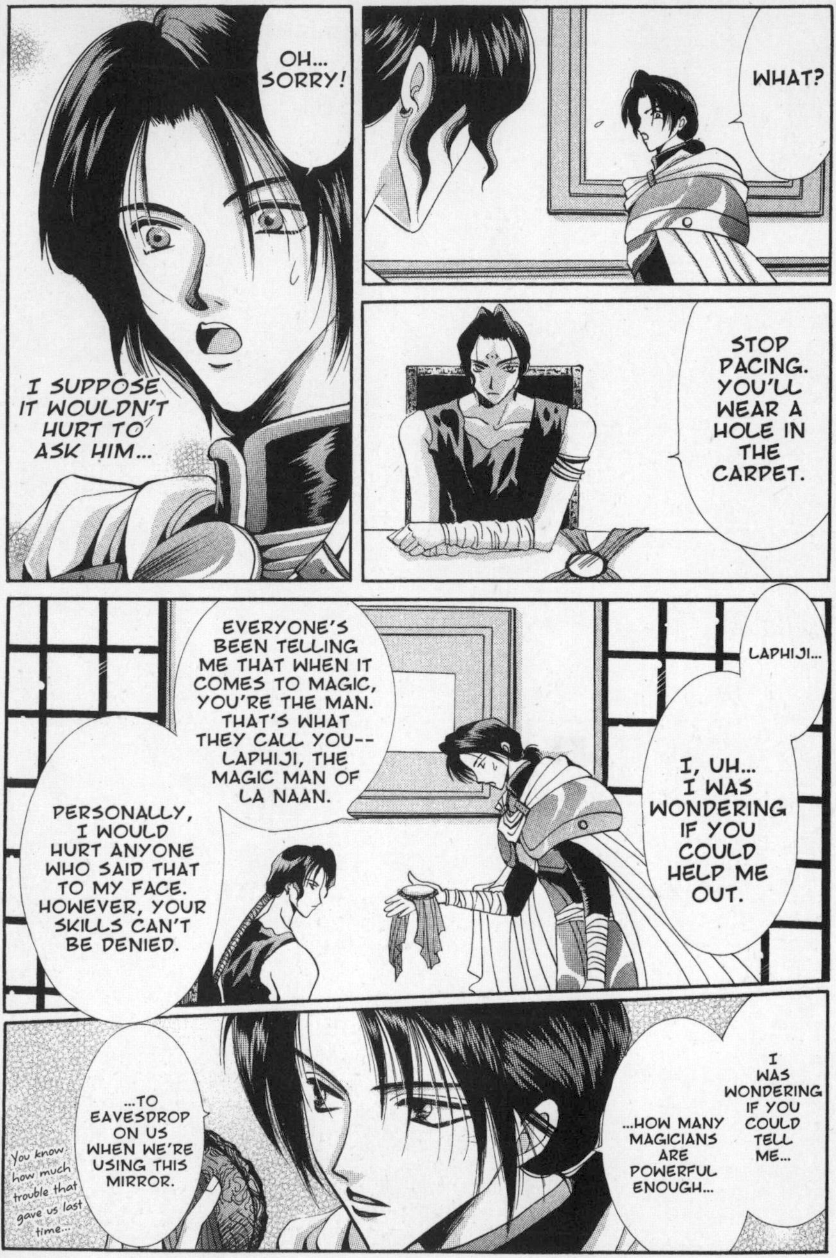
WHAT?
STOP PACING. YOU'LL WEAR A HOLE IN THE CARPET.
OH... SORRY!
I SUPPOSE IT WOULDN'T HURT TO ASK HIM...
LAPHIJI...
I, UH... I WAS WONDERING IF YOU COULD HELP ME OUT.
EVERYONE'S BEEN TELLING ME THAT WHEN IT COMES TO MAGIC, YOU'RE THE MAN. THAT'S WHAT THEY CALL YOU-- LAPHIJI, THE MAGIC MAN OF LA NAAN.
PERSONALLY, I WOULD HURT ANYONE WHO SAID THAT TO MY FACE. HOWEVER, YOUR SKILLS CAN'T BE DENIED.
I WAS WONDERING IF YOU COULD TELL ME...
...HOW MANY MAGICIANS ARE POWERFUL ENOUGH...
...TO EAVESDROP ON US WHEN WE'RE USING THIS MIRROR.
You know how much trouble that gave us last time...

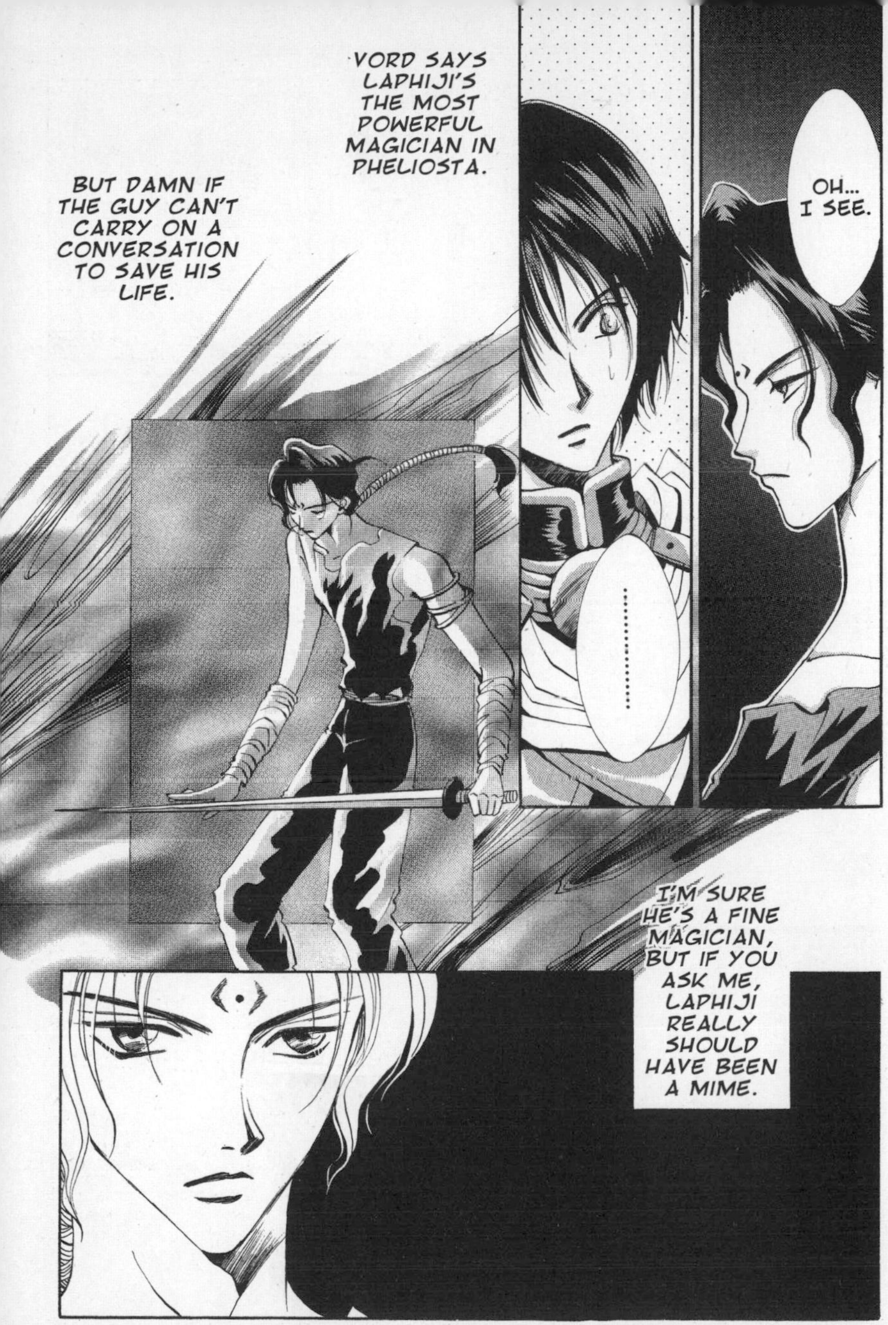
OH... I SEE.
......
VORD SAYS LAPHIJI'S THE MOST POWERFUL MAGICIAN IN PHELIOSTA.
BUT DAMN IF THE GUY CAN'T CARRY ON A CONVERSATION TO SAVE HIS LIFE.
I'M SURE HE'S A FINE MAGICIAN, BUT IF YOU ASK ME, LAPHIJI REALLY SHOULD HAVE BEEN A MIME.

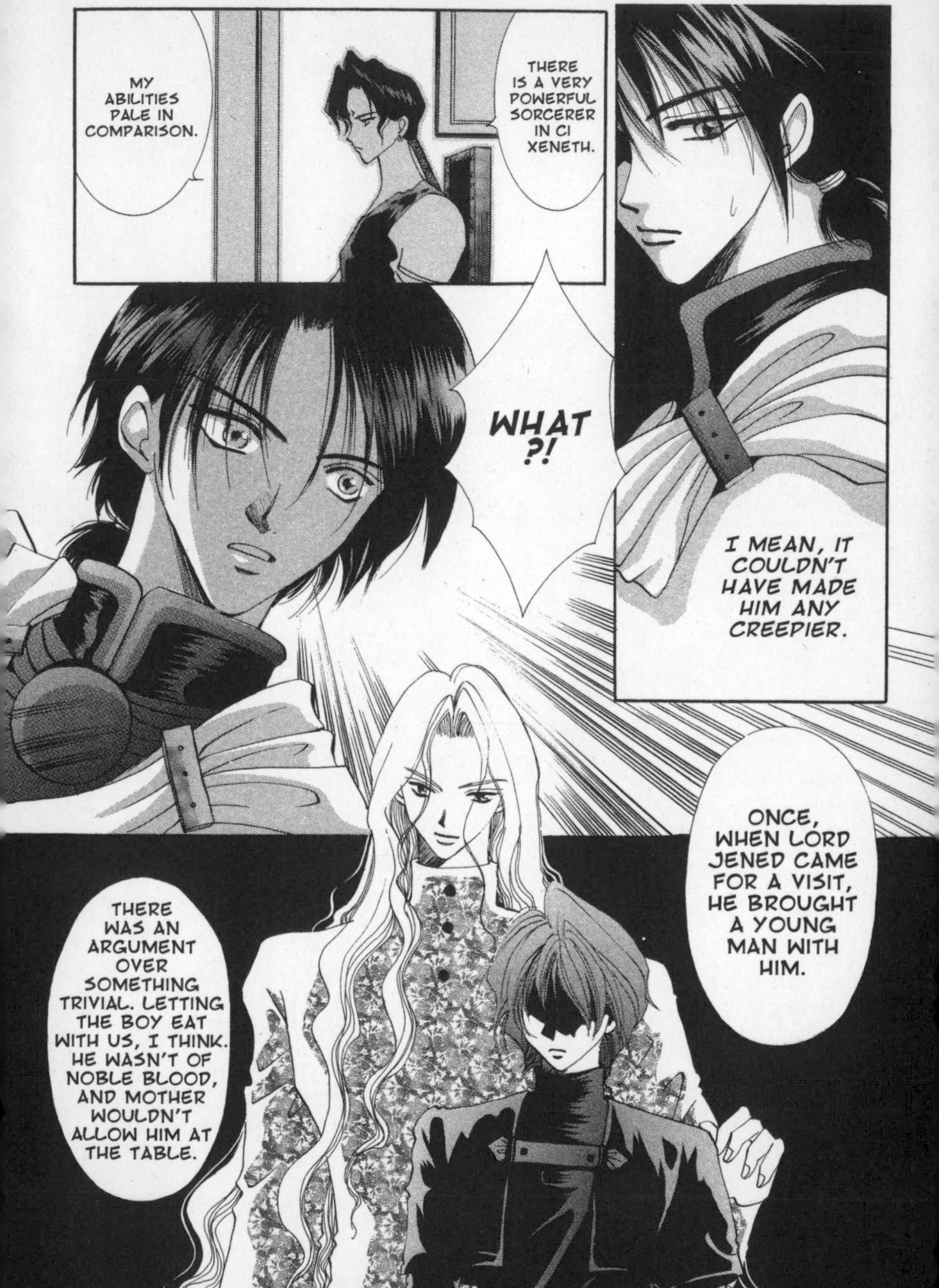
I MEAN, IT COULDN'T HAVE MADE HIM ANY CREEPIER.
THERE IS A VERY POWERFUL SORCERER IN CI XENETH.
MY ABILITIES PALE IN COMPARISON.
WHAT?!
ONCE, WHEN LORD JENED CAME FOR A VISIT, HE BROUGHT A YOUNG MAN WITH HIM.
THERE WAS AN ARGUMENT OVER SOMETHING TRIVIAL. LETTING THE BOY EAT WITH US, I THINK. HE WASN'T OF NOBLE BLOOD, AND MOTHER WOULDN'T ALLOW HIM AT THE TABLE.

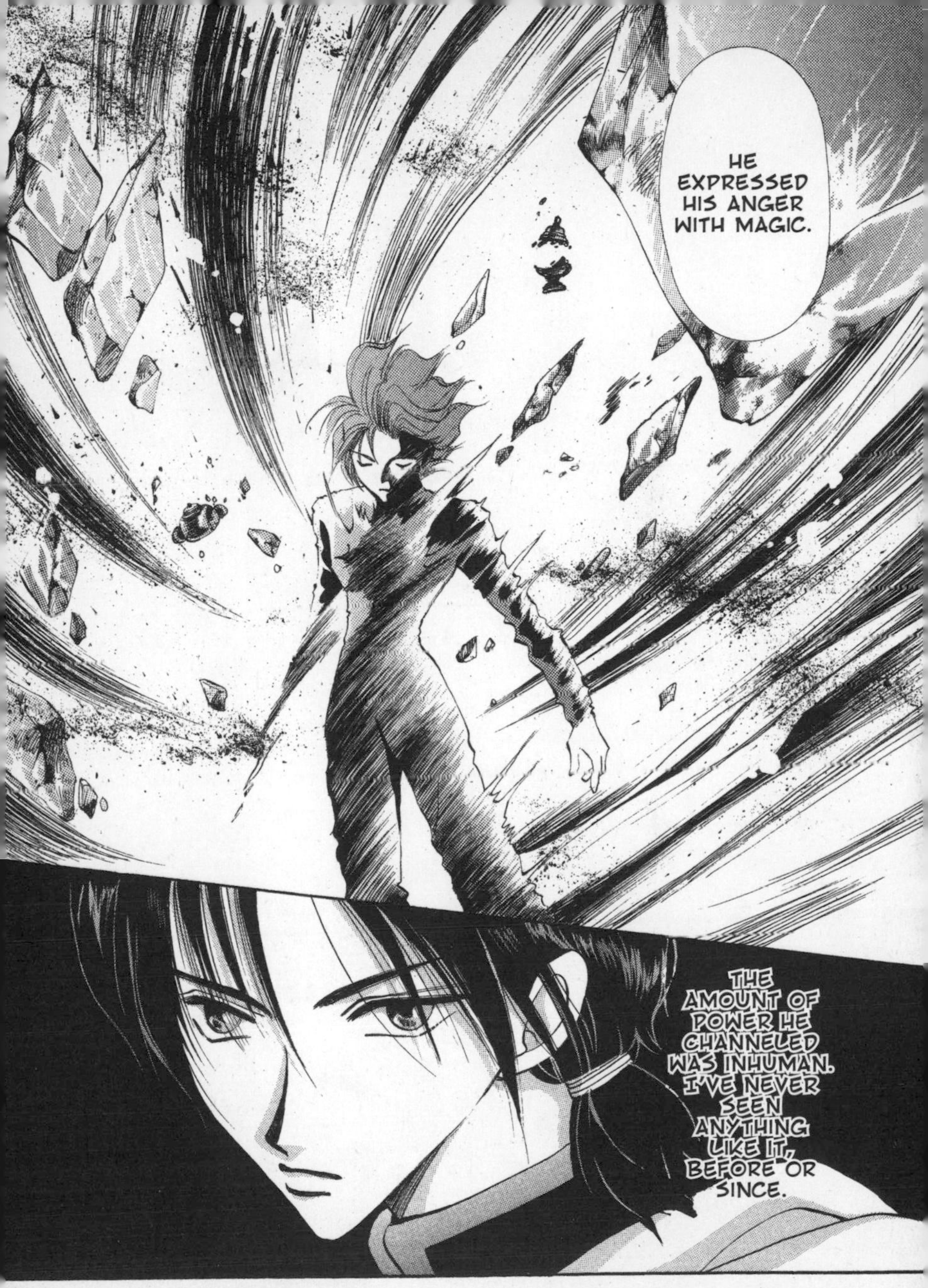
HE EXPRESSED HIS ANGER WITH MAGIC.
THE AMOUNT OF POWER HE CHANNELED WAS INHUMAN. I'VE NEVER SEEN ANYTHING LIKE IT, BEFORE OR SINCE.

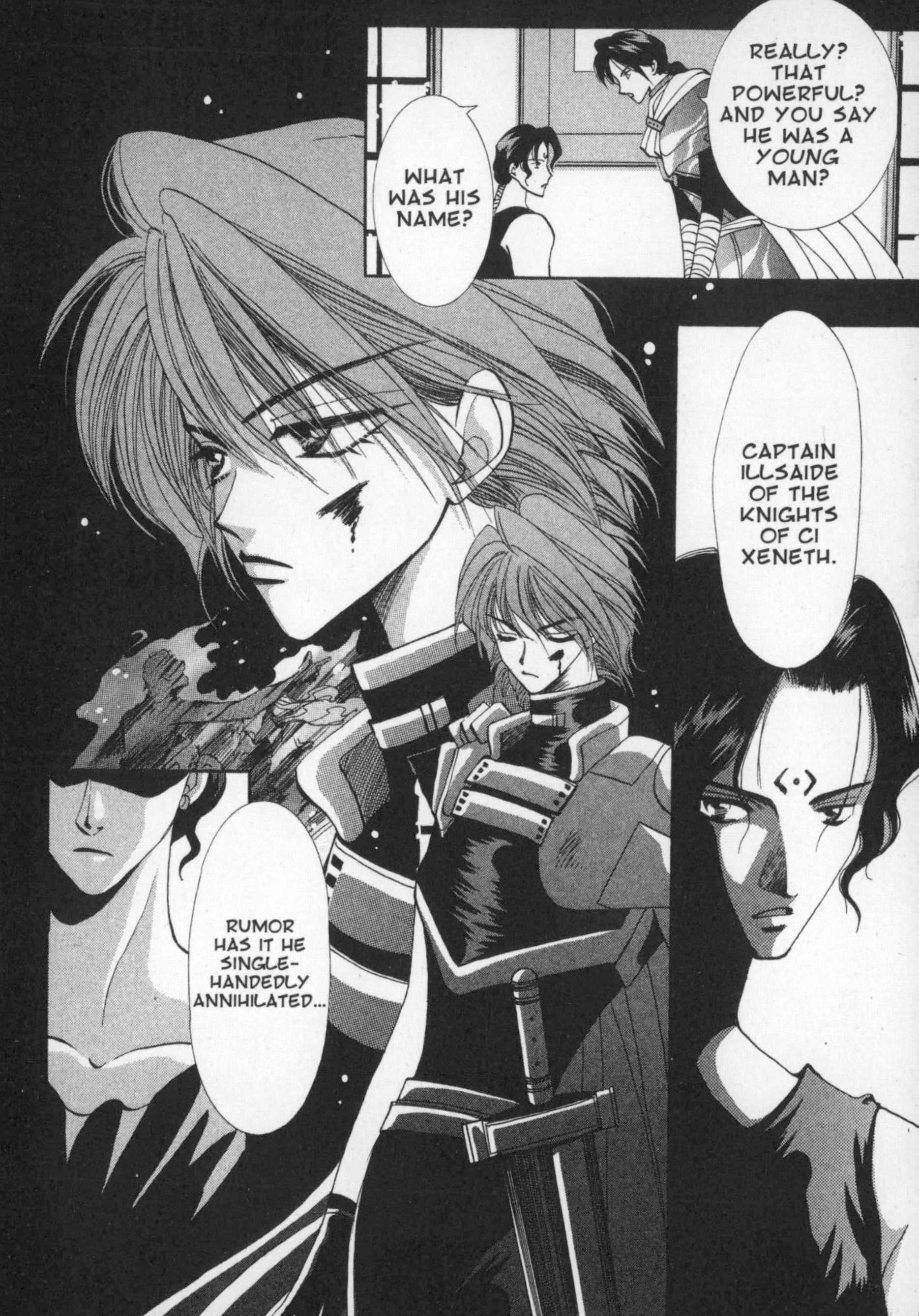
REALLY? THAT POWERFUL? AND YOU SAY HE WAS A YOUNG MAN?
WHAT WAS HIS NAME?
CAPTAIN ILLSAIDE OF THE KNIGHTS OF CI XENETH.
RUMOR HAS IT HE SINGLE-HANDEDLY ANNIHILATED...

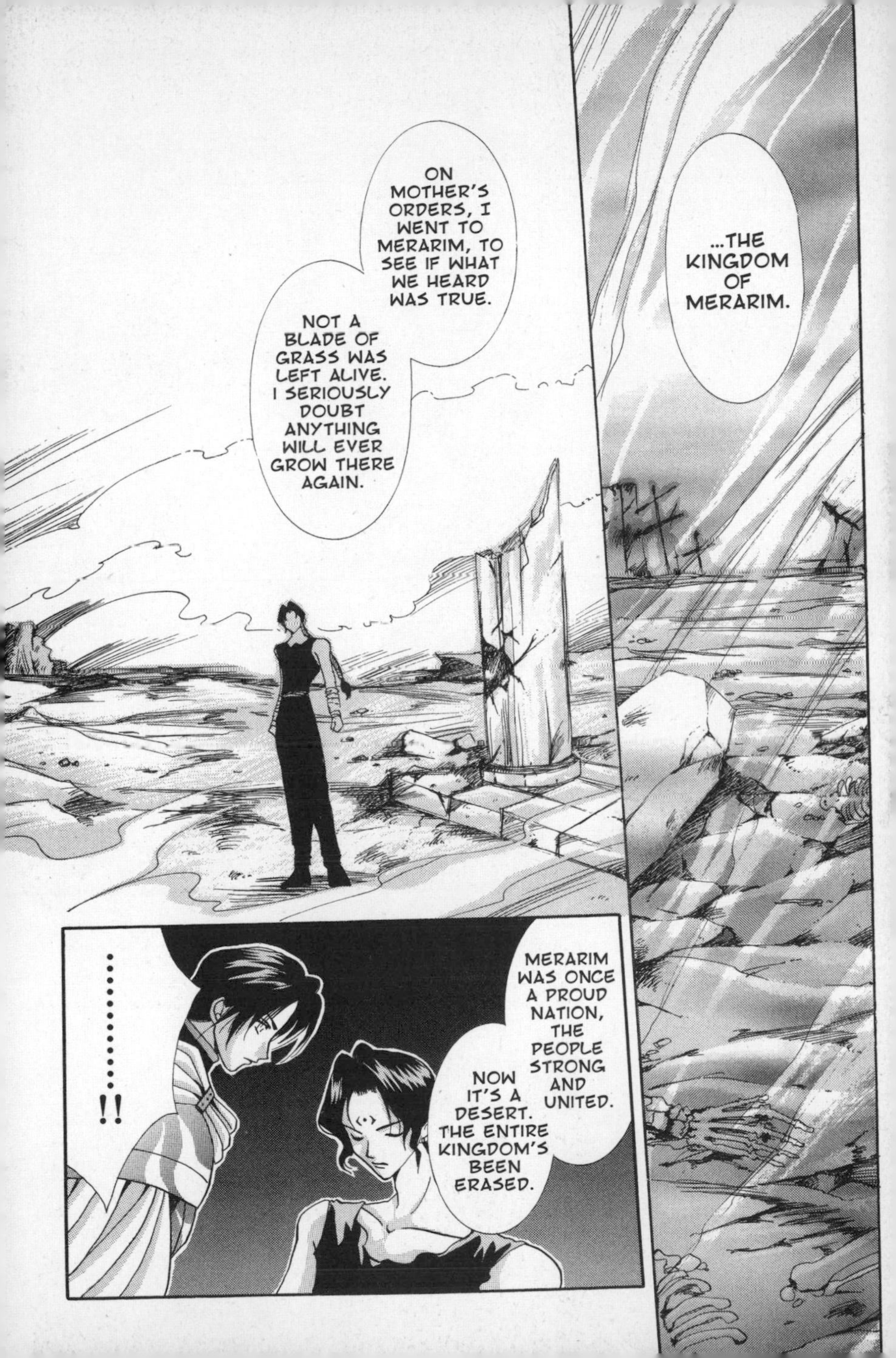
...THE KINGDOM OF MERARIM.
ON MOTHER'S ORDERS, I WENT TO MERARIM, TO SEE IF WHAT WE HEARD WAS TRUE.
NOT A BLADE OF GRASS WAS LEFT ALIVE. I SERIOUSLY DOUBT ANYTHING WILL EVER GROW THERE AGAIN.
MERARIM WAS ONCE A PROUD NATION, THE PEOPLE STRONG AND UNITED.
NOW IT'S A DESERT. THE ENTIRE KINGDOM'S BEEN ERASED.
........!!

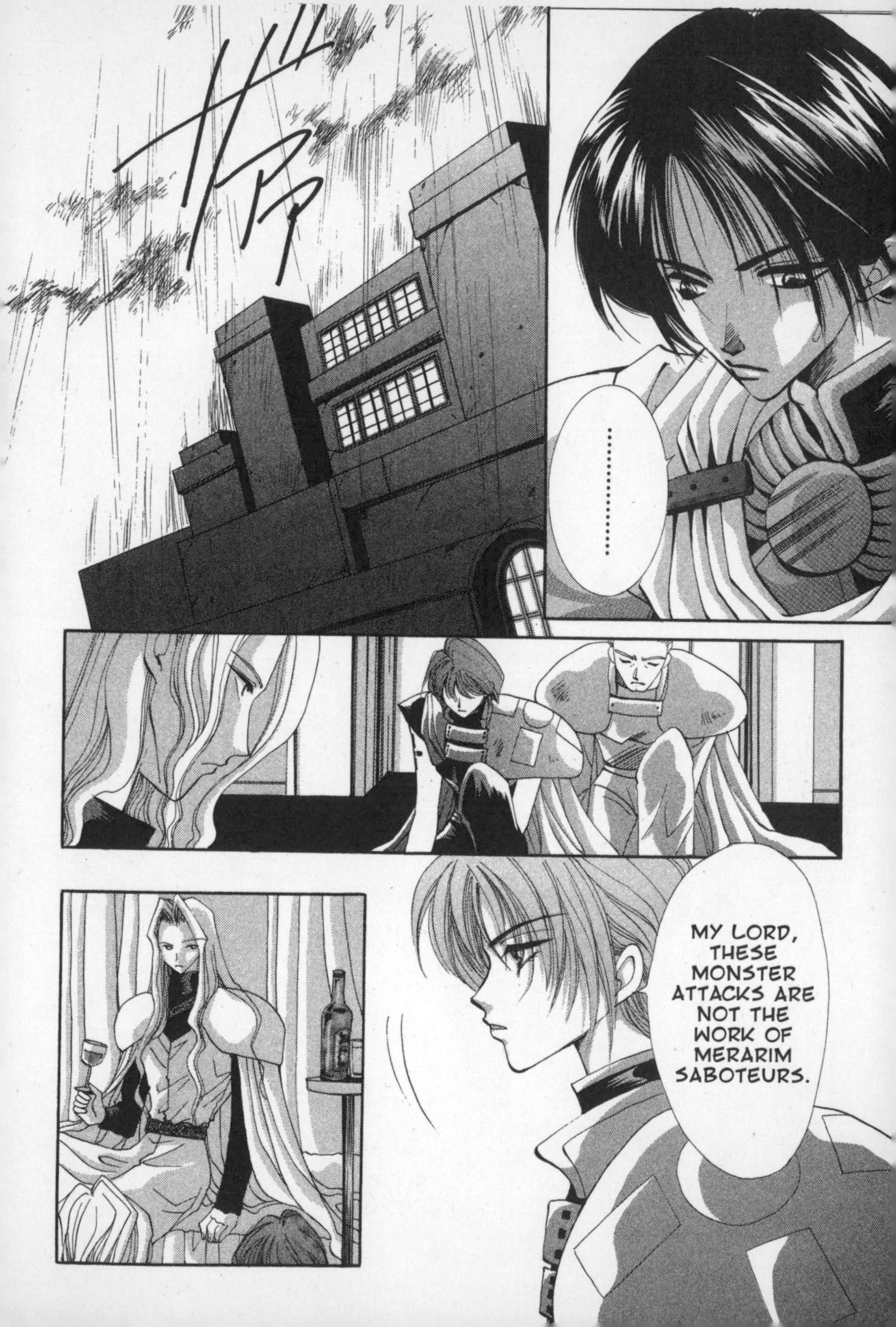

......
MY LORD, THESE MONSTER ATTACKS ARE NOT THE WORK OF MERARIM SABOTEURS.

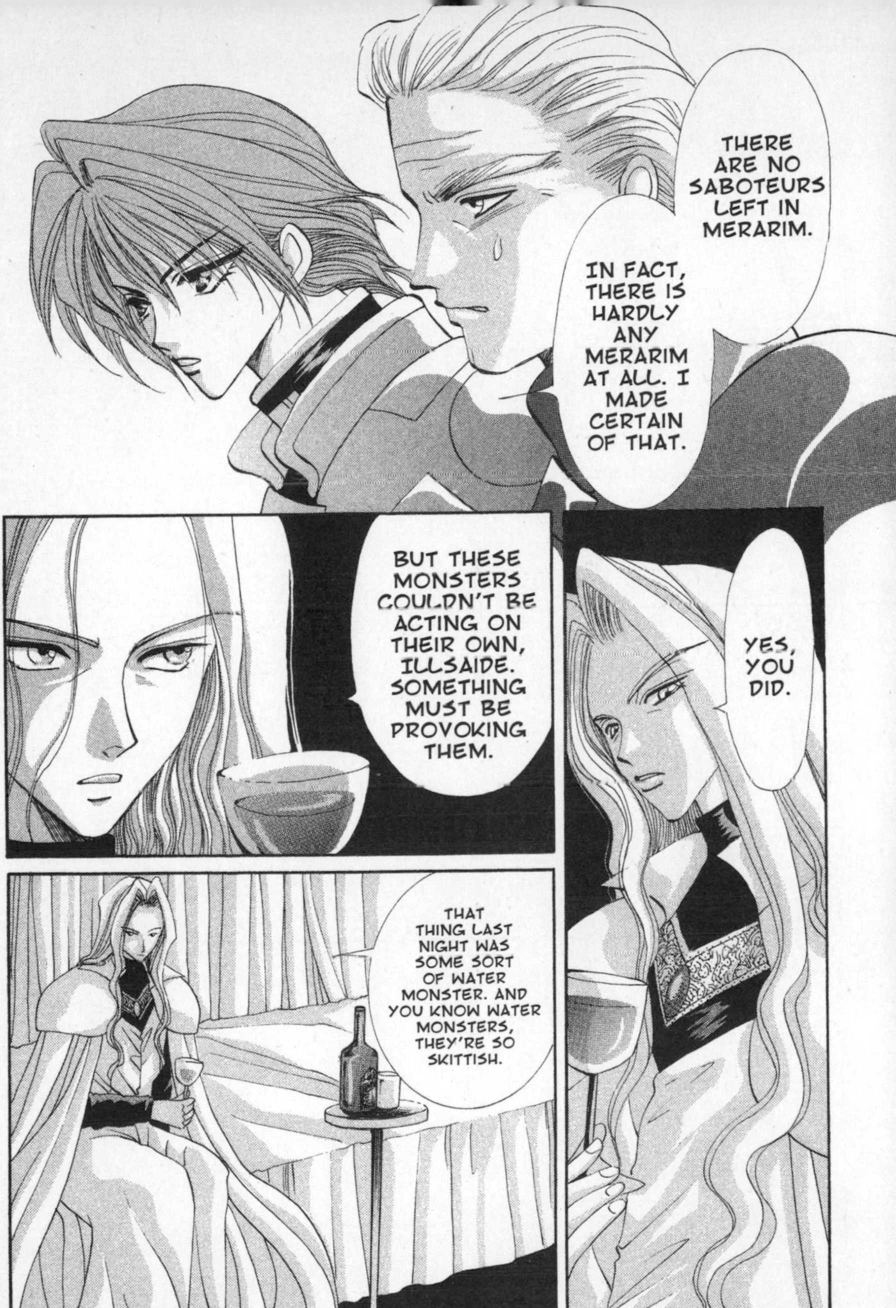
THERE ARE NO SABOTEURS LEFT IN MERARIM.
IN FACT, THERE IS HARDLY ANY MERARIM AT ALL. I MADE CERTAIN OF THAT.
YES, YOU DID.
BUT THESE MONSTERS COULDN'T BE ACTING ON THEIR OWN, ILLSAIDE. SOMETHING MUST BE PROVOKING THEM.
THAT THING LAST NIGHT WAS SOME SORT OF WATER MONSTER. AND YOU KNOW WATER MONSTERS, THEY'RE SO SKITTISH.

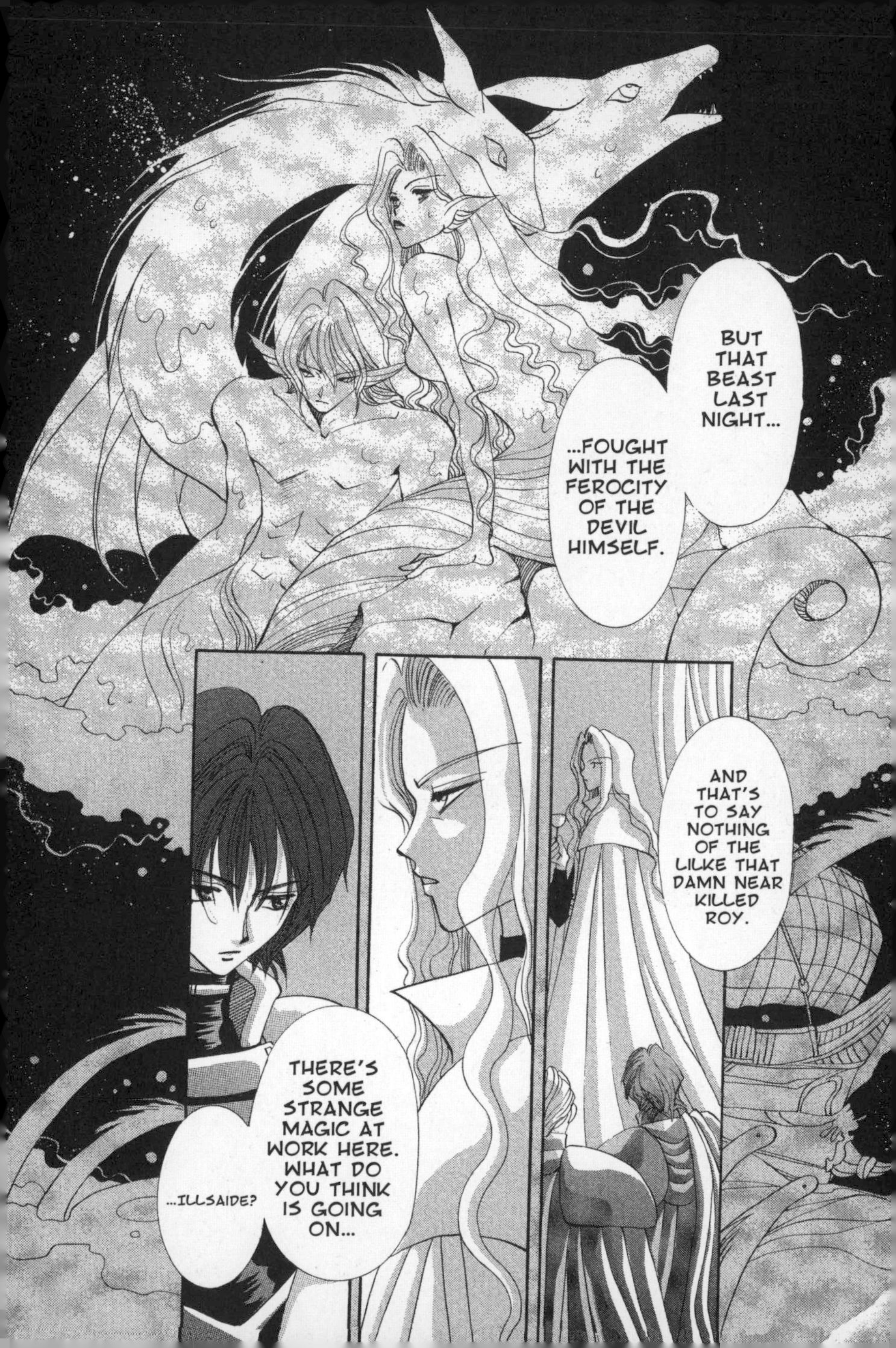
BUT THAT BEAST LAST NIGHT...
...FOUGHT WITH THE FEROCITY OF THE DEVIL HIMSELF.
AND THAT'S TO SAY NOTHING OF THE LILKE THAT DAMN NEAR KILLED ROY.
THERE'S SOME STRANGE MAGIC AT WORK HERE. WHAT DO YOU THINK IS GOING ON...
...ILLSAIDE?

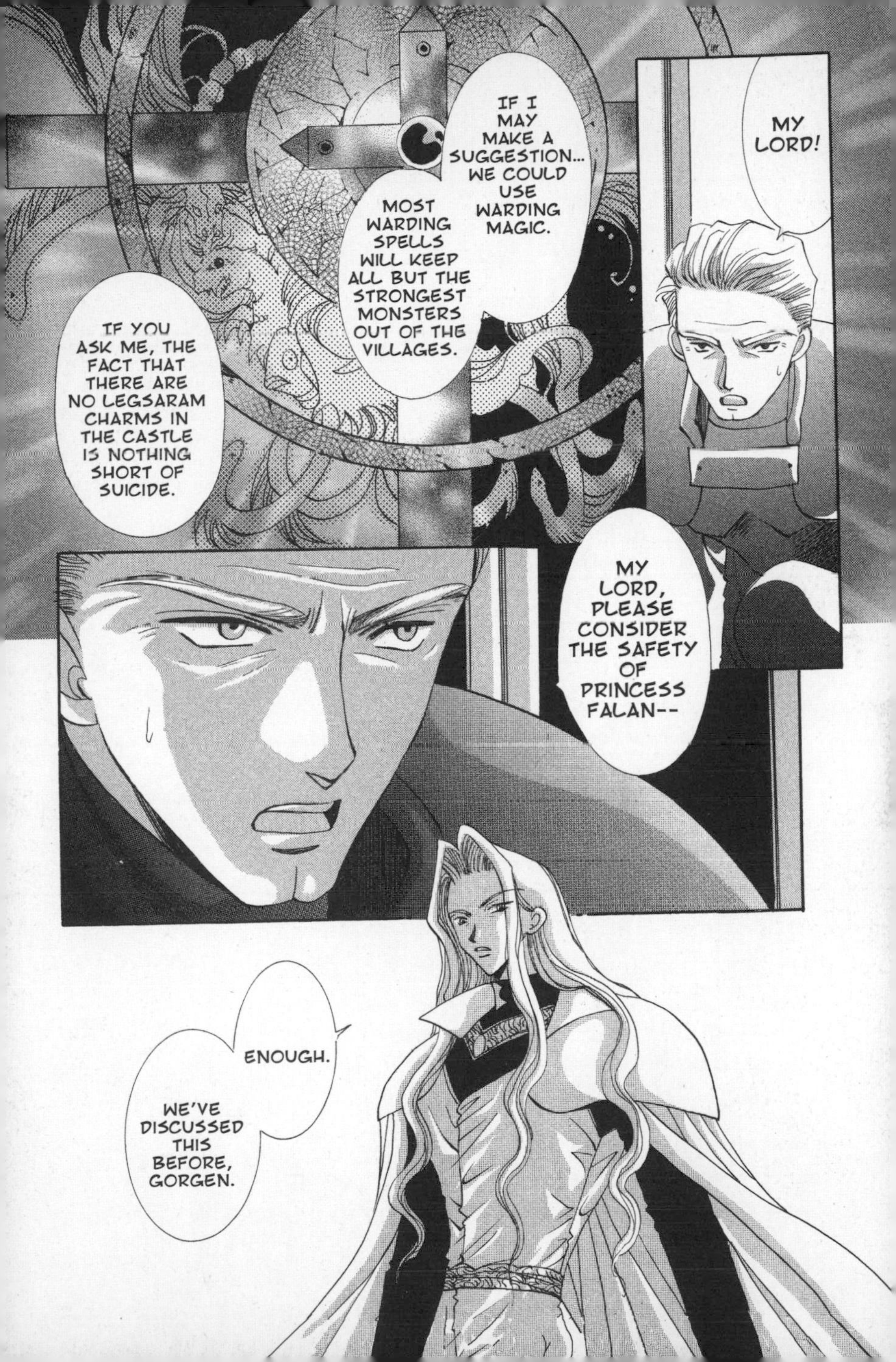

MY LORD!
IF I MAY MAKE A SUGGESTION... WE COULD USE WARDING MAGIC.
MOST WARDING SPELLS WILL KEEP ALL BUT THE STRONGEST MONSTERS OUT OF THE VILLAGES.
IF YOU ASK ME, THE FACT THAT THERE ARE NO LEGSARAM CHARMS IN THE CASTLE IS NOTHING SHORT OF SUICIDE.
MY LORD, PLEASE CONSIDER THE SAFETY OF PRINCESS FALAN--
ENOUGH.
WE'VE DISCUSSED THIS BEFORE, GORGEN.

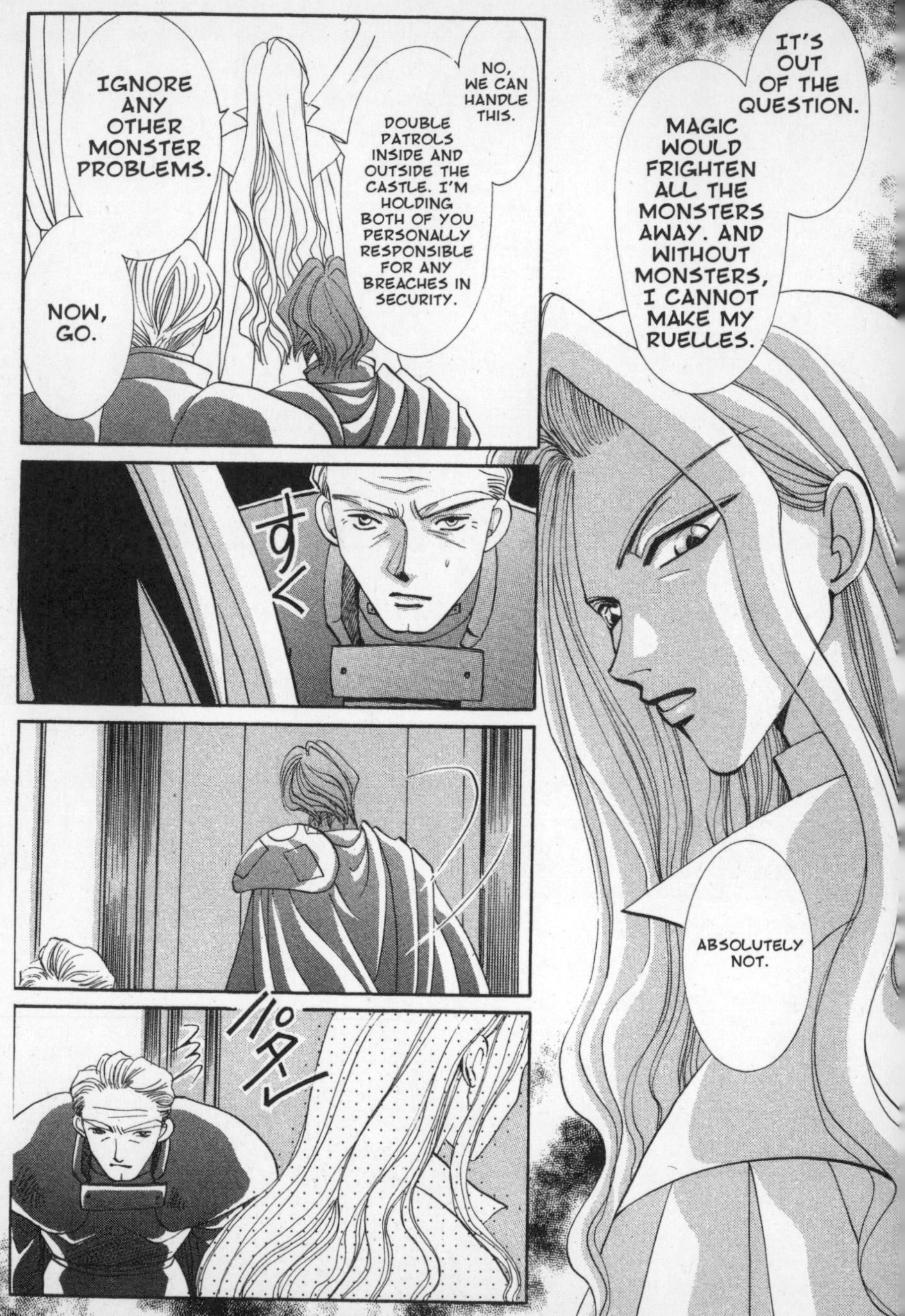
IT'S OUT OF THE QUESTION.
MAGIC WOULD FRIGHTEN ALL THE MONSTERS AWAY. AND WITHOUT MONSTERS, I CANNOT MAKE MY RUELLES.
ABSOLUTELY NOT.
NO, WE CAN HANDLE THIS.
DOUBLE PATROLS INSIDE AND OUTSIDE THE CASTLE. I'M HOLDING BOTH OF YOU PERSONALLY RESPONSIBLE FOR ANY BREACHES IN SECURITY.
IGNORE ANY OTHER MONSTER PROBLEMS.
NOW, GO.
すく
パタン

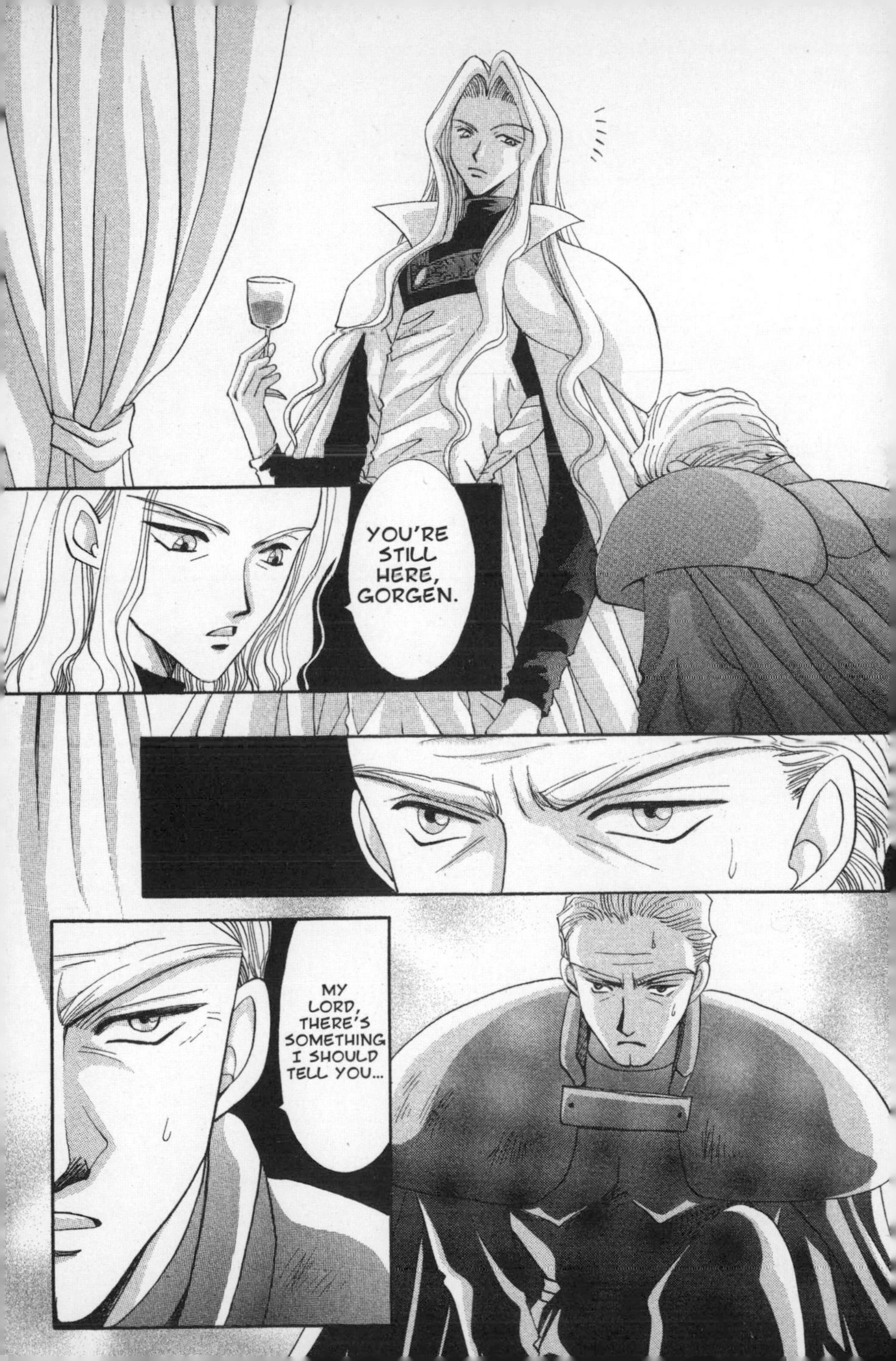
YOU'RE STILL HERE, GORGEN.
MY LORD, THERE'S SOMETHING I SHOULD TELL YOU...

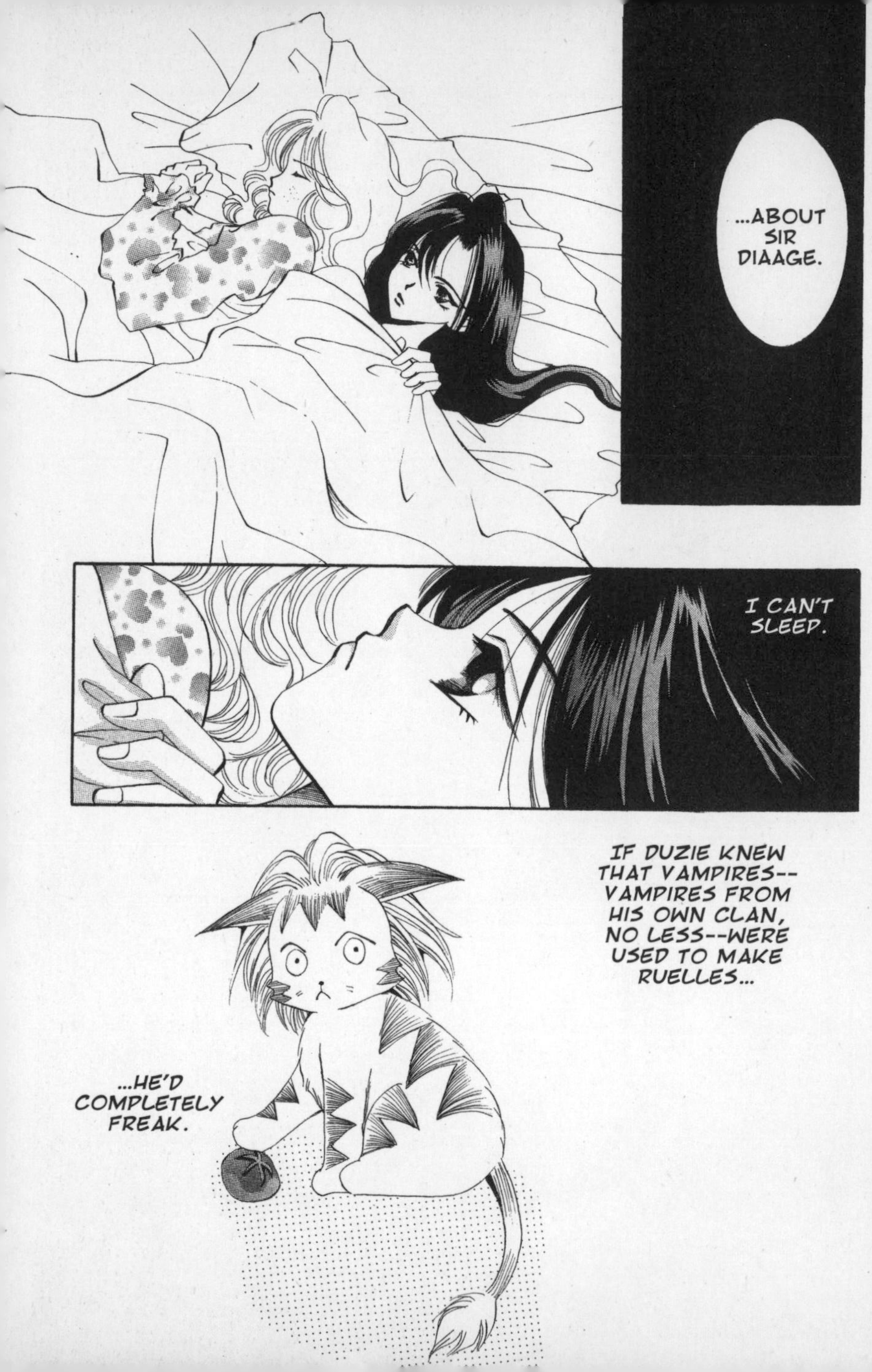
...ABOUT SIR DIAAGE.
I CAN'T SLEEP.
IF DUZIE KNEW THAT VAMPIRES-- VAMPIRES FROM HIS OWN CLAN, NO LESS--WERE USED TO MAKE RUELLES...
...HE'D COMPLETELY FREAK.

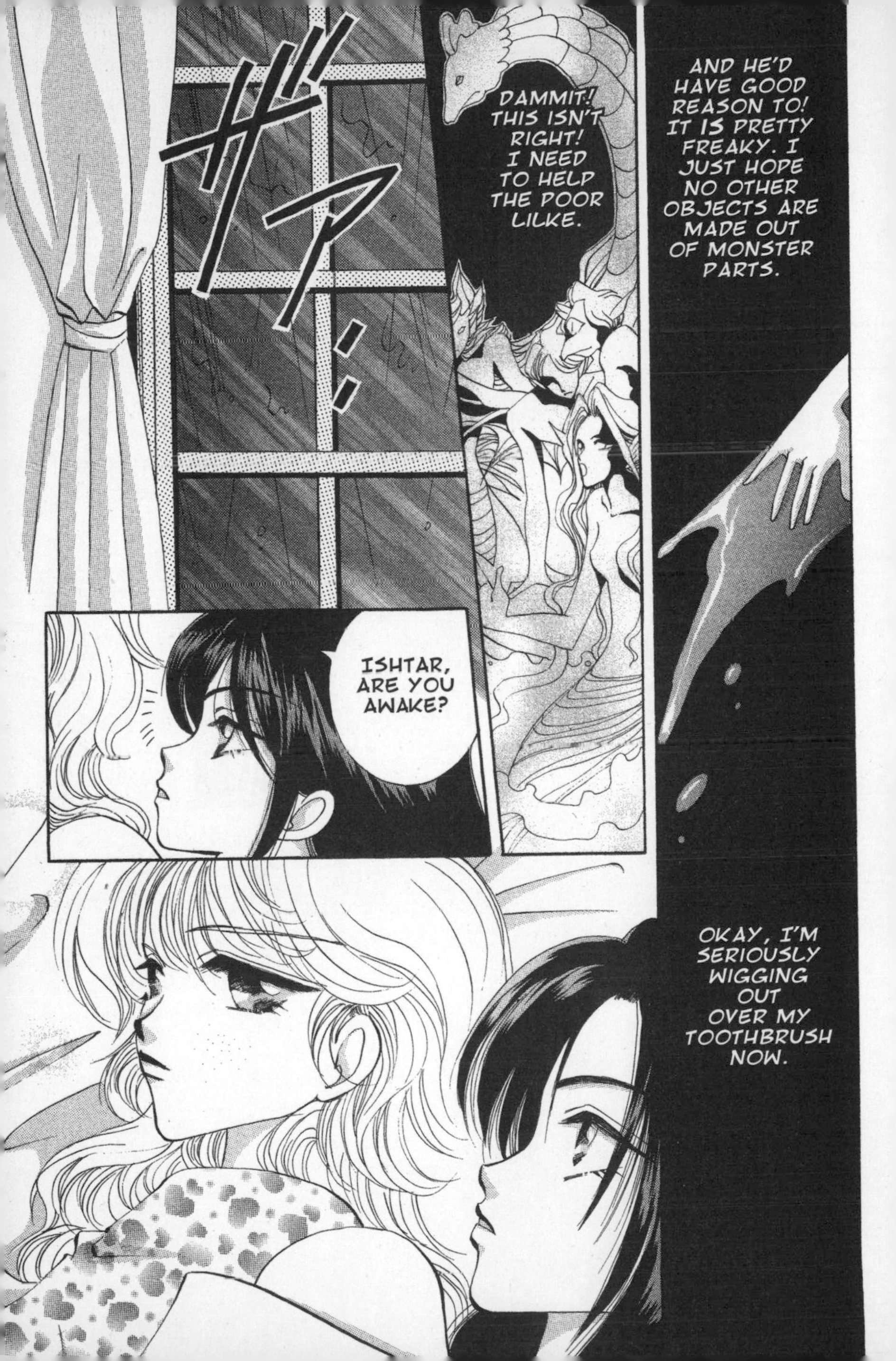
AND HE'D HAVE GOOD REASON TO! IT IS PRETTY FREAKY. I JUST HOPE NO OTHER OBJECTS ARE MADE OUT OF MONSTER PARTS.
DAMMIT! THIS ISN'T RIGHT! I NEED TO HELP THE POOR LILKE.
ザァ
ISHTAR, ARE YOU AWAKE?
OKAY, I'M SERIOUSLY WIGGING OUT OVER MY TOOTHBRUSH NOW.

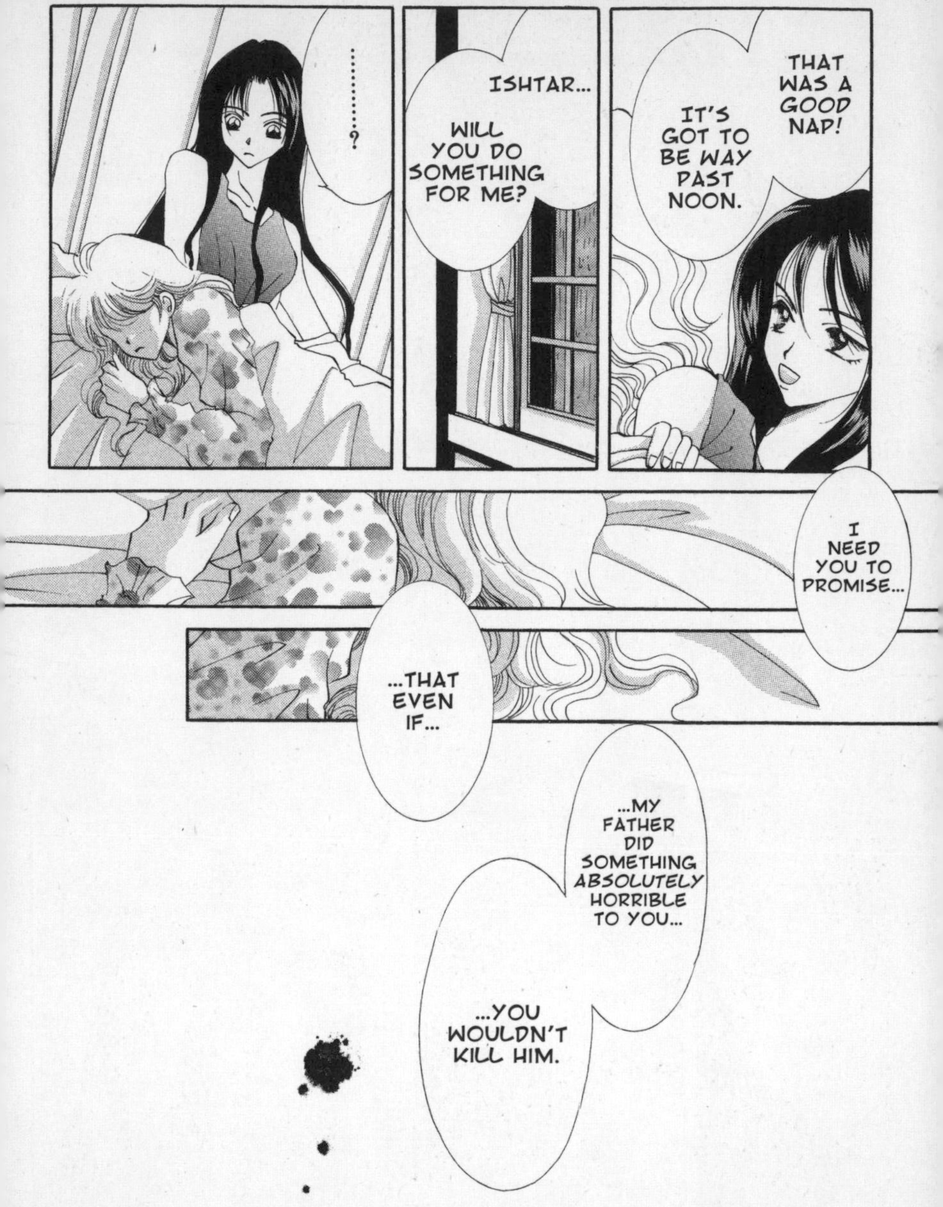
THAT WAS A GOOD NAP!
IT'S GOT TO BE WAY PAST NOON.
ISHTAR...
WILL YOU DO SOMETHING FOR ME?
......?
I NEED YOU TO PROMISE...
...THAT EVEN IF...
...MY FATHER DID SOMETHING ABSOLUTELY HORRIBLE TO YOU...
...YOU WOULDN'T KILL HIM.

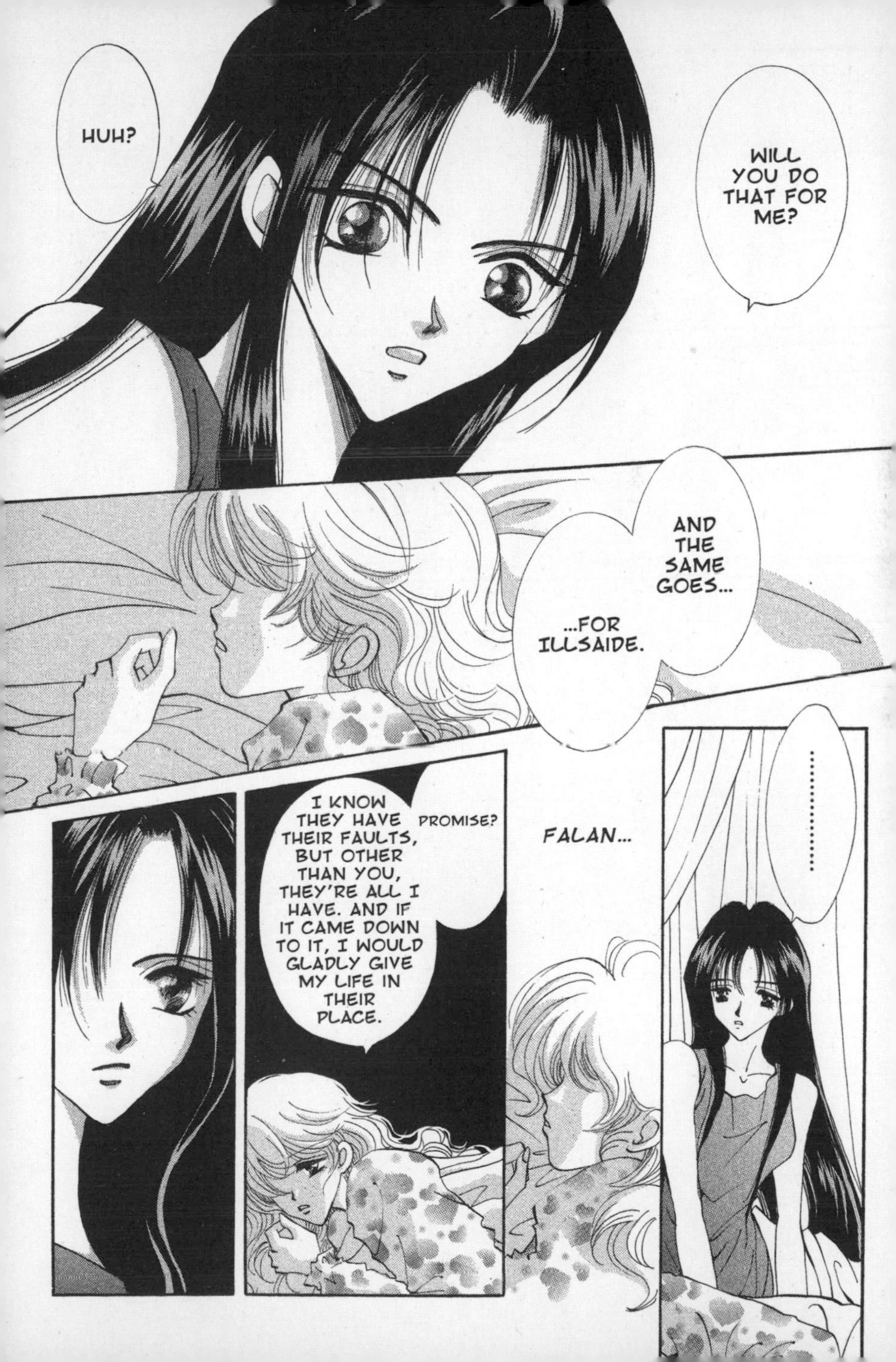
WILL YOU DO THAT FOR ME?
HUH?
AND THE SAME GOES...
...FOR ILLSAIDE.
......
FALAN...
PROMISE?
I KNOW THEY HAVE THEIR FAULTS, BUT OTHER THAN YOU, THEY'RE ALL I HAVE. AND IF IT CAME DOWN TO IT, I WOULD GLADLY GIVE MY LIFE IN THEIR PLACE.

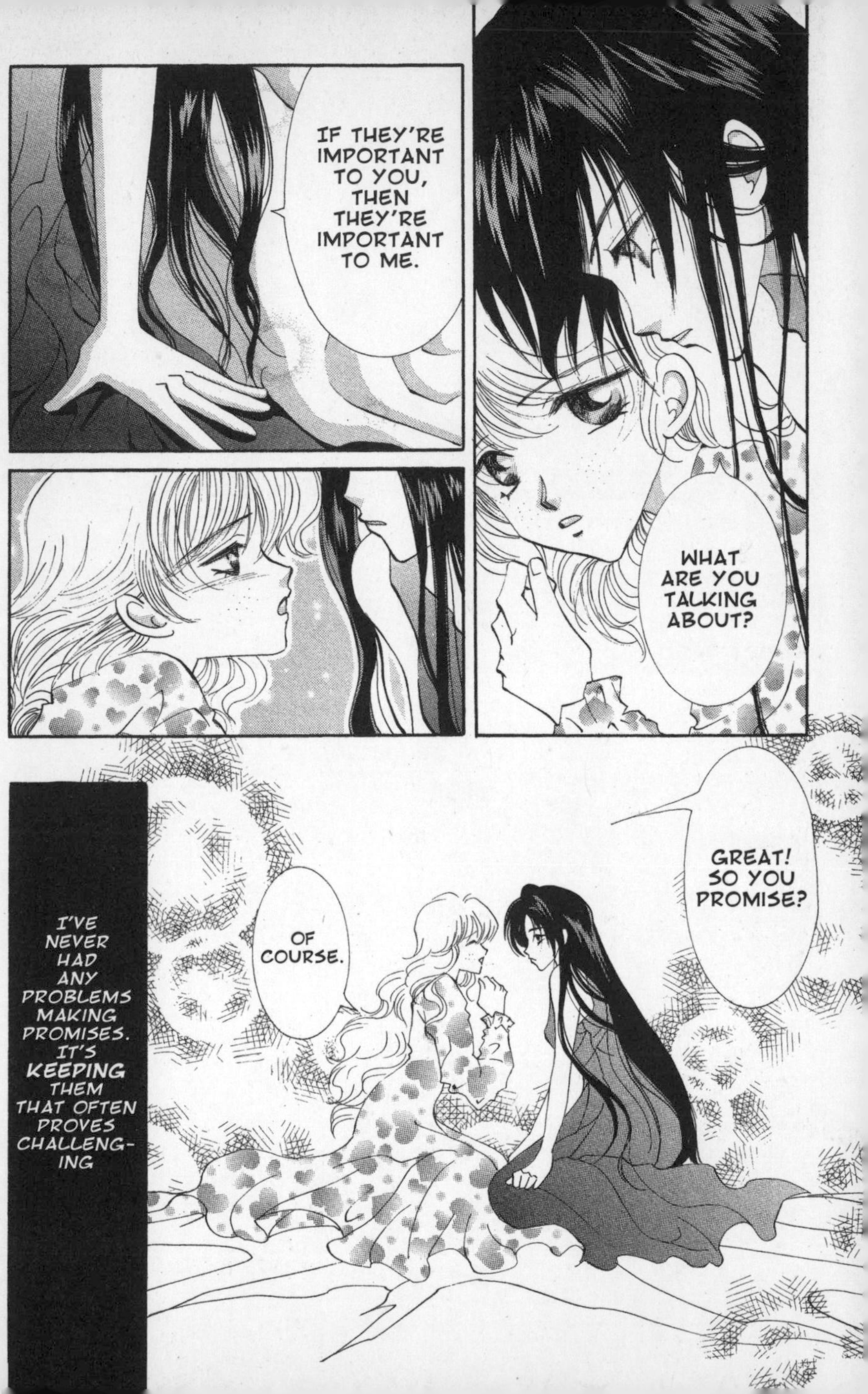
WHAT ARE YOU TALKING ABOUT?
IF THEY'RE IMPORTANT TO YOU, THEN THEY'RE IMPORTANT TO ME.
GREAT! SO YOU PROMISE?
OF COURSE.
I'VE NEVER HAD ANY PROBLEMS MAKING PROMISES. IT'S **KEEPING** THEM THAT OFTEN PROVES CHALLENG-ING

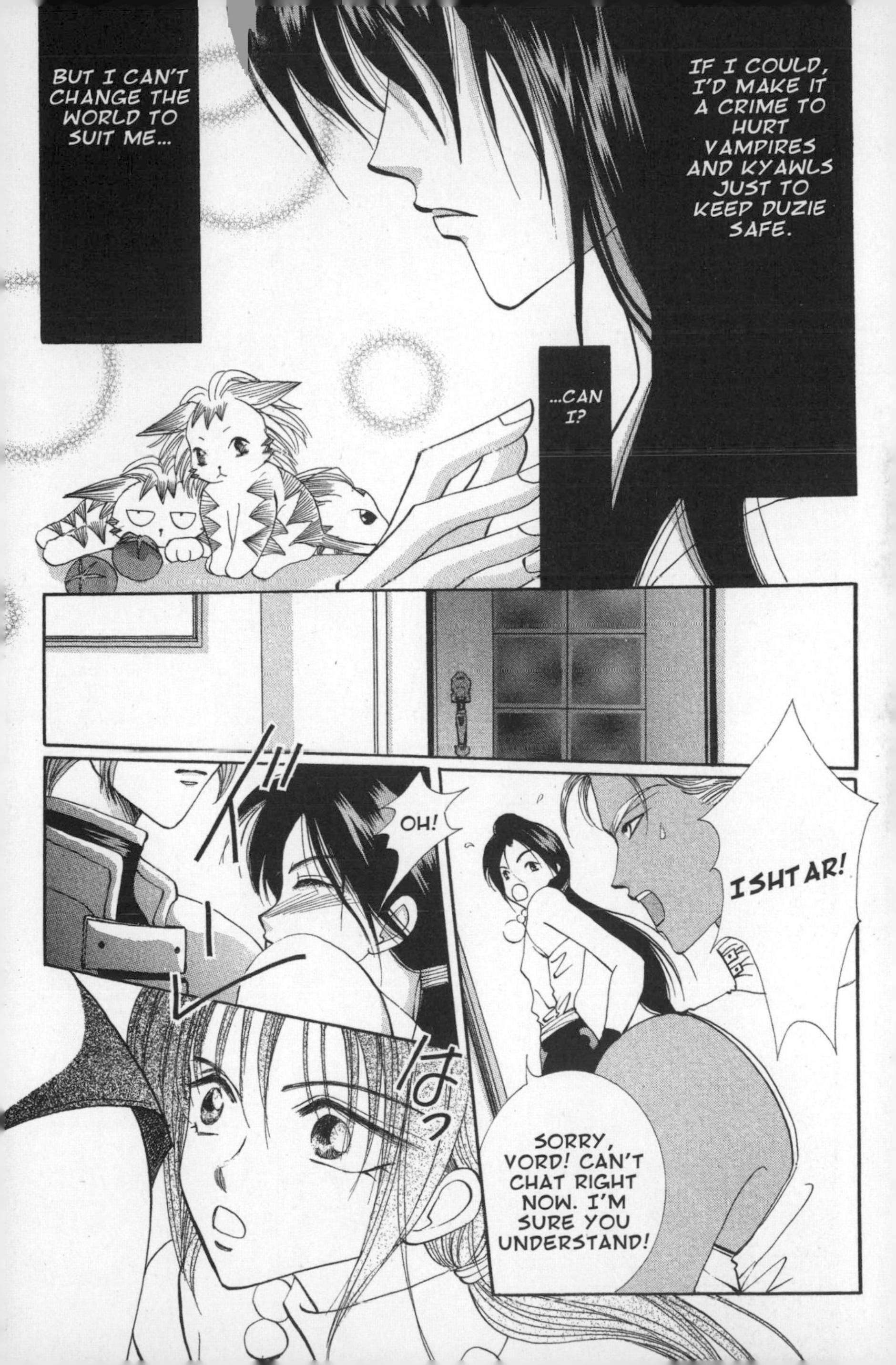
IF I COULD, I'D MAKE IT A CRIME TO HURT VAMPIRES AND KYAWLS JUST TO KEEP DUZIE SAFE.
BUT I CAN'T CHANGE THE WORLD TO SUIT ME...
...CAN I?
ISHTAR!
SORRY, VORD! CAN'T CHAT RIGHT NOW. I'M SURE YOU UNDERSTAND!
OH!
はっ

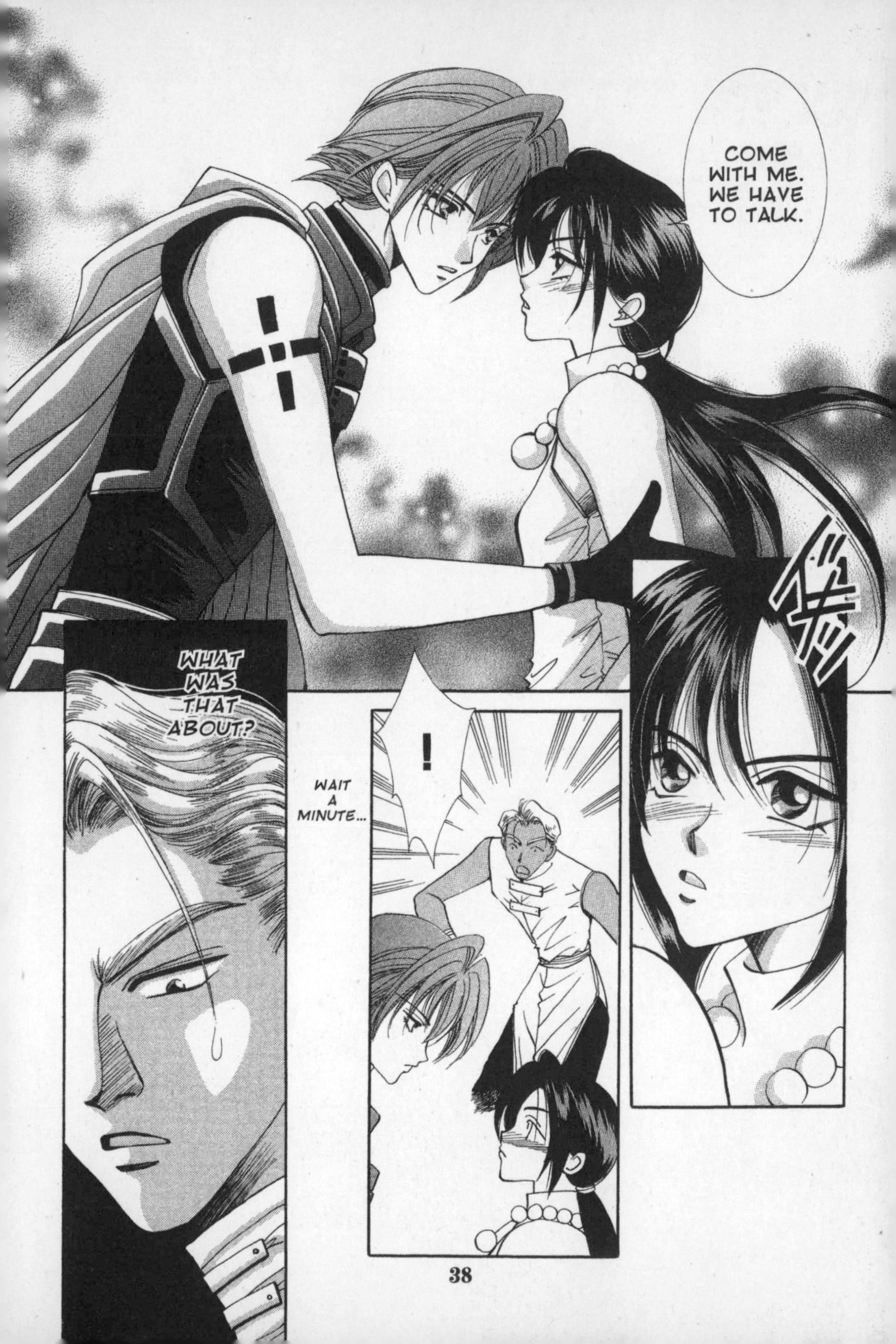
COME WITH ME. WE HAVE TO TALK.
!
WAIT A MINUTE...
WHAT WAS THAT ABOUT?

吸血遊戯
東領篇（シー・ゼネス）
Act.9

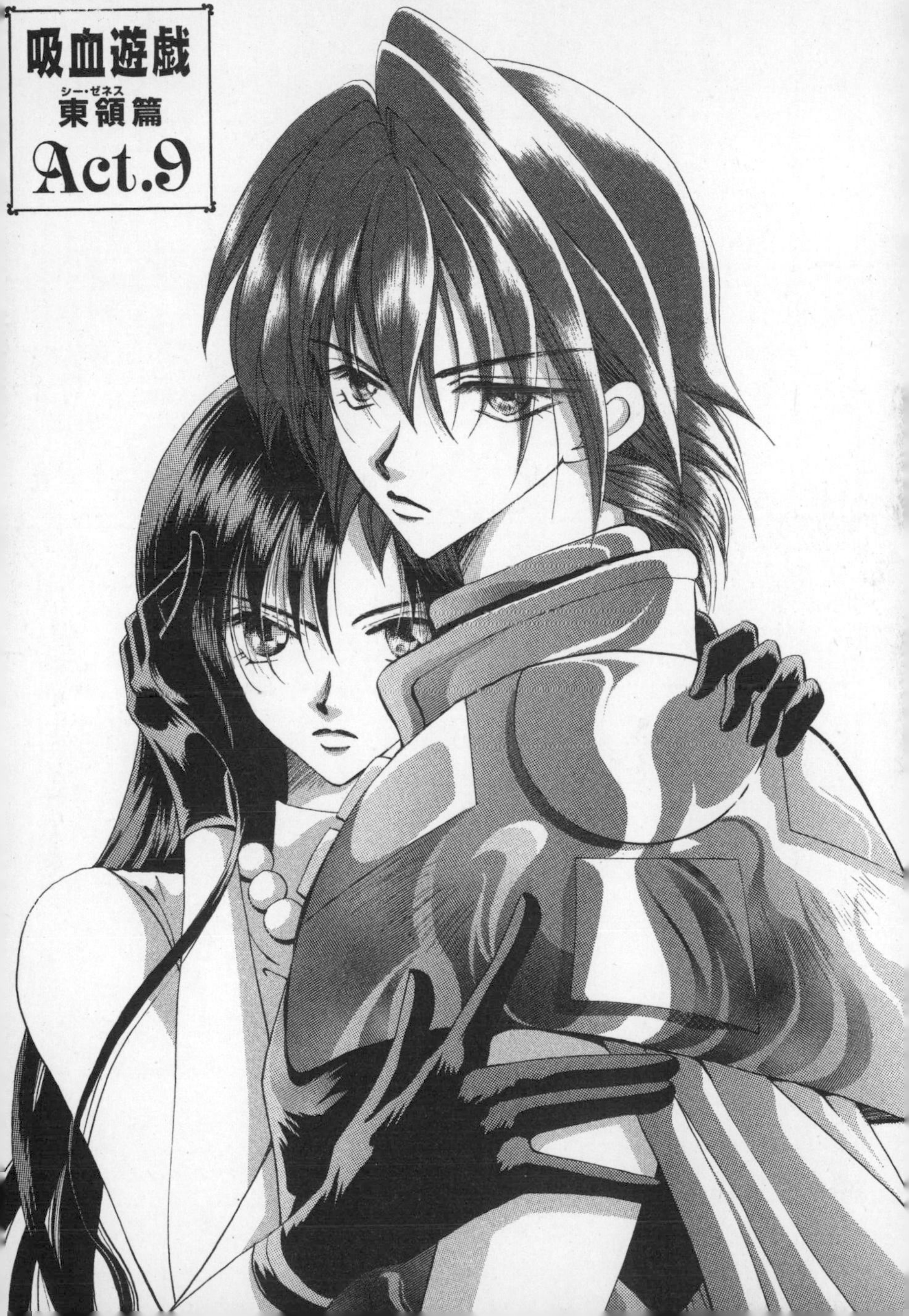

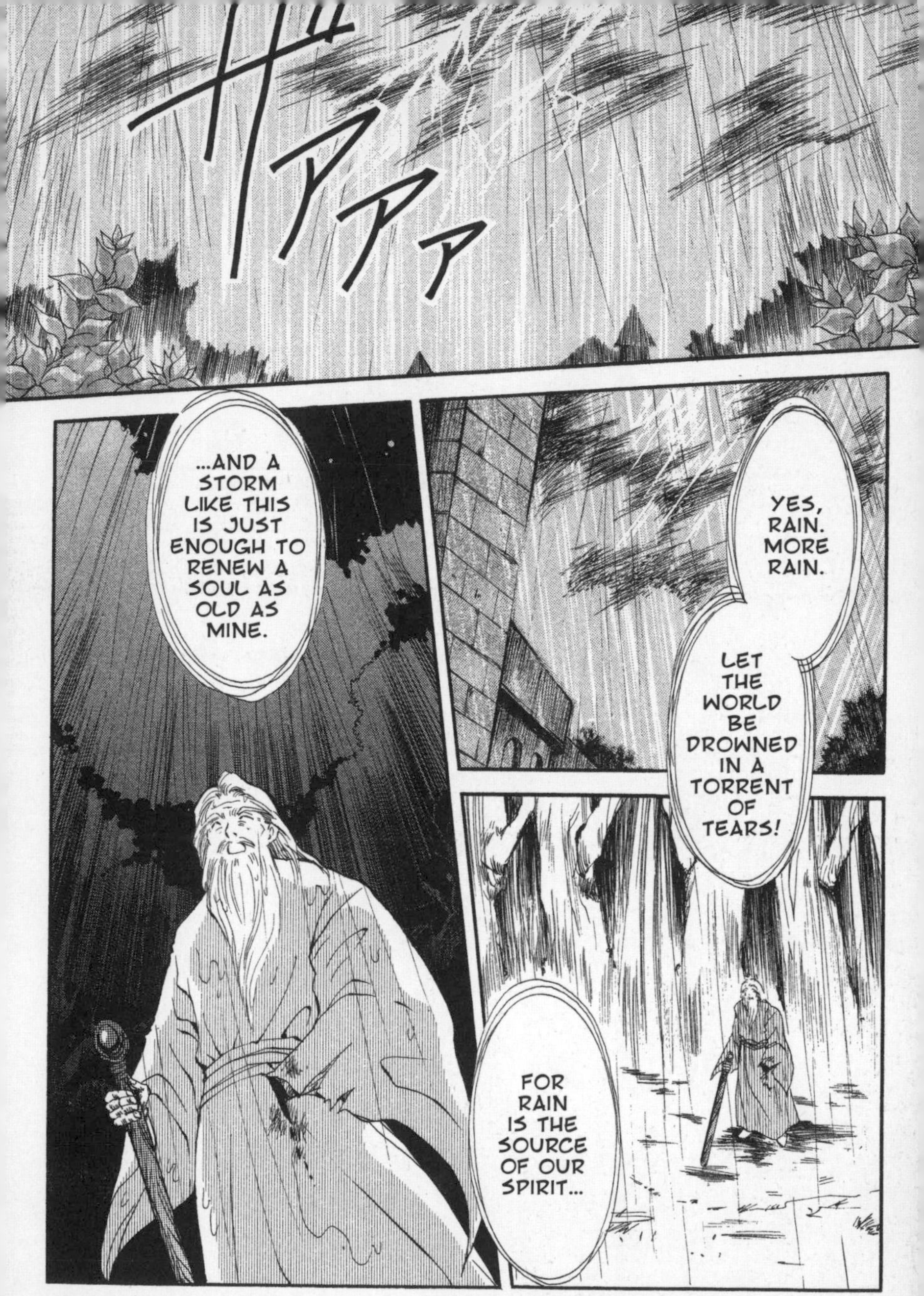
ザァァァ
YES, RAIN. MORE RAIN.
LET THE WORLD BE DROWNED IN A TORRENT OF TEARS!
FOR RAIN IS THE SOURCE OF OUR SPIRIT...
...AND A STORM LIKE THIS IS JUST ENOUGH TO RENEW A SOUL AS OLD AS MINE.

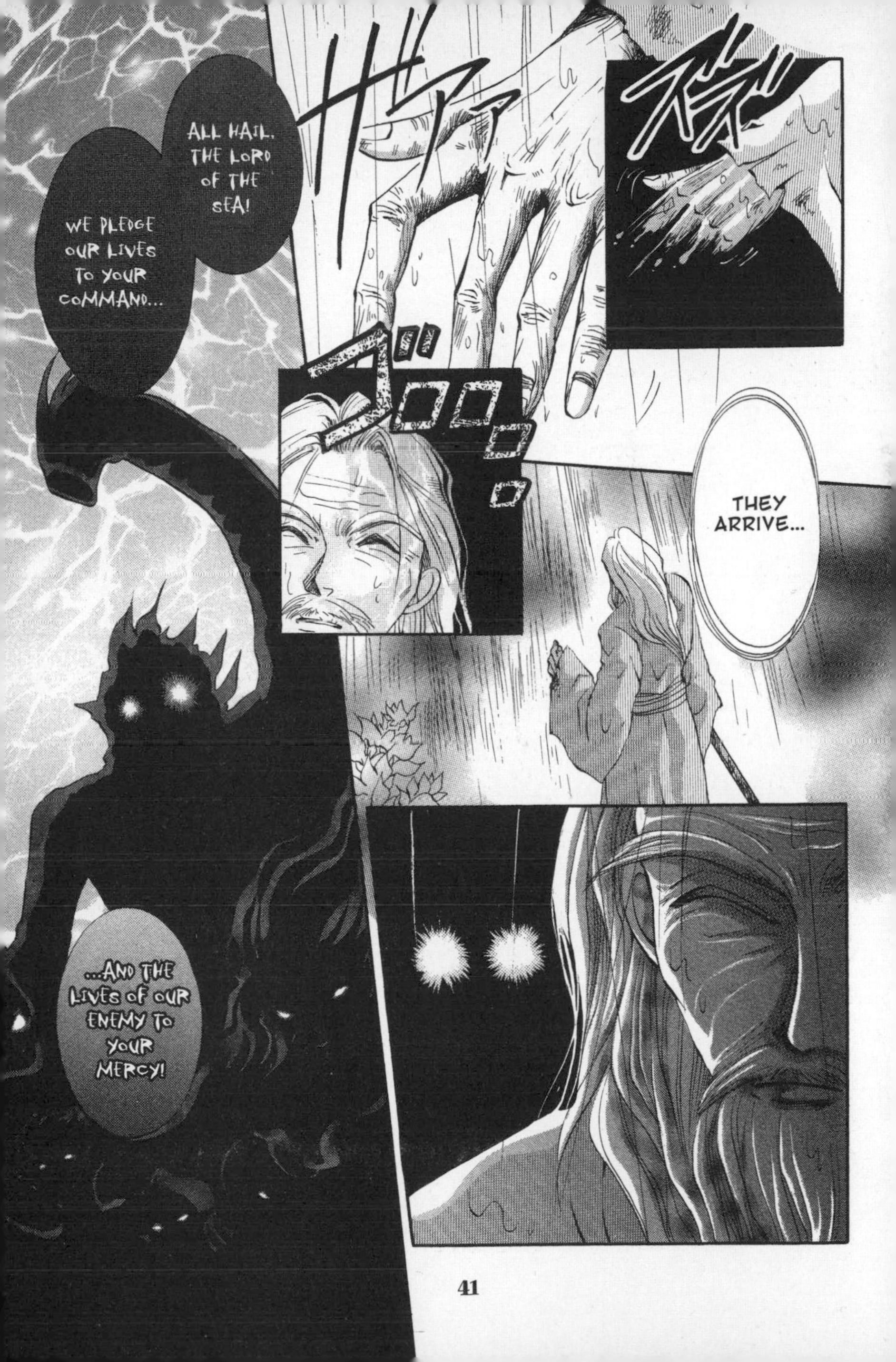
THEY ARRIVE...
ALL HAIL, THE LORD OF THE SEA!
WE PLEDGE OUR LIVES TO YOUR COMMAND...
...AND THE LIVES OF OUR ENEMY TO YOUR MERCY!

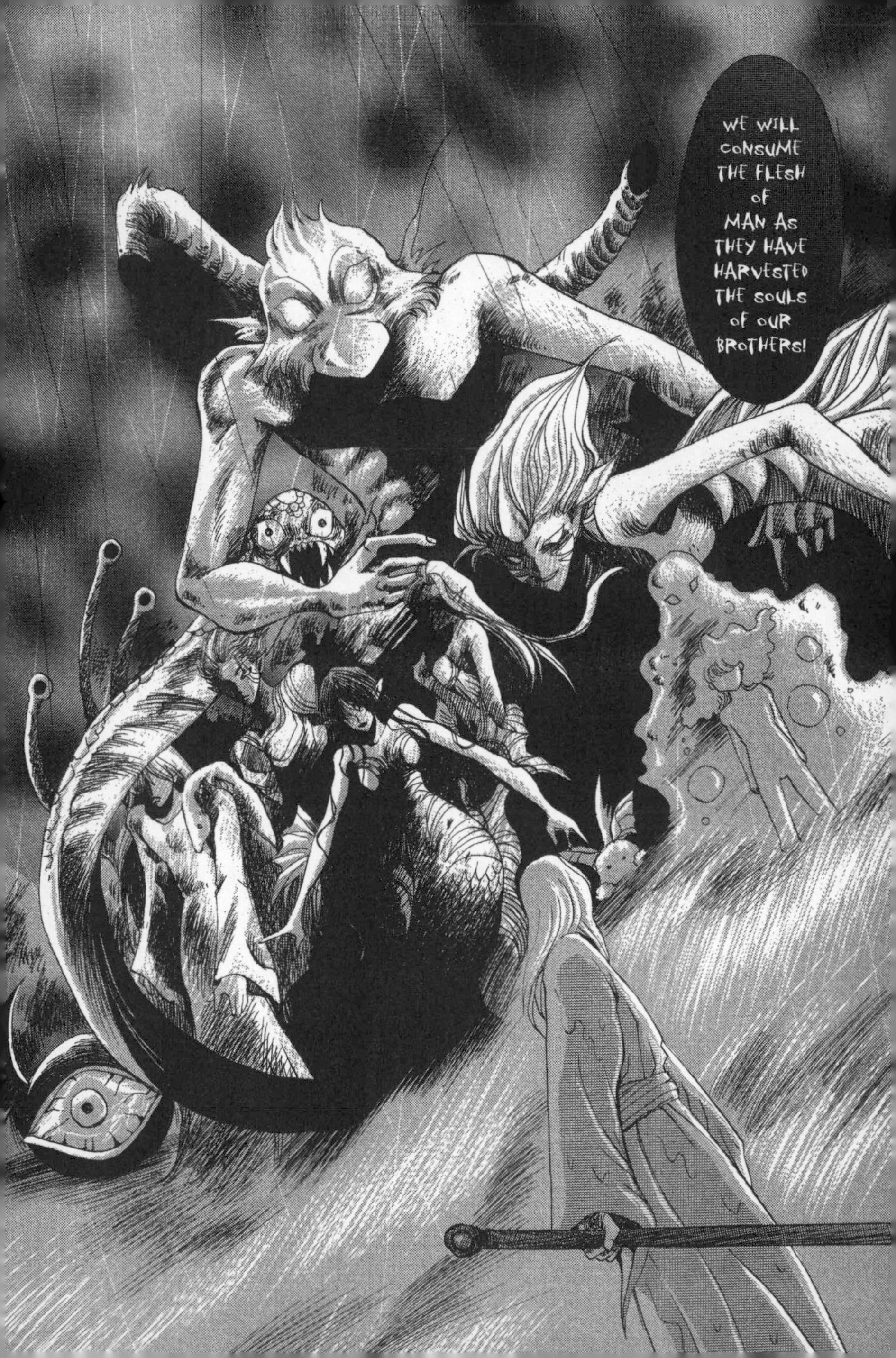
WE WILL CONSUME THE FLESH OF MAN AS THEY HAVE HARVESTED THE SOULS OF OUR BROTHERS!

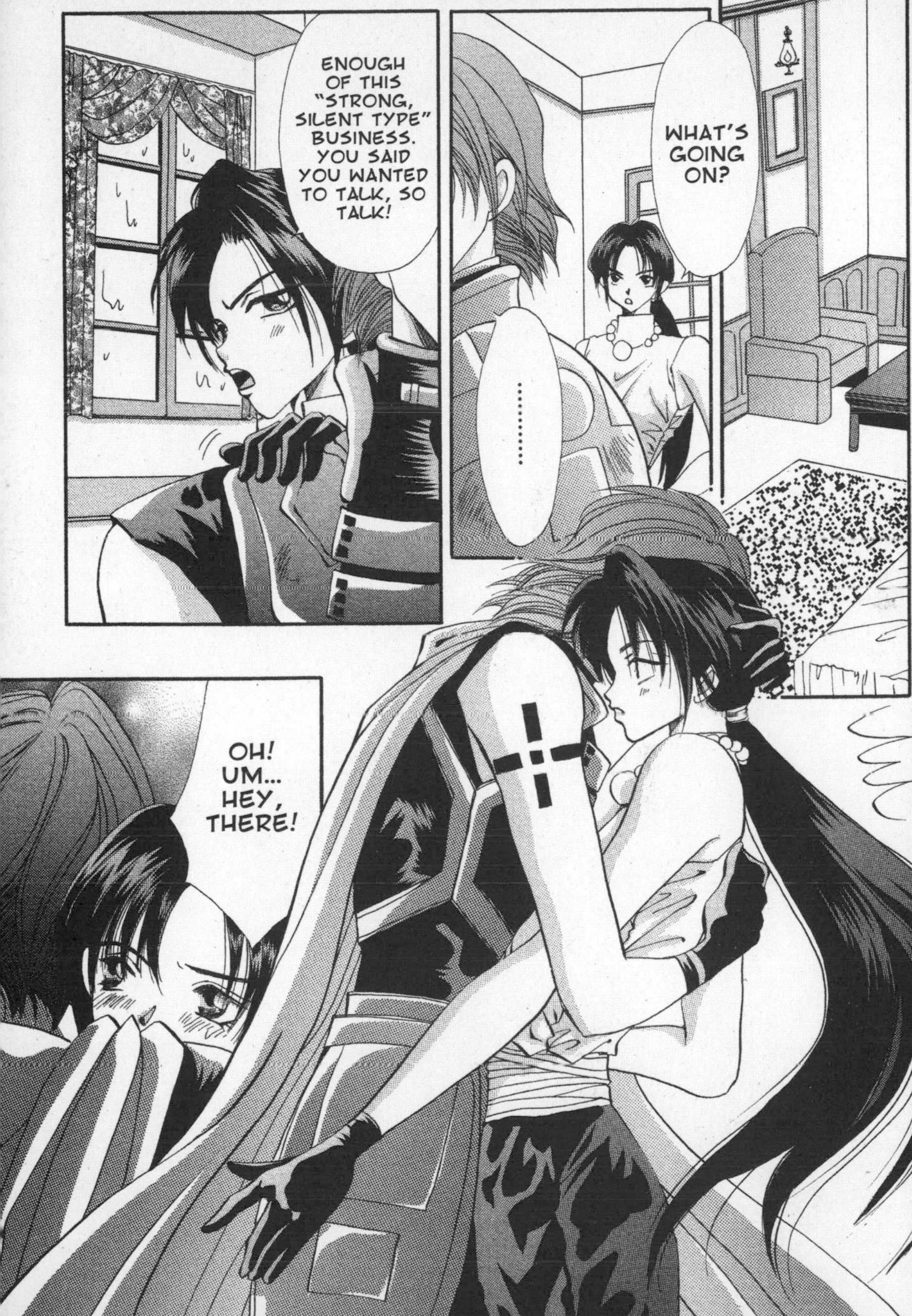
WHAT'S GOING ON?
......
ENOUGH OF THIS "STRONG, SILENT TYPE" BUSINESS. YOU SAID YOU WANTED TO TALK, SO TALK!
OH! UM... HEY, THERE!

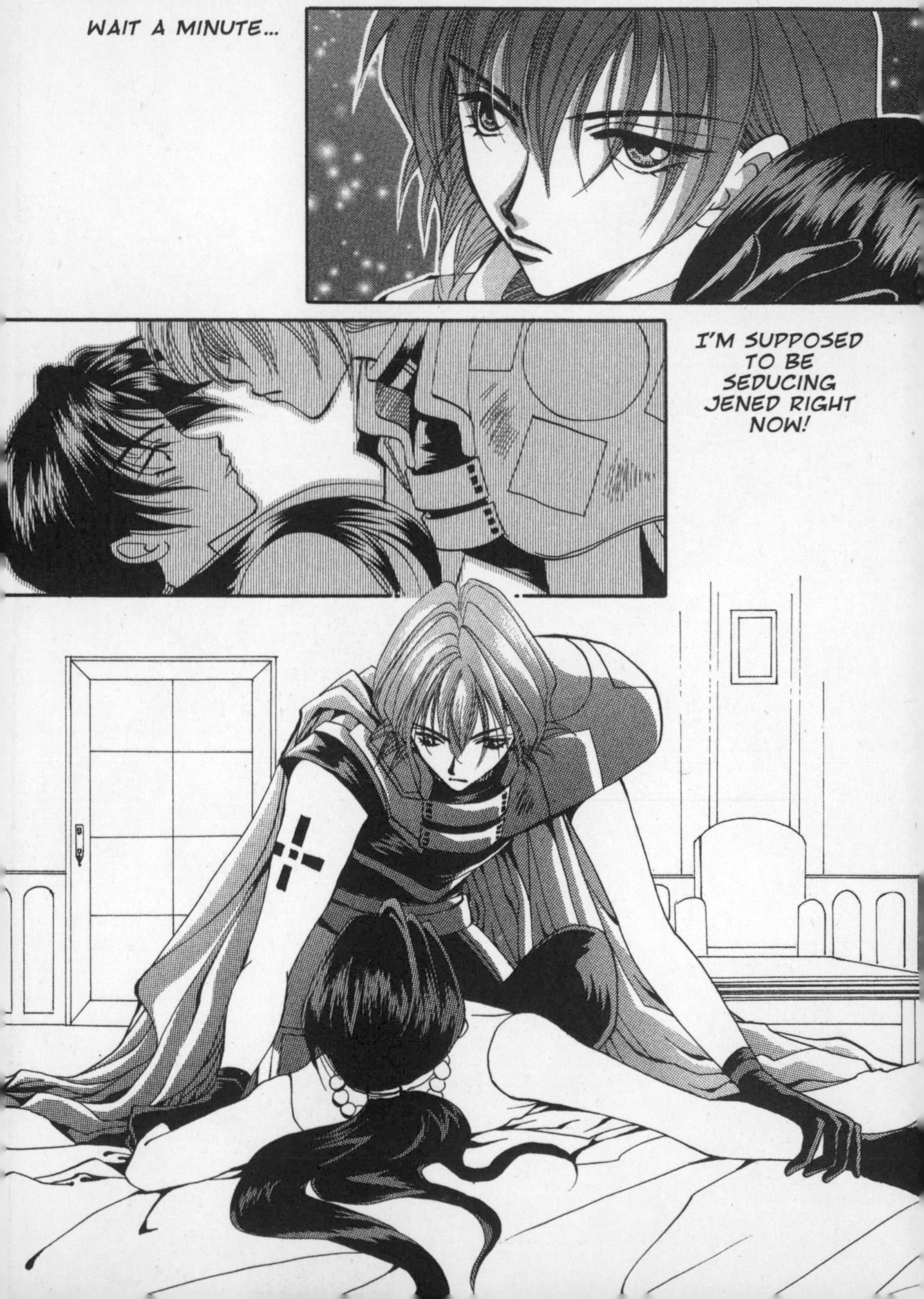
WAIT A MINUTE...
I'M SUPPOSED TO BE SEDUCING JENED RIGHT NOW!

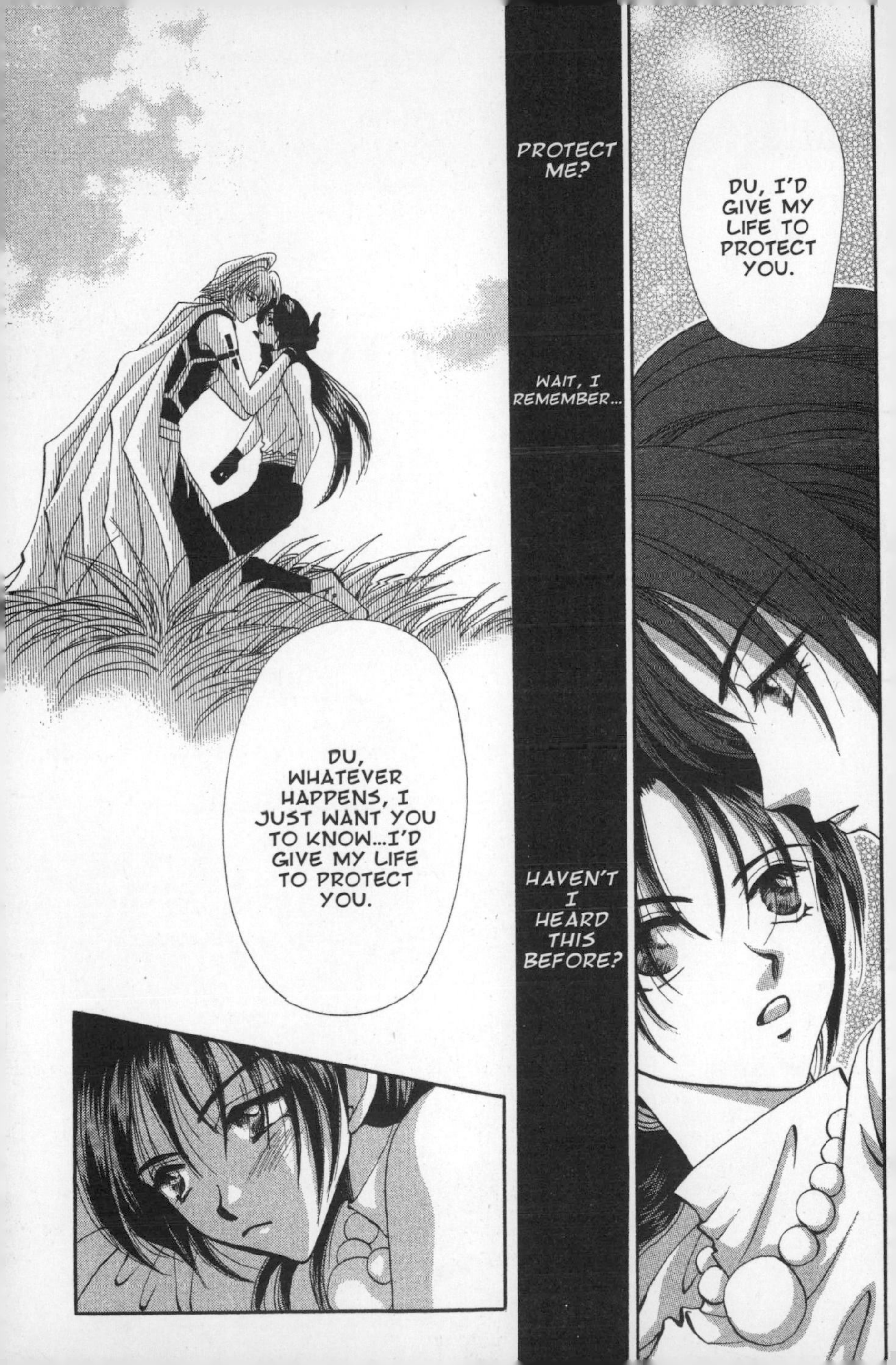
DU, I'D GIVE MY LIFE TO PROTECT YOU.
PROTECT ME?
WAIT, I REMEMBER...
HAVEN'T I HEARD THIS BEFORE?
DU, WHATEVER HAPPENS, I JUST WANT YOU TO KNOW...I'D GIVE MY LIFE TO PROTECT YOU.

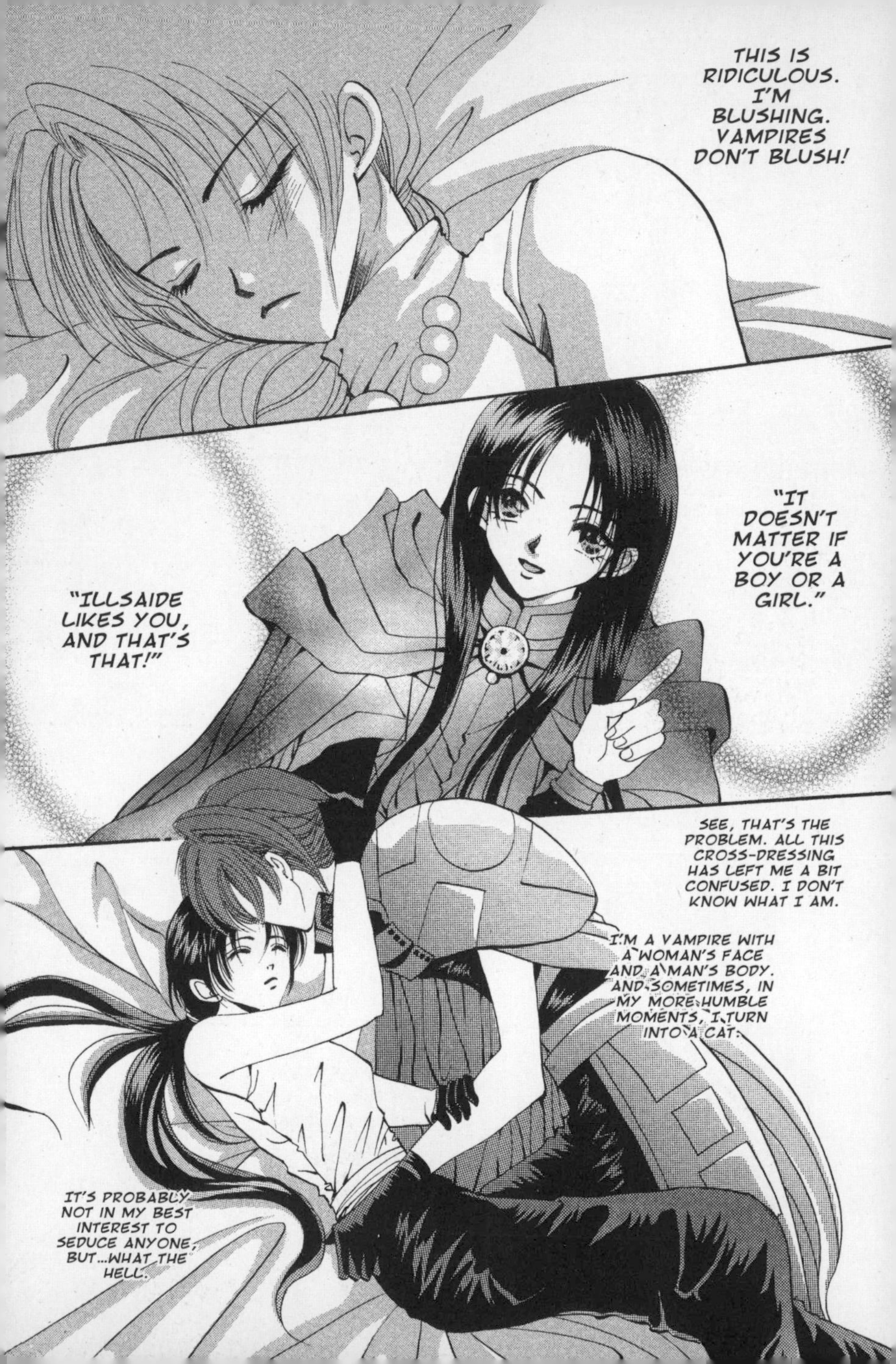
THIS IS RIDICULOUS. I'M BLUSHING. VAMPIRES DON'T BLUSH!
"IT DOESN'T MATTER IF YOU'RE A BOY OR A GIRL."
"ILLSAIDE LIKES YOU, AND THAT'S THAT!"
SEE, THAT'S THE PROBLEM. ALL THIS CROSS-DRESSING HAS LEFT ME A BIT CONFUSED. I DON'T KNOW WHAT I AM.
I'M A VAMPIRE WITH A WOMAN'S FACE AND A MAN'S BODY. AND SOMETIMES, IN MY MORE HUMBLE MOMENTS, I TURN INTO A CAT.
IT'S PROBABLY NOT IN MY BEST INTEREST TO SEDUCE ANYONE, BUT...WHAT THE HELL.

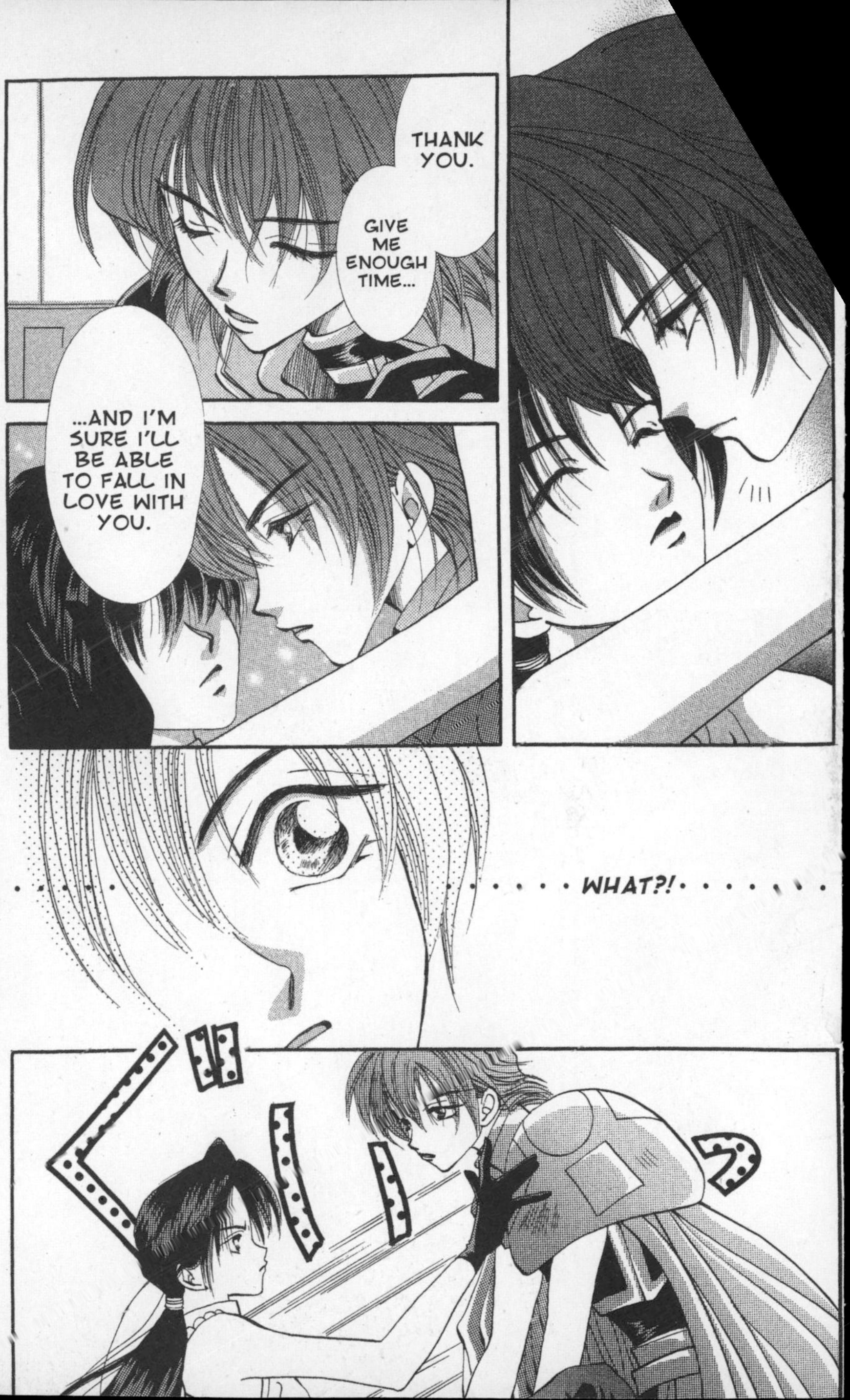
THANK YOU.
GIVE ME ENOUGH TIME...
...AND I'M SURE I'LL BE ABLE TO FALL IN LOVE WITH YOU.
WHAT?!

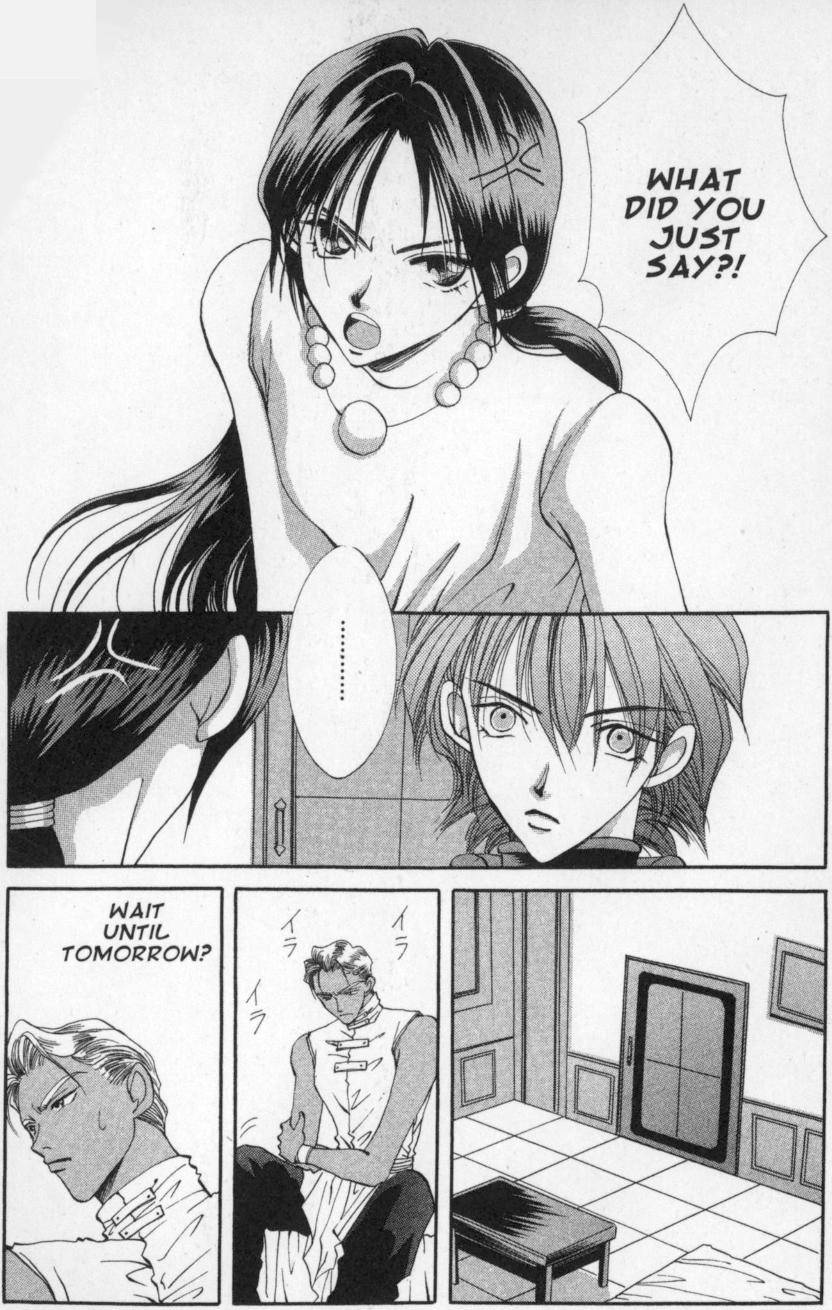
WHAT DID YOU JUST SAY?!
......
イラ
イラ
イラ
WAIT UNTIL TOMORROW?

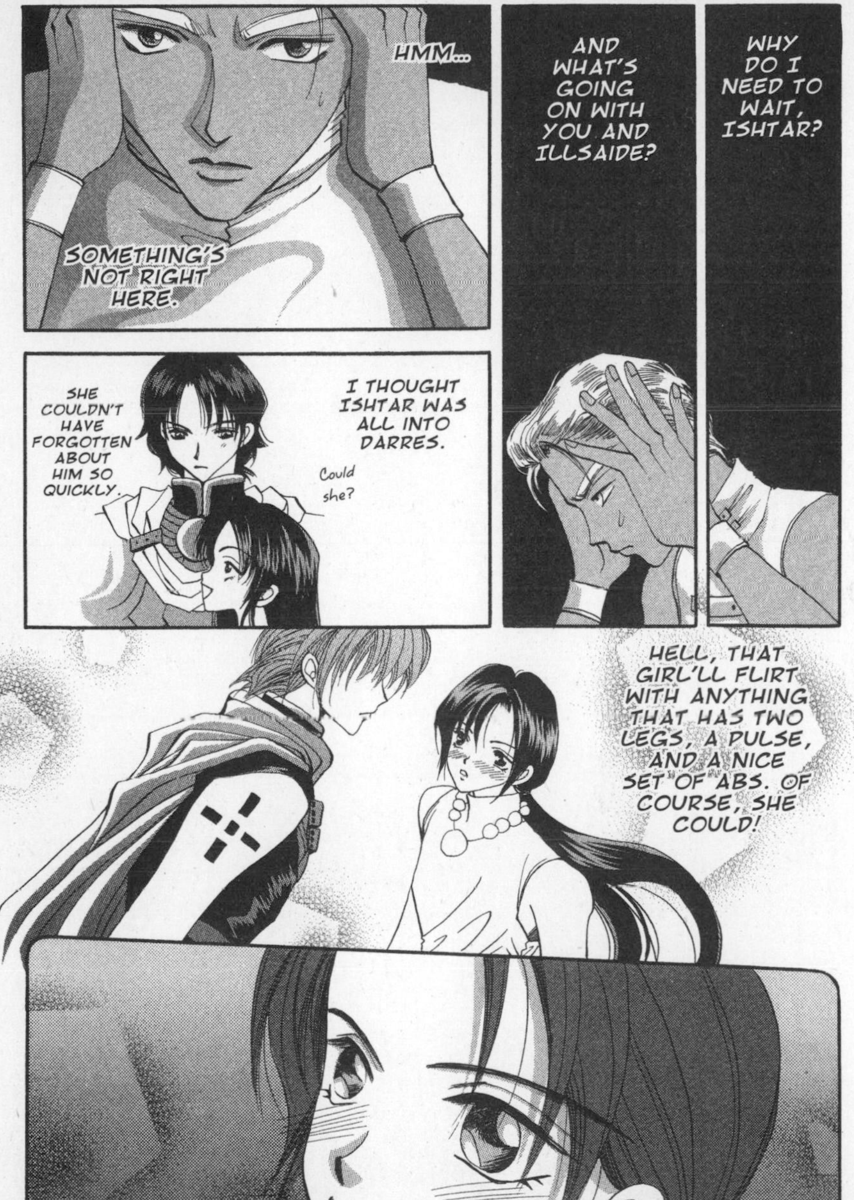
WHY DO I NEED TO WAIT, ISHTAR?
AND WHAT'S GOING ON WITH YOU AND ILLSAIDE?
HMM...
SOMETHING'S NOT RIGHT HERE.
I THOUGHT ISHTAR WAS ALL INTO DARRES.
Could she?
SHE COULDN'T HAVE FORGOTTEN ABOUT HIM SO QUICKLY.
HELL, THAT GIRL'LL FLIRT WITH ANYTHING THAT HAS TWO LEGS, A PULSE, AND A NICE SET OF ABS. OF COURSE, SHE COULD!

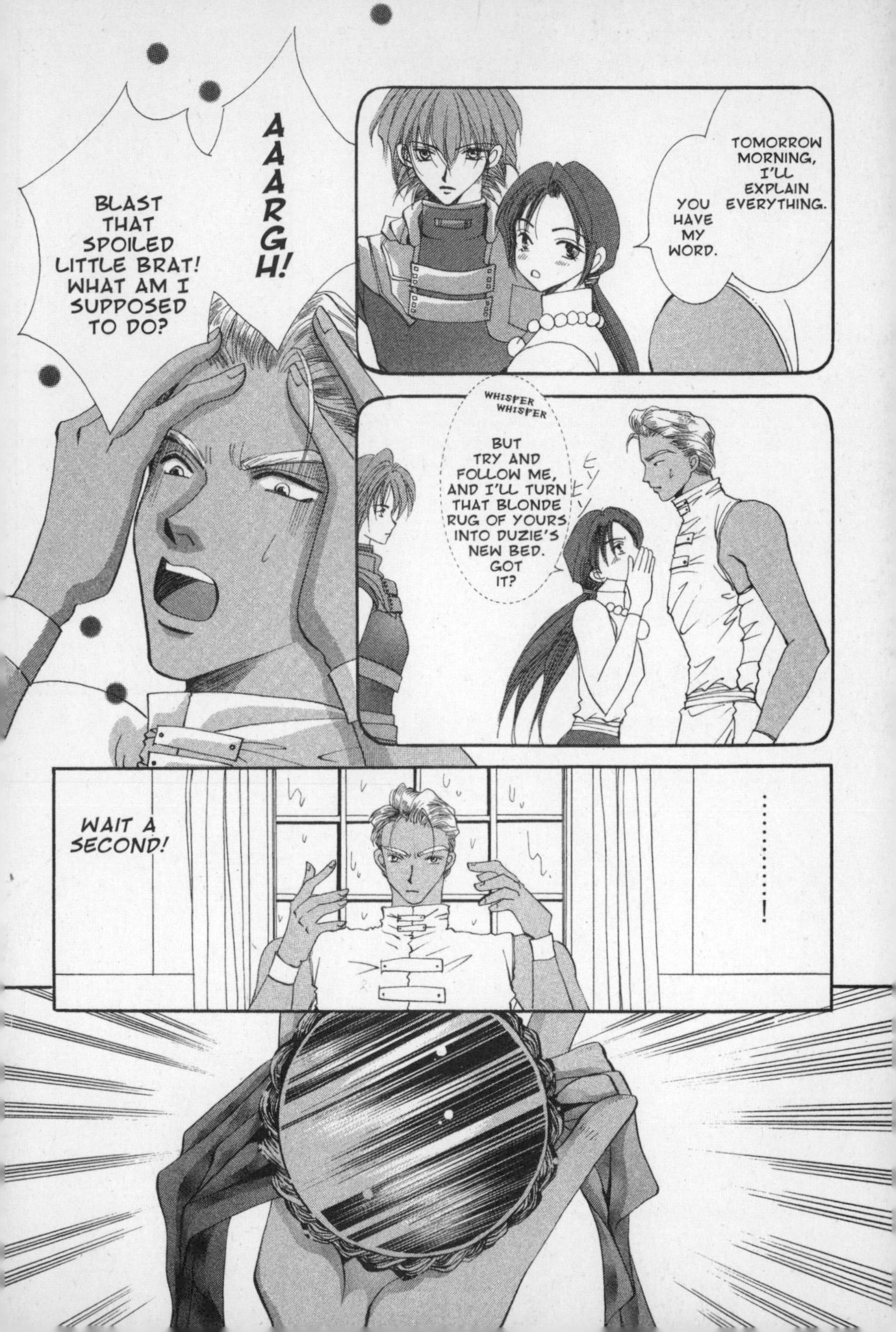
TOMORROW MORNING, I'LL EXPLAIN EVERYTHING.
YOU HAVE MY WORD.
WHISPER WHISPER
BUT TRY AND FOLLOW ME, AND I'LL TURN THAT BLONDE RUG OF YOURS INTO DUZIE'S NEW BED. GOT IT?
AAAARGH!
BLAST THAT SPOILED LITTLE BRAT! WHAT AM I SUPPOSED TO DO?
......!
WAIT A SECOND!

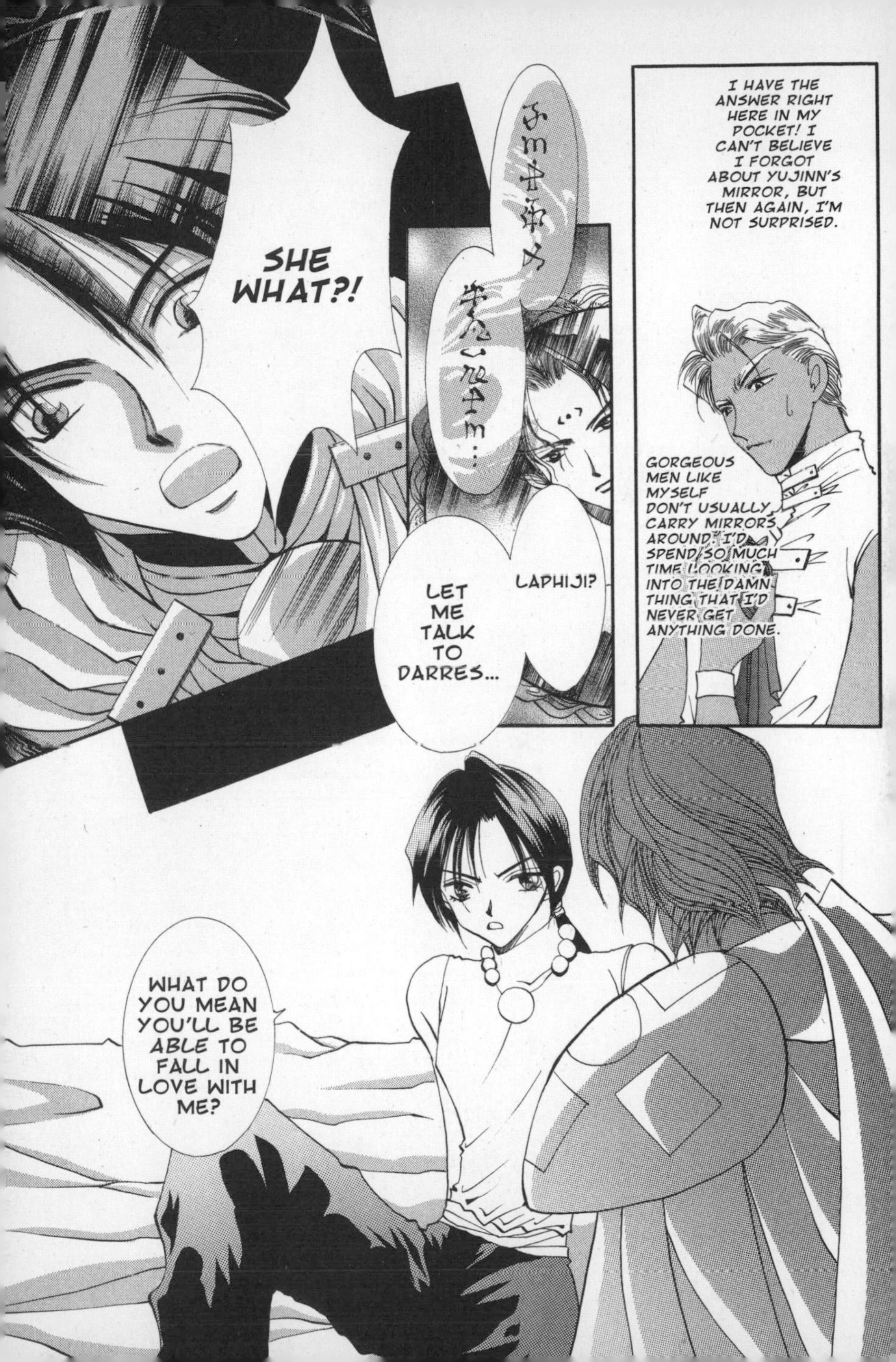
I HAVE THE ANSWER RIGHT HERE IN MY POCKET! I CAN'T BELIEVE I FORGOT ABOUT YUJINN'S MIRROR, BUT THEN AGAIN, I'M NOT SURPRISED.
GORGEOUS MEN LIKE MYSELF DON'T USUALLY CARRY MIRRORS AROUND. I'D SPEND SO MUCH TIME LOOKING INTO THE DAMN THING THAT I'D NEVER GET ANYTHING DONE.
LAPHIJI?
LET ME TALK TO DARRES...
SHE WHAT?!
WHAT DO YOU MEAN YOU'LL BE ABLE TO FALL IN LOVE WITH ME?

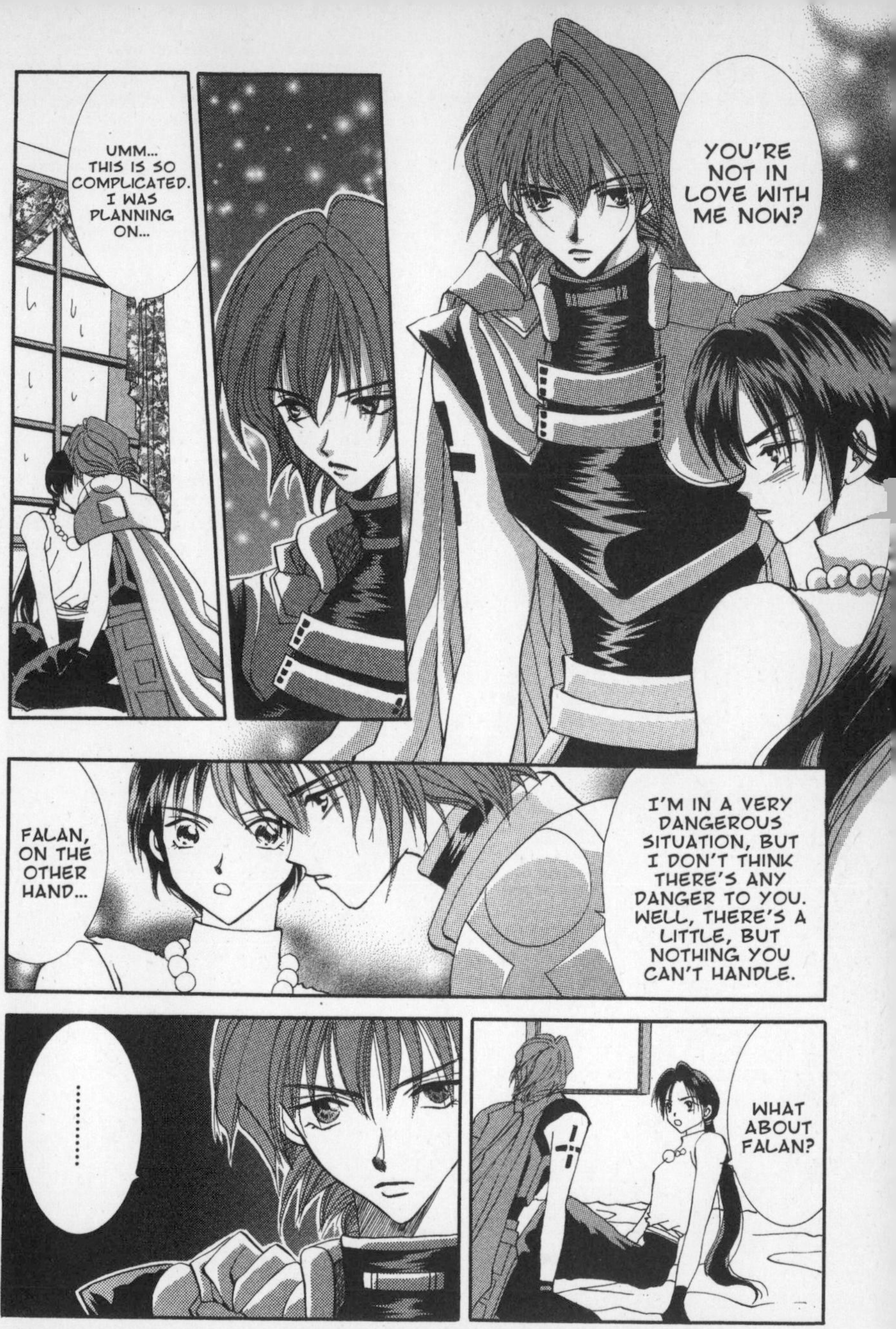
YOU'RE NOT IN LOVE WITH ME NOW?
UMM... THIS IS SO COMPLICATED. I WAS PLANNING ON...
I'M IN A VERY DANGEROUS SITUATION, BUT I DON'T THINK THERE'S ANY DANGER TO YOU. WELL, THERE'S A LITTLE, BUT NOTHING YOU CAN'T HANDLE.
FALAN, ON THE OTHER HAND...
WHAT ABOUT FALAN?
....

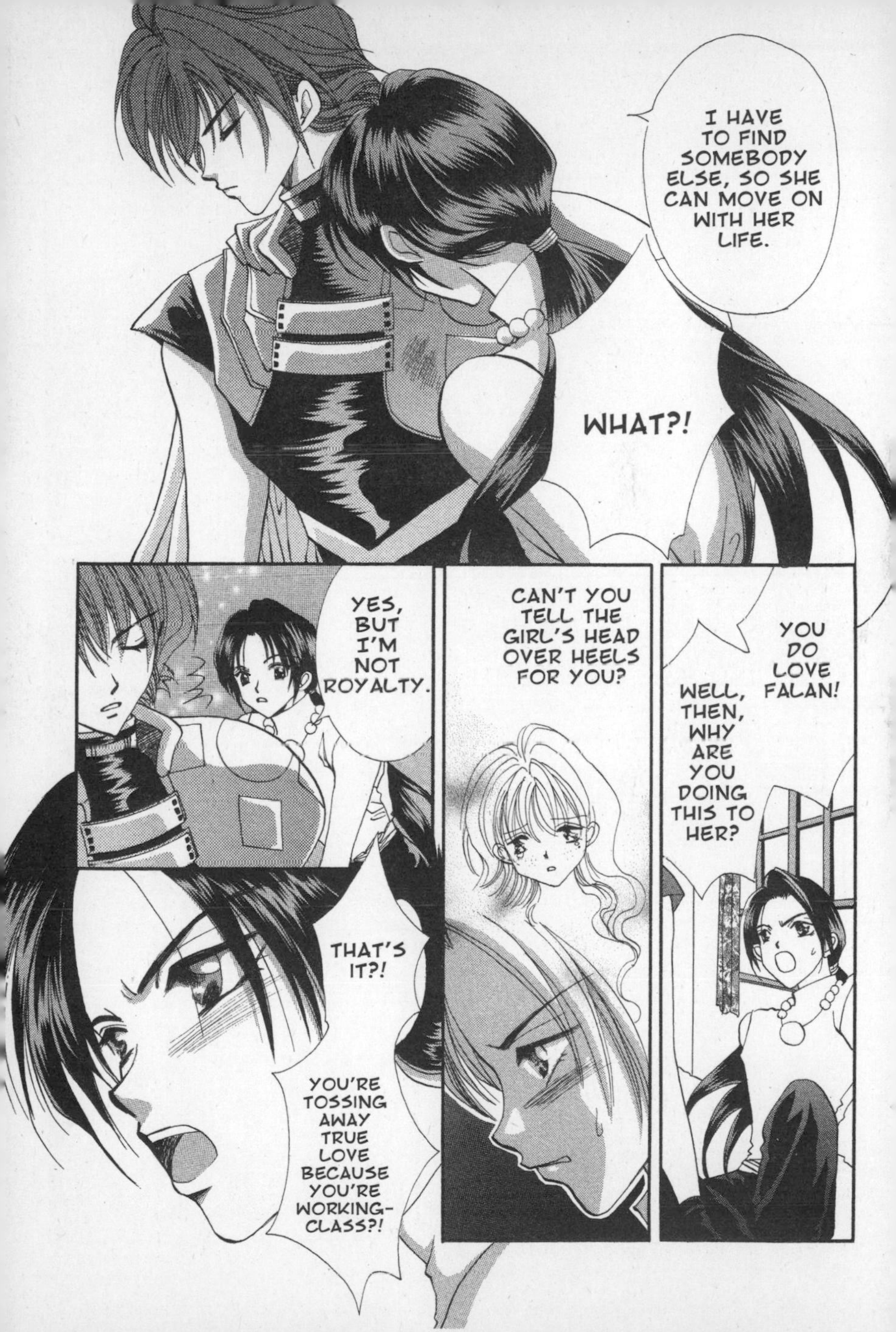
I HAVE TO FIND SOMEBODY ELSE, SO SHE CAN MOVE ON WITH HER LIFE.
WHAT?!
YOU DO LOVE FALAN!
WELL, THEN, WHY ARE YOU DOING THIS TO HER?
CAN'T YOU TELL THE GIRL'S HEAD OVER HEELS FOR YOU?
YES, BUT I'M NOT ROYALTY.
THAT'S IT?!
YOU'RE TOSSING AWAY TRUE LOVE BECAUSE YOU'RE WORKING-CLASS?!

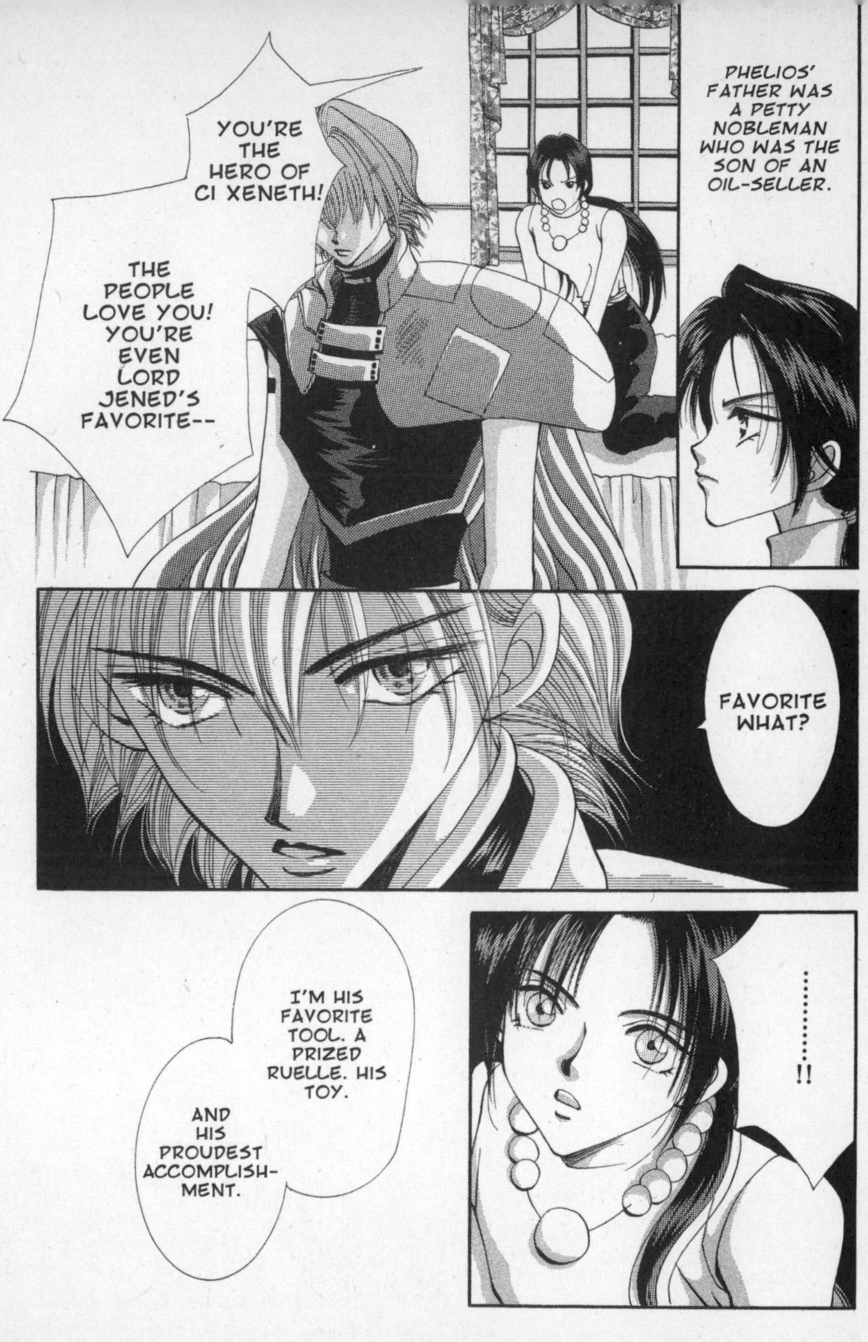
PHELIOS' FATHER WAS A PETTY NOBLEMAN WHO WAS THE SON OF AN OIL-SELLER.
YOU'RE THE HERO OF CI XENETH!
THE PEOPLE LOVE YOU! YOU'RE EVEN LORD JENED'S FAVORITE--
FAVORITE WHAT?
......!!
I'M HIS FAVORITE TOOL. A PRIZED RUELLE. HIS TOY.
AND HIS PROUDEST ACCOMPLISHMENT.

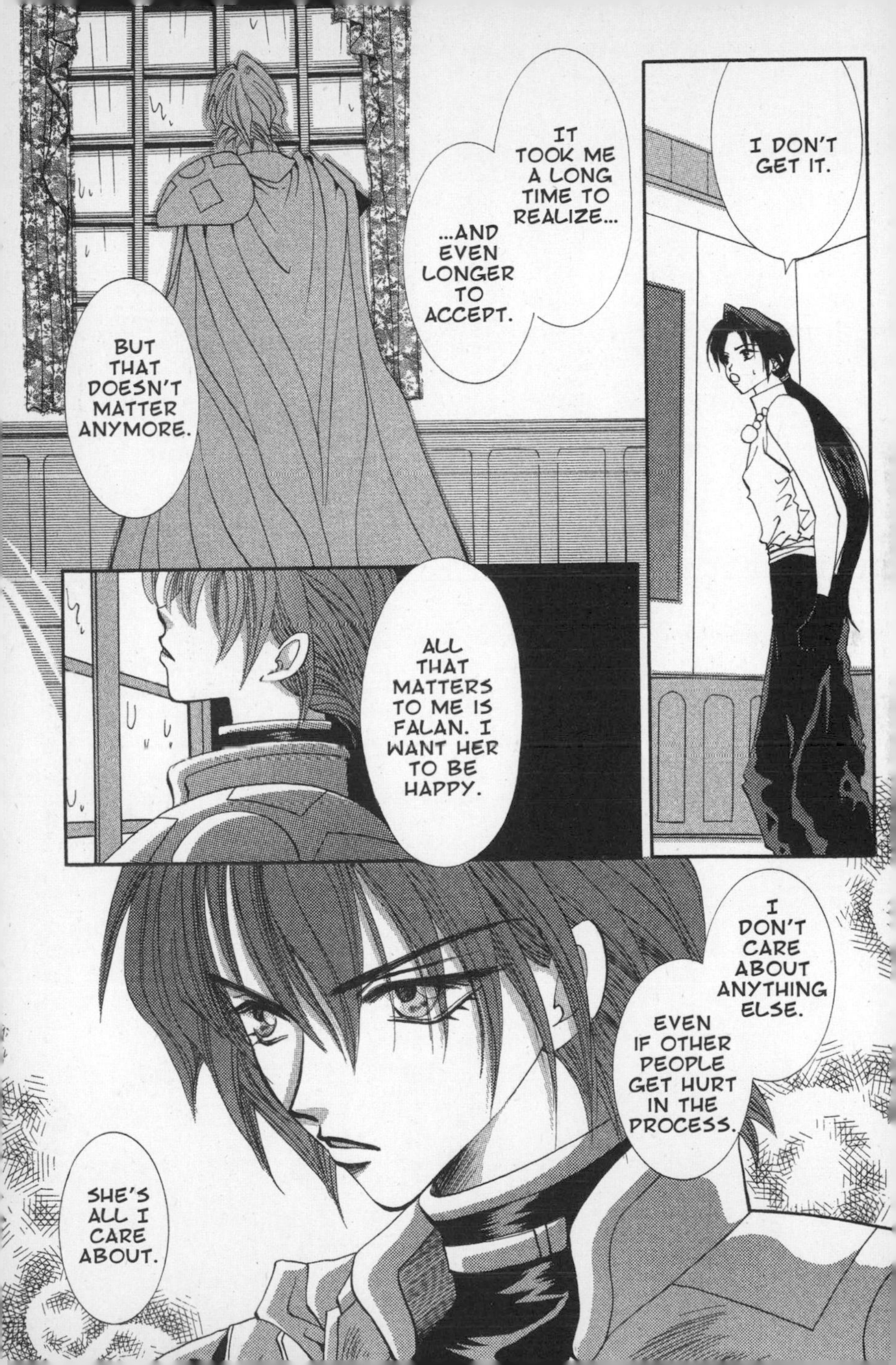
I DON'T GET IT.
IT TOOK ME A LONG TIME TO REALIZE...
...AND EVEN LONGER TO ACCEPT.
BUT THAT DOESN'T MATTER ANYMORE.
ALL THAT MATTERS TO ME IS FALAN. I WANT HER TO BE HAPPY.
I DON'T CARE ABOUT ANYTHING ELSE.
EVEN IF OTHER PEOPLE GET HURT IN THE PROCESS.
SHE'S ALL I CARE ABOUT.

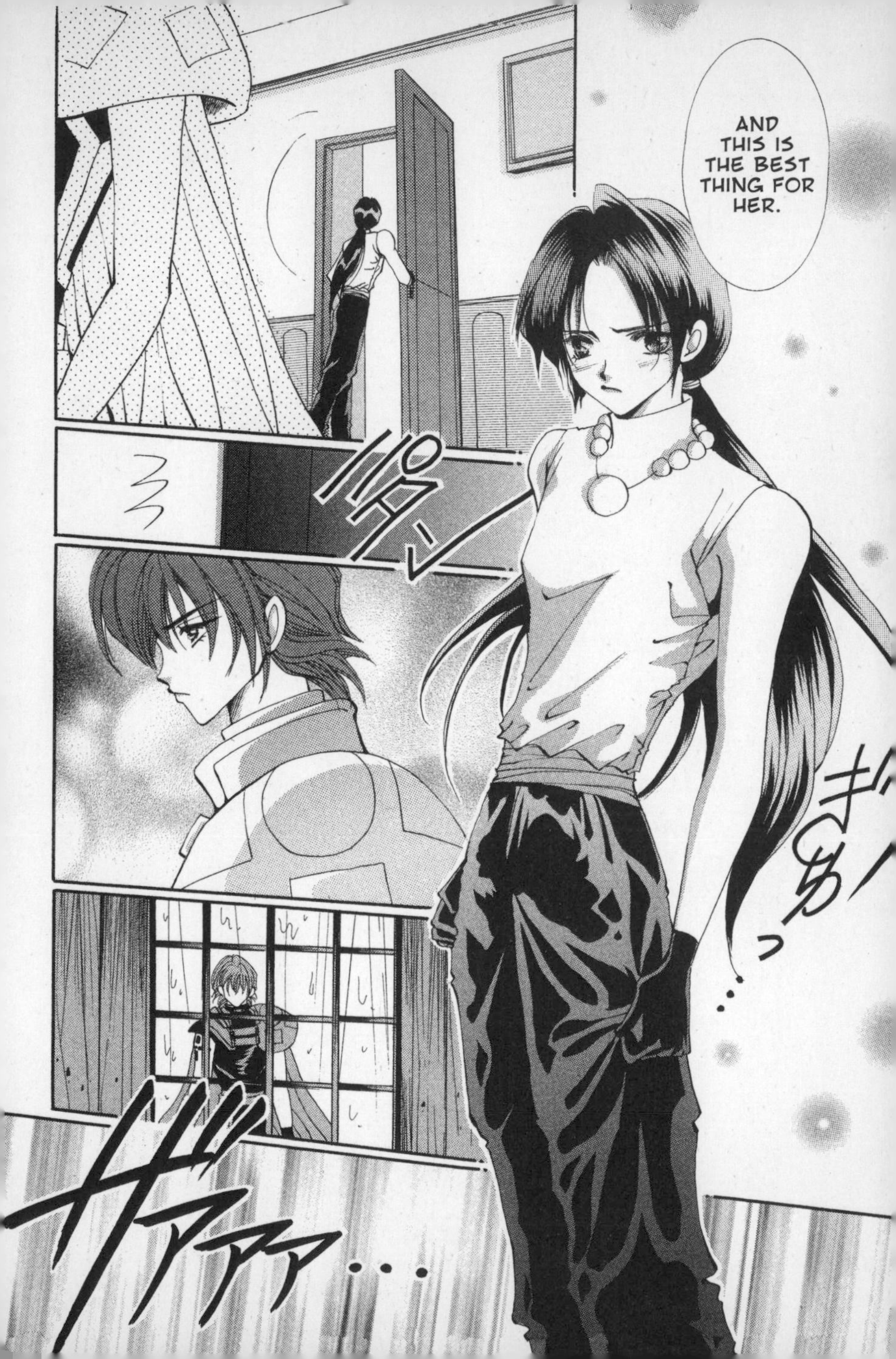
AND THIS IS THE BEST THING FOR HER.

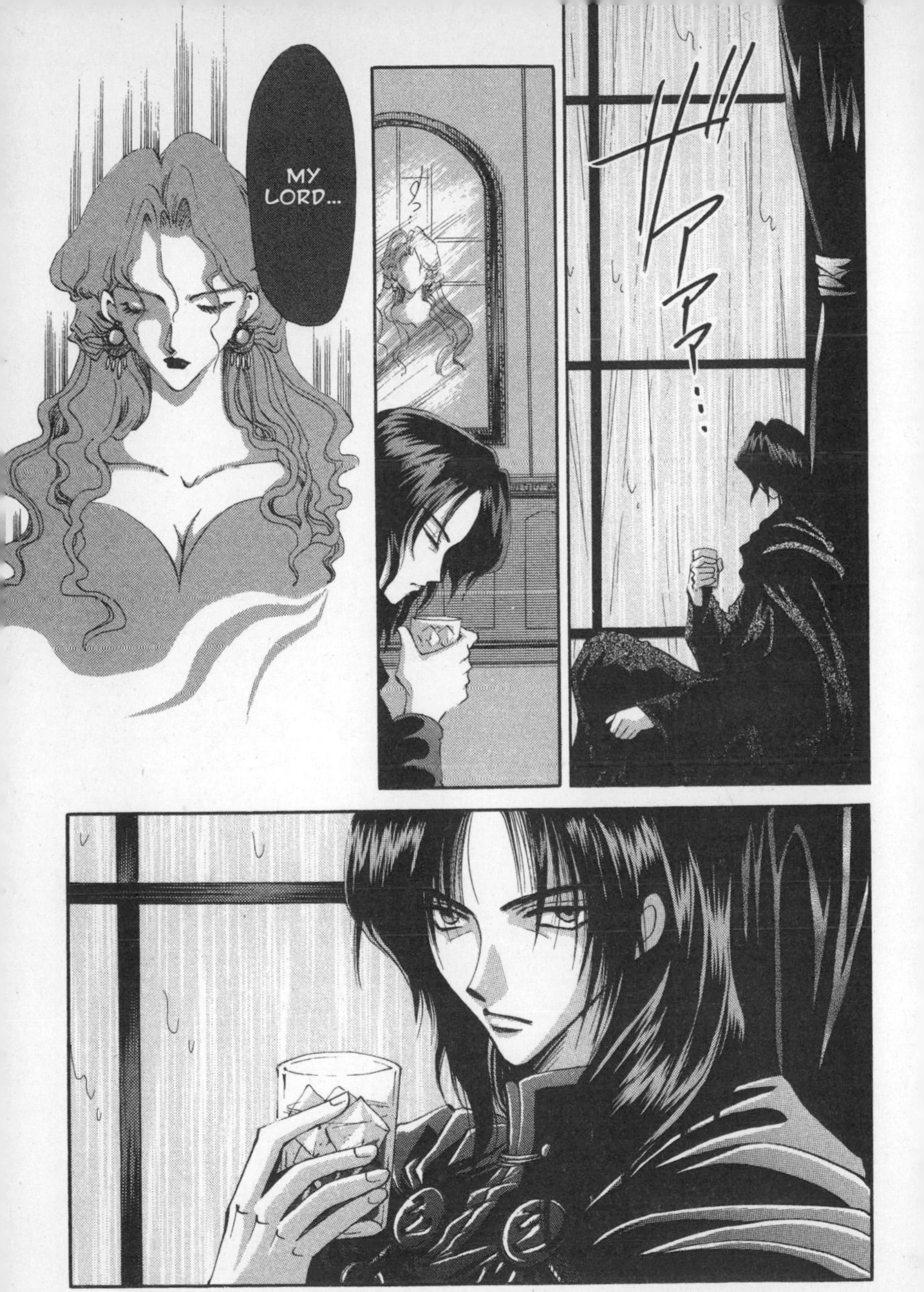
ザアァァ…
MY LORD...

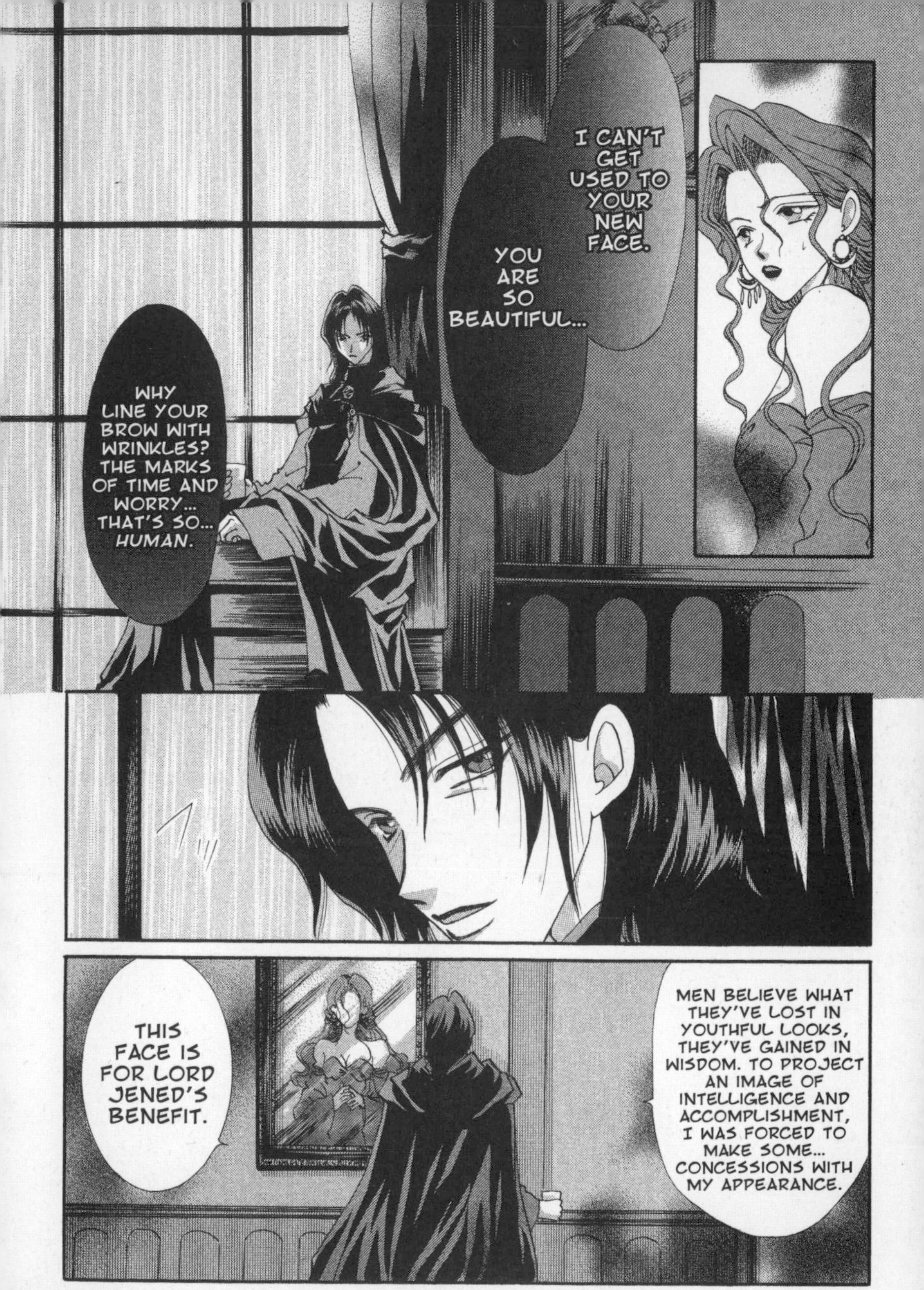
I CAN'T GET USED TO YOUR NEW FACE.
YOU ARE SO BEAUTIFUL...
WHY LINE YOUR BROW WITH WRINKLES? THE MARKS OF TIME AND WORRY... THAT'S SO... HUMAN.
MEN BELIEVE WHAT THEY'VE LOST IN YOUTHFUL LOOKS, THEY'VE GAINED IN WISDOM. TO PROJECT AN IMAGE OF INTELLIGENCE AND ACCOMPLISHMENT, I WAS FORCED TO MAKE SOME... CONCESSIONS WITH MY APPEARANCE.
THIS FACE IS FOR LORD JENED'S BENEFIT.

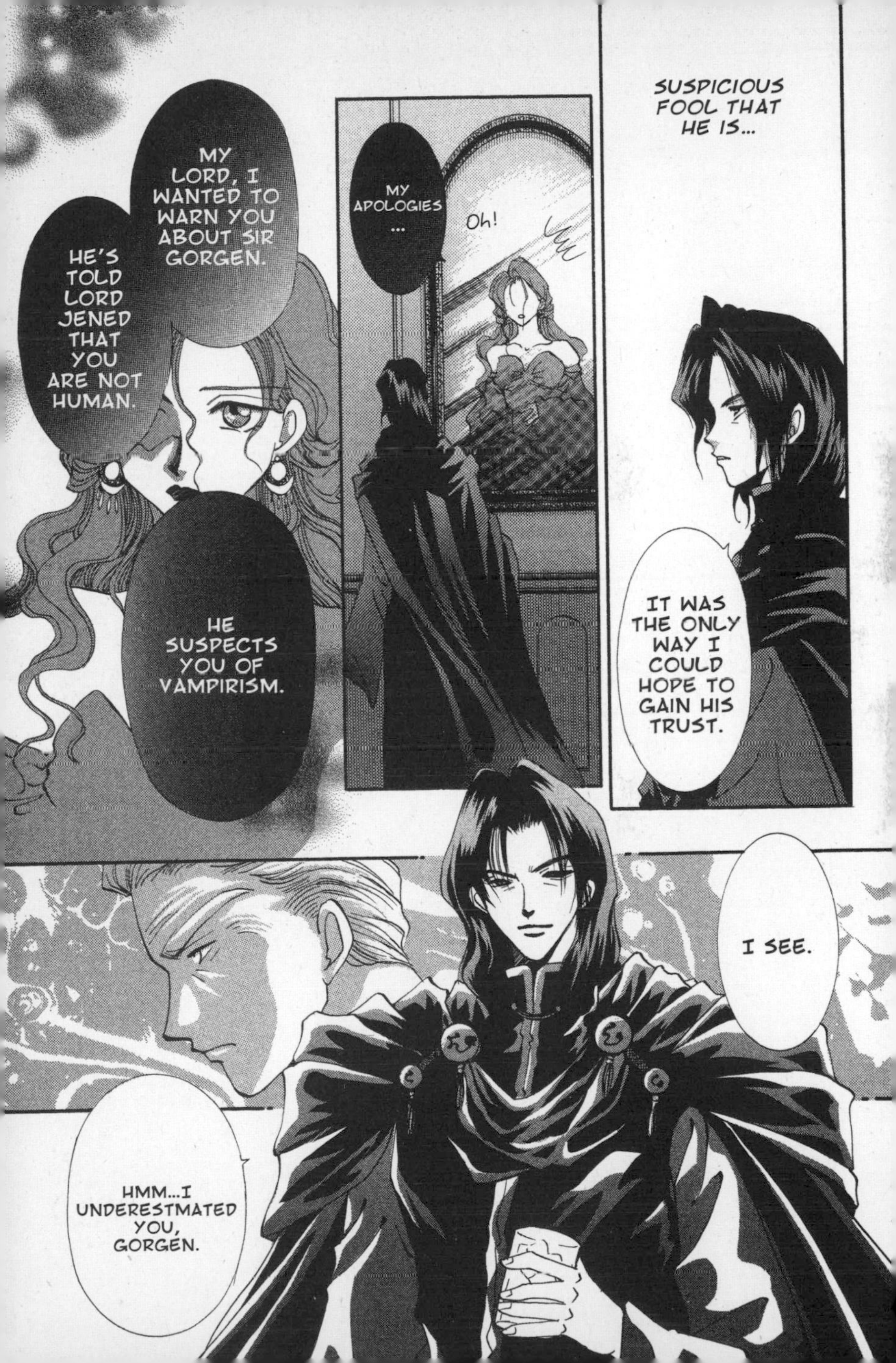
SUSPICIOUS FOOL THAT HE IS...
IT WAS THE ONLY WAY I COULD HOPE TO GAIN HIS TRUST.
Oh!
MY APOLOGIES ...
MY LORD, I WANTED TO WARN YOU ABOUT SIR GORGEN.
HE'S TOLD LORD JENED THAT YOU ARE NOT HUMAN.
HE SUSPECTS YOU OF VAMPIRISM.
I SEE.
HMM...I UNDERESTMATED YOU, GORGEN.

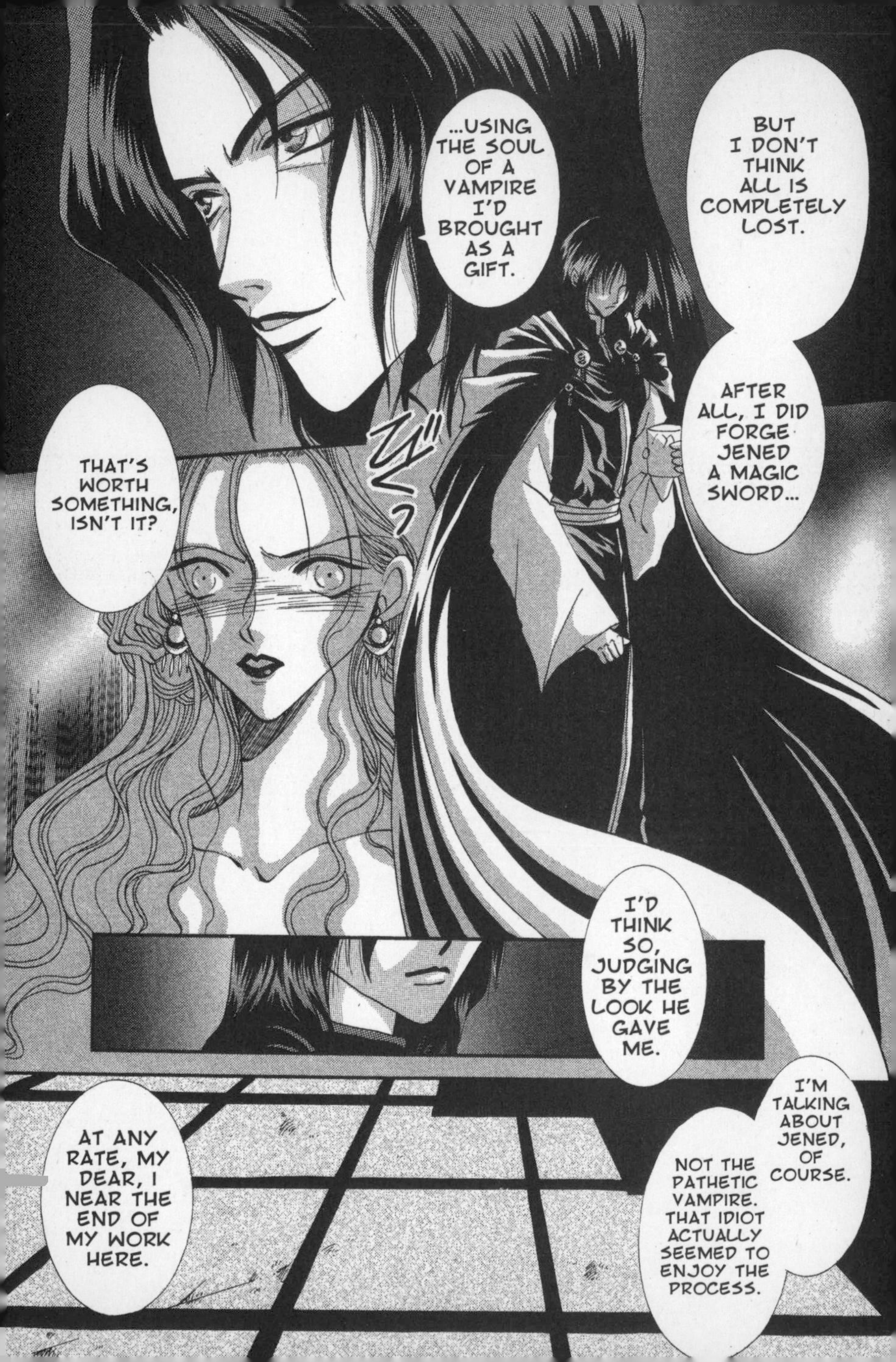
BUT I DON'T THINK ALL IS COMPLETELY LOST.
AFTER ALL, I DID FORGE JENED A MAGIC SWORD...
...USING THE SOUL OF A VAMPIRE I'D BROUGHT AS A GIFT.
THAT'S WORTH SOMETHING, ISN'T IT?
I'D THINK SO, JUDGING BY THE LOOK HE GAVE ME.
I'M TALKING ABOUT JENED, OF COURSE.
NOT THE PATHETIC VAMPIRE. THAT IDIOT ACTUALLY SEEMED TO ENJOY THE PROCESS.
AT ANY RATE, MY DEAR, I NEAR THE END OF MY WORK HERE.

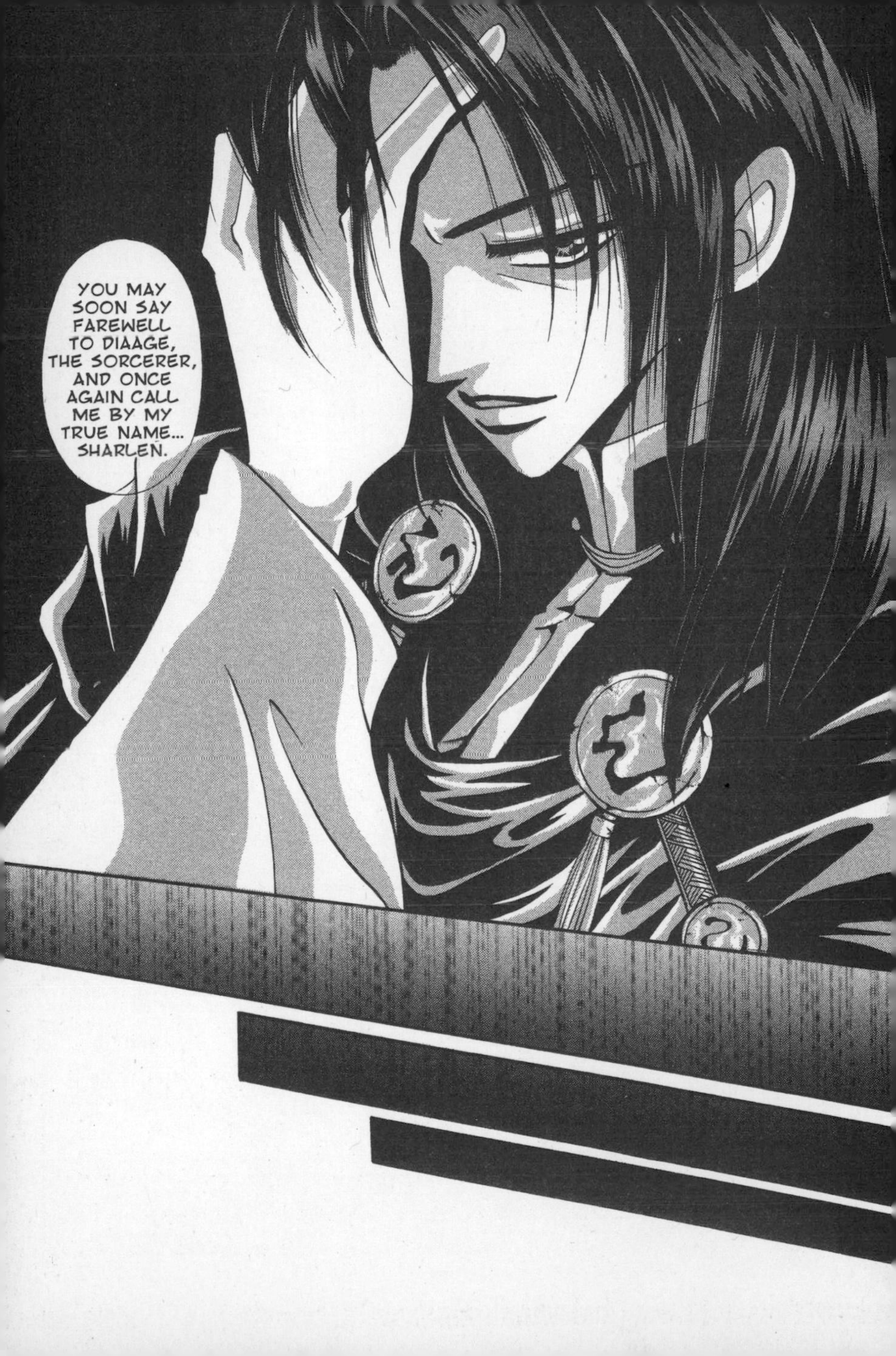
YOU MAY SOON SAY FAREWELL TO DIAAGE, THE SORCERER, AND ONCE AGAIN CALL ME BY MY TRUE NAME... SHARLEN.

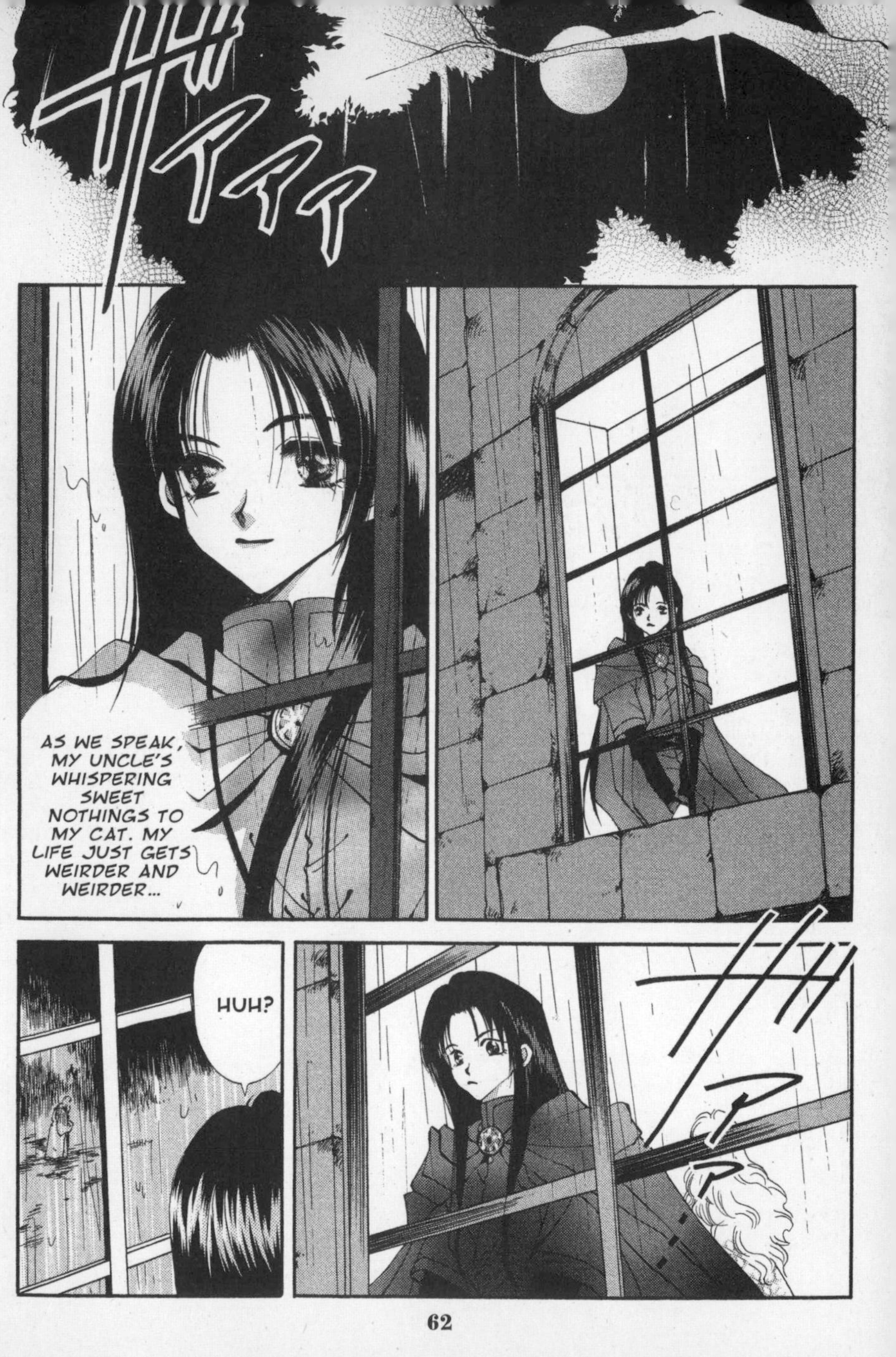
AS WE SPEAK, MY UNCLE'S WHISPERING SWEET NOTHINGS TO MY CAT. MY LIFE JUST GETS WEIRDER AND WEIRDER...
HUH?

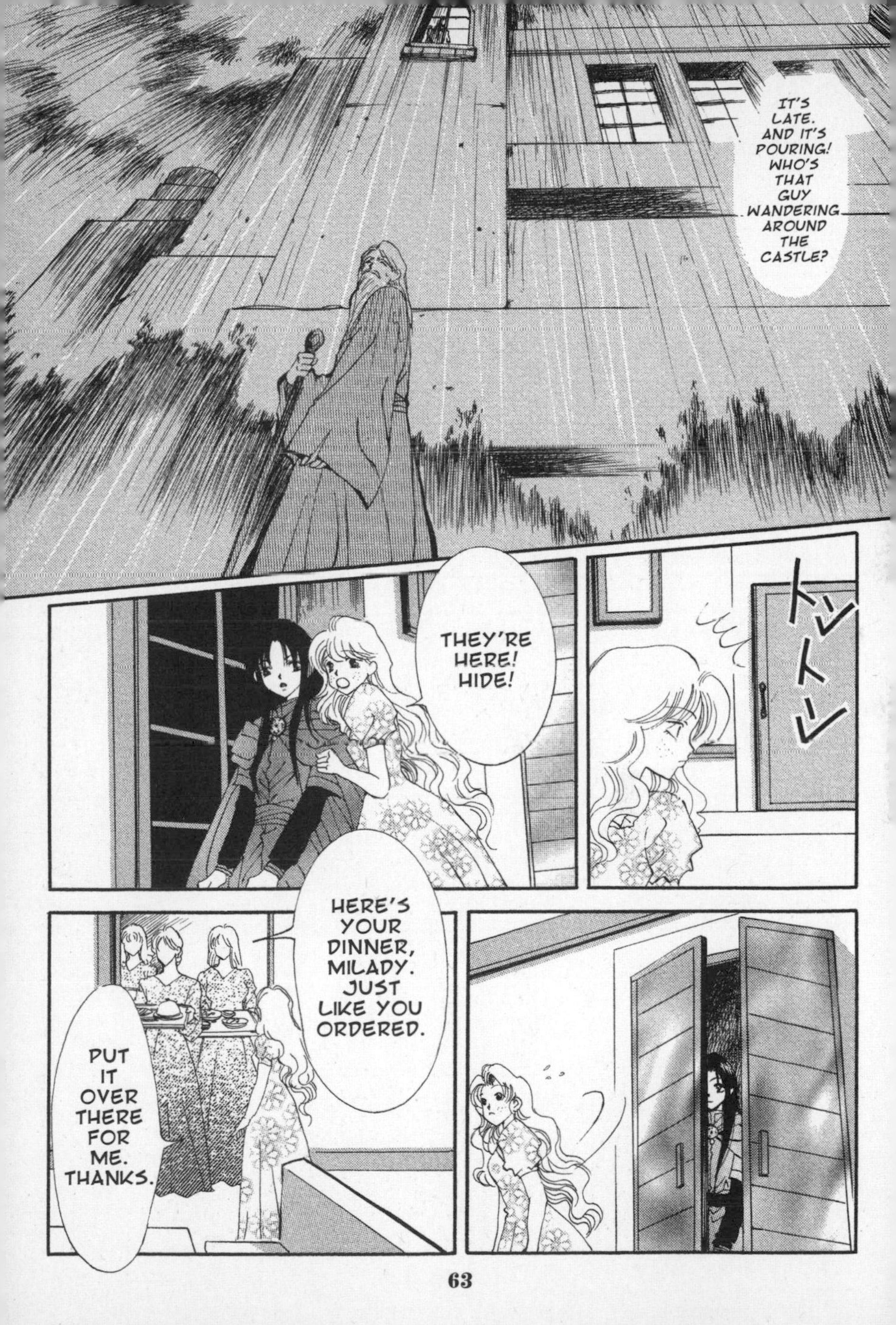
IT'S LATE. AND IT'S POURING! WHO'S THAT GUY WANDERING AROUND THE CASTLE?
トントン
THEY'RE HERE! HIDE!
HERE'S YOUR DINNER, MILADY. JUST LIKE YOU ORDERED.
PUT IT OVER THERE FOR ME. THANKS.

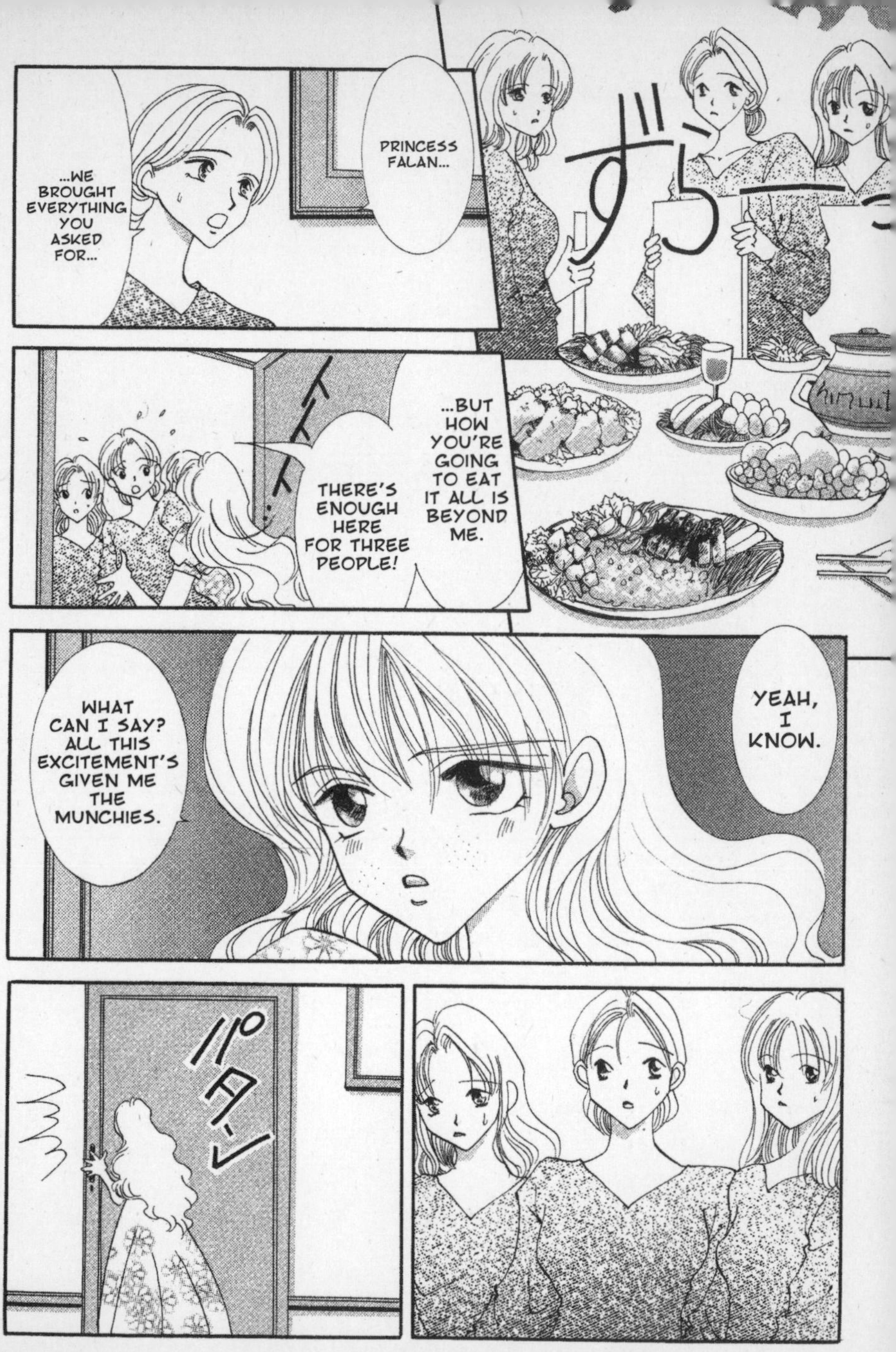
ずらーっ
PRINCESS FALAN...
...WE BROUGHT EVERYTHING YOU ASKED FOR...
...BUT HOW YOU'RE GOING TO EAT IT ALL IS BEYOND ME.
THERE'S ENOUGH HERE FOR THREE PEOPLE!
YEAH, I KNOW.
WHAT CAN I SAY? ALL THIS EXCITEMENT'S GIVEN ME THE MUNCHIES.
パタン

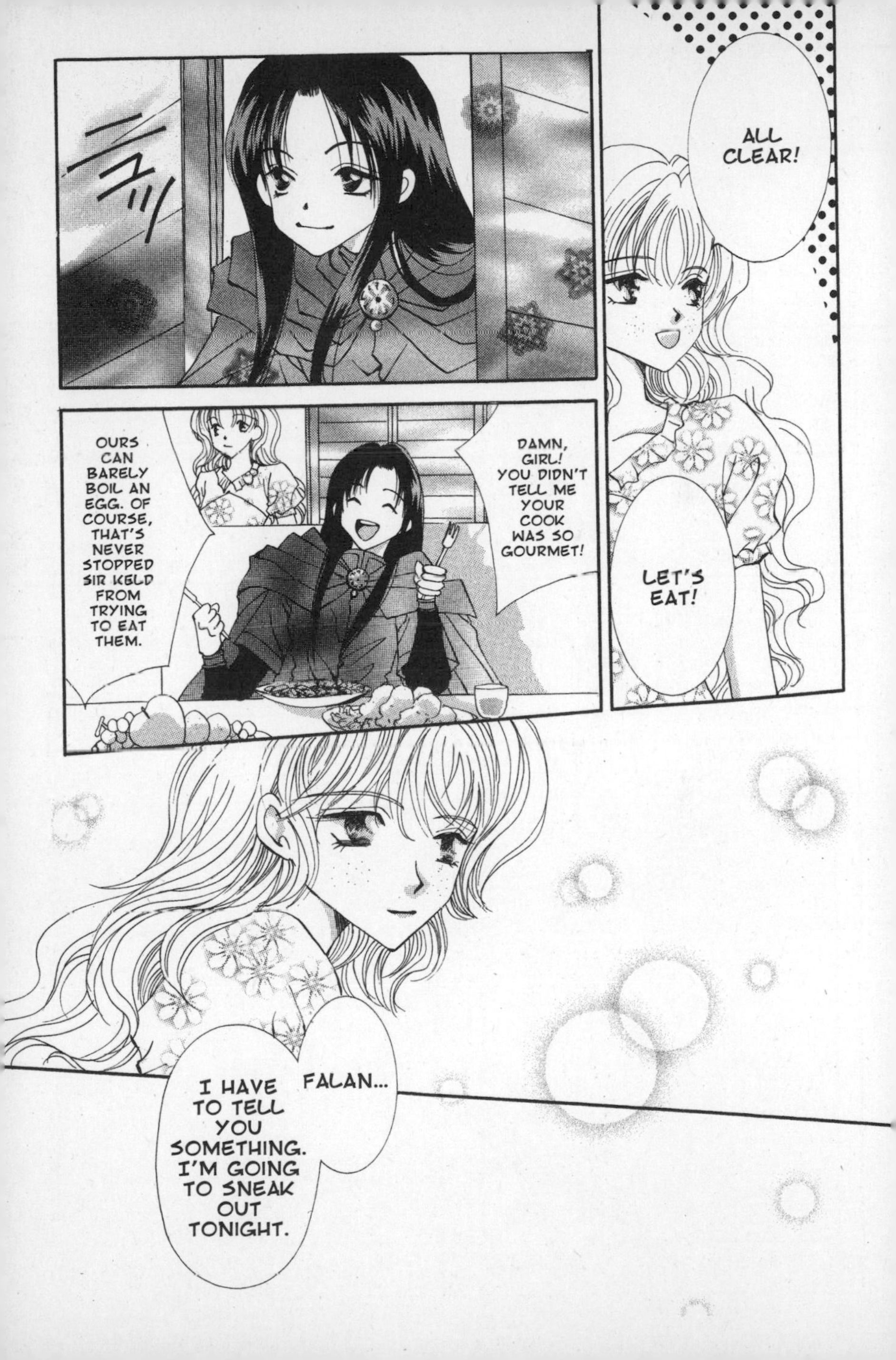
ALL CLEAR!
LET'S EAT!
ニコッ
DAMN, GIRL! YOU DIDN'T TELL ME YOUR COOK WAS SO GOURMET!
OURS CAN BARELY BOIL AN EGG. OF COURSE, THAT'S NEVER STOPPED SIR KELD FROM TRYING TO EAT THEM.
FALAN...
I HAVE TO TELL YOU SOMETHING. I'M GOING TO SNEAK OUT TONIGHT.

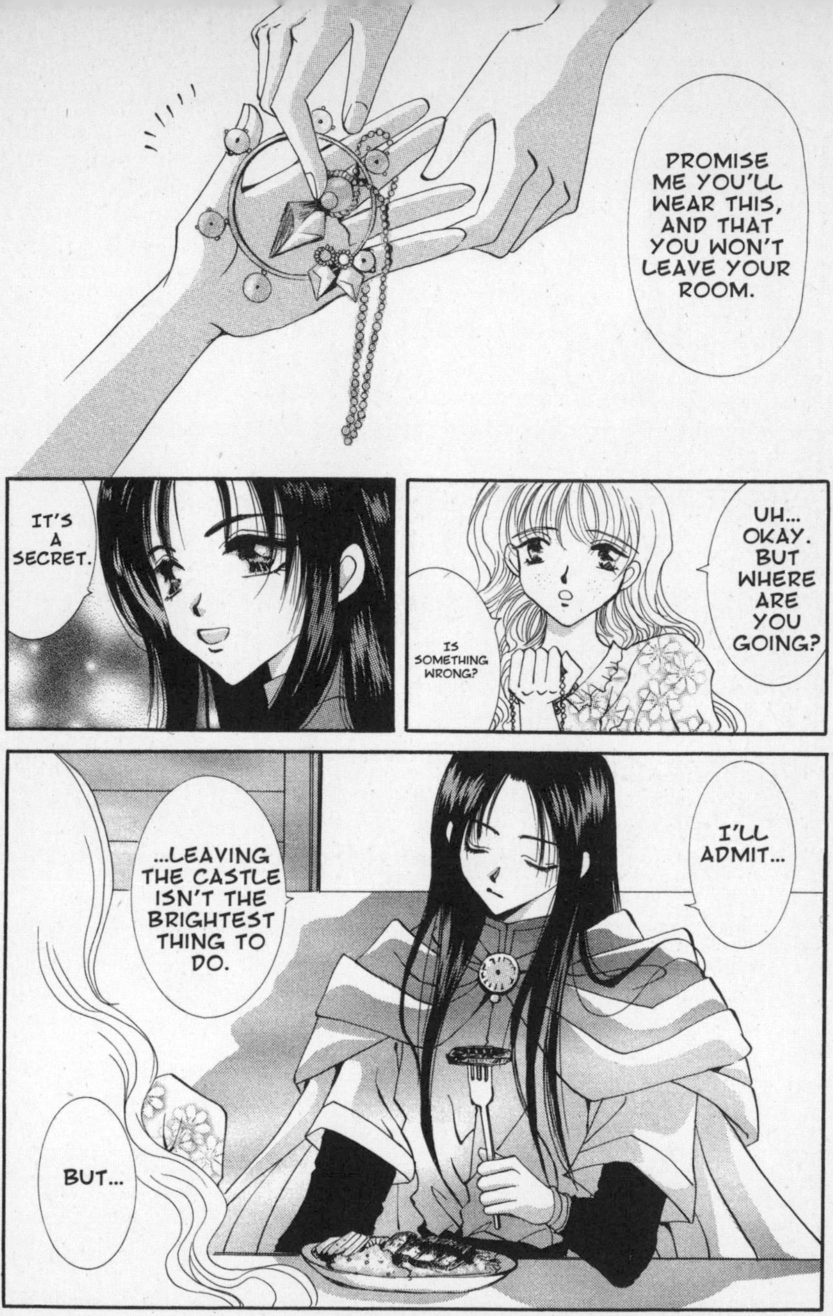
PROMISE ME YOU'LL WEAR THIS, AND THAT YOU WON'T LEAVE YOUR ROOM.
UH... OKAY. BUT WHERE ARE YOU GOING?
IS SOMETHING WRONG?
IT'S A SECRET.
I'LL ADMIT...
...LEAVING THE CASTLE ISN'T THE BRIGHTEST THING TO DO.
BUT...

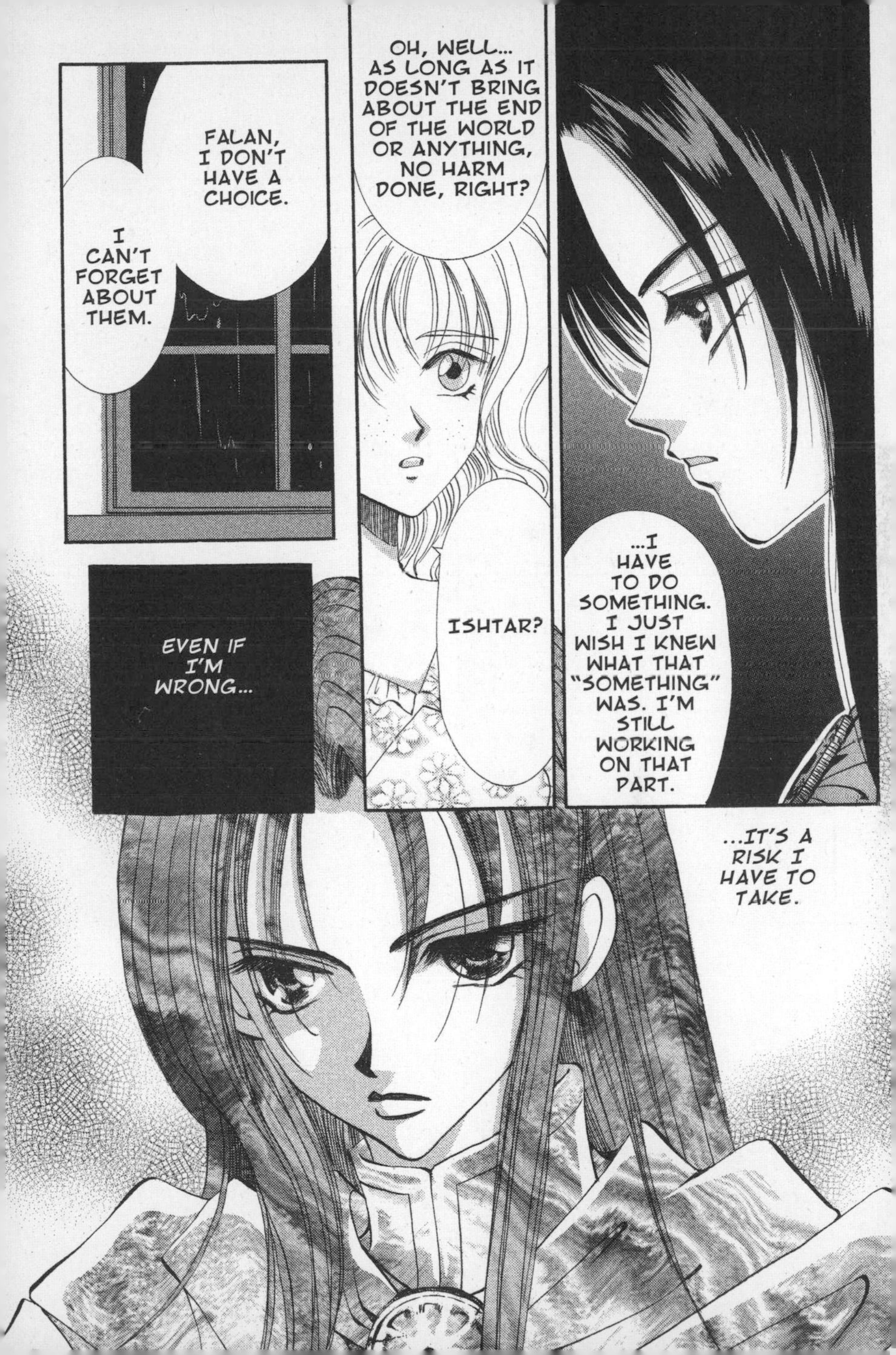
...I HAVE TO DO SOMETHING. I JUST WISH I KNEW WHAT THAT "SOMETHING" WAS. I'M STILL WORKING ON THAT PART.
OH, WELL... AS LONG AS IT DOESN'T BRING ABOUT THE END OF THE WORLD OR ANYTHING, NO HARM DONE, RIGHT?
ISHTAR?
FALAN, I DON'T HAVE A CHOICE.
I CAN'T FORGET ABOUT THEM.
EVEN IF I'M WRONG...
...IT'S A RISK I HAVE TO TAKE.

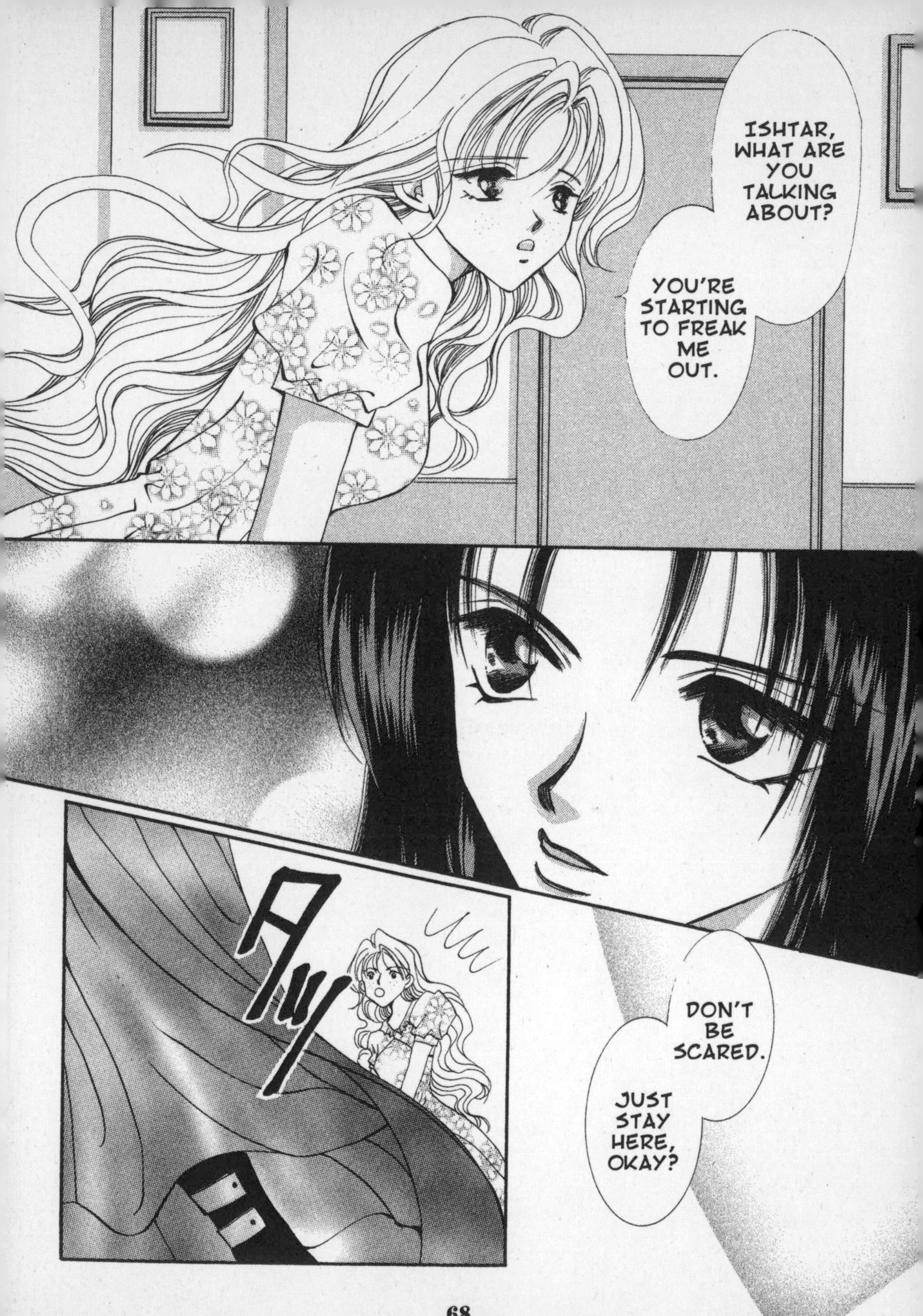
ISHTAR, WHAT ARE YOU TALKING ABOUT?
YOU'RE STARTING TO FREAK ME OUT.
DON'T BE SCARED.
JUST STAY HERE, OKAY?

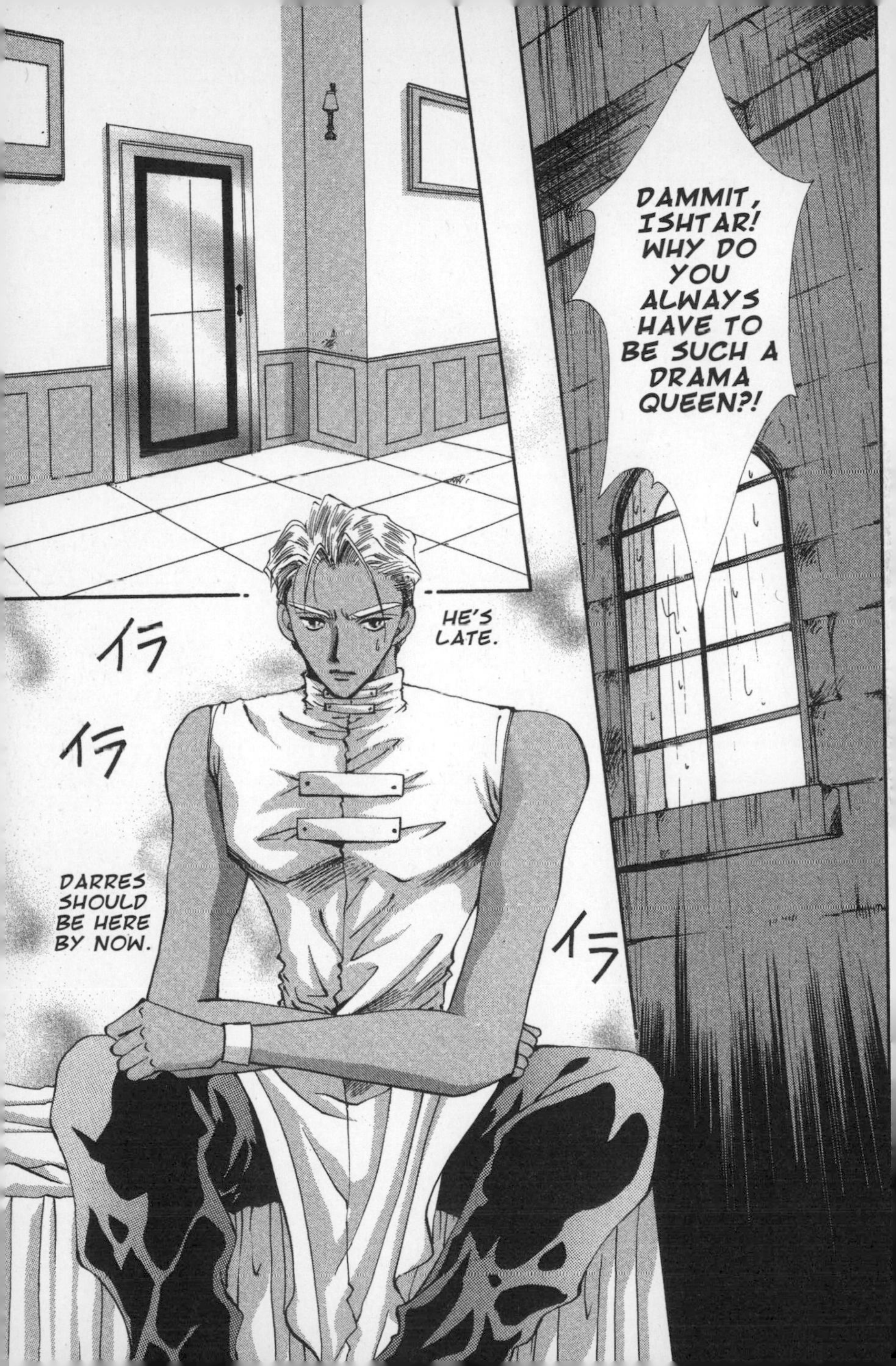
DAMMIT, ISHTAR! WHY DO YOU ALWAYS HAVE TO BE SUCH A DRAMA QUEEN?!
HE'S LATE.
イラ
イラ
DARRES SHOULD BE HERE BY NOW.
イラ

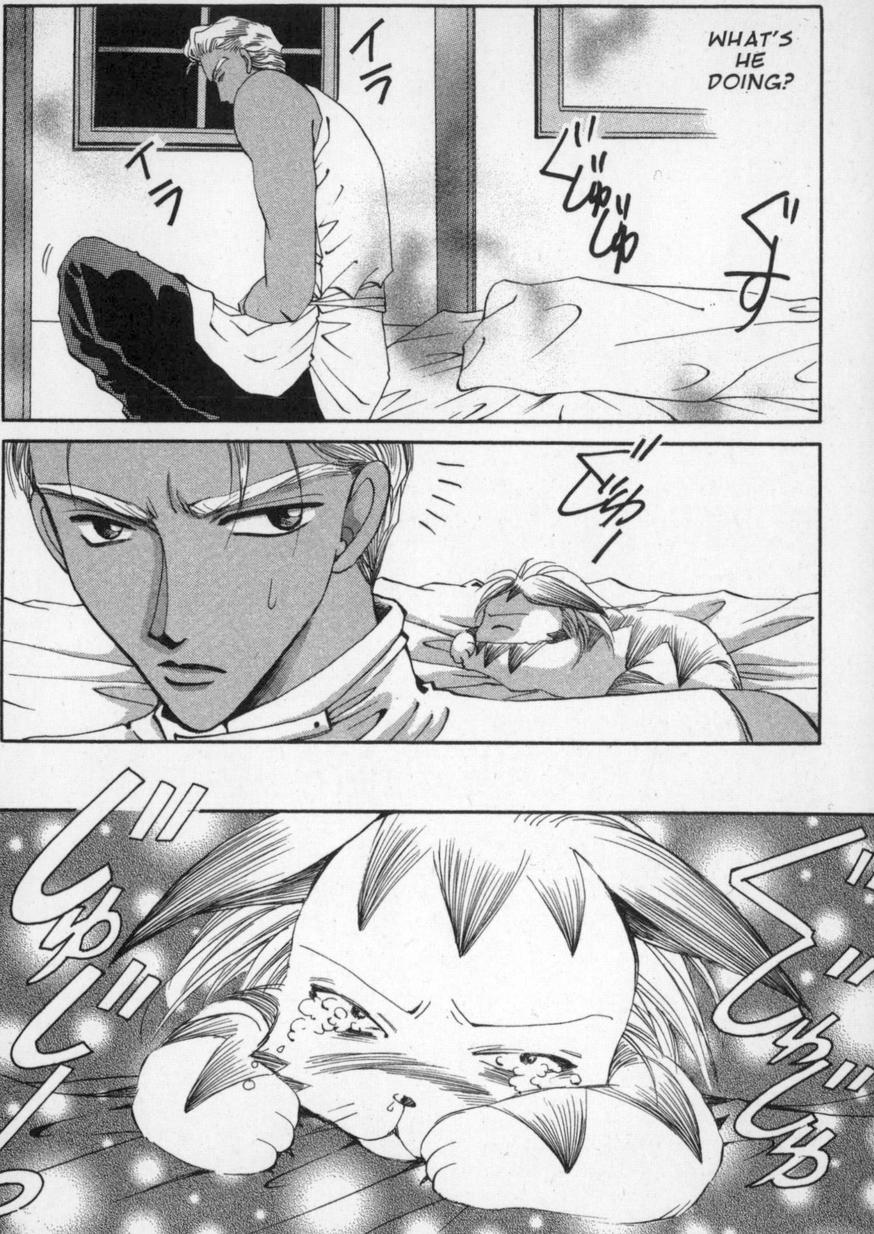
WHAT'S HE DOING?
イラ
イラ

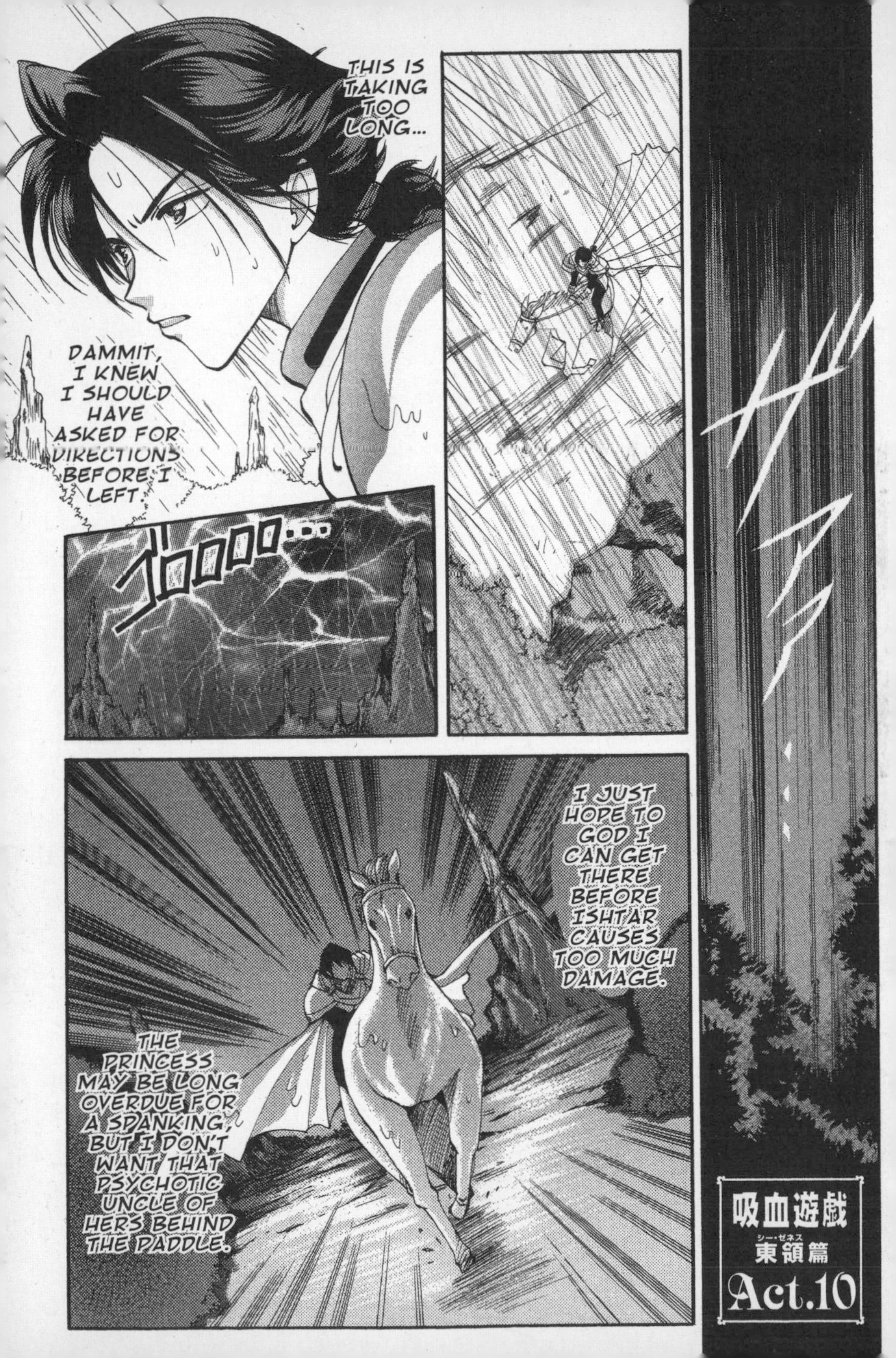
ザァァァ…
吸血遊戯
シー・ゼネス
東領篇
Act.10
THIS IS TAKING TOO LONG...
DAMMIT, I KNEW I SHOULD HAVE ASKED FOR DIRECTIONS BEFORE I LEFT.
ゴロロロロ…
I JUST HOPE TO GOD I CAN GET THERE BEFORE ISHTAR CAUSES TOO MUCH DAMAGE.
THE PRINCESS MAY BE LONG OVERDUE FOR A SPANKING, BUT I DON'T WANT THAT PSYCHOTIC UNCLE OF HERS BEHIND THE PADDLE.

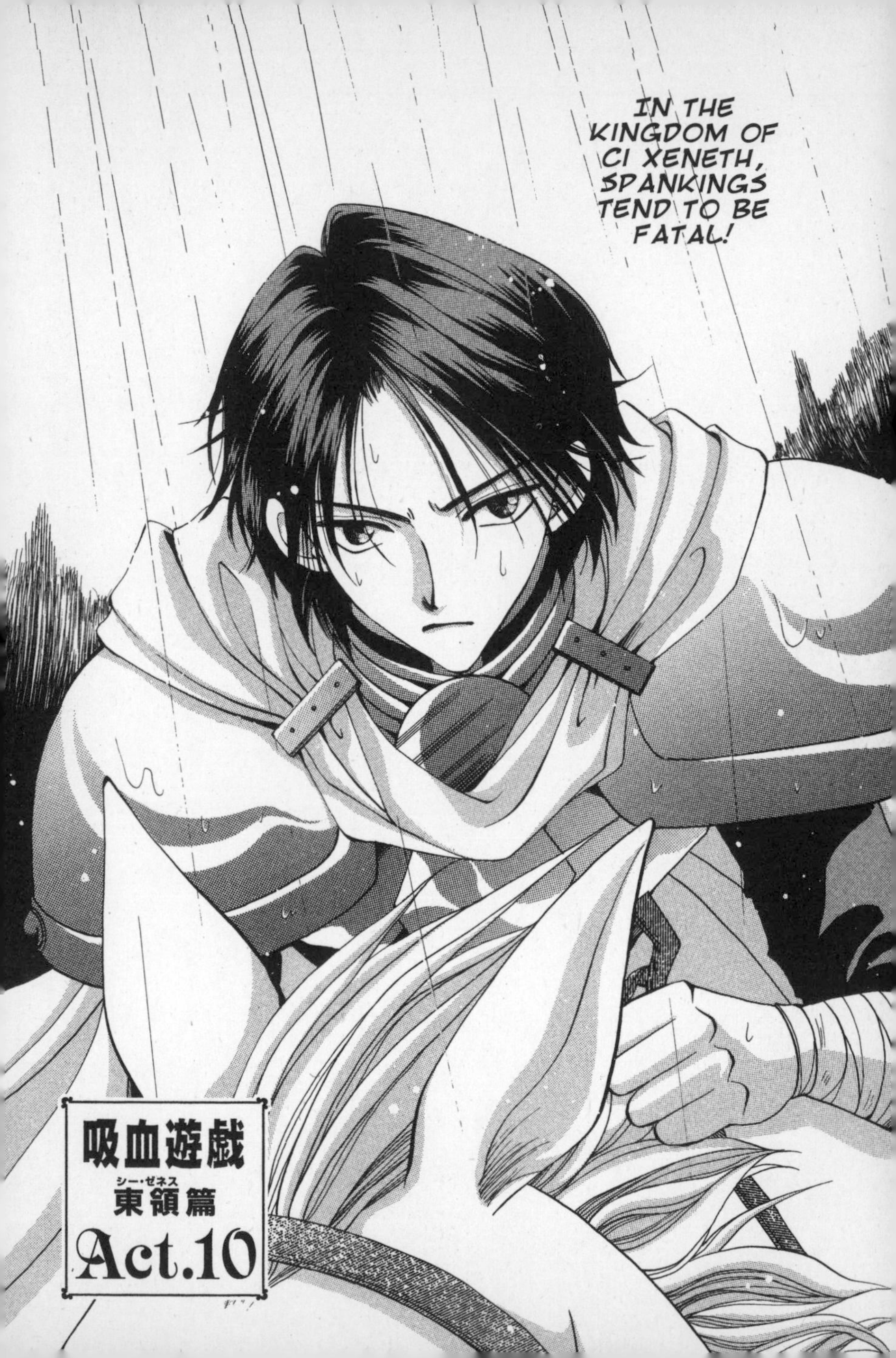
IN THE KINGDOM OF CI XENETH, SPANKINGS TEND TO BE FATAL!
吸血遊戯
シー・ゼネス
東領篇
Act.10

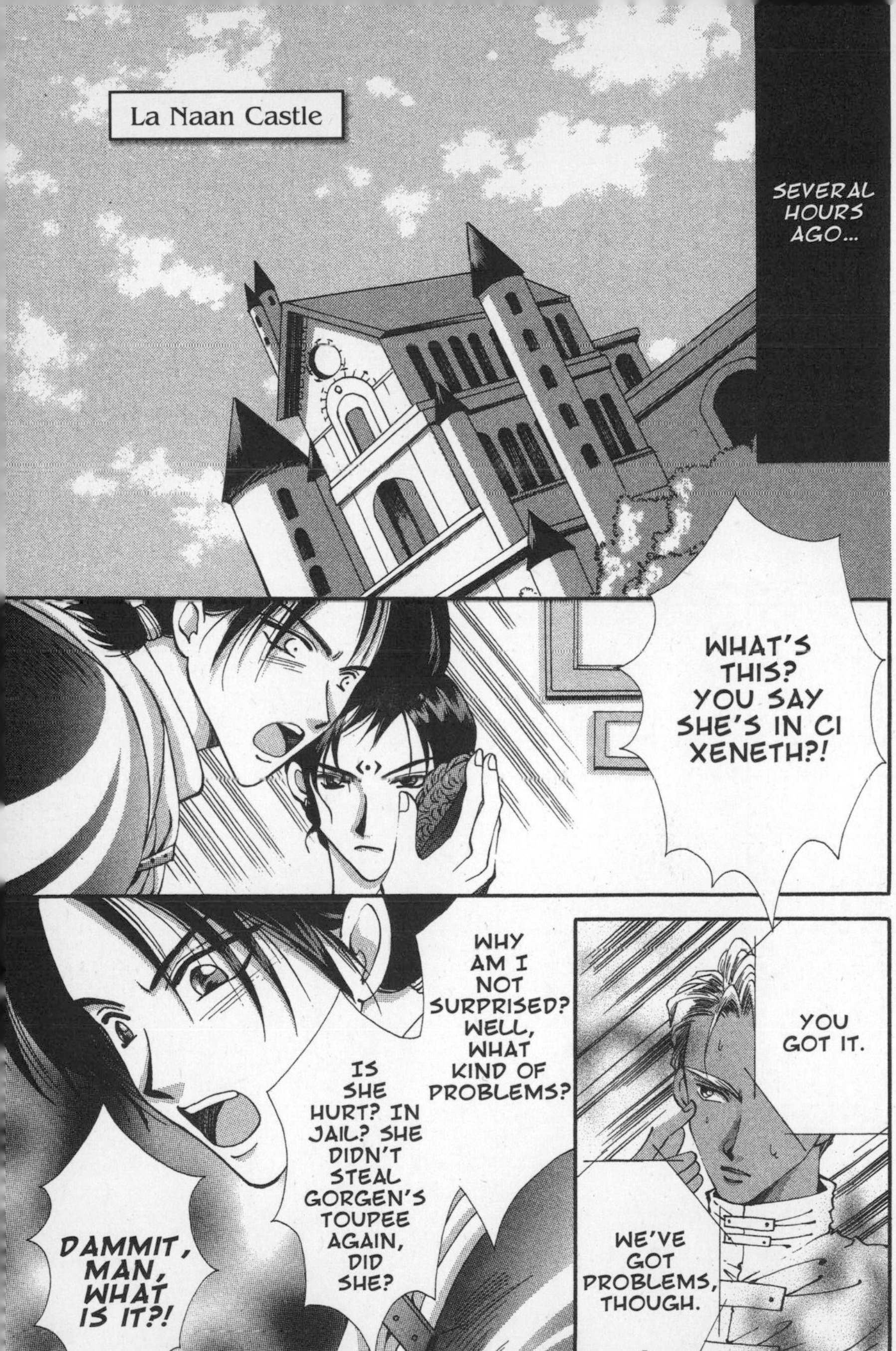
SEVERAL HOURS AGO...
La Naan Castle
WHAT'S THIS? YOU SAY SHE'S IN CI XENETH?!
YOU GOT IT.
WE'VE GOT PROBLEMS, THOUGH.
WHY AM I NOT SURPRISED? WELL, WHAT KIND OF PROBLEMS?
IS SHE HURT? IN JAIL? SHE DIDN'T STEAL GORGEN'S TOUPEE AGAIN, DID SHE?
DAMMIT, MAN, WHAT IS IT?!

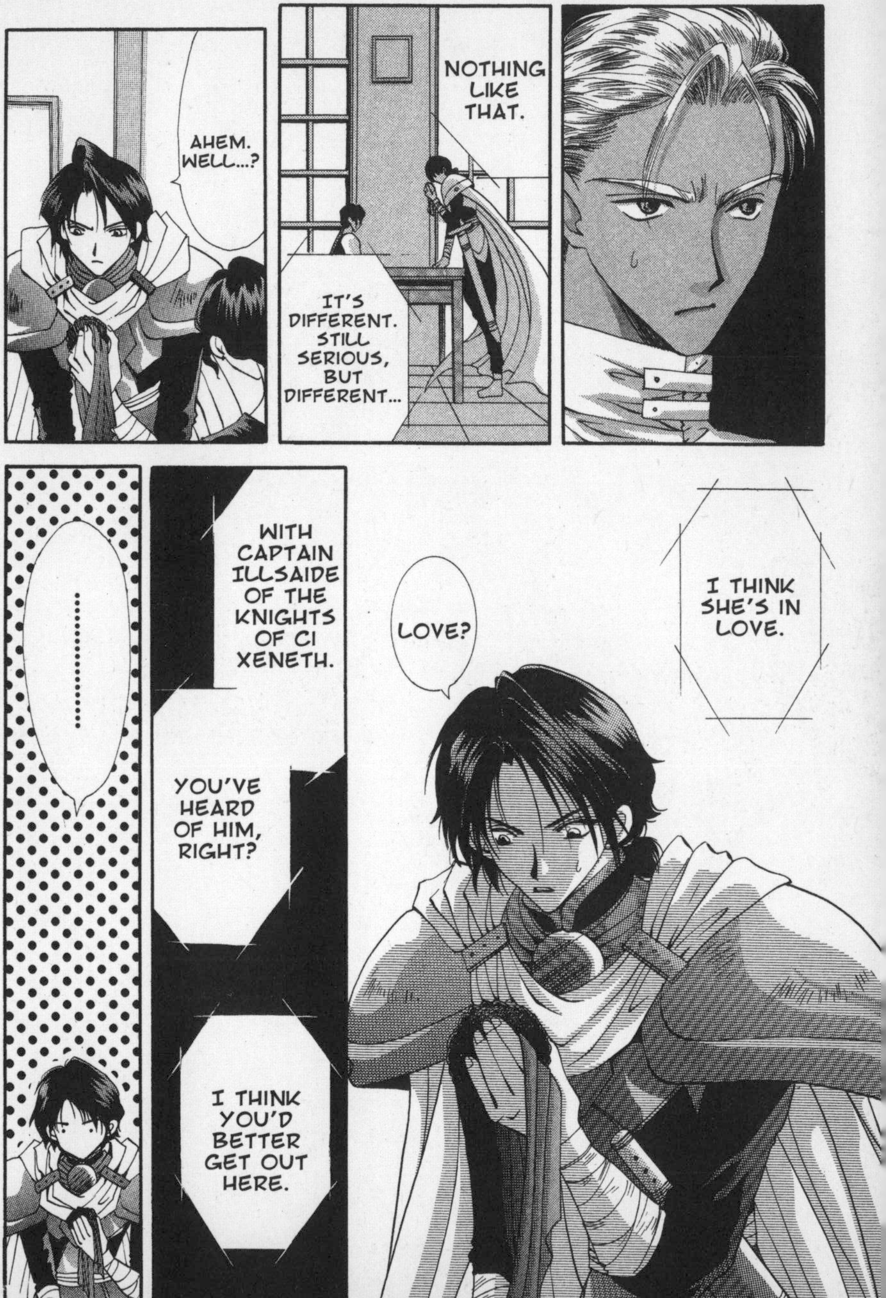
NOTHING LIKE THAT.
IT'S DIFFERENT. STILL SERIOUS, BUT DIFFERENT...
AHEM. WELL...?
I THINK SHE'S IN LOVE.
LOVE?
WITH CAPTAIN ILLSAIDE OF THE KNIGHTS OF CI XENETH.
YOU'VE HEARD OF HIM, RIGHT?
I THINK YOU'D BETTER GET OUT HERE.
....

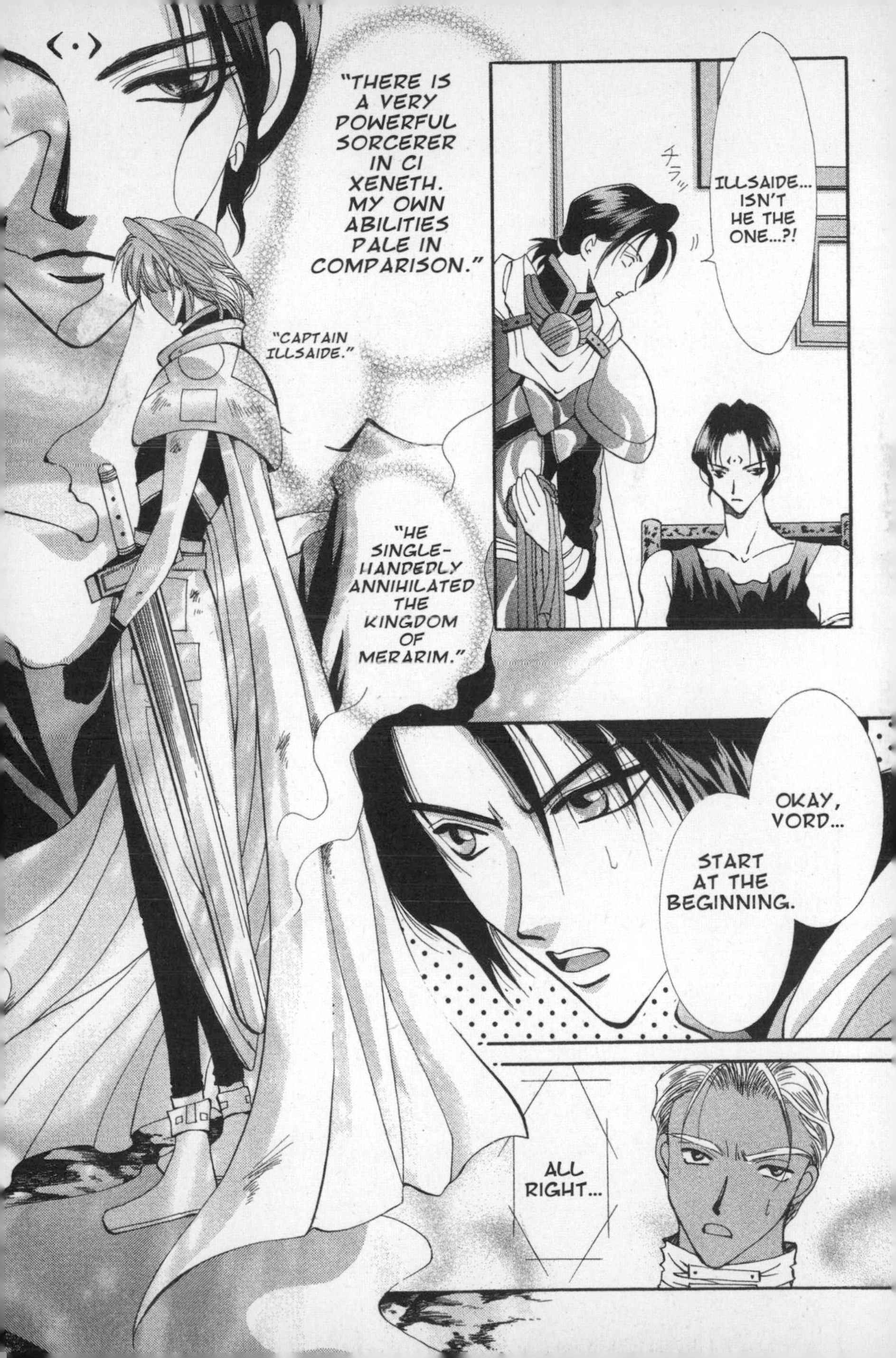

チラッ
ILLSAIDE... ISN'T HE THE ONE...?!
OKAY, VORD...
START AT THE BEGINNING.
ALL RIGHT...
"THERE IS A VERY POWERFUL SORCERER IN CI XENETH. MY OWN ABILITIES PALE IN COMPARISON."
"CAPTAIN ILLSAIDE."
"HE SINGLE-HANDEDLY ANNIHILATED THE KINGDOM OF MERARIM."

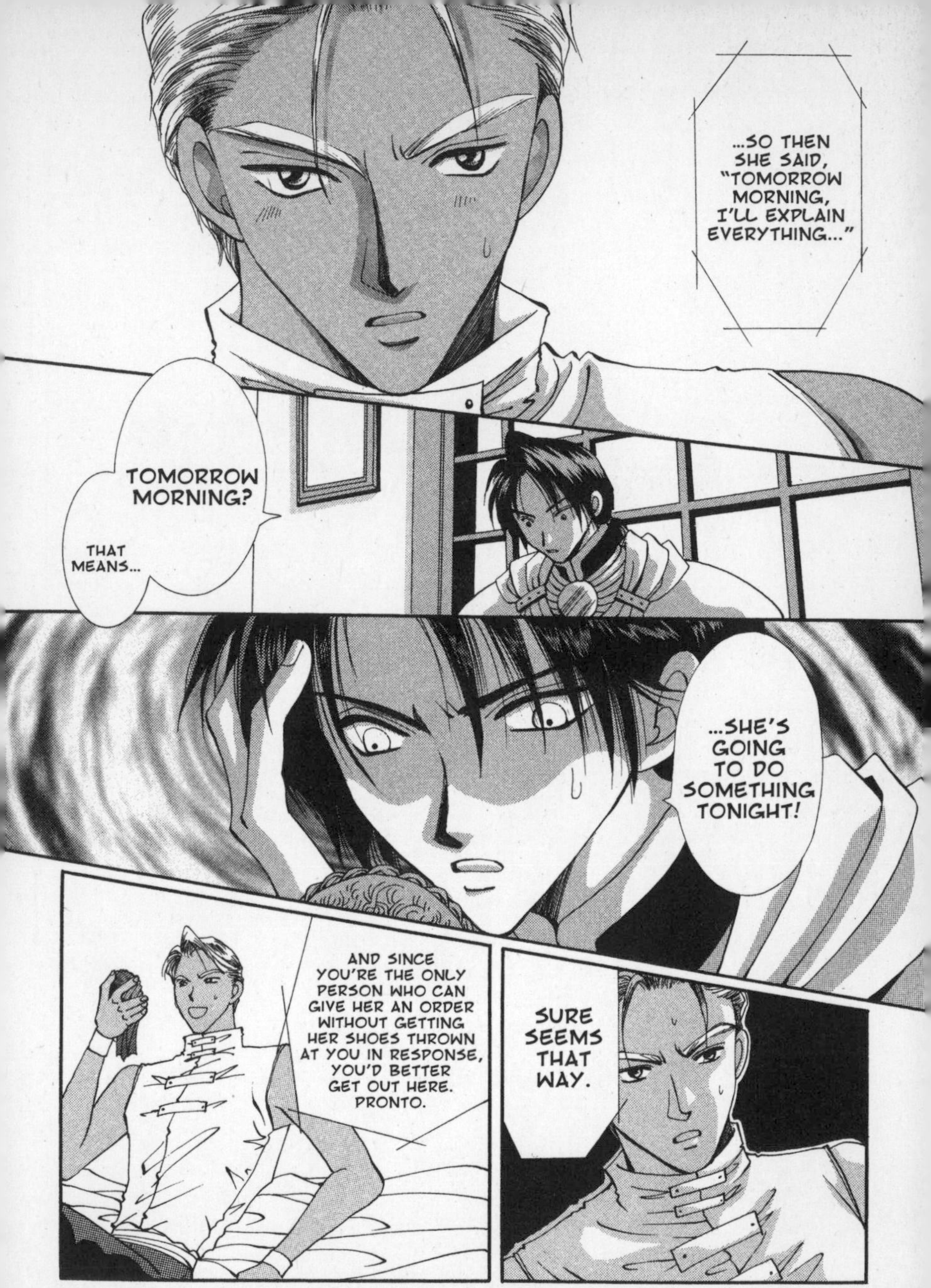
...SO THEN SHE SAID, "TOMORROW MORNING, I'LL EXPLAIN EVERYTHING..."
TOMORROW MORNING?
THAT MEANS...
...SHE'S GOING TO DO SOMETHING TONIGHT!
SURE SEEMS THAT WAY.
AND SINCE YOU'RE THE ONLY PERSON WHO CAN GIVE HER AN ORDER WITHOUT GETTING HER SHOES THROWN AT YOU IN RESPONSE, YOU'D BETTER GET OUT HERE. PRONTO.

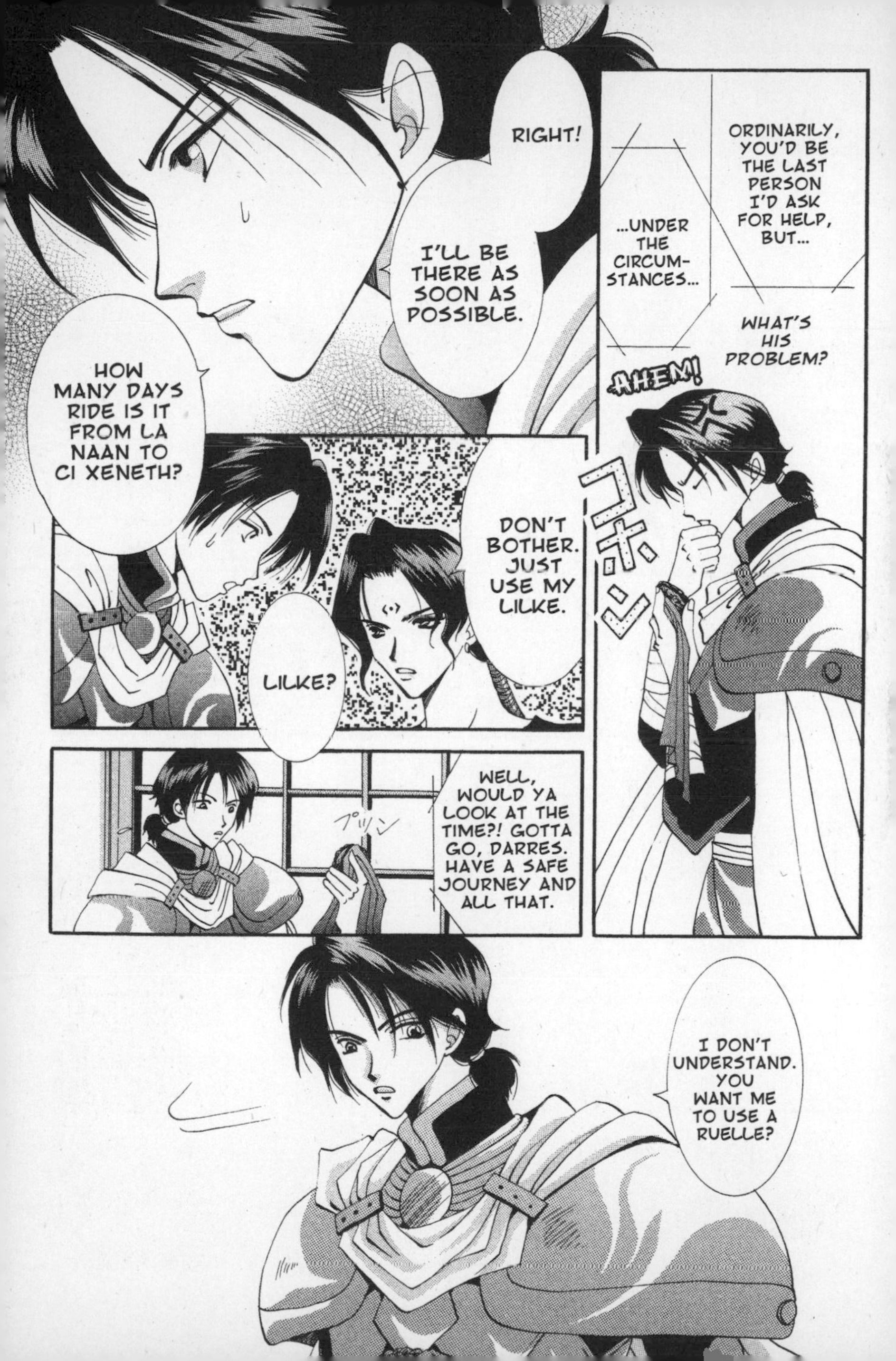
ORDINARILY, YOU'D BE THE LAST PERSON I'D ASK FOR HELP, BUT...
...UNDER THE CIRCUM-STANCES...
WHAT'S HIS PROBLEM?
AHEM!
コホン
RIGHT!
I'LL BE THERE AS SOON AS POSSIBLE.
HOW MANY DAYS RIDE IS IT FROM LA NAAN TO CI XENETH?
DON'T BOTHER. JUST USE MY LILKE.
LILKE?
WELL, WOULD YA LOOK AT THE TIME?! GOTTA GO, DARRES. HAVE A SAFE JOURNEY AND ALL THAT.
プツン
I DON'T UNDERSTAND. YOU WANT ME TO USE A RUELLE?

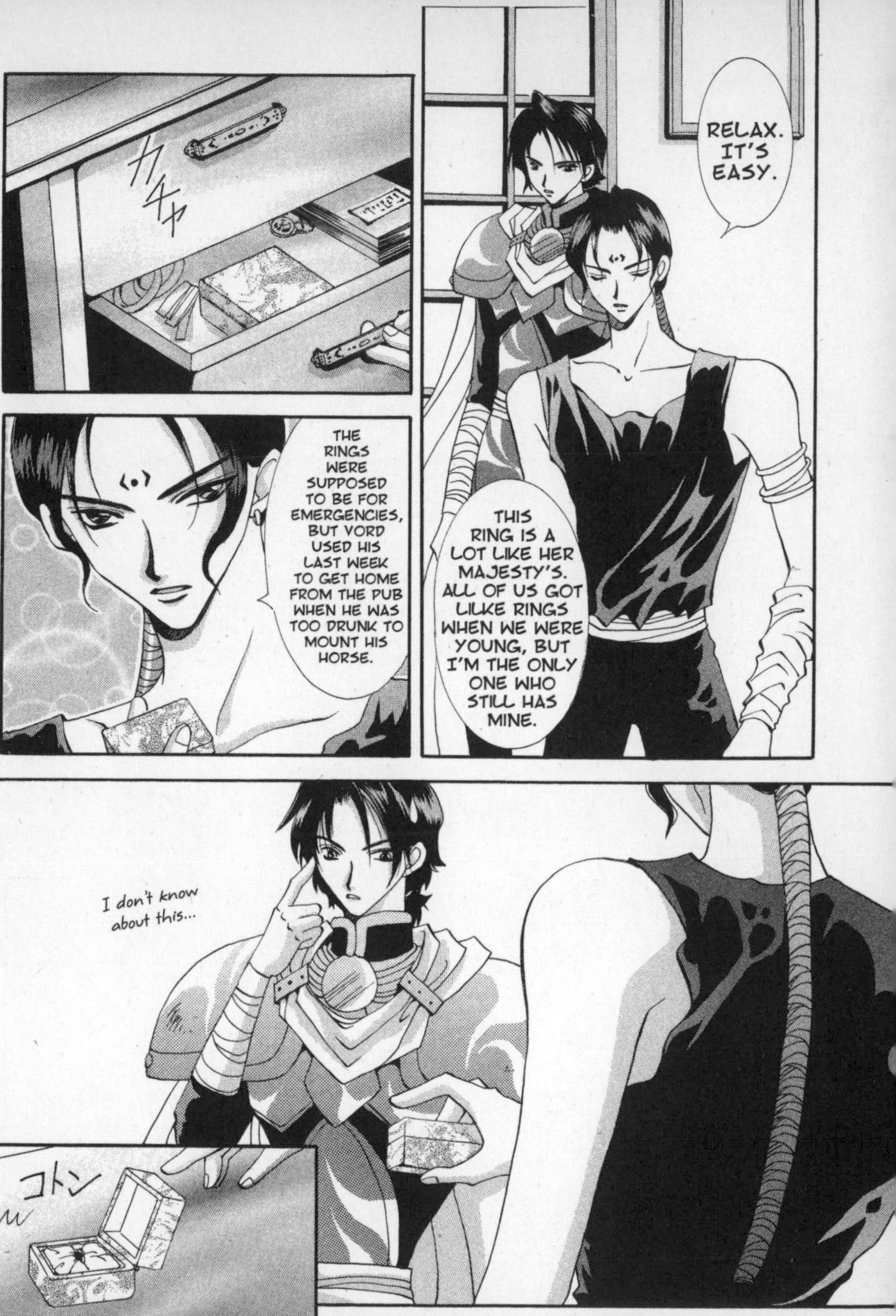
RELAX. IT'S EASY.
THIS RING IS A LOT LIKE HER MAJESTY'S. ALL OF US GOT LILKE RINGS WHEN WE WERE YOUNG, BUT I'M THE ONLY ONE WHO STILL HAS MINE.
カチャ
THE RINGS WERE SUPPOSED TO BE FOR EMERGENCIES, BUT VORD USED HIS LAST WEEK TO GET HOME FROM THE PUB WHEN HE WAS TOO DRUNK TO MOUNT HIS HORSE.
I don't know about this...
コトン

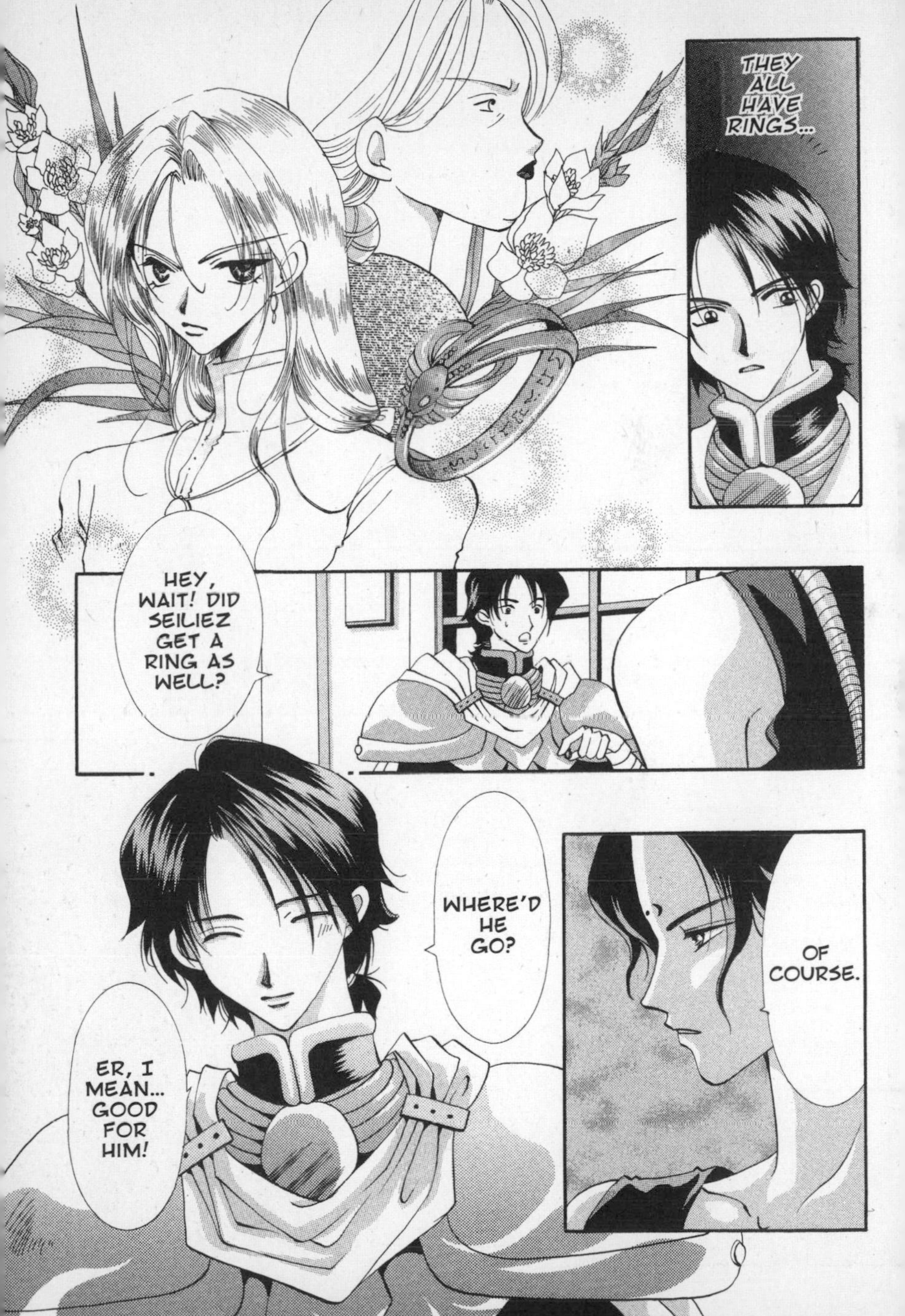
THEY ALL HAVE RINGS...
HEY, WAIT! DID SEILIEZ GET A RING AS WELL?
OF COURSE.
WHERE'D HE GO?
ER, I MEAN... GOOD FOR HIM!

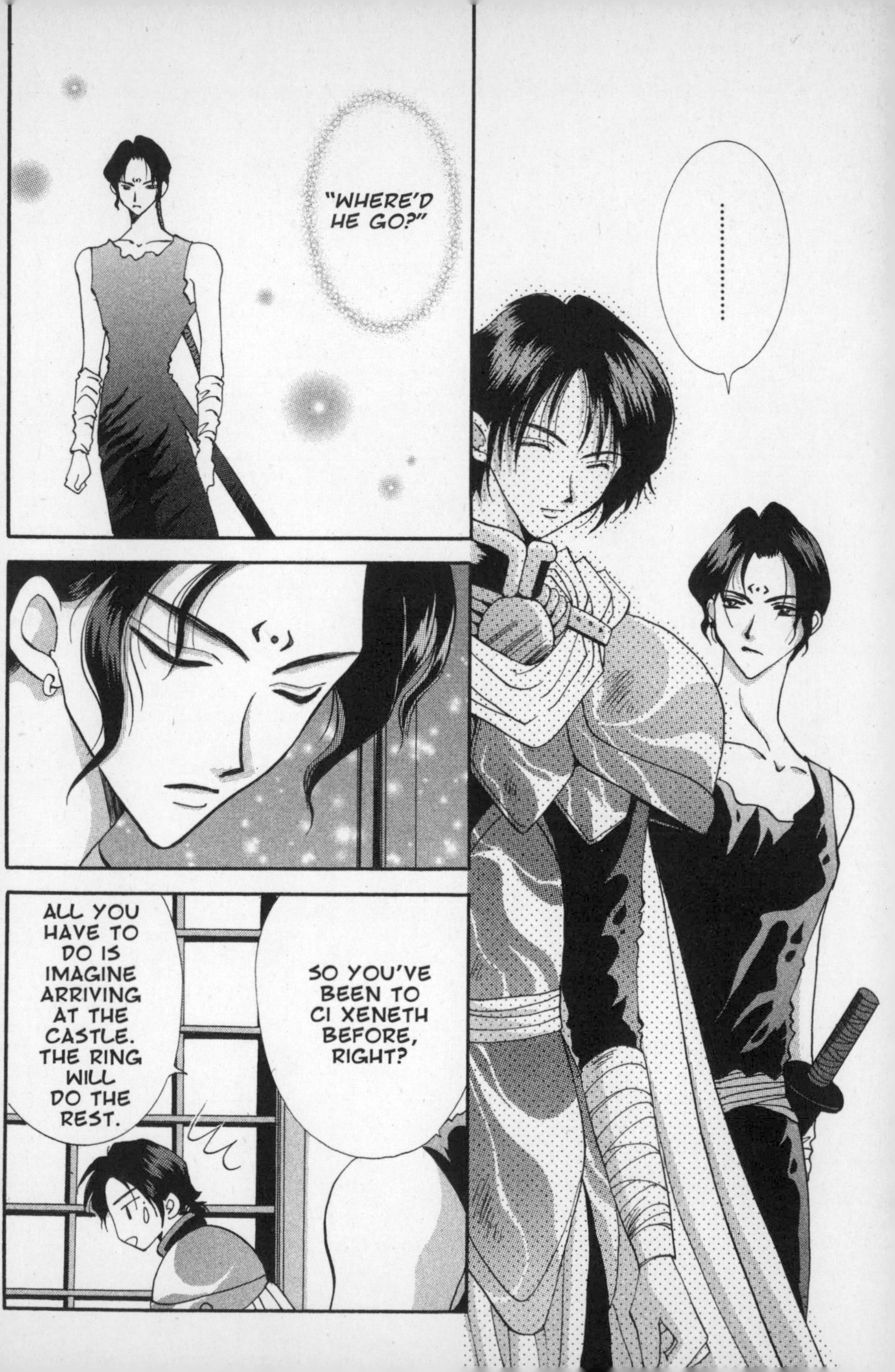
……
"WHERE'D HE GO?"
SO YOU'VE BEEN TO CI XENETH BEFORE, RIGHT?
ALL YOU HAVE TO DO IS IMAGINE ARRIVING AT THE CASTLE. THE RING WILL DO THE REST.

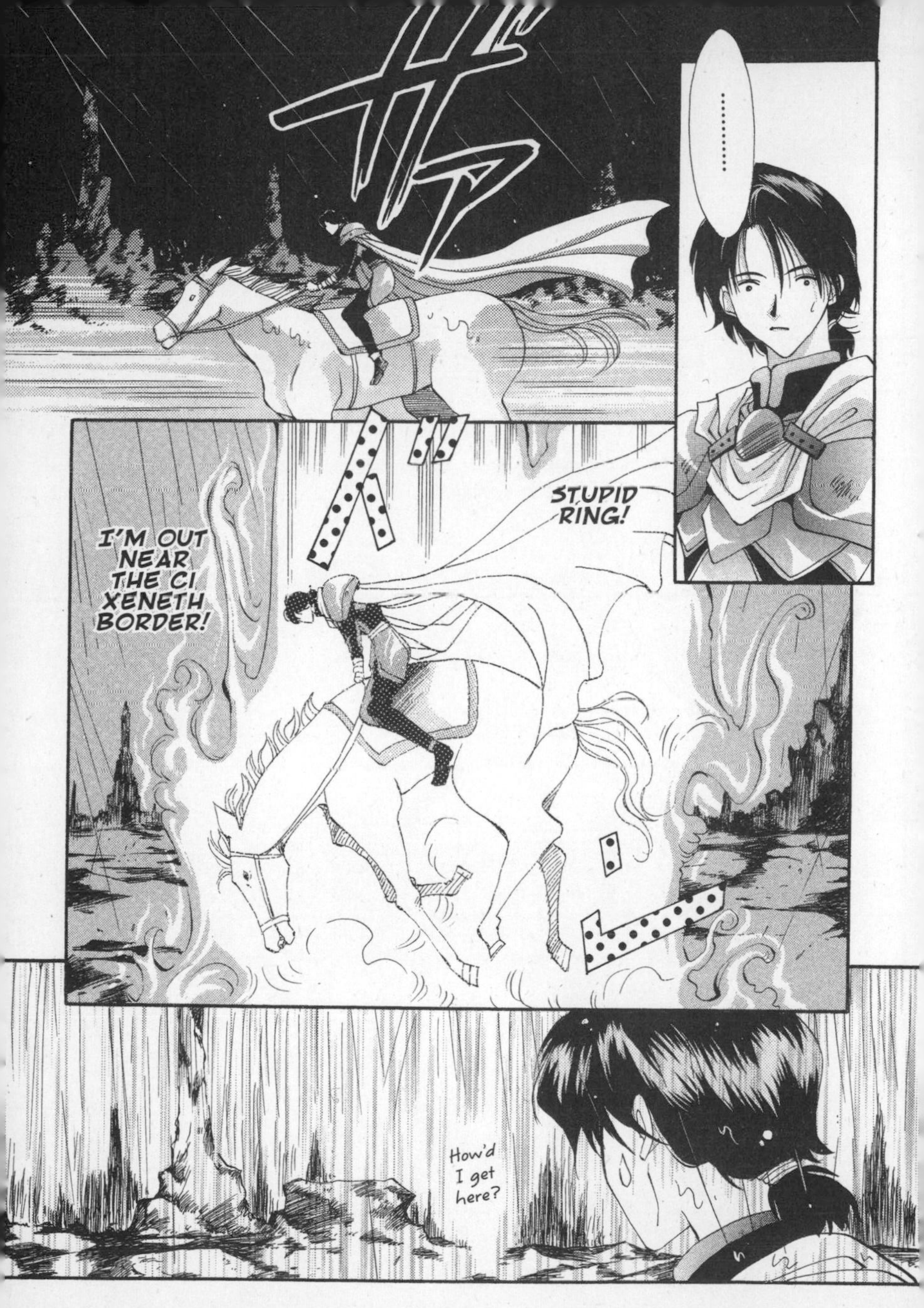
......
STUPID RING!
I'M OUT NEAR THE CI XENETH BORDER!
How'd I get here?

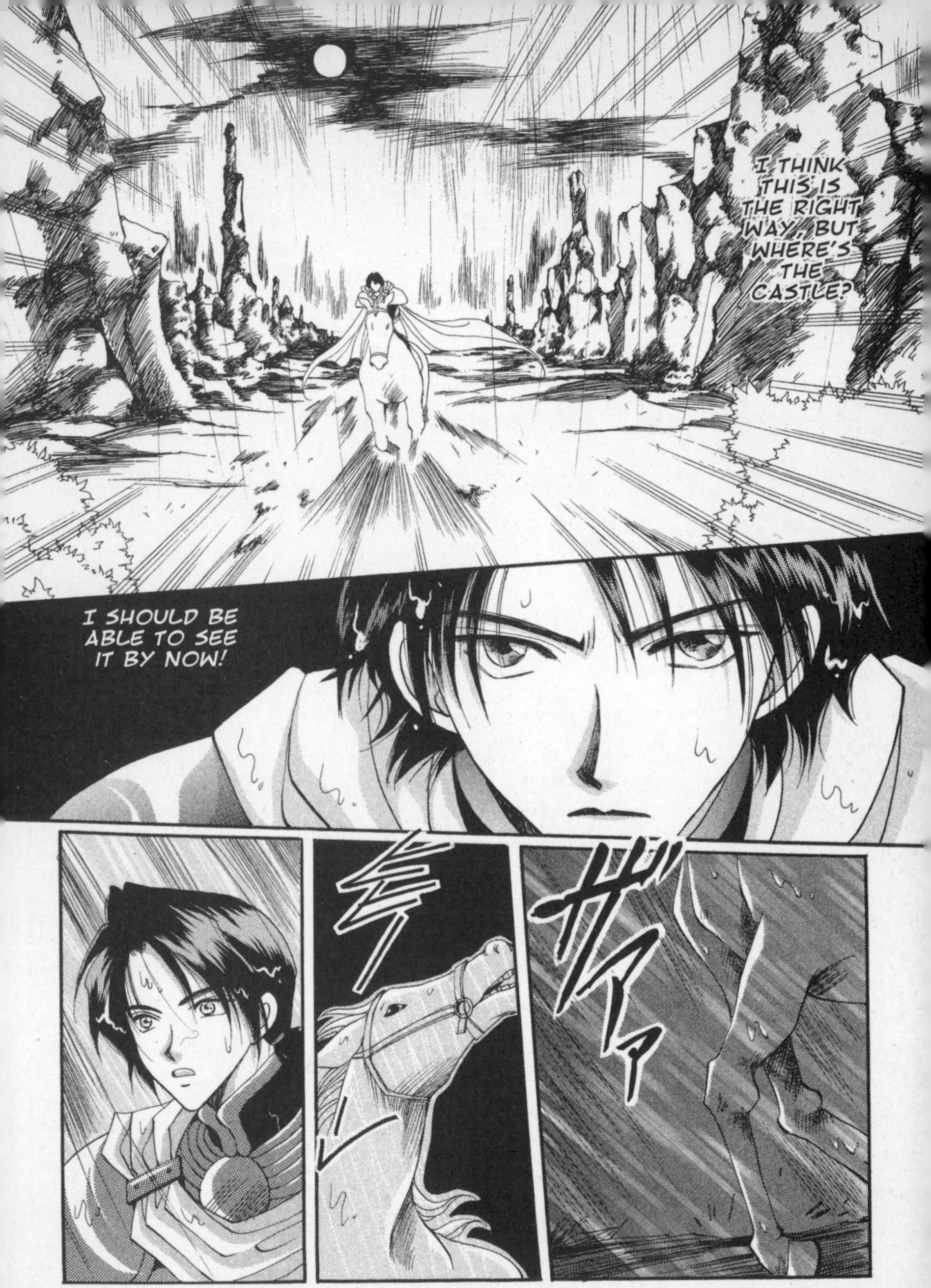
I THINK THIS IS THE RIGHT WAY, BUT WHERE'S THE CASTLE?
I SHOULD BE ABLE TO SEE IT BY NOW!

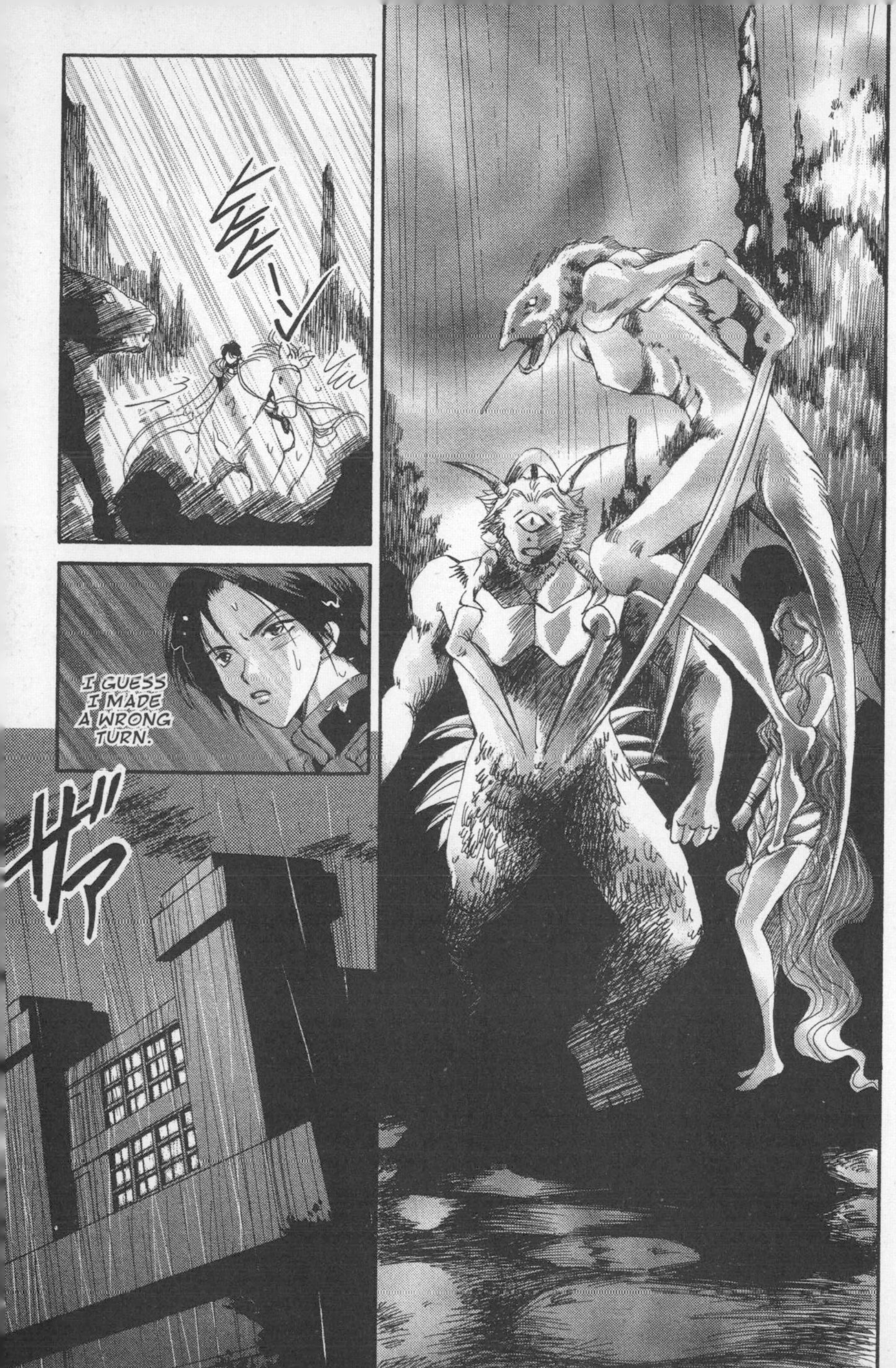
I GUESS I MADE A WRONG TURN.
ザァ

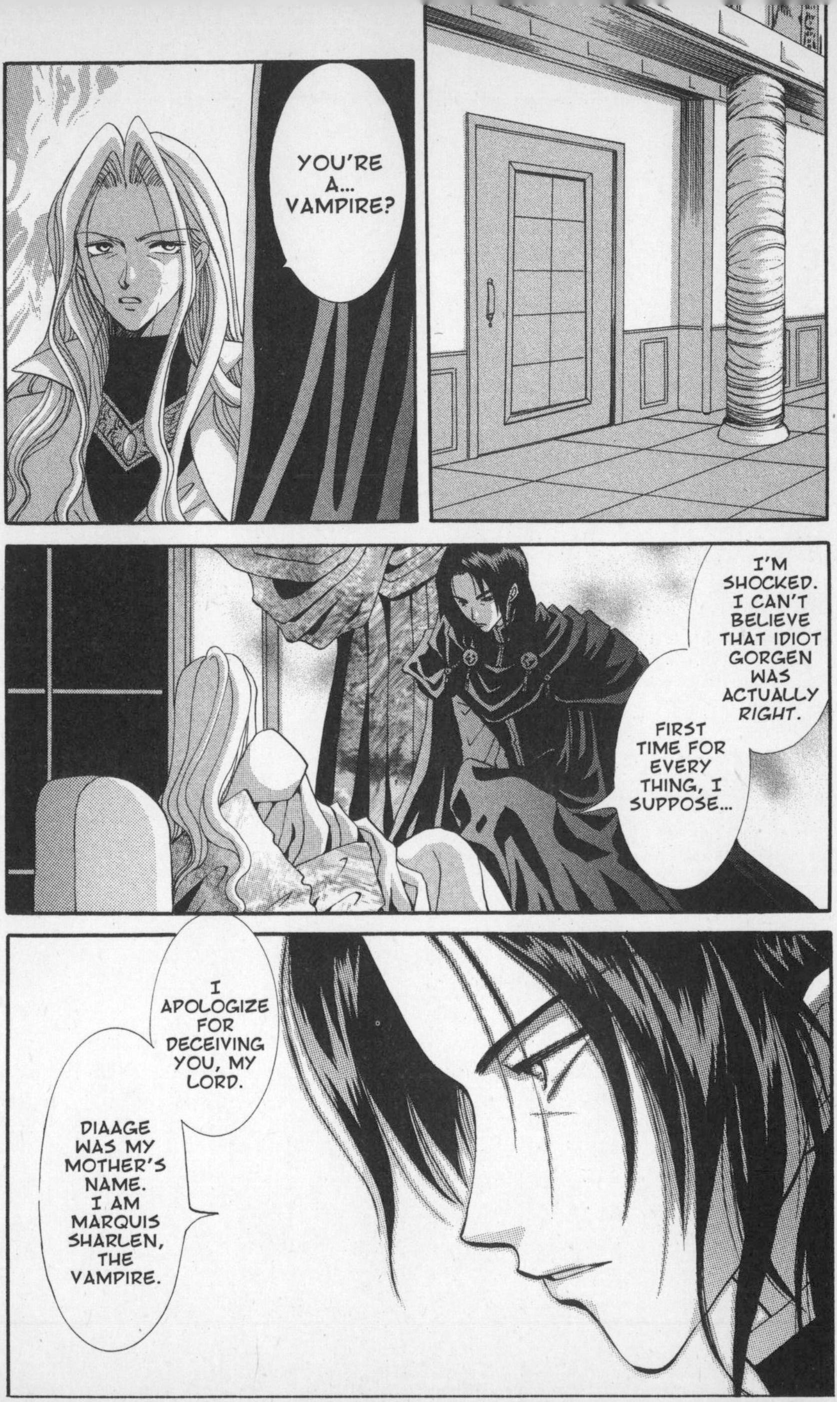
YOU'RE A... VAMPIRE?
I'M SHOCKED. I CAN'T BELIEVE THAT IDIOT GORGEN WAS ACTUALLY RIGHT.
FIRST TIME FOR EVERY THING, I SUPPOSE...
I APOLOGIZE FOR DECEIVING YOU, MY LORD.
DIAAGE WAS MY MOTHER'S NAME. I AM MARQUIS SHARLEN, THE VAMPIRE.

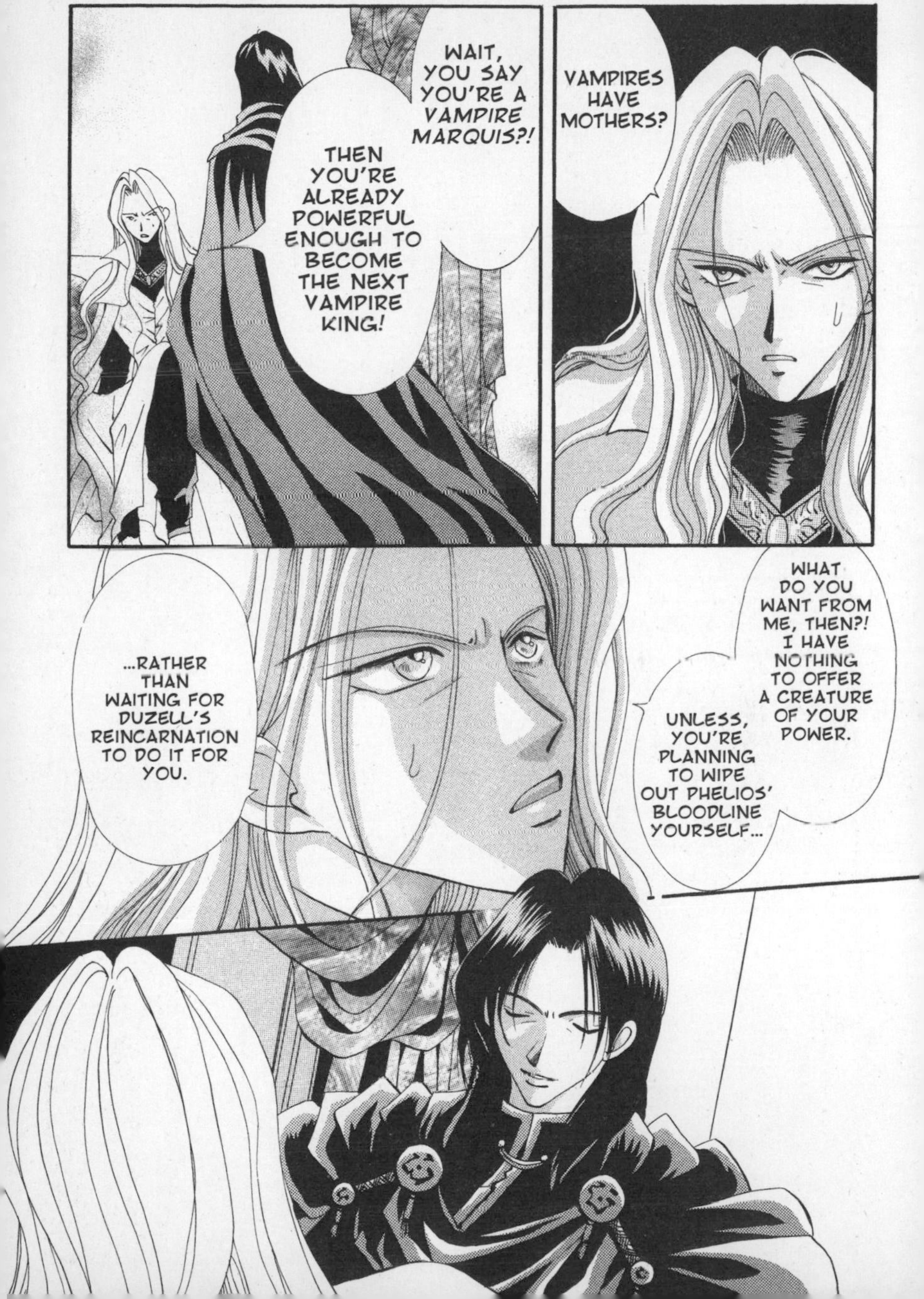
VAMPIRES HAVE MOTHERS?
WAIT, YOU SAY YOU'RE A VAMPIRE MARQUIS?!
THEN YOU'RE ALREADY POWERFUL ENOUGH TO BECOME THE NEXT VAMPIRE KING!
WHAT DO YOU WANT FROM ME, THEN?! I HAVE NOTHING TO OFFER A CREATURE OF YOUR POWER.
UNLESS, YOU'RE PLANNING TO WIPE OUT PHELIOS' BLOODLINE YOURSELF...
...RATHER THAN WAITING FOR DUZELL'S REINCARNATION TO DO IT FOR YOU.

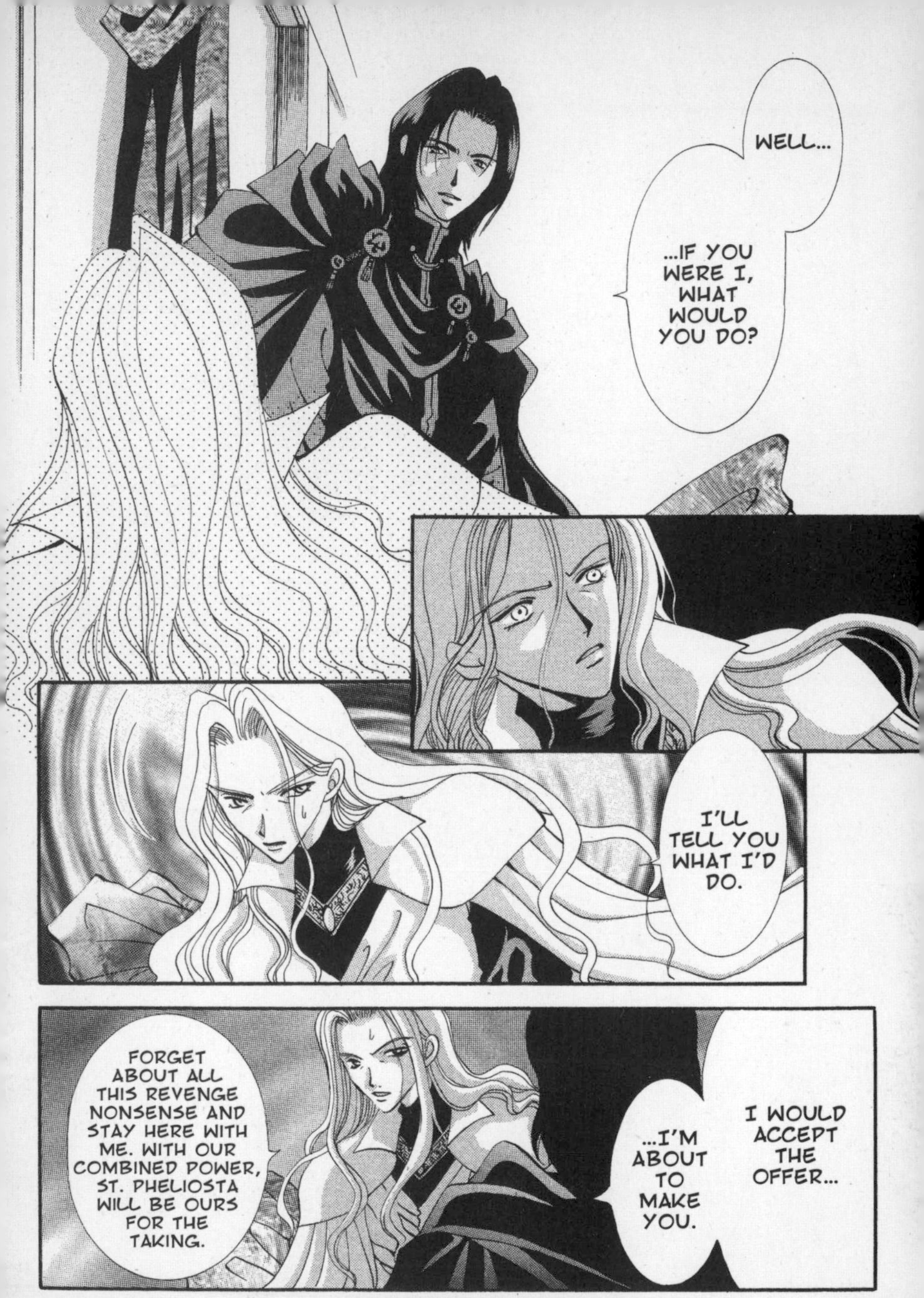
WELL...
...IF YOU WERE I, WHAT WOULD YOU DO?
I'LL TELL YOU WHAT I'D DO.
I WOULD ACCEPT THE OFFER...
...I'M ABOUT TO MAKE YOU.
FORGET ABOUT ALL THIS REVENGE NONSENSE AND STAY HERE WITH ME. WITH OUR COMBINED POWER, ST. PHELIOSTA WILL BE OURS FOR THE TAKING.

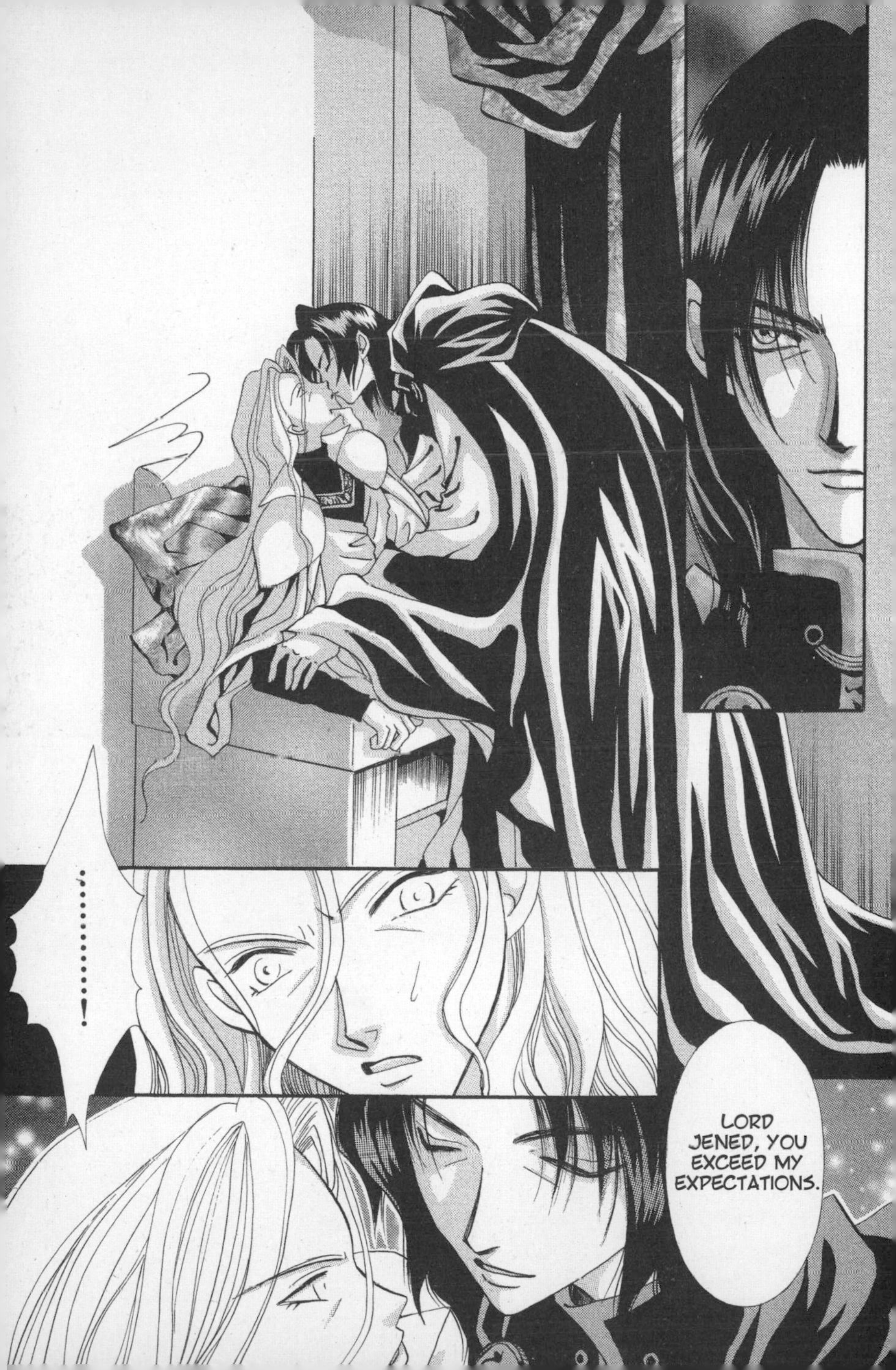
LORD JENED, YOU EXCEED MY EXPECTATIONS.
......!

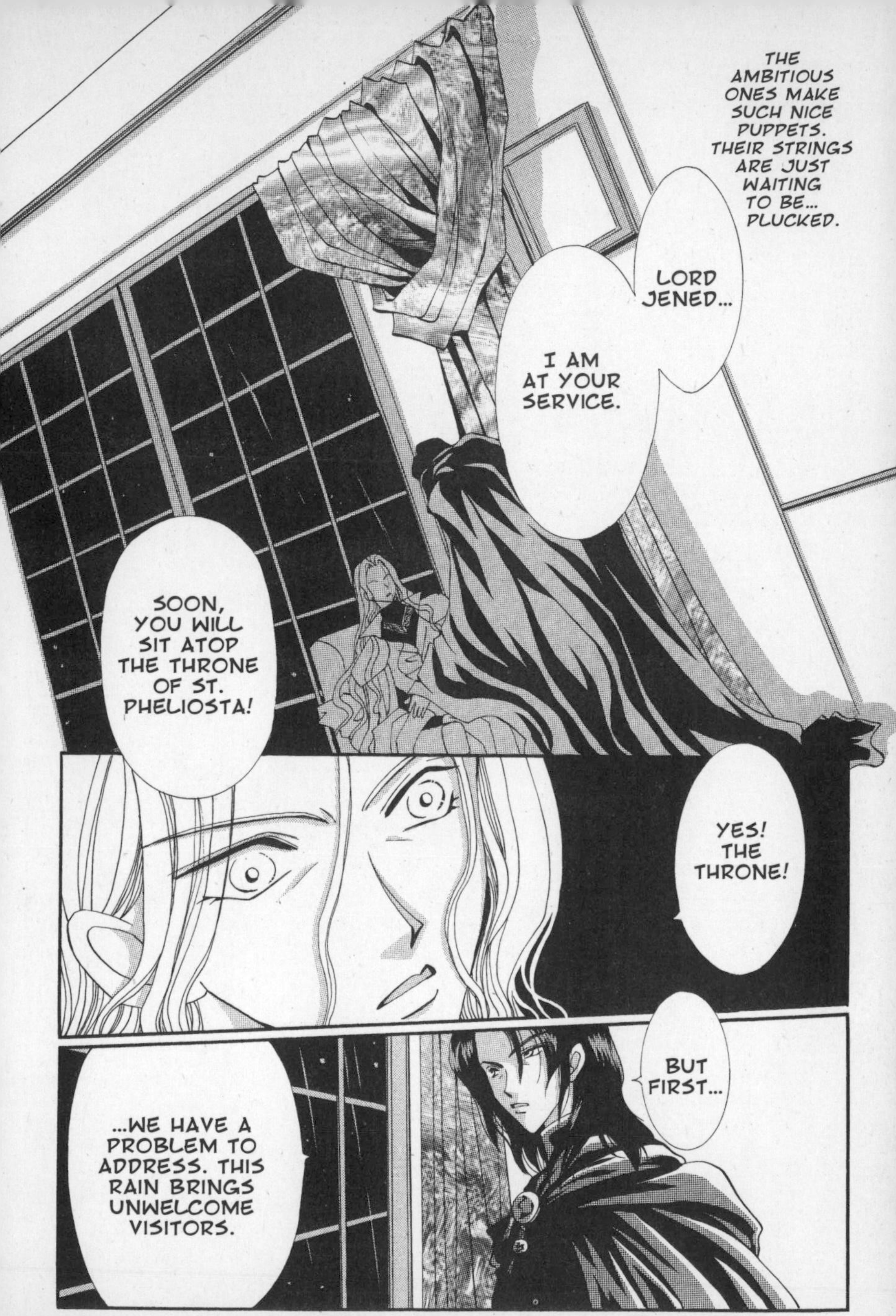
THE AMBITIOUS ONES MAKE SUCH NICE PUPPETS. THEIR STRINGS ARE JUST WAITING TO BE... PLUCKED.
LORD JENED...
I AM AT YOUR SERVICE.
SOON, YOU WILL SIT ATOP THE THRONE OF ST. PHELIOSTA!
YES! THE THRONE!
BUT FIRST...
...WE HAVE A PROBLEM TO ADDRESS. THIS RAIN BRINGS UNWELCOME VISITORS.

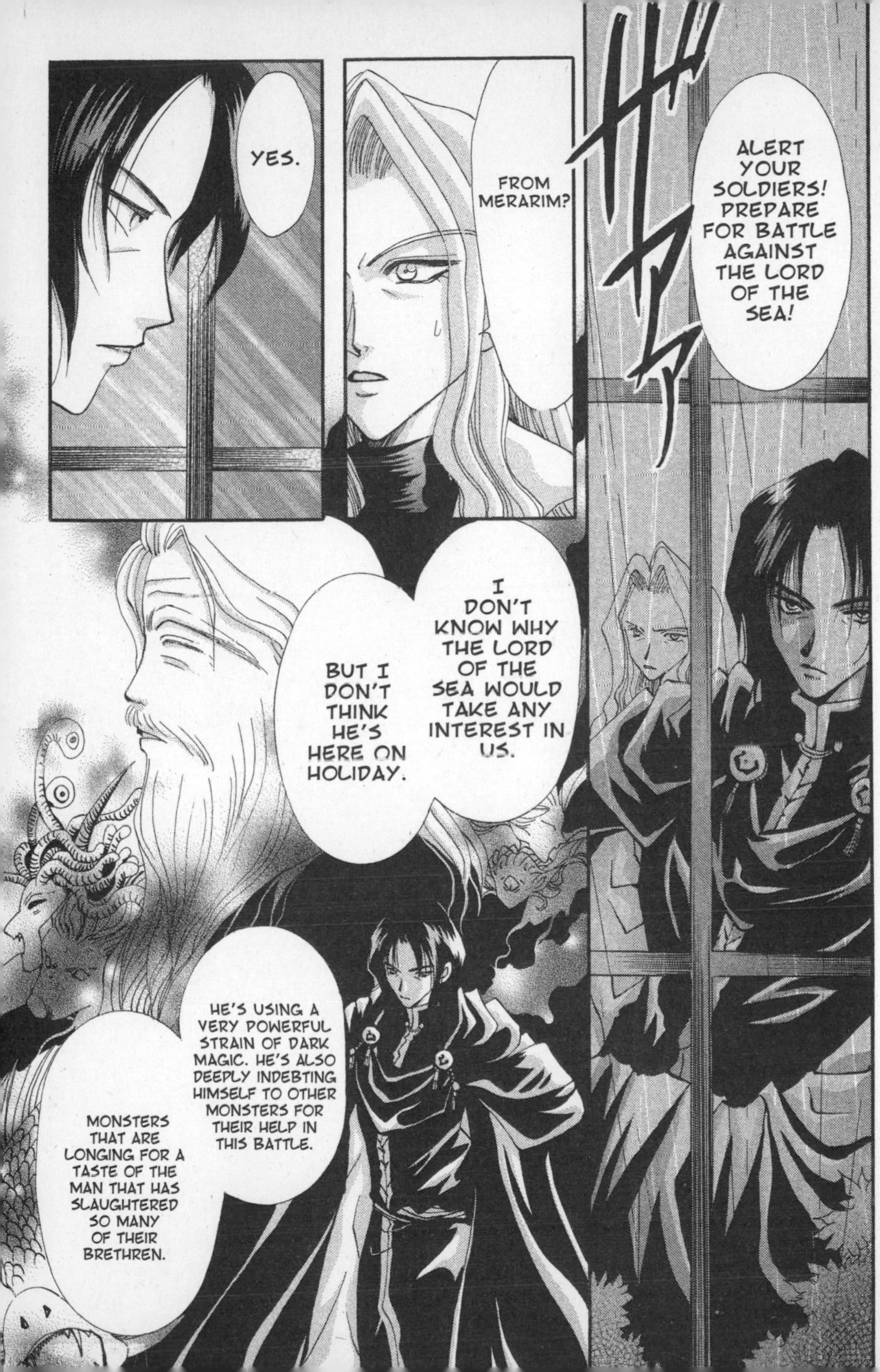
ALERT YOUR SOLDIERS! PREPARE FOR BATTLE AGAINST THE LORD OF THE SEA!
FROM MERARIM?
YES.
I DON'T KNOW WHY THE LORD OF THE SEA WOULD TAKE ANY INTEREST IN US.
BUT I DON'T THINK HE'S HERE ON HOLIDAY.
HE'S USING A VERY POWERFUL STRAIN OF DARK MAGIC. HE'S ALSO DEEPLY INDEBTING HIMSELF TO OTHER MONSTERS FOR THEIR HELP IN THIS BATTLE.
MONSTERS THAT ARE LONGING FOR A TASTE OF THE MAN THAT HAS SLAUGHTERED SO MANY OF THEIR BRETHREN.

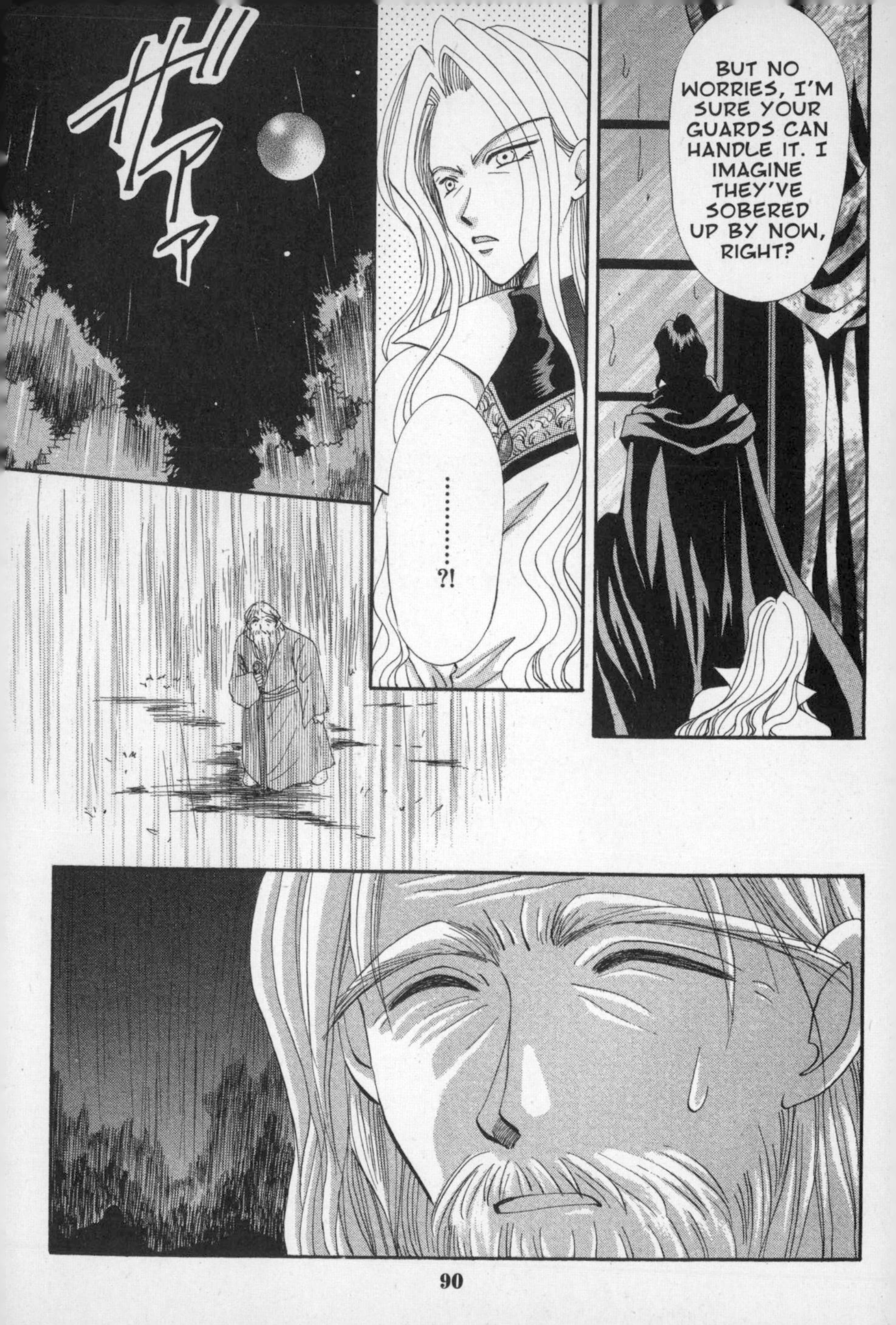
BUT NO WORRIES, I'M SURE YOUR GUARDS CAN HANDLE IT. I IMAGINE THEY'VE SOBERED UP BY NOW, RIGHT?
......?!

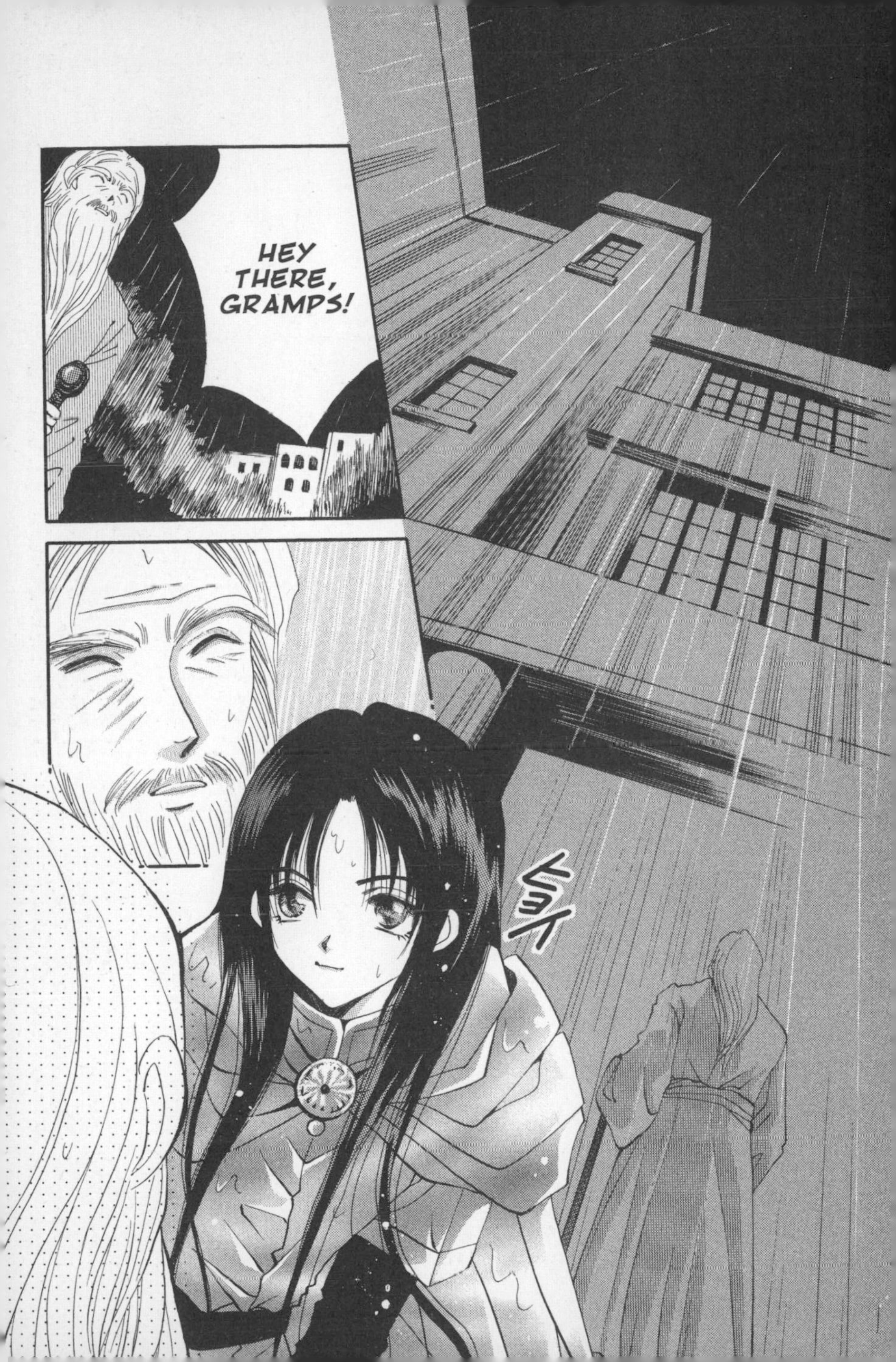
HEY THERE, GRAMPS!

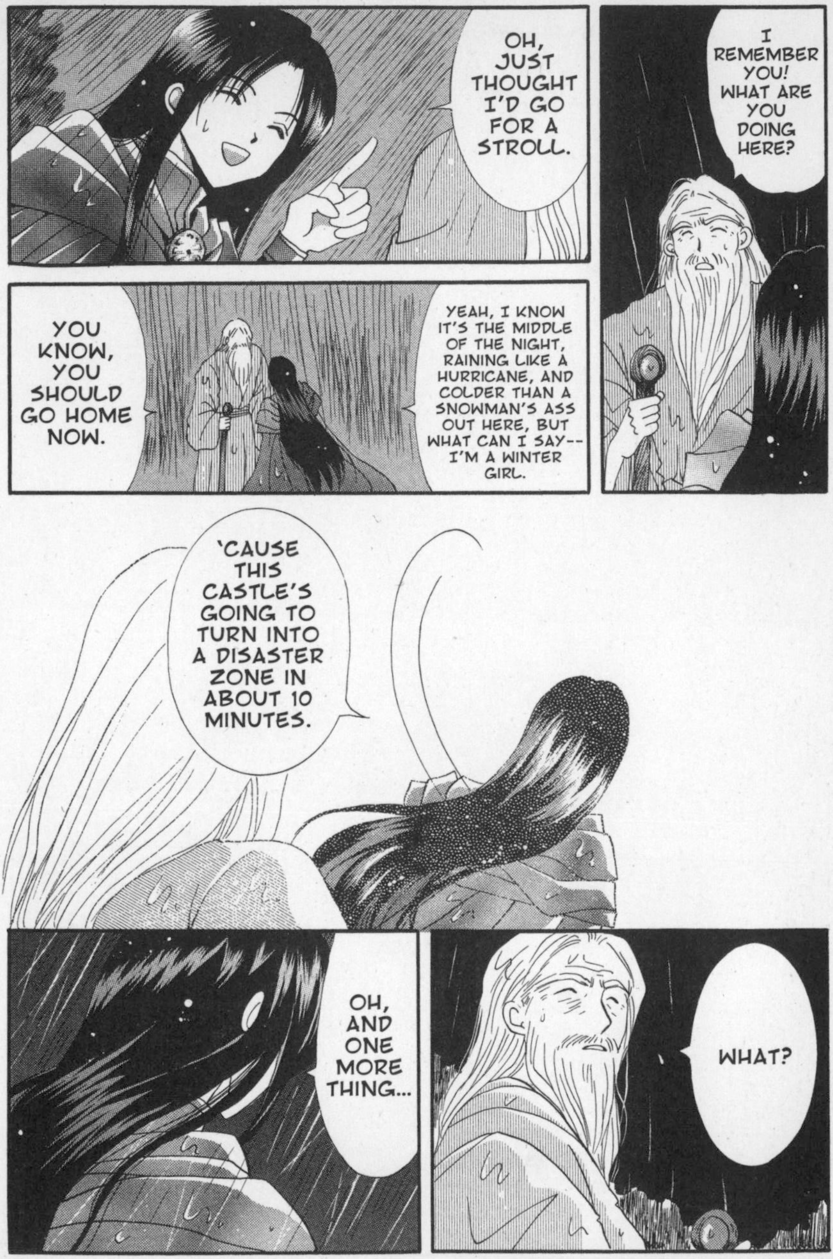
I REMEMBER YOU! WHAT ARE YOU DOING HERE?
OH, JUST THOUGHT I'D GO FOR A STROLL.
YEAH, I KNOW IT'S THE MIDDLE OF THE NIGHT, RAINING LIKE A HURRICANE, AND COLDER THAN A SNOWMAN'S ASS OUT HERE, BUT WHAT CAN I SAY-- I'M A WINTER GIRL.
YOU KNOW, YOU SHOULD GO HOME NOW.
'CAUSE THIS CASTLE'S GOING TO TURN INTO A DISASTER ZONE IN ABOUT 10 MINUTES.
WHAT?
OH, AND ONE MORE THING...

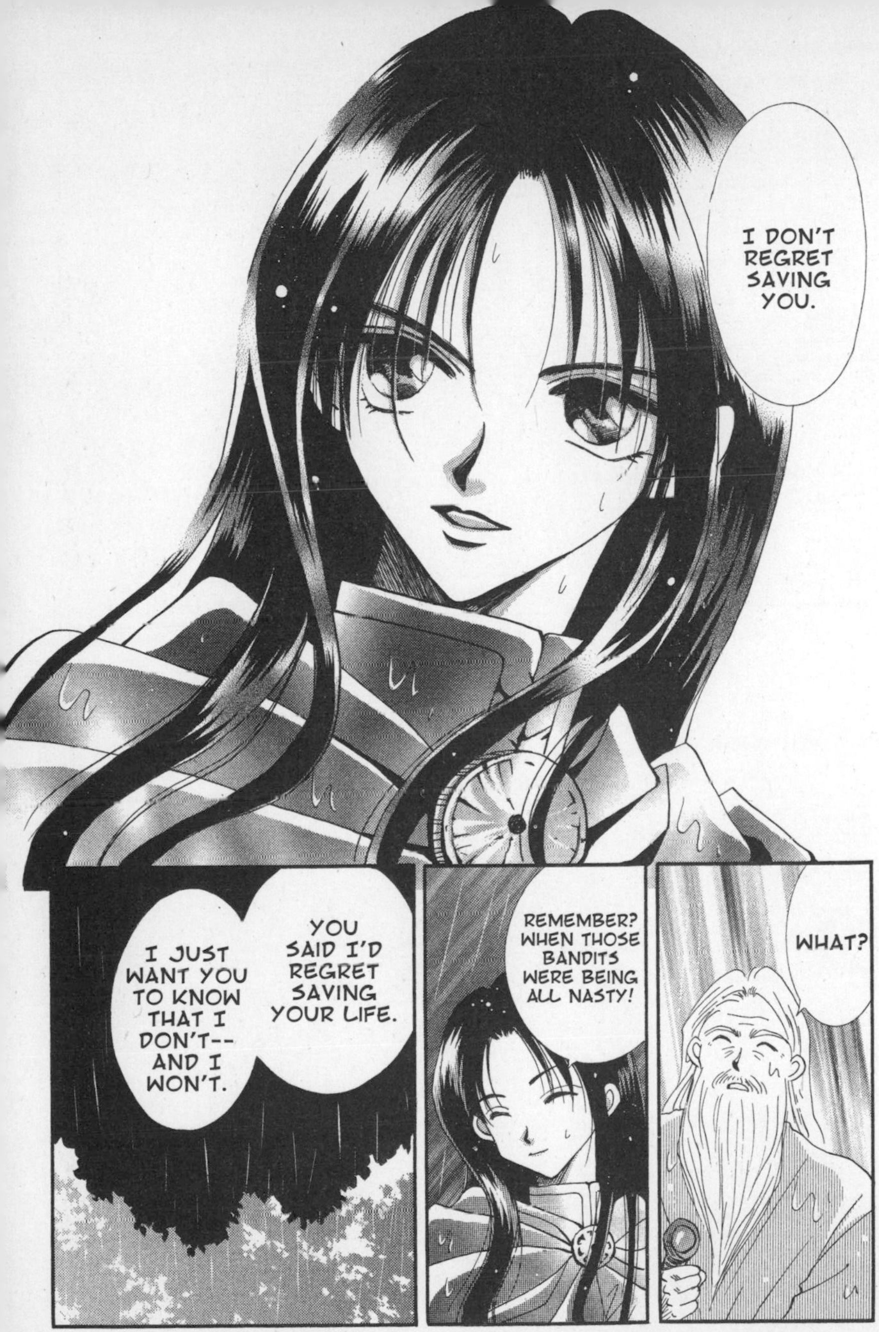
I DON'T REGRET SAVING YOU.
WHAT?
REMEMBER? WHEN THOSE BANDITS WERE BEING ALL NASTY!
YOU SAID I'D REGRET SAVING YOUR LIFE.
I JUST WANT YOU TO KNOW THAT I DON'T-- AND I WON'T.

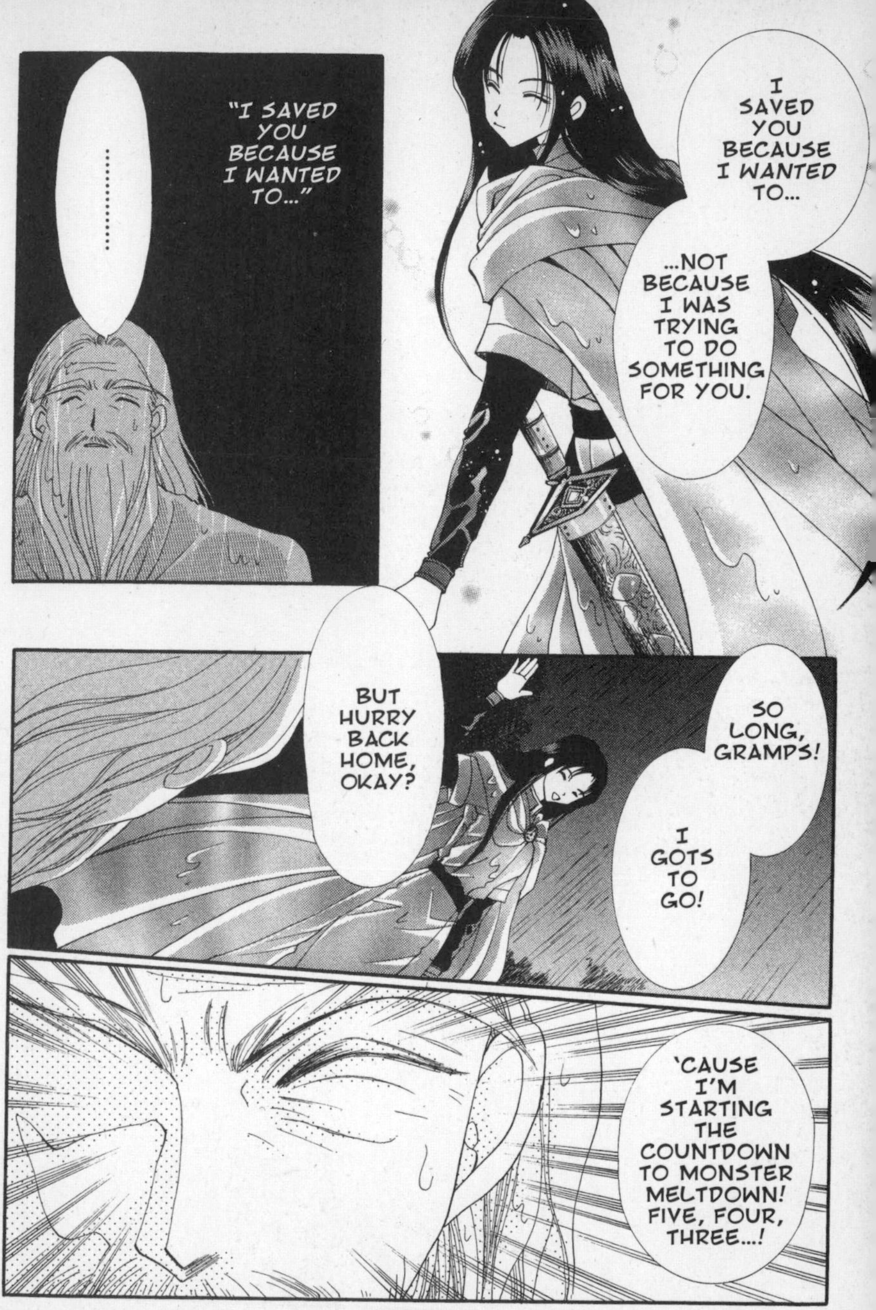
I SAVED YOU BECAUSE I WANTED TO...
...NOT BECAUSE I WAS TRYING TO DO SOMETHING FOR YOU.
......
"I SAVED YOU BECAUSE I WANTED TO..."
BUT HURRY BACK HOME, OKAY?
SO LONG, GRAMPS!
I GOTS TO GO!
'CAUSE I'M STARTING THE COUNTDOWN TO MONSTER MELTDOWN! FIVE, FOUR, THREE...!

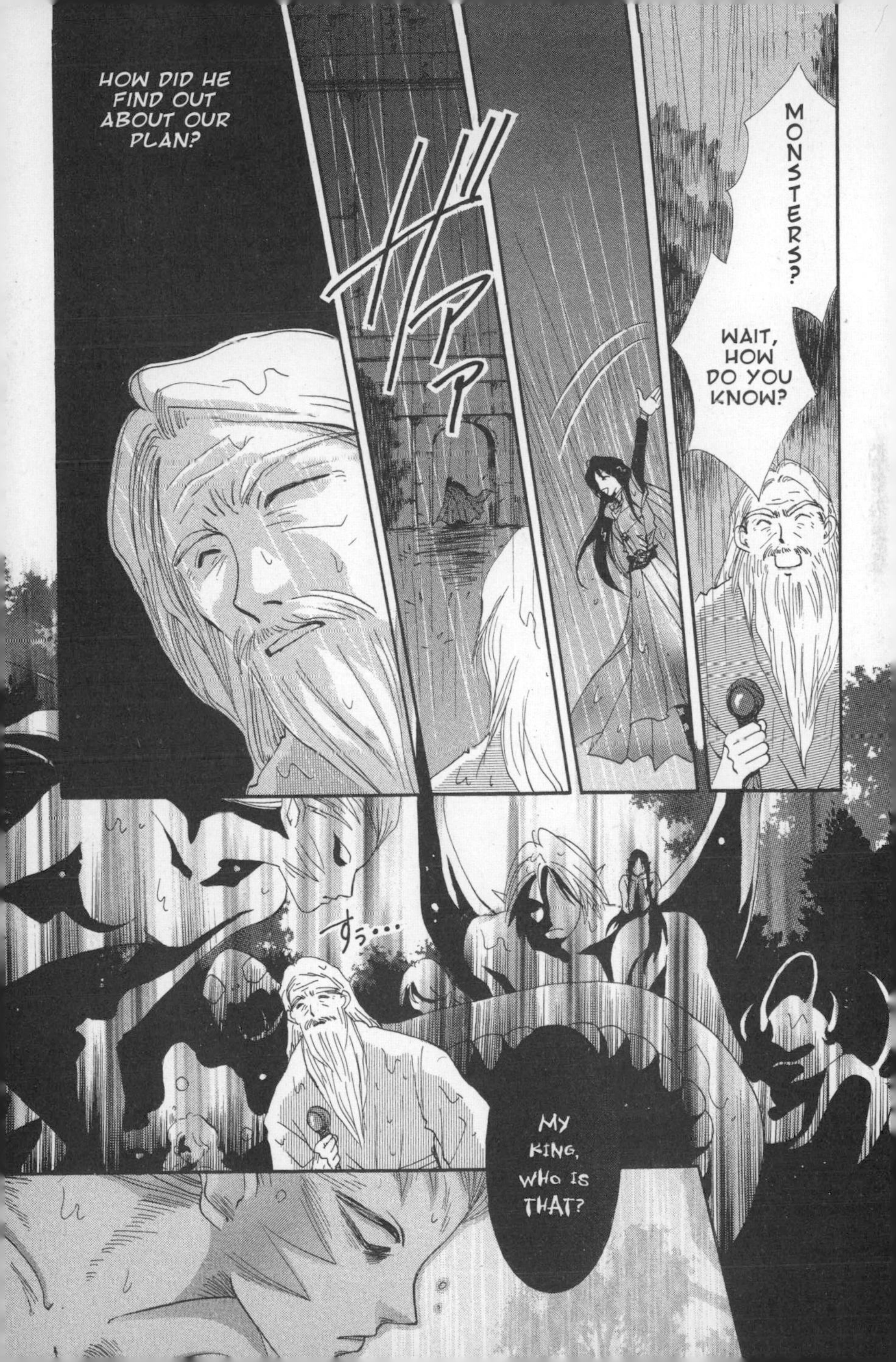
MONSTERS?
WAIT, HOW DO YOU KNOW?
HOW DID HE FIND OUT ABOUT OUR PLAN?
すぅ…
MY KING, WHO IS THAT?

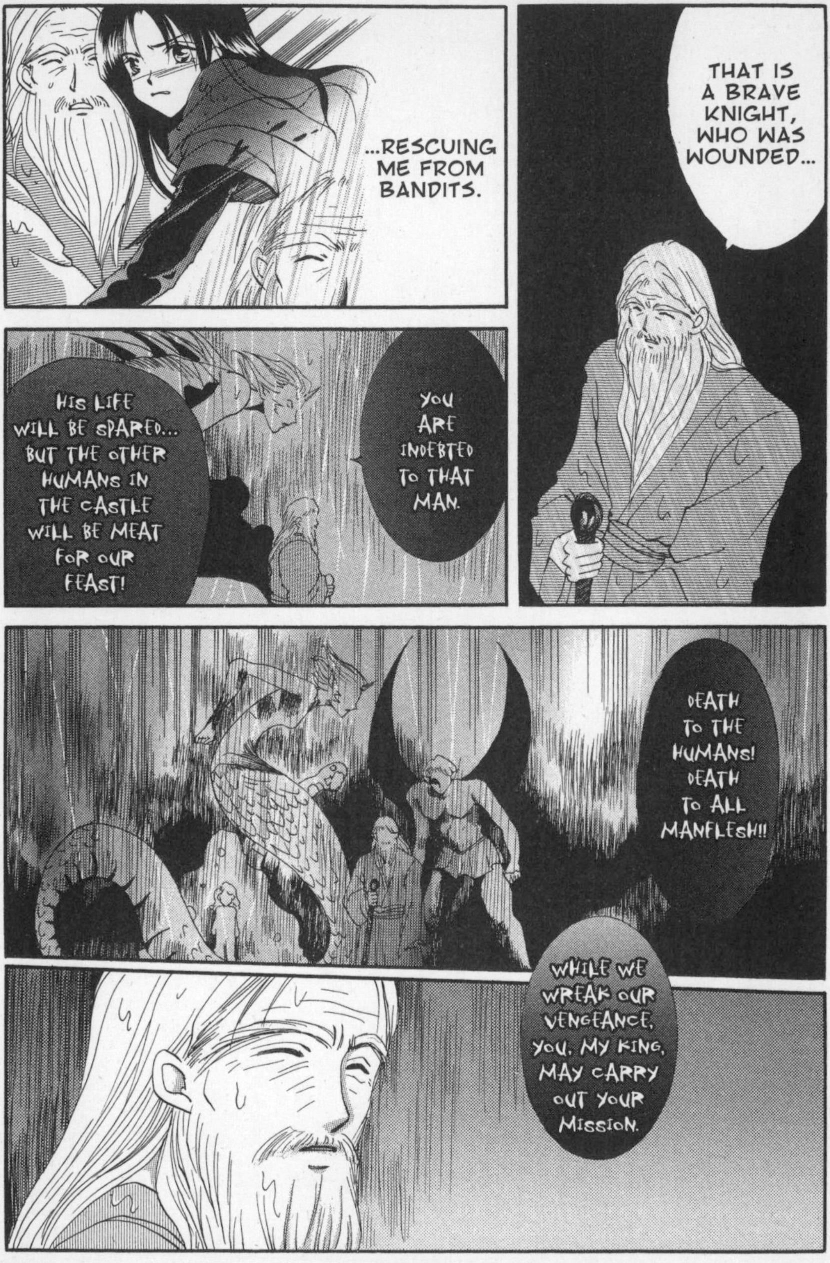
THAT IS A BRAVE KNIGHT, WHO WAS WOUNDED...
...RESCUING ME FROM BANDITS.
YOU ARE INDEBTED TO THAT MAN.
HIS LIFE WILL BE SPARED... BUT THE OTHER HUMANS IN THE CASTLE WILL BE MEAT FOR OUR FEAST!
DEATH TO THE HUMANS! DEATH TO ALL MANFLESH!!
WHILE WE WREAK OUR VENGEANCE, YOU, MY KING, MAY CARRY OUT YOUR MISSION.

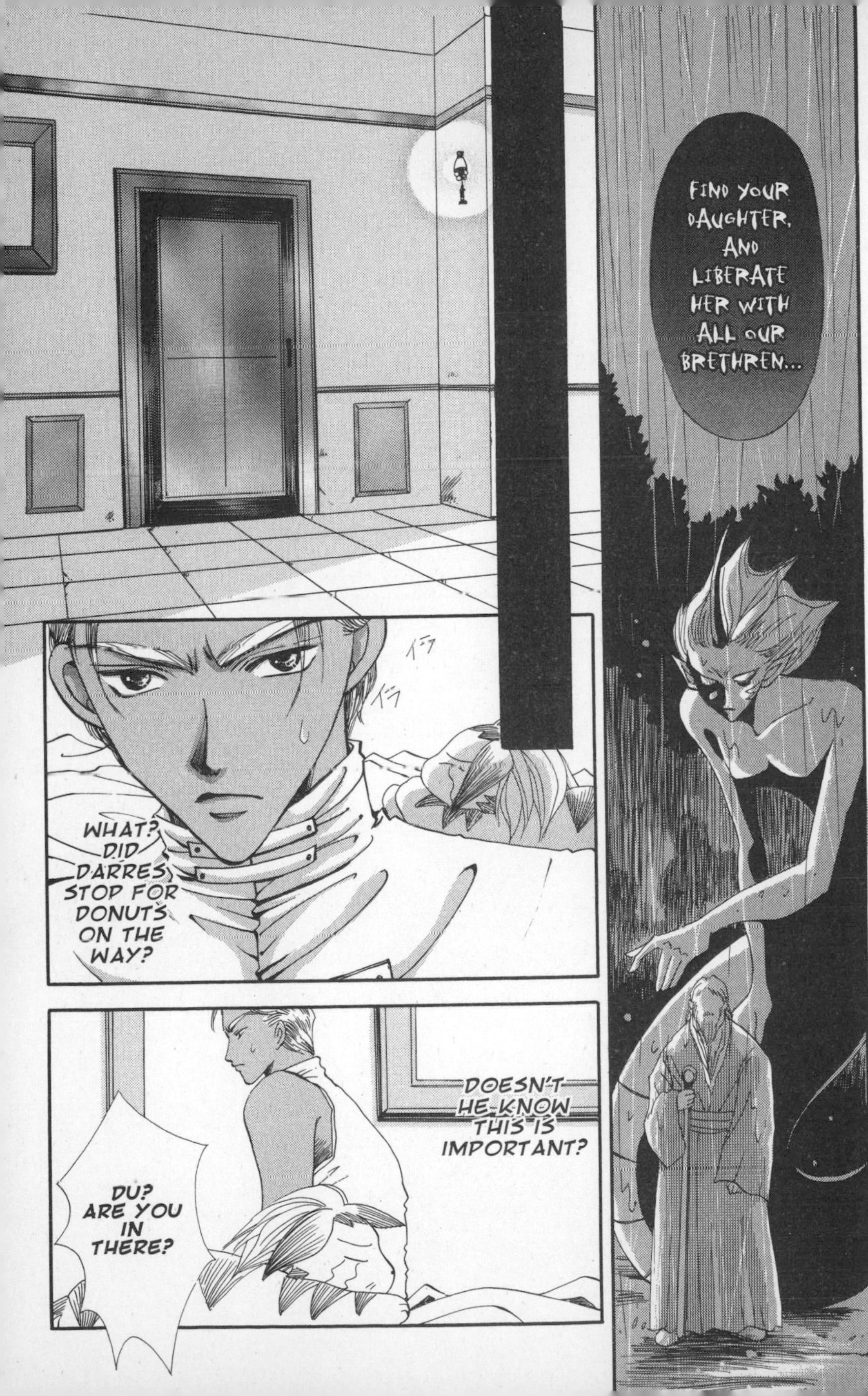
FIND YOUR DAUGHTER, AND LIBERATE HER WITH ALL OUR BRETHREN...
WHAT? DID DARRES STOP FOR DONUTS ON THE WAY?
DOESN'T HE KNOW THIS IS IMPORTANT?
DU? ARE YOU IN THERE?

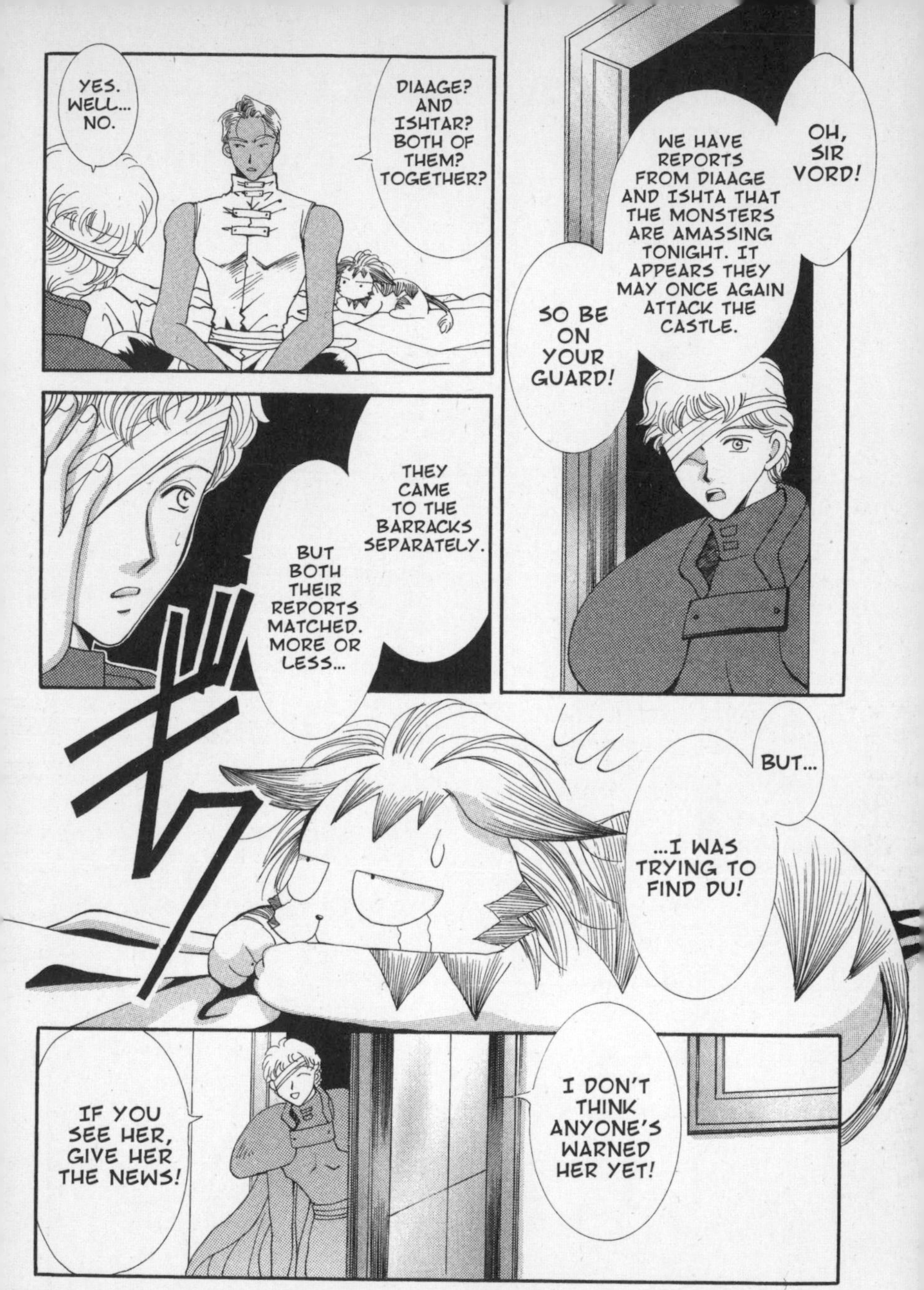
OH, SIR VORD!
WE HAVE REPORTS FROM DIAAGE AND ISHTA THAT THE MONSTERS ARE AMASSING TONIGHT. IT APPEARS THEY MAY ONCE AGAIN ATTACK THE CASTLE.
SO BE ON YOUR GUARD!
DIAAGE? AND ISHTAR? BOTH OF THEM? TOGETHER?
YES. WELL... NO.
THEY CAME TO THE BARRACKS SEPARATELY.
BUT BOTH THEIR REPORTS MATCHED. MORE OR LESS...
BUT...
...I WAS TRYING TO FIND DU!
I DON'T THINK ANYONE'S WARNED HER YET!
IF YOU SEE HER, GIVE HER THE NEWS!

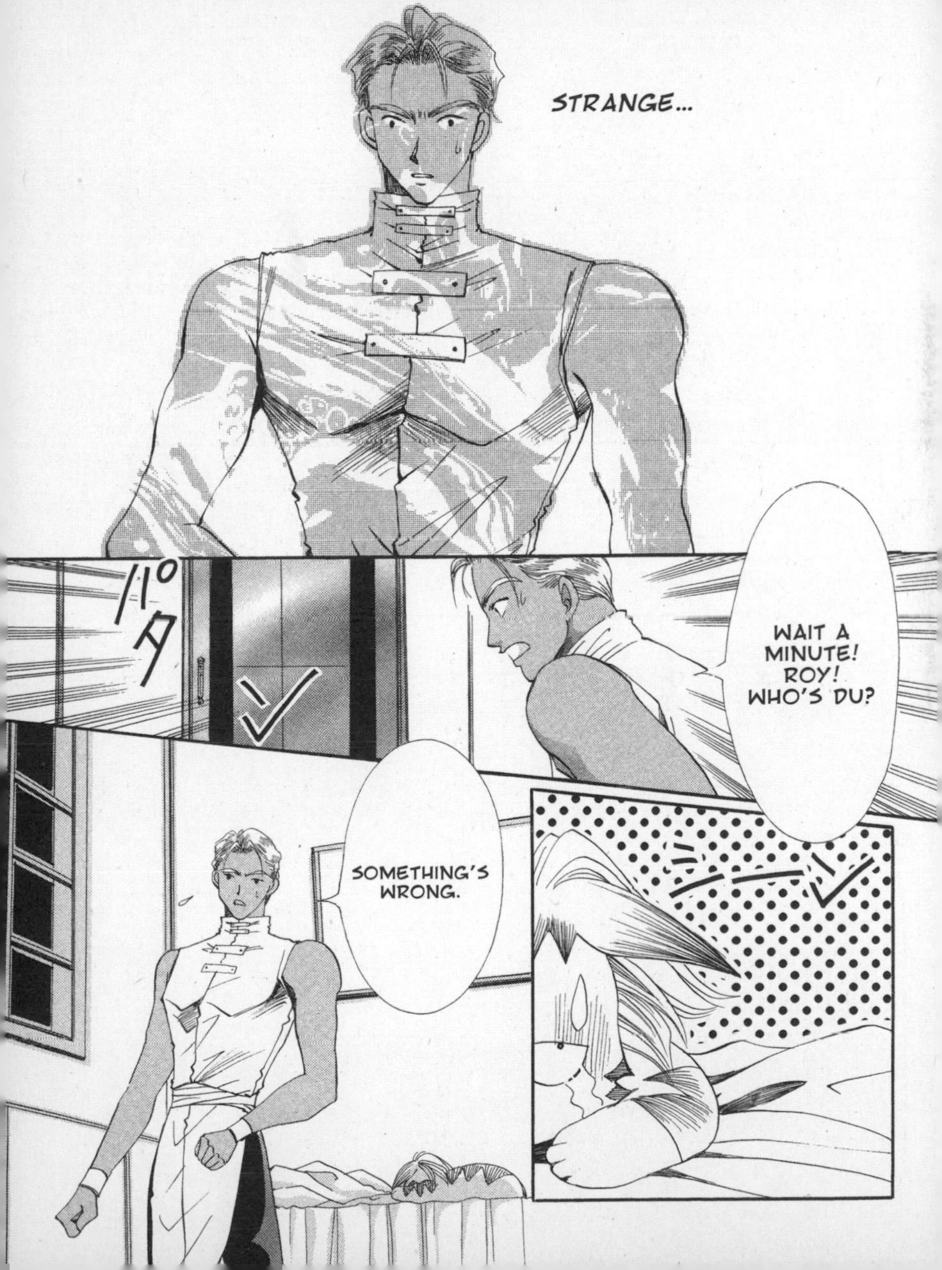
STRANGE...
WAIT A MINUTE! ROY! WHO'S DU?
パタ
SOMETHING'S WRONG.

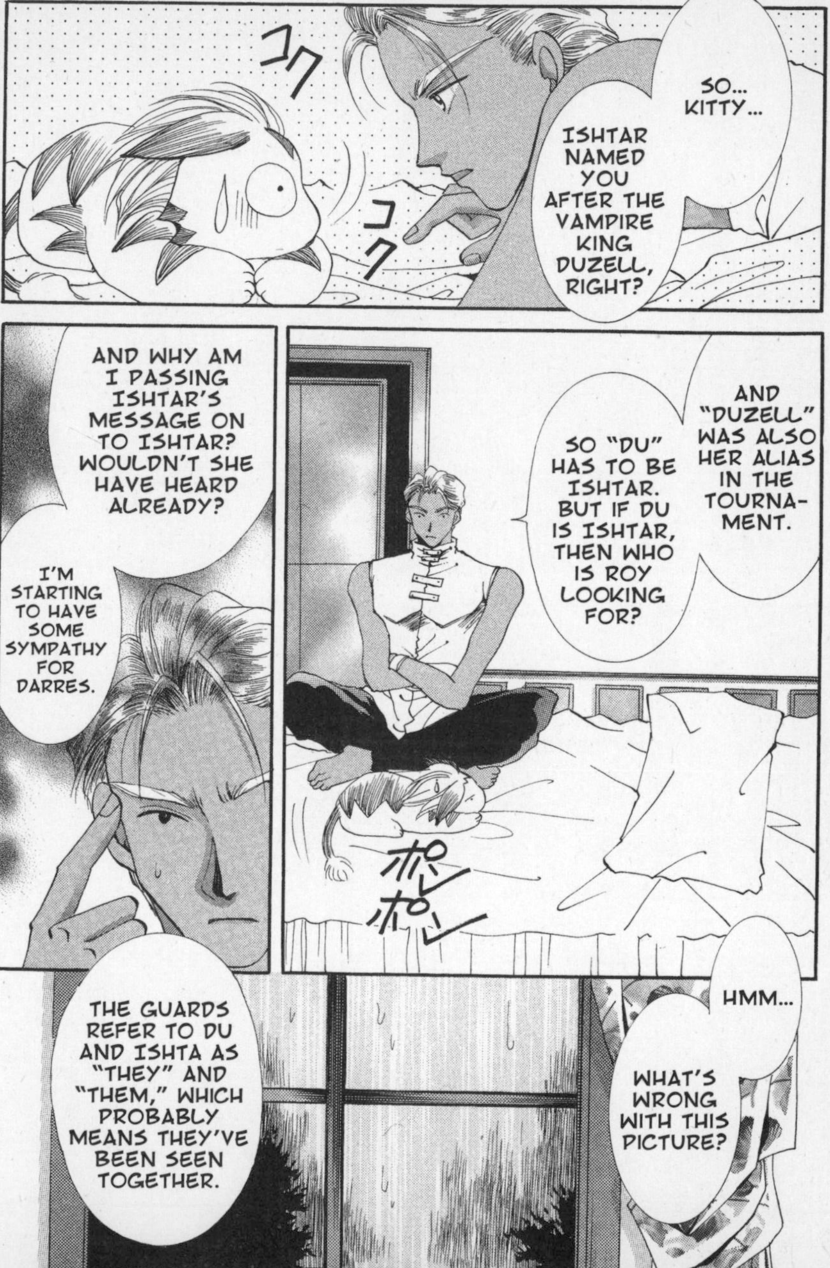
コク
コク
SO... KITTY...
ISHTAR NAMED YOU AFTER THE VAMPIRE KING DUZELL, RIGHT?
AND "DUZELL" WAS ALSO HER ALIAS IN THE TOURNA-MENT.
SO "DU" HAS TO BE ISHTAR. BUT IF DU IS ISHTAR, THEN WHO IS ROY LOOKING FOR?
ポンポン
AND WHY AM I PASSING ISHTAR'S MESSAGE ON TO ISHTAR? WOULDN'T SHE HAVE HEARD ALREADY?
I'M STARTING TO HAVE SOME SYMPATHY FOR DARRES.
HMM...
WHAT'S WRONG WITH THIS PICTURE?
THE GUARDS REFER TO DU AND ISHTA AS "THEY" AND "THEM," WHICH PROBABLY MEANS THEY'VE BEEN SEEN TOGETHER.

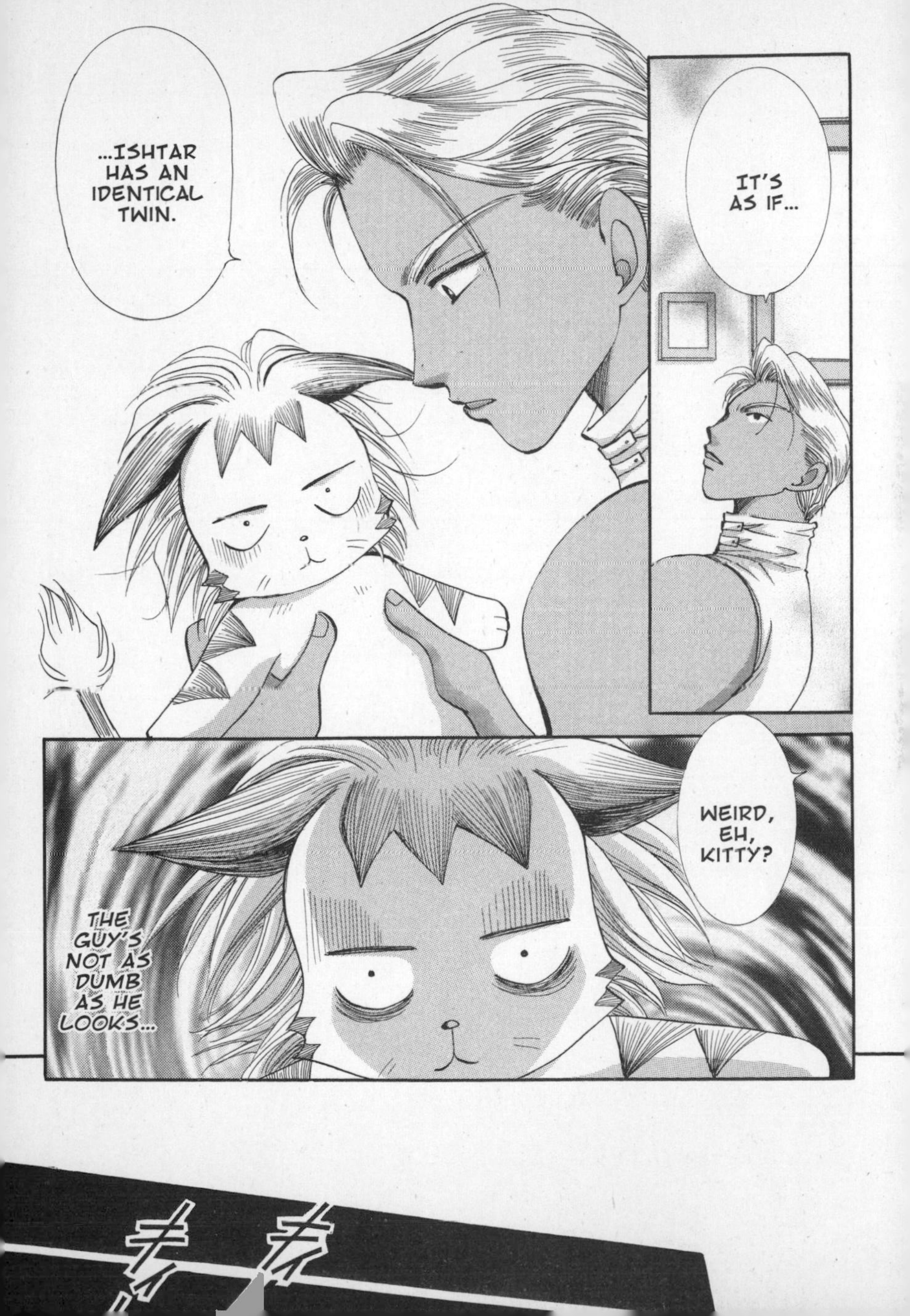
IT'S AS IF...
...ISHTAR HAS AN IDENTICAL TWIN.
WEIRD, EH, KITTY?
THE GUY'S NOT AS DUMB AS HE LOOKS...

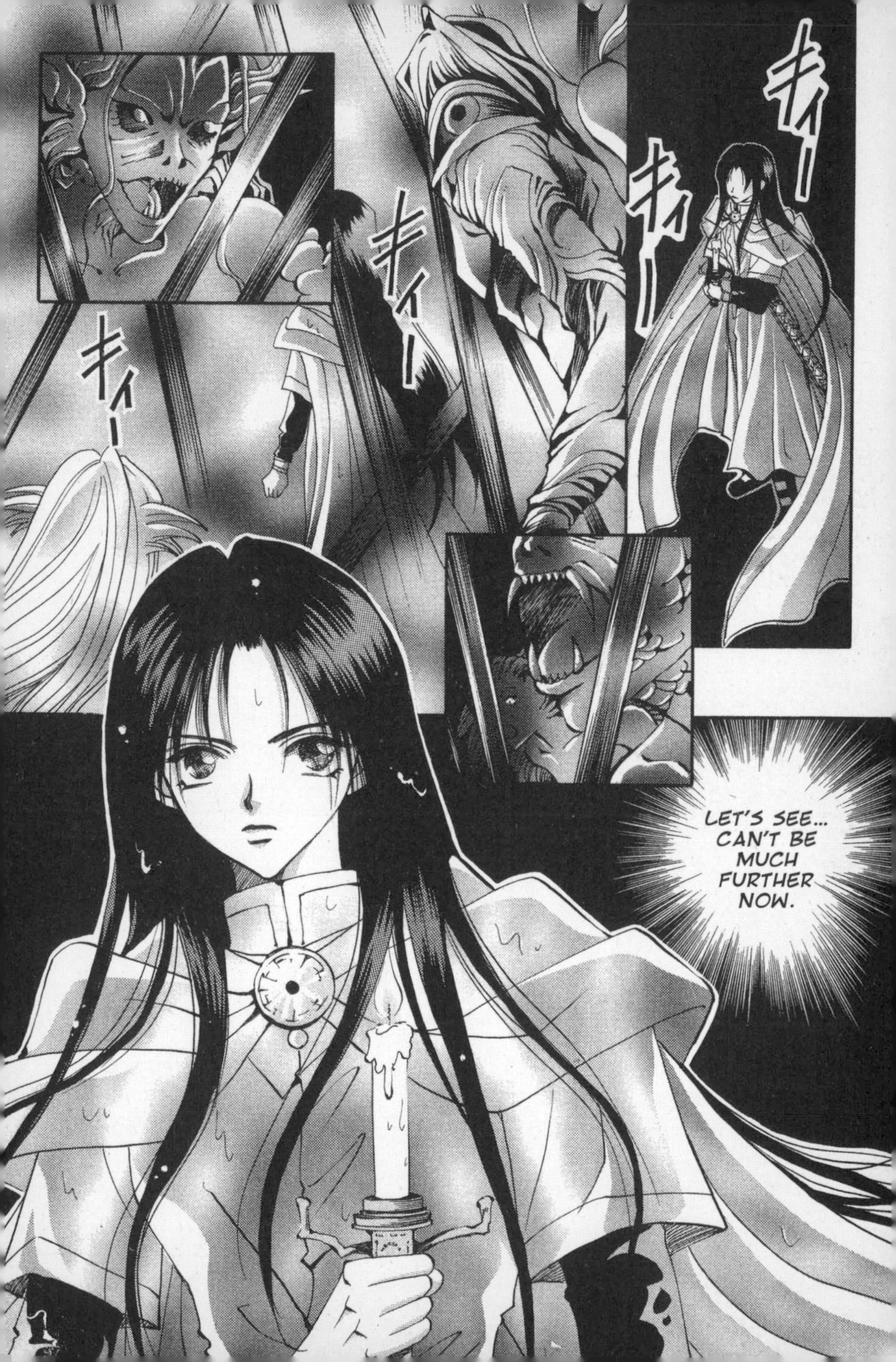
キィー
キィー
キィー
キィー
LET'S SEE...
CAN'T BE
MUCH
FURTHER
NOW.

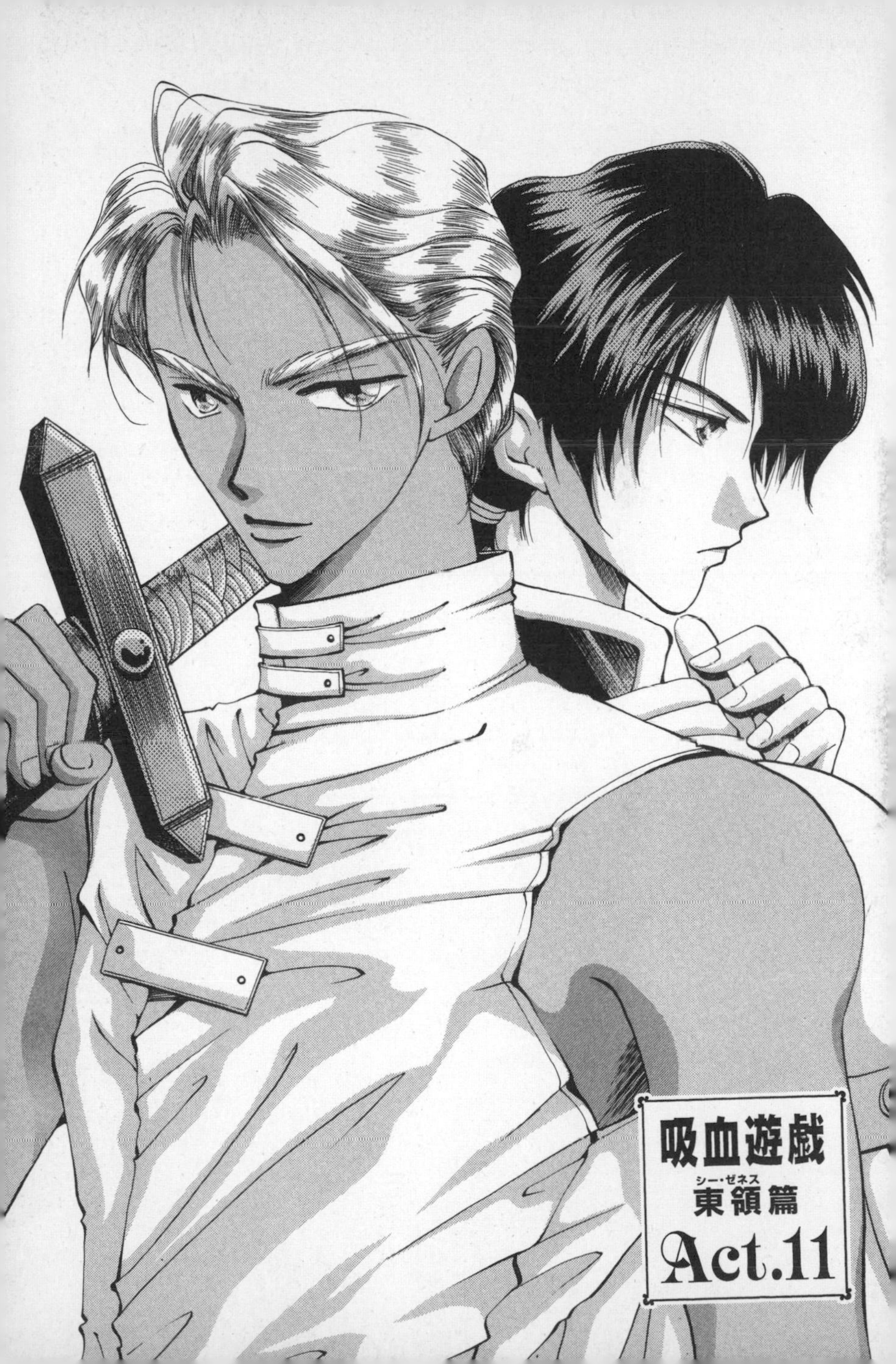
吸血遊戯
シー・ゼネス
東領篇
Act.11

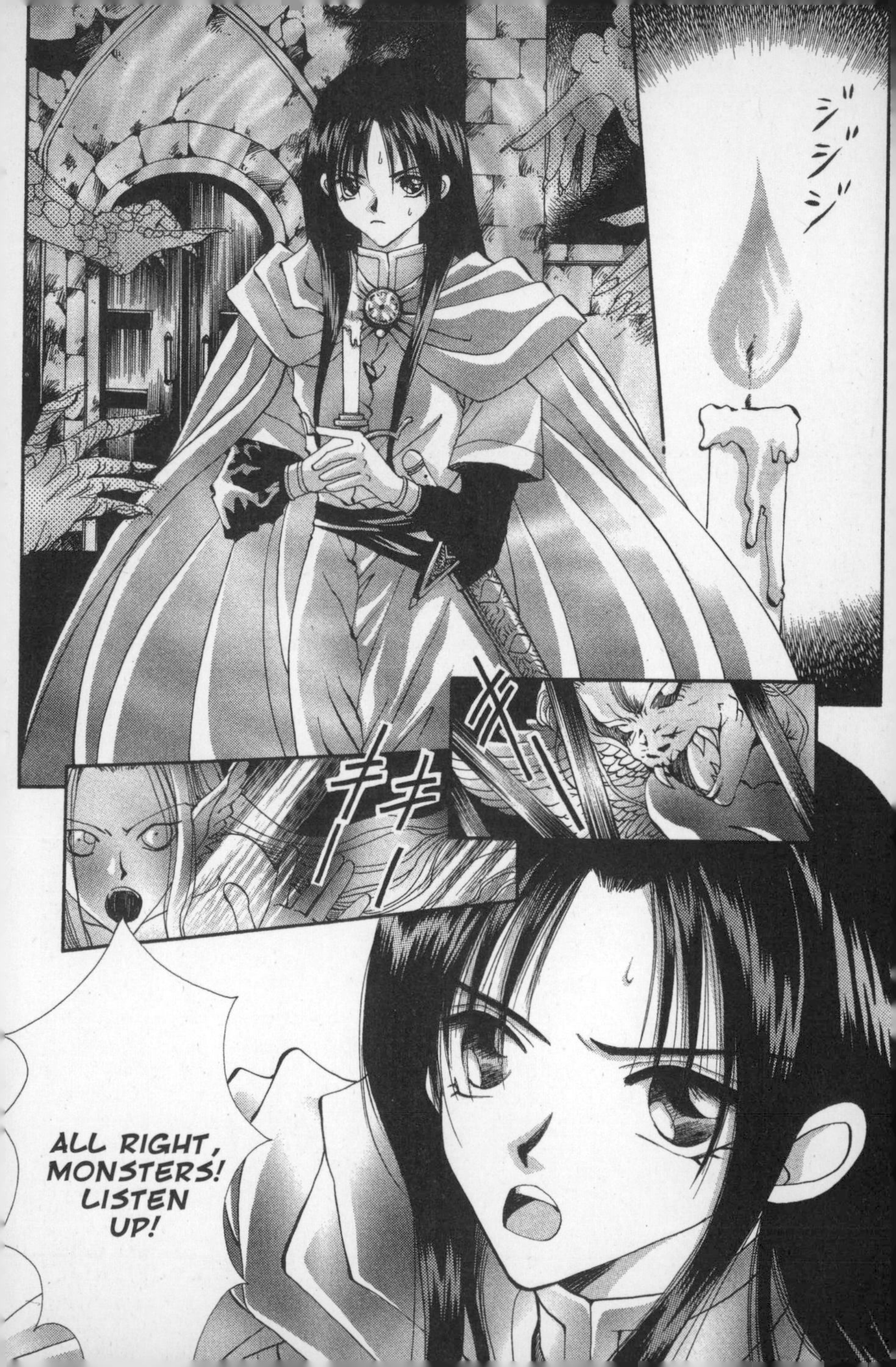
ジジジジ
キキー
ALL RIGHT, MONSTERS! LISTEN UP!

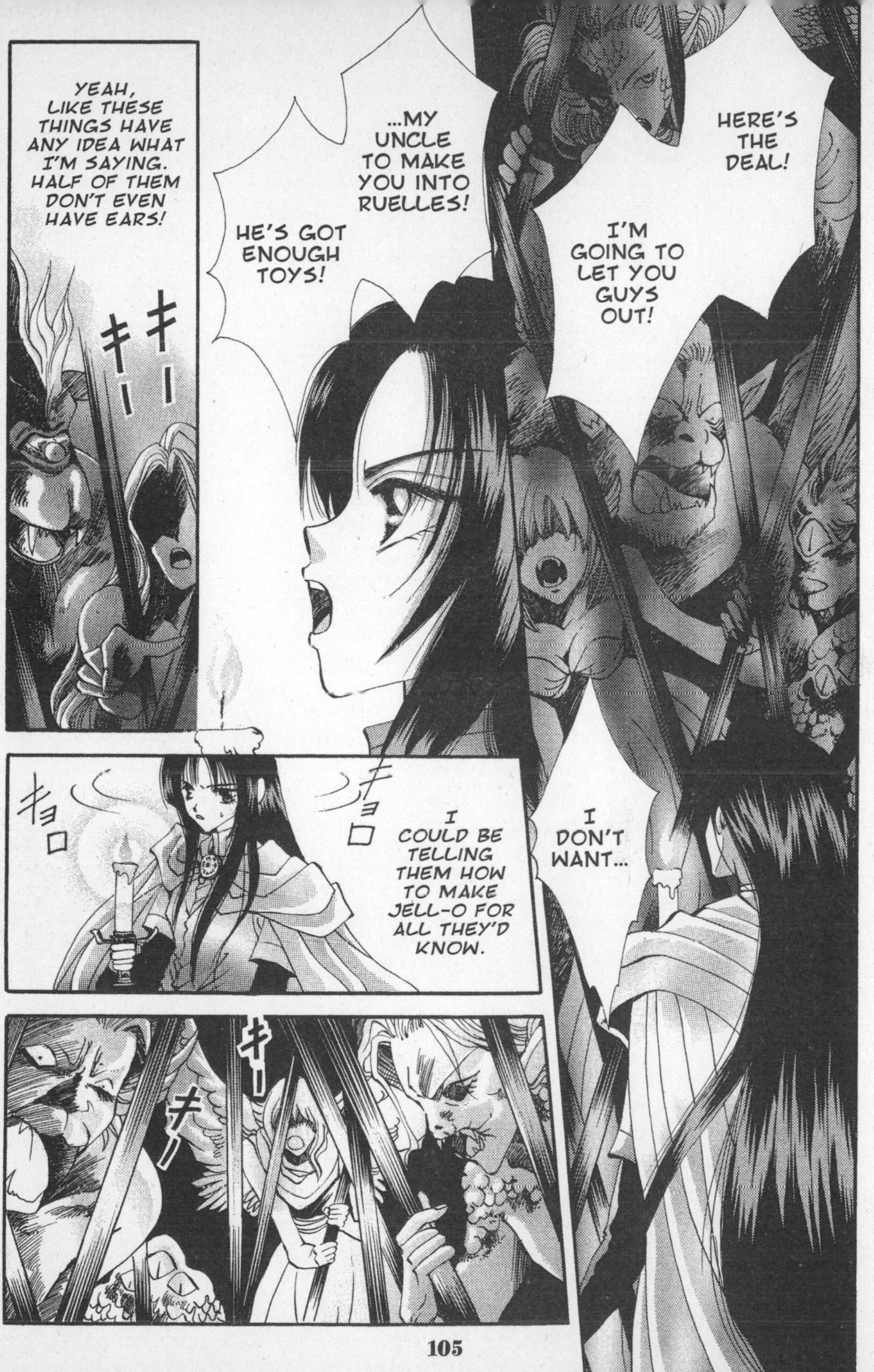
HERE'S THE DEAL!
I'M GOING TO LET YOU GUYS OUT!
I DON'T WANT...
...MY UNCLE TO MAKE YOU INTO RUELLES!
HE'S GOT ENOUGH TOYS!
YEAH, LIKE THESE THINGS HAVE ANY IDEA WHAT I'M SAYING. HALF OF THEM DON'T EVEN HAVE EARS!
キー
キー
キョロ
キョロ
I COULD BE TELLING THEM HOW TO MAKE JELL-O FOR ALL THEY'D KNOW.
キー
キー

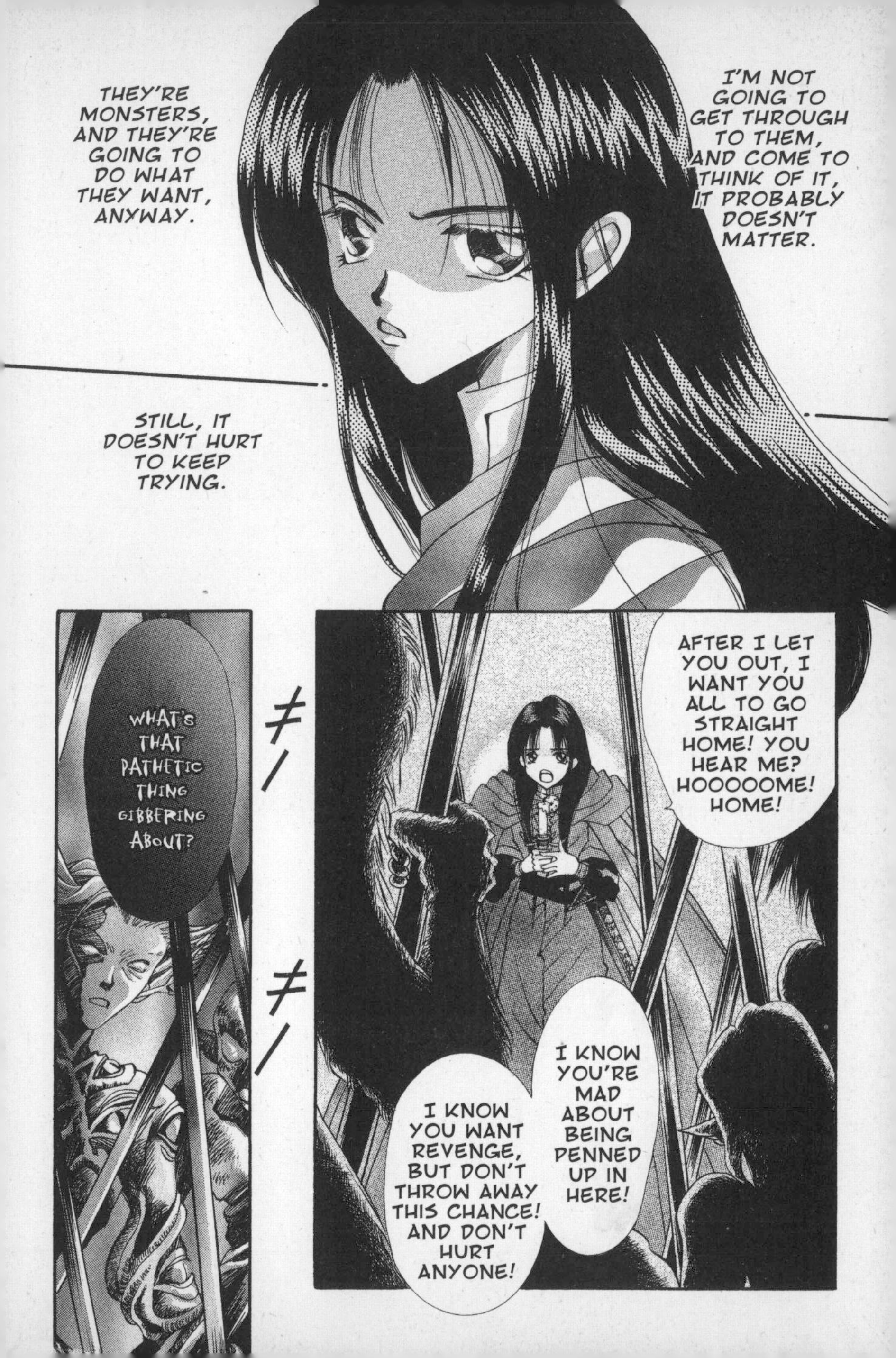
I'M NOT GOING TO GET THROUGH TO THEM, AND COME TO THINK OF IT, IT PROBABLY DOESN'T MATTER.
THEY'RE MONSTERS, AND THEY'RE GOING TO DO WHAT THEY WANT, ANYWAY.
STILL, IT DOESN'T HURT TO KEEP TRYING.
AFTER I LET YOU OUT, I WANT YOU ALL TO GO STRAIGHT HOME! YOU HEAR ME? HOOOOOME! HOME!
I KNOW YOU'RE MAD ABOUT BEING PENNED UP IN HERE!
I KNOW YOU WANT REVENGE, BUT DON'T THROW AWAY THIS CHANCE! AND DON'T HURT ANYONE!
WHAT'S THAT PATHETIC THING GIBBERING ABOUT?

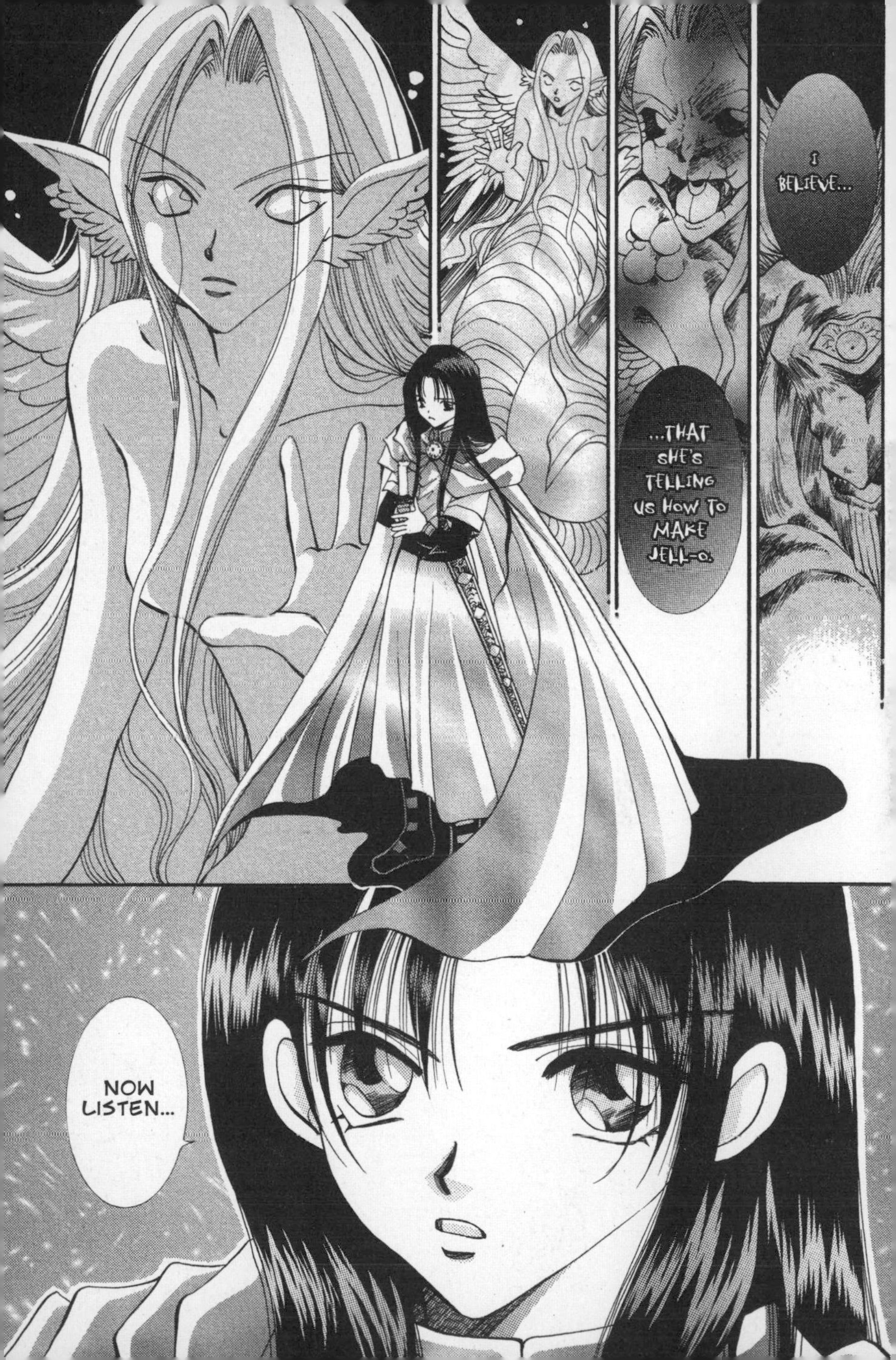
I BELIEVE...
...THAT SHE'S TELLING US HOW TO MAKE JELL-O.
NOW LISTEN...

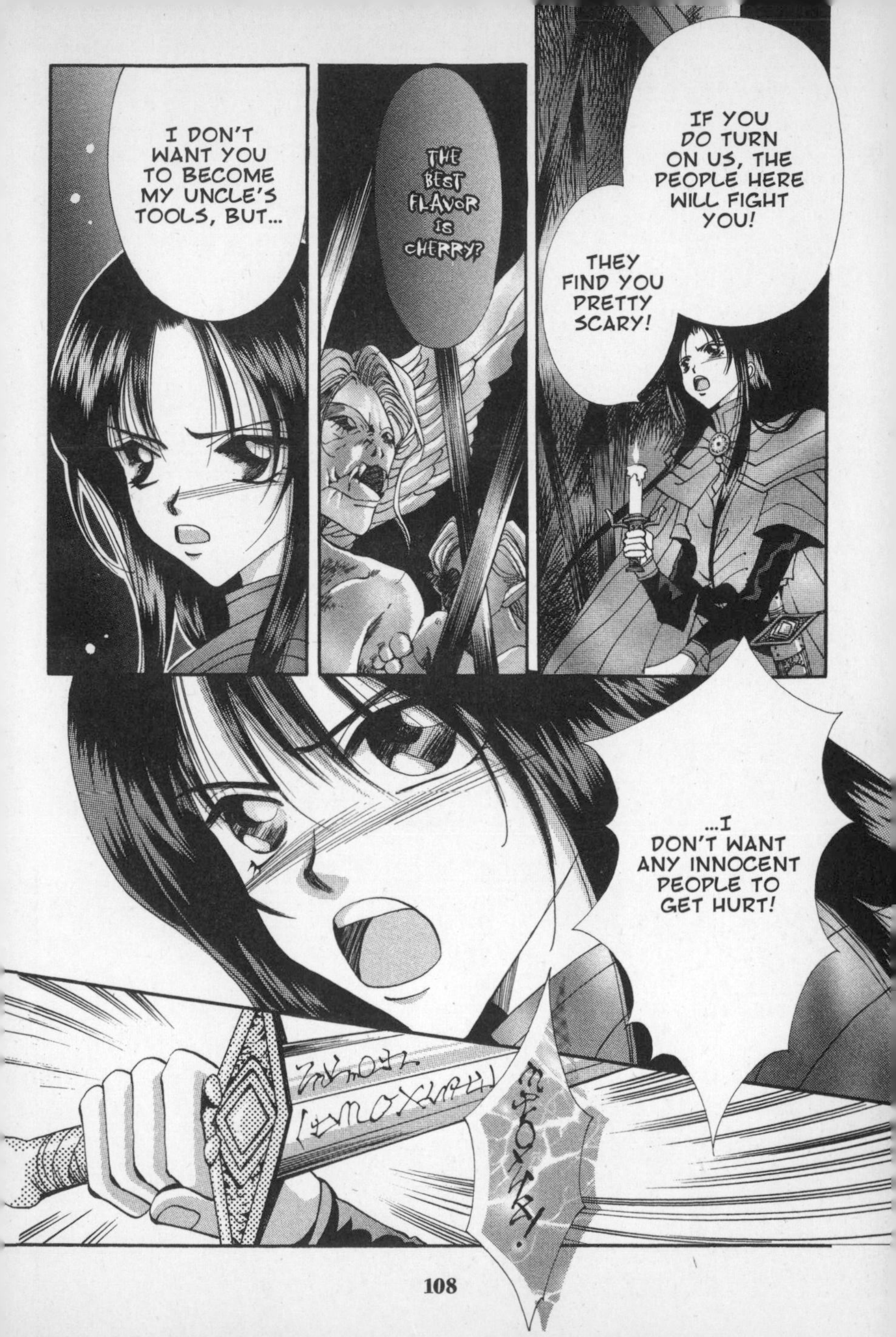
IF YOU DO TURN ON US, THE PEOPLE HERE WILL FIGHT YOU!
THEY FIND YOU PRETTY SCARY!
THE BEST FLAVOR IS CHERRY?
I DON'T WANT YOU TO BECOME MY UNCLE'S TOOLS, BUT...
...I DON'T WANT ANY INNOCENT PEOPLE TO GET HURT!

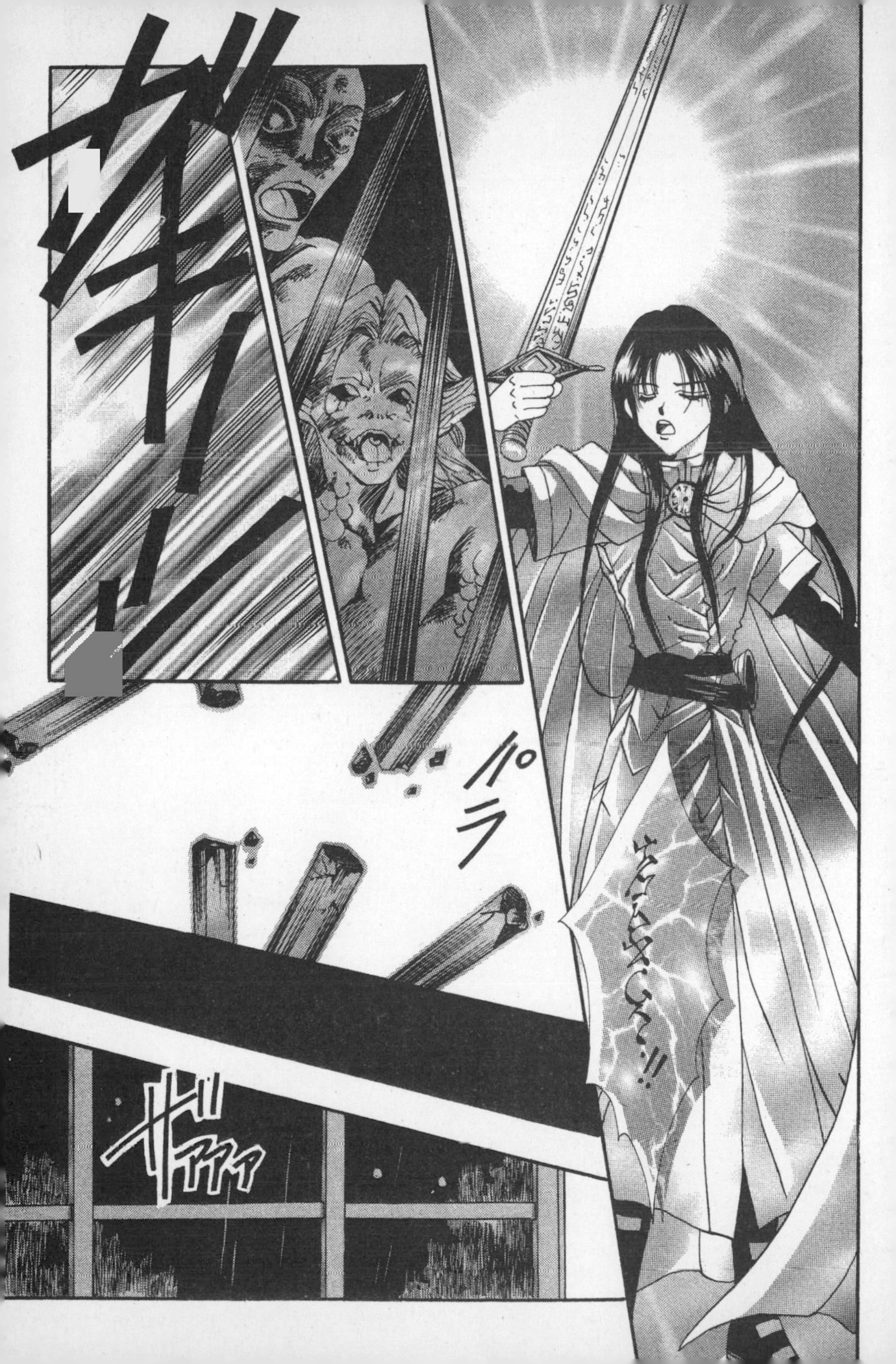
パラ

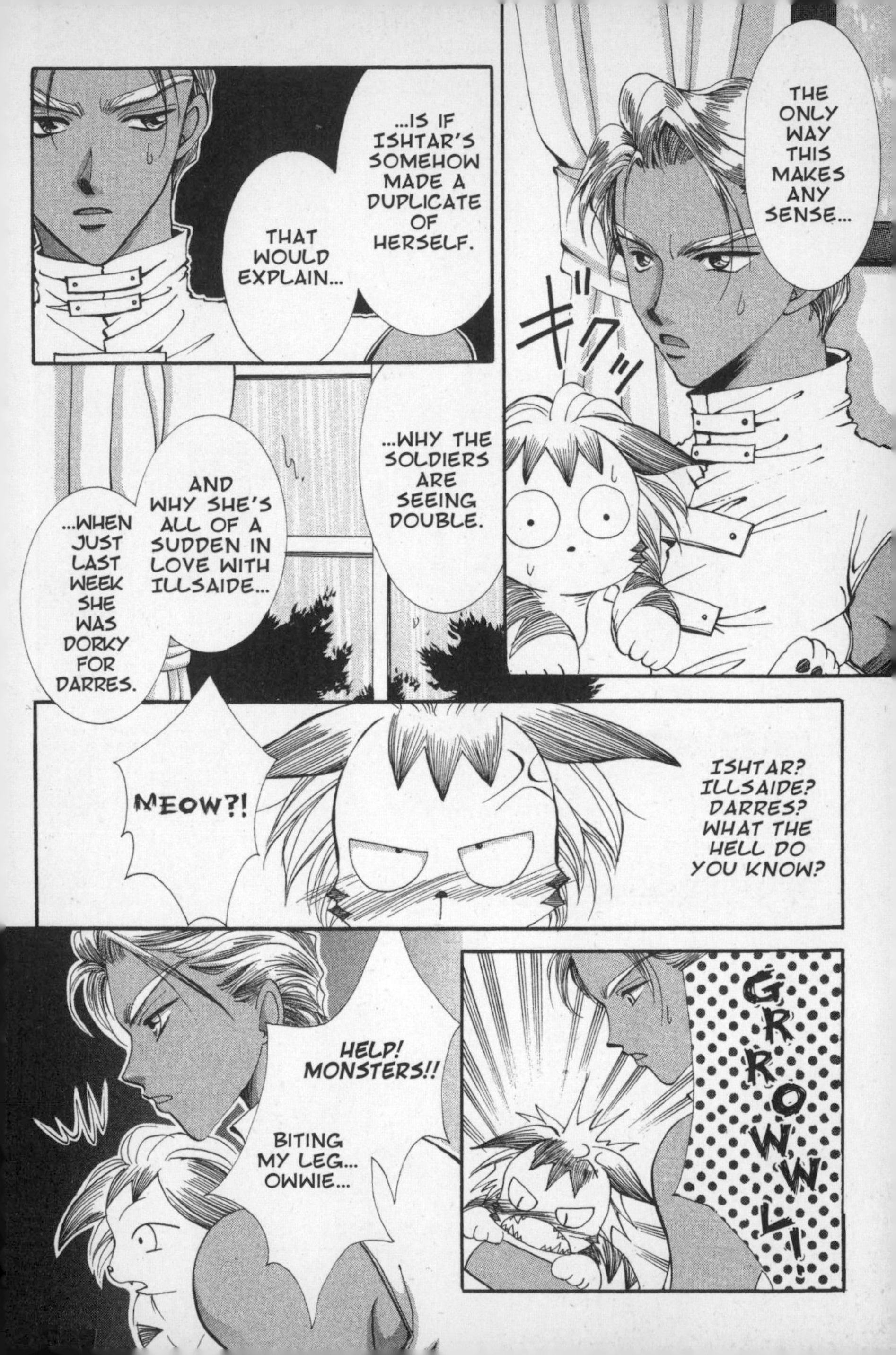
THE ONLY WAY THIS MAKES ANY SENSE...
ギクッ
...IS IF ISHTAR'S SOMEHOW MADE A DUPLICATE OF HERSELF.
THAT WOULD EXPLAIN...
...WHY THE SOLDIERS ARE SEEING DOUBLE.
AND WHY SHE'S ALL OF A SUDDEN IN LOVE WITH ILLSAIDE...
...WHEN JUST LAST WEEK SHE WAS DORKY FOR DARRES.
ISHTAR? ILLSAIDE? DARRES? WHAT THE HELL DO YOU KNOW?
MEOW?!
GRROWWL!
HELP! MONSTERS!!
BITING MY LEG... OWWIE...

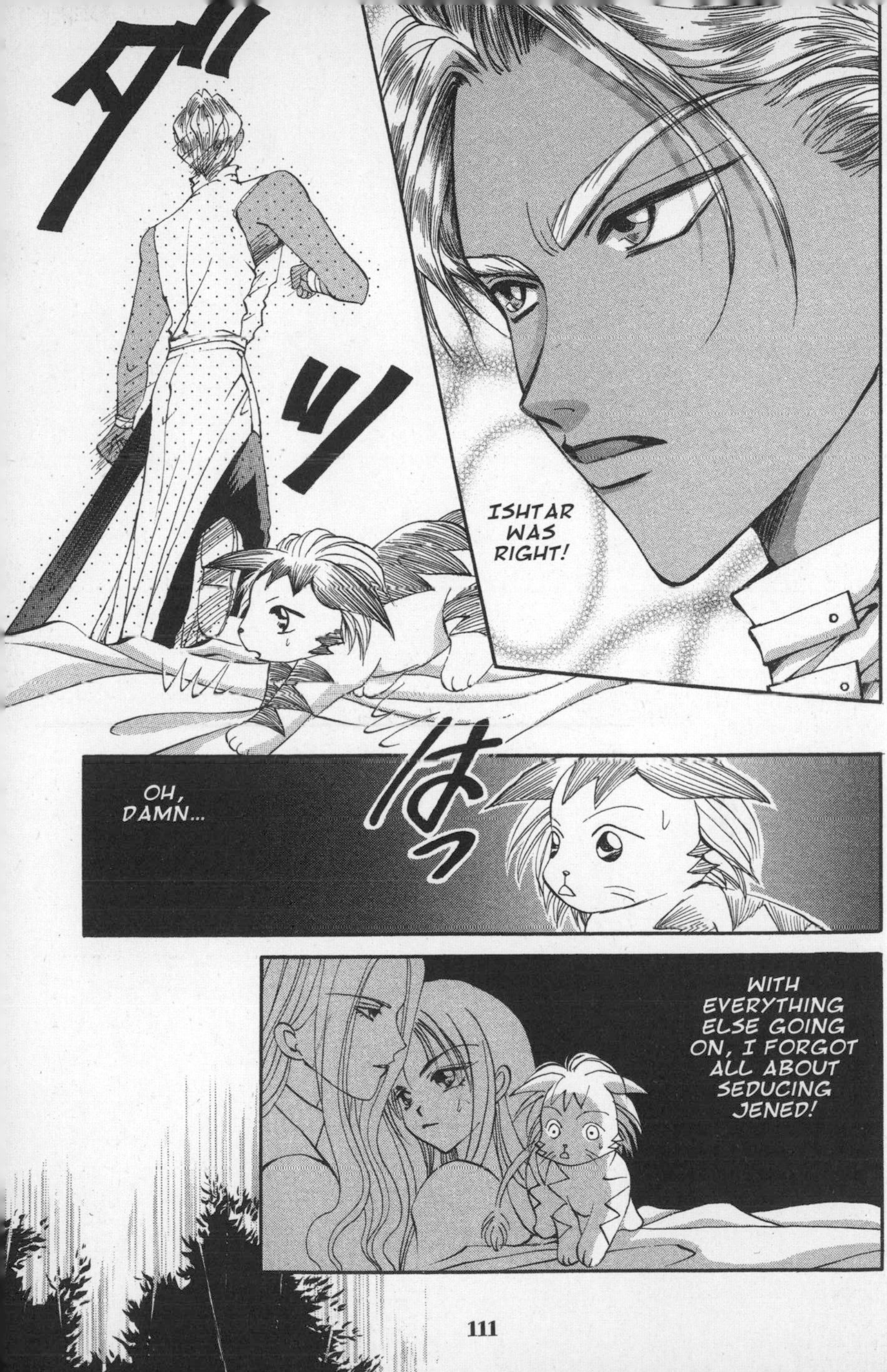
ISHTAR WAS RIGHT!
ダッ
はっ
OH, DAMN...
WITH EVERYTHING ELSE GOING ON, I FORGOT ALL ABOUT SEDUCING JENED!

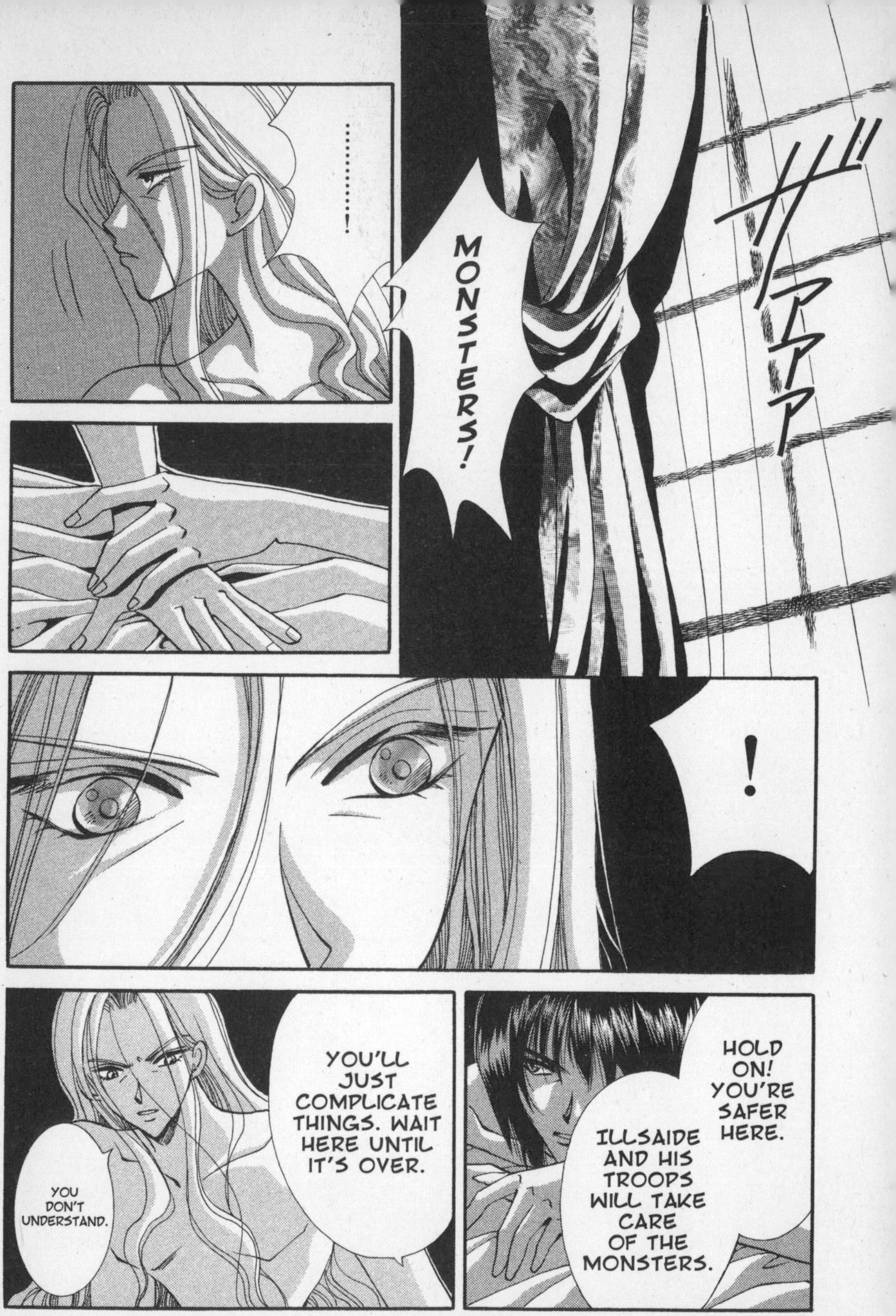
MONSTERS!
……!
!
HOLD ON! YOU'RE SAFER HERE.
ILLSAIDE AND HIS TROOPS WILL TAKE CARE OF THE MONSTERS.
YOU'LL JUST COMPLICATE THINGS. WAIT HERE UNTIL IT'S OVER.
YOU DON'T UNDERSTAND.

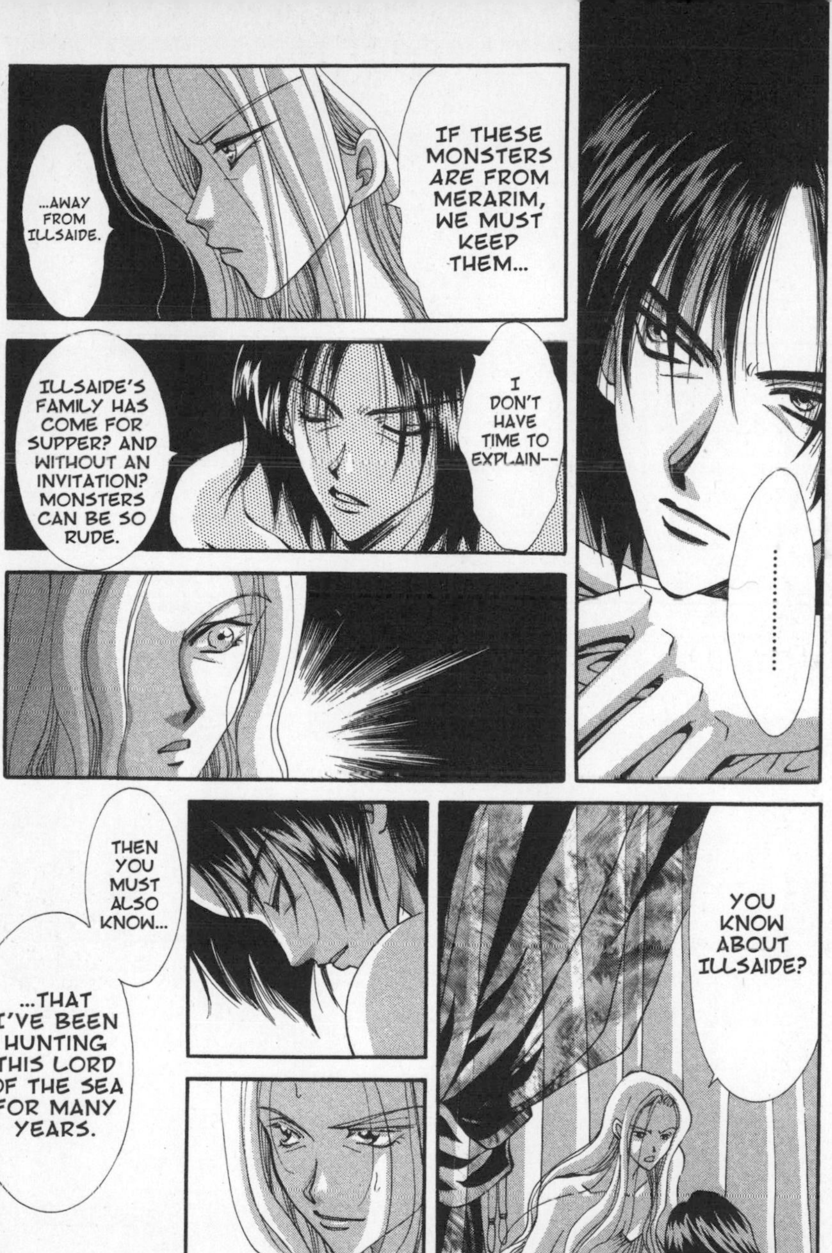
......
IF THESE MONSTERS ARE FROM MERARIM, WE MUST KEEP THEM...
...AWAY FROM ILLSAIDE.
I DON'T HAVE TIME TO EXPLAIN--
ILLSAIDE'S FAMILY HAS COME FOR SUPPER? AND WITHOUT AN INVITATION? MONSTERS CAN BE SO RUDE.
YOU KNOW ABOUT ILLSAIDE?
THEN YOU MUST ALSO KNOW...
...THAT I'VE BEEN HUNTING THIS LORD OF THE SEA FOR MANY YEARS.

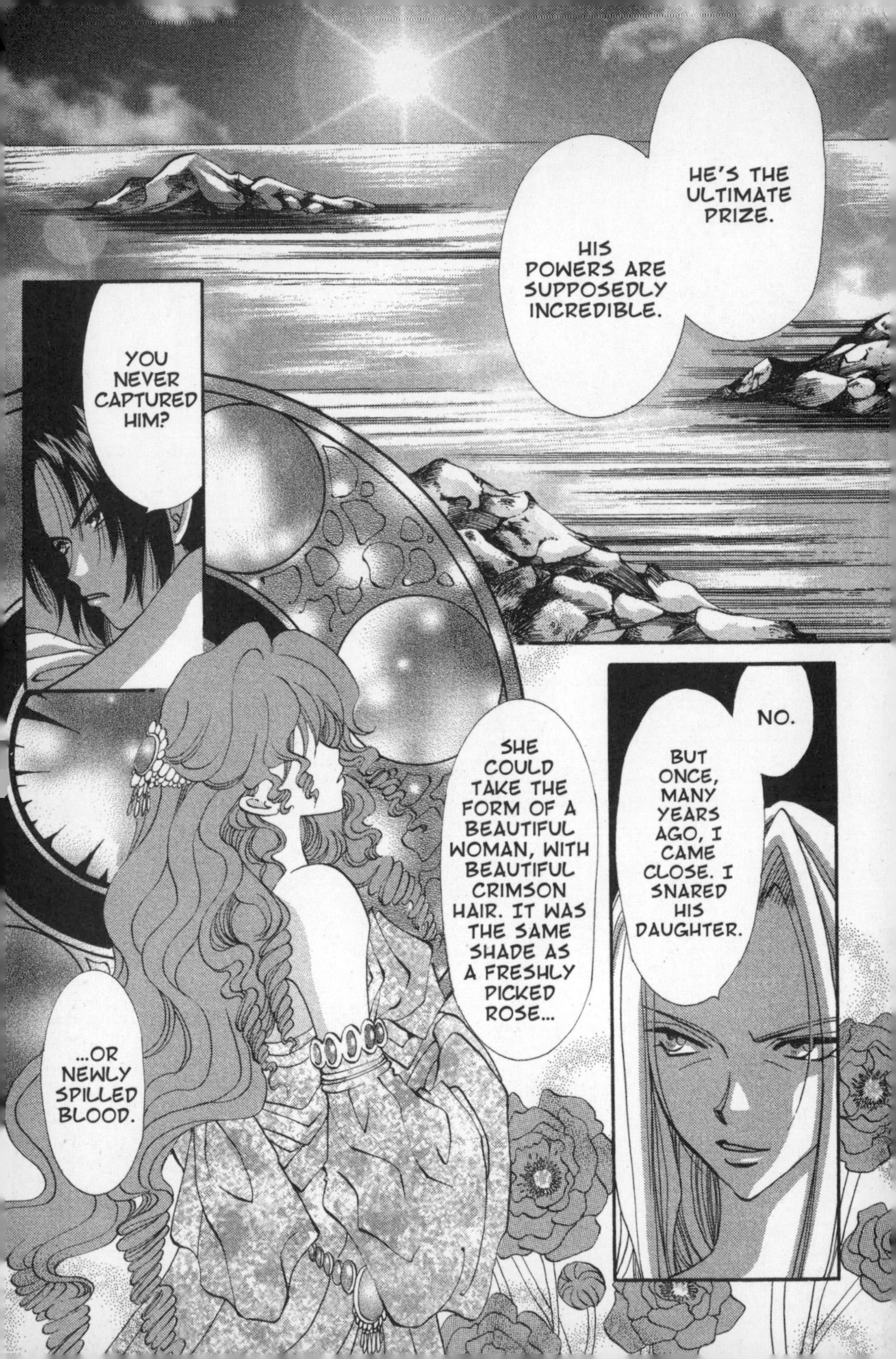
HE'S THE ULTIMATE PRIZE.
HIS POWERS ARE SUPPOSEDLY INCREDIBLE.
YOU NEVER CAPTURED HIM?
NO.
BUT ONCE, MANY YEARS AGO, I CAME CLOSE. I SNARED HIS DAUGHTER.
SHE COULD TAKE THE FORM OF A BEAUTIFUL WOMAN, WITH BEAUTIFUL CRIMSON HAIR. IT WAS THE SAME SHADE AS A FRESHLY PICKED ROSE...
...OR NEWLY SPILLED BLOOD.

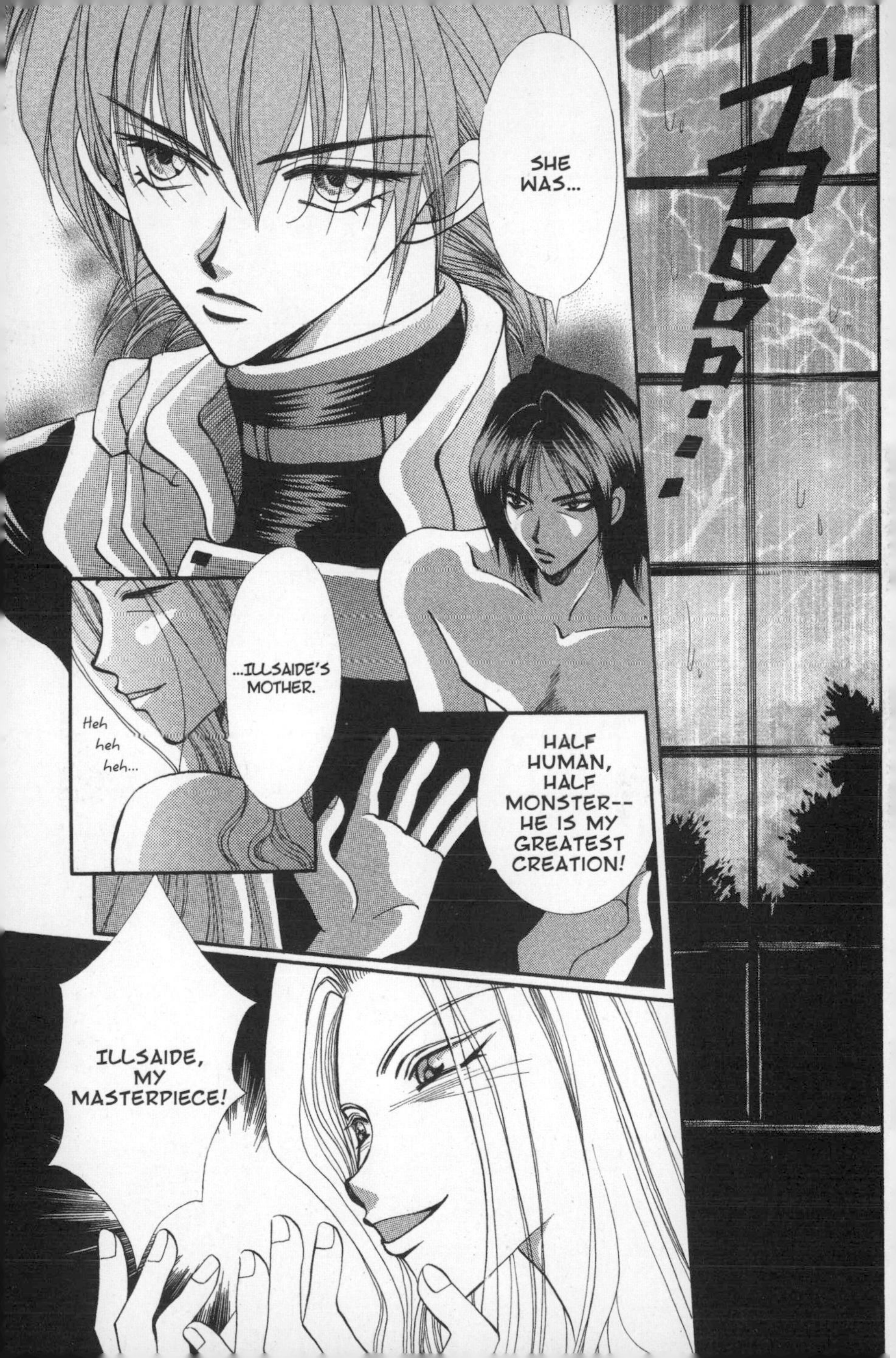
ゴロロロ…
SHE WAS...
...ILLSAIDE'S MOTHER.
Heh heh heh...
HALF HUMAN, HALF MONSTER-- HE IS MY GREATEST CREATION!
ILLSAIDE, MY MASTERPIECE!

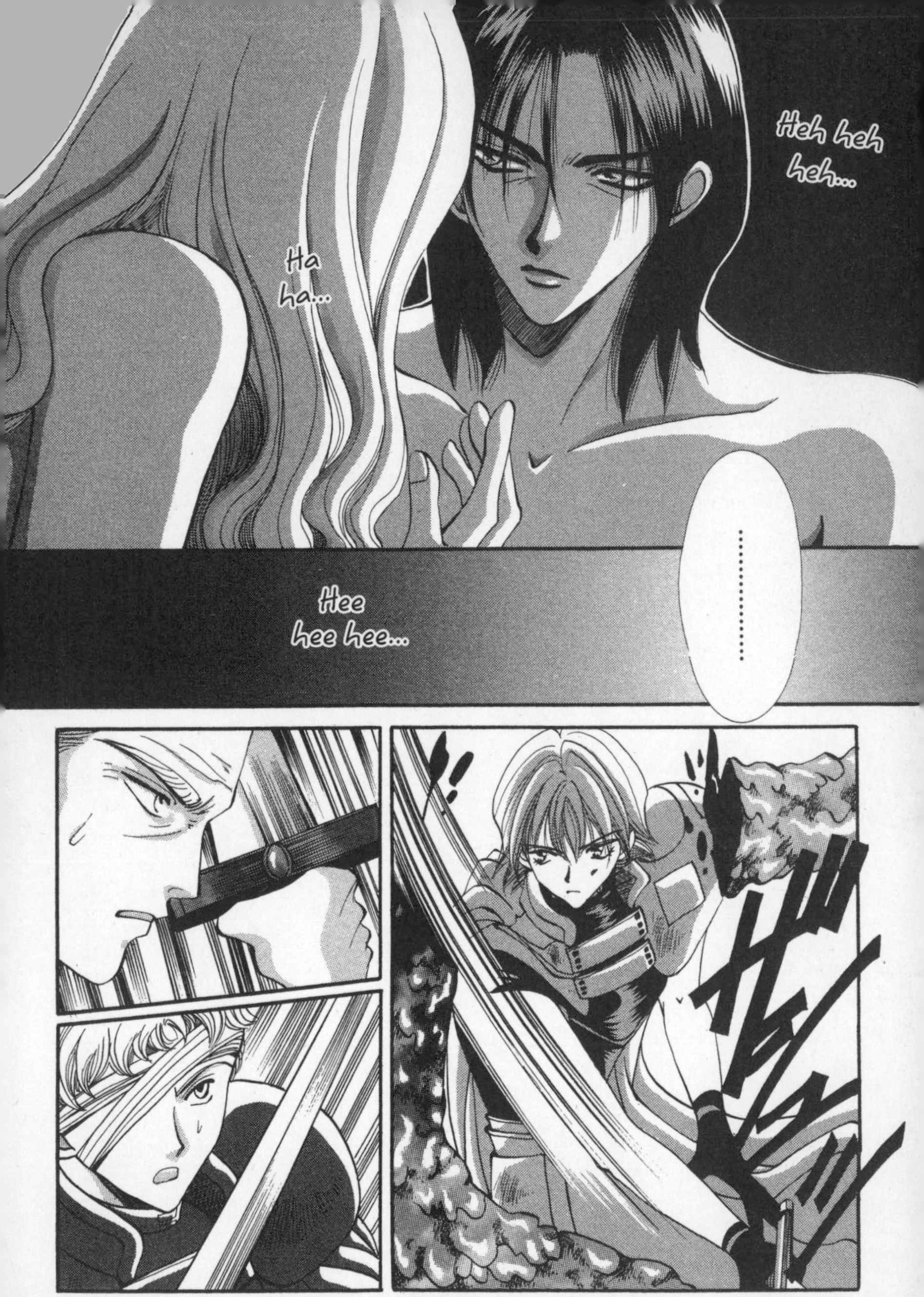
Heh heh heh...
Ha ha...
....
Hee hee hee...
!!
!!

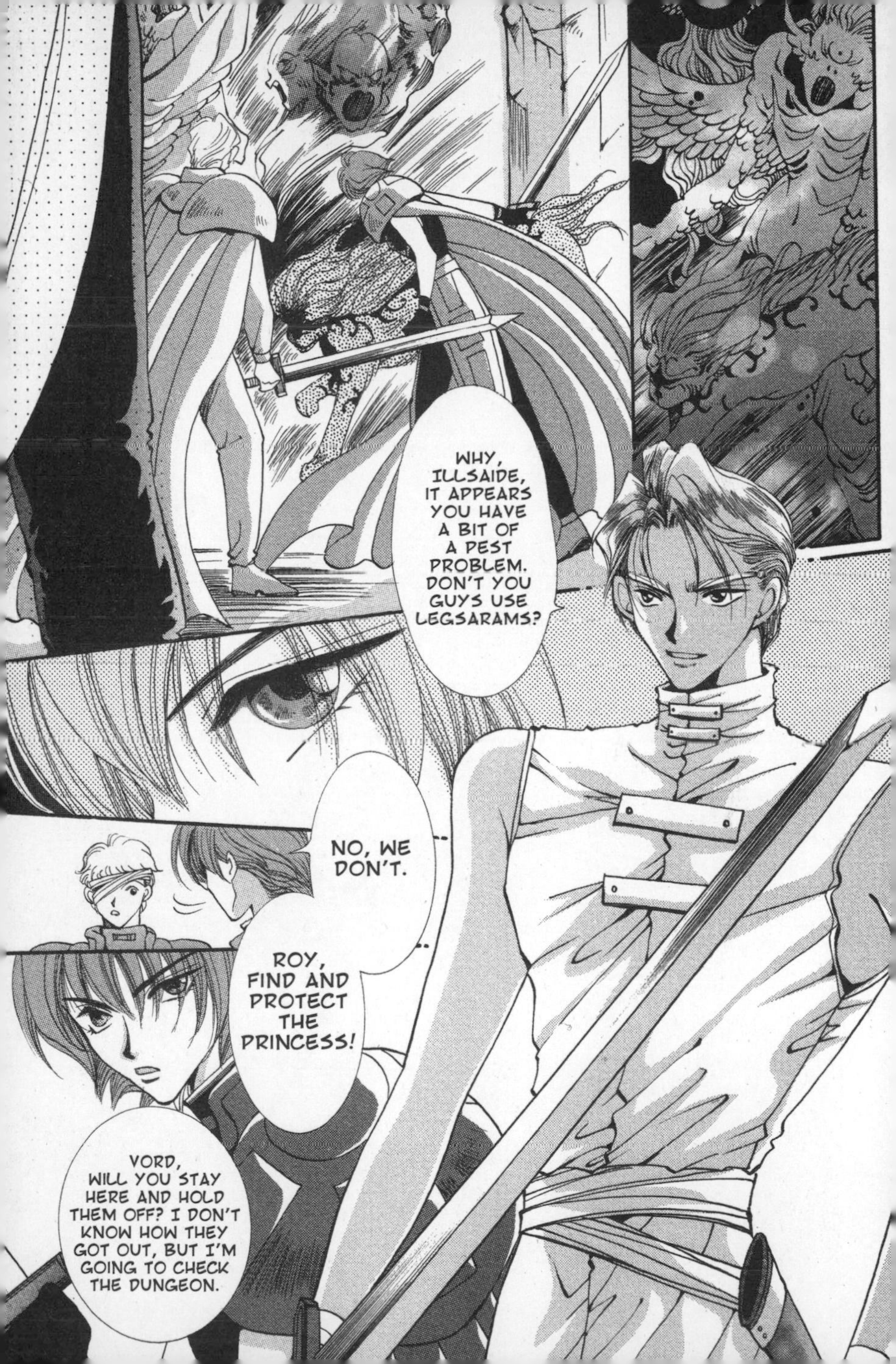
WHY, ILLSAIDE, IT APPEARS YOU HAVE A BIT OF A PEST PROBLEM. DON'T YOU GUYS USE LEGSARAMS?
NO, WE DON'T.
ROY, FIND AND PROTECT THE PRINCESS!
VORD, WILL YOU STAY HERE AND HOLD THEM OFF? I DON'T KNOW HOW THEY GOT OUT, BUT I'M GOING TO CHECK THE DUNGEON.

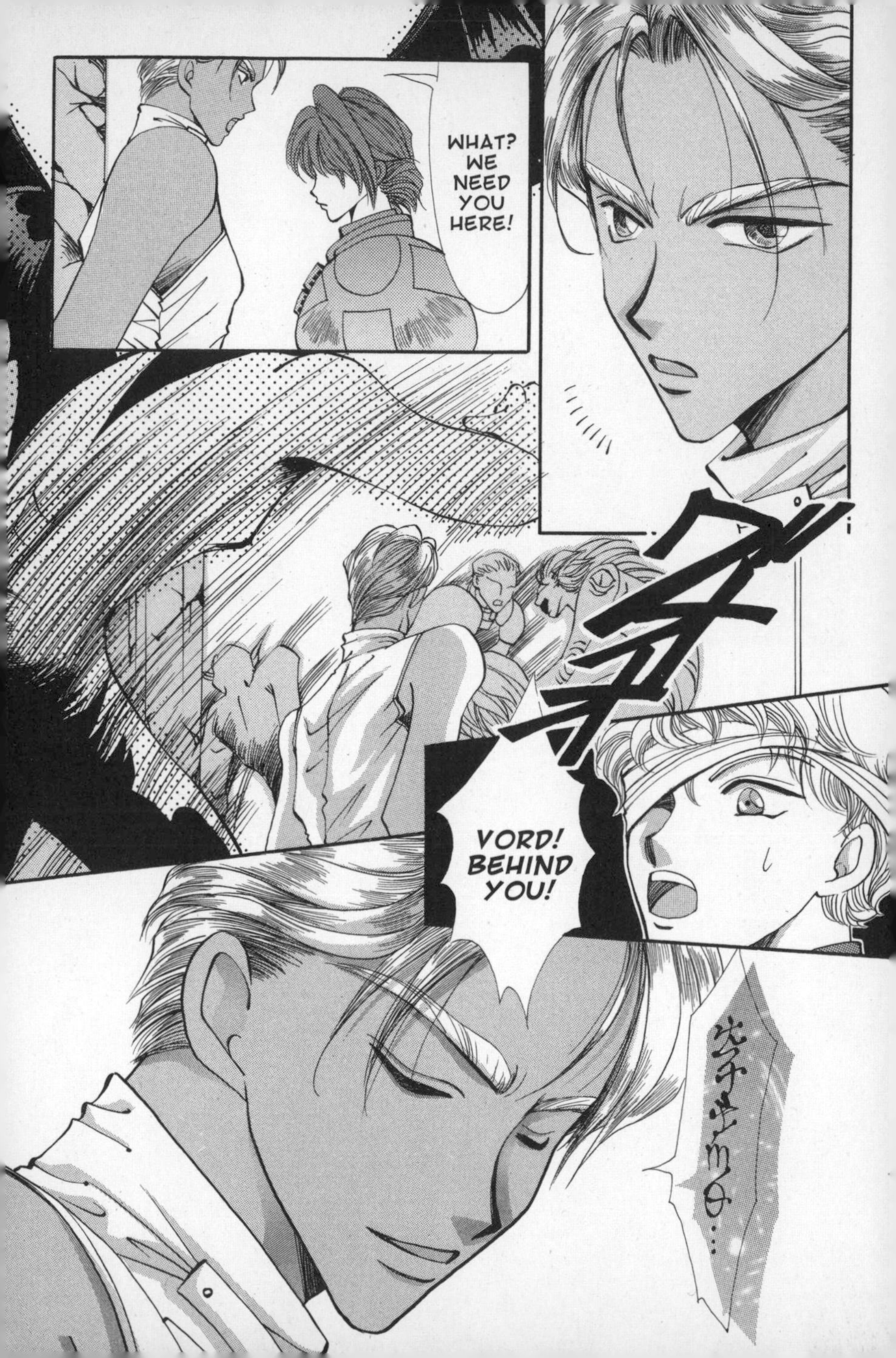
WHAT? WE NEED YOU HERE!
VORD! BEHIND YOU!

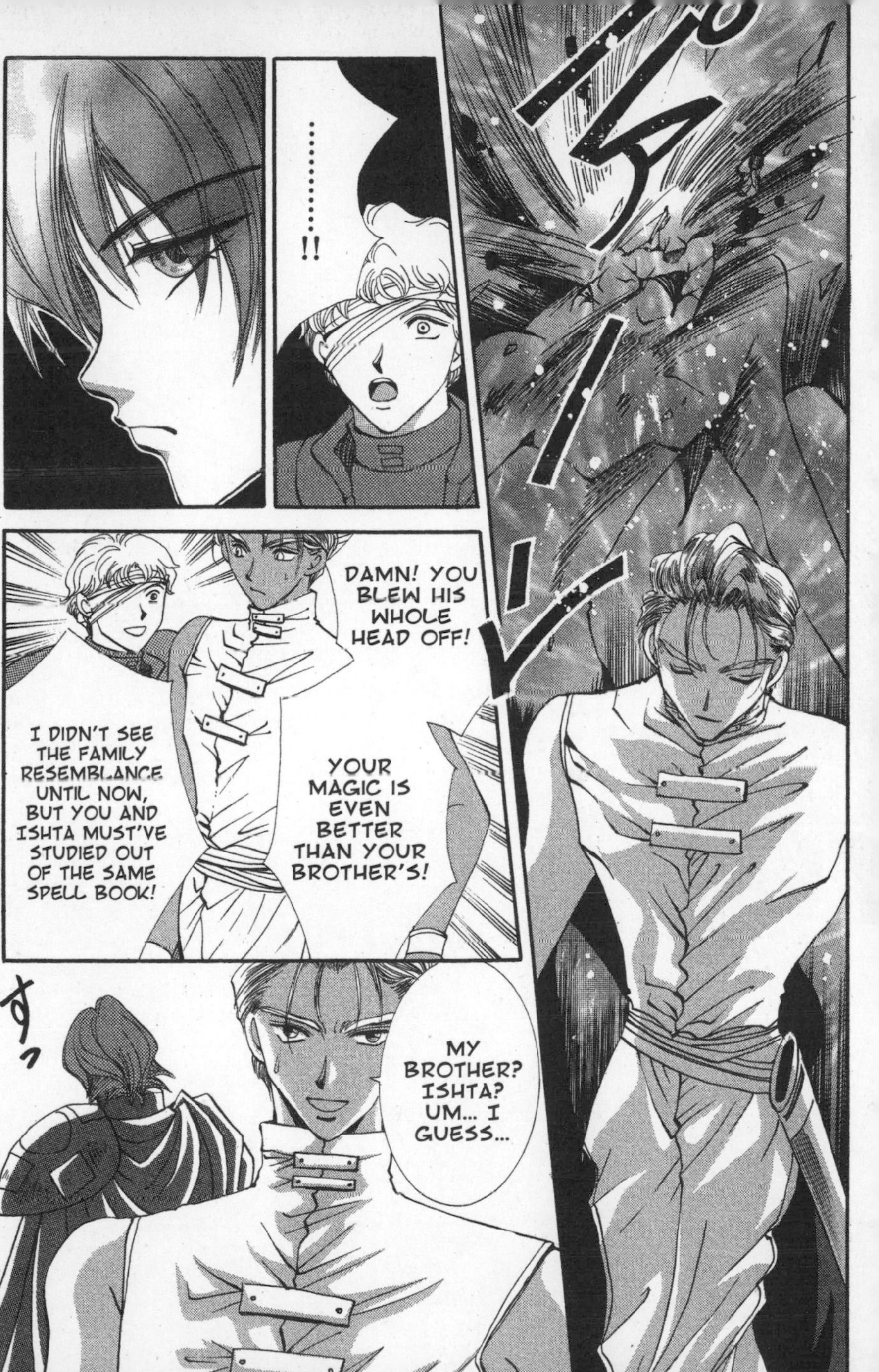
......!!
DAMN! YOU BLEW HIS WHOLE HEAD OFF!
YOUR MAGIC IS EVEN BETTER THAN YOUR BROTHER'S!
I DIDN'T SEE THE FAMILY RESEMBLANCE UNTIL NOW, BUT YOU AND ISHTA MUST'VE STUDIED OUT OF THE SAME SPELL BOOK!
MY BROTHER? ISHTA? UM... I GUESS...
すっ

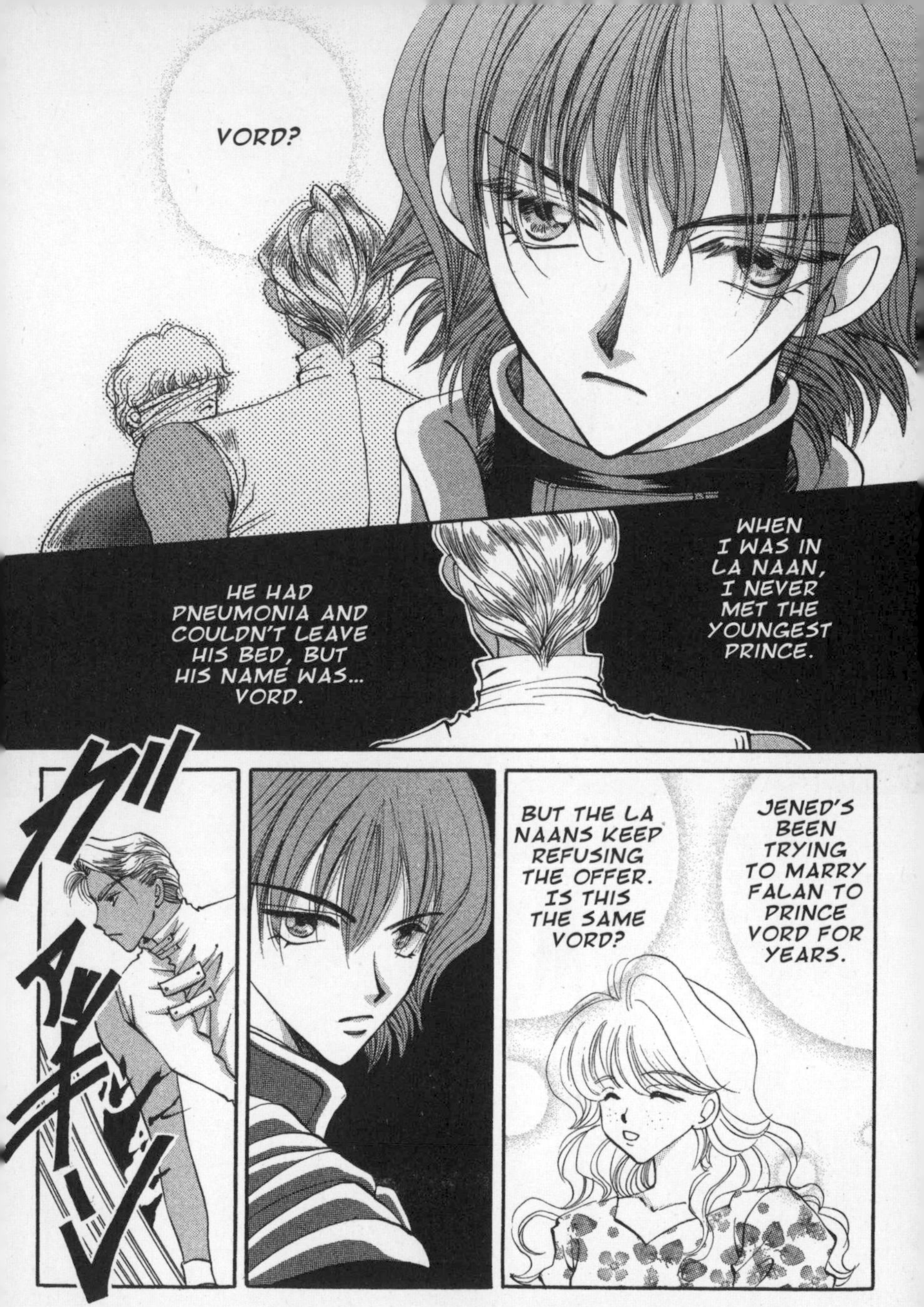
VORD?
WHEN I WAS IN LA NAAN, I NEVER MET THE YOUNGEST PRINCE.
HE HAD PNEUMONIA AND COULDN'T LEAVE HIS BED, BUT HIS NAME WAS... VORD.
JENED'S BEEN TRYING TO MARRY FALAN TO PRINCE VORD FOR YEARS.
BUT THE LA NAANS KEEP REFUSING THE OFFER. IS THIS THE SAME VORD?

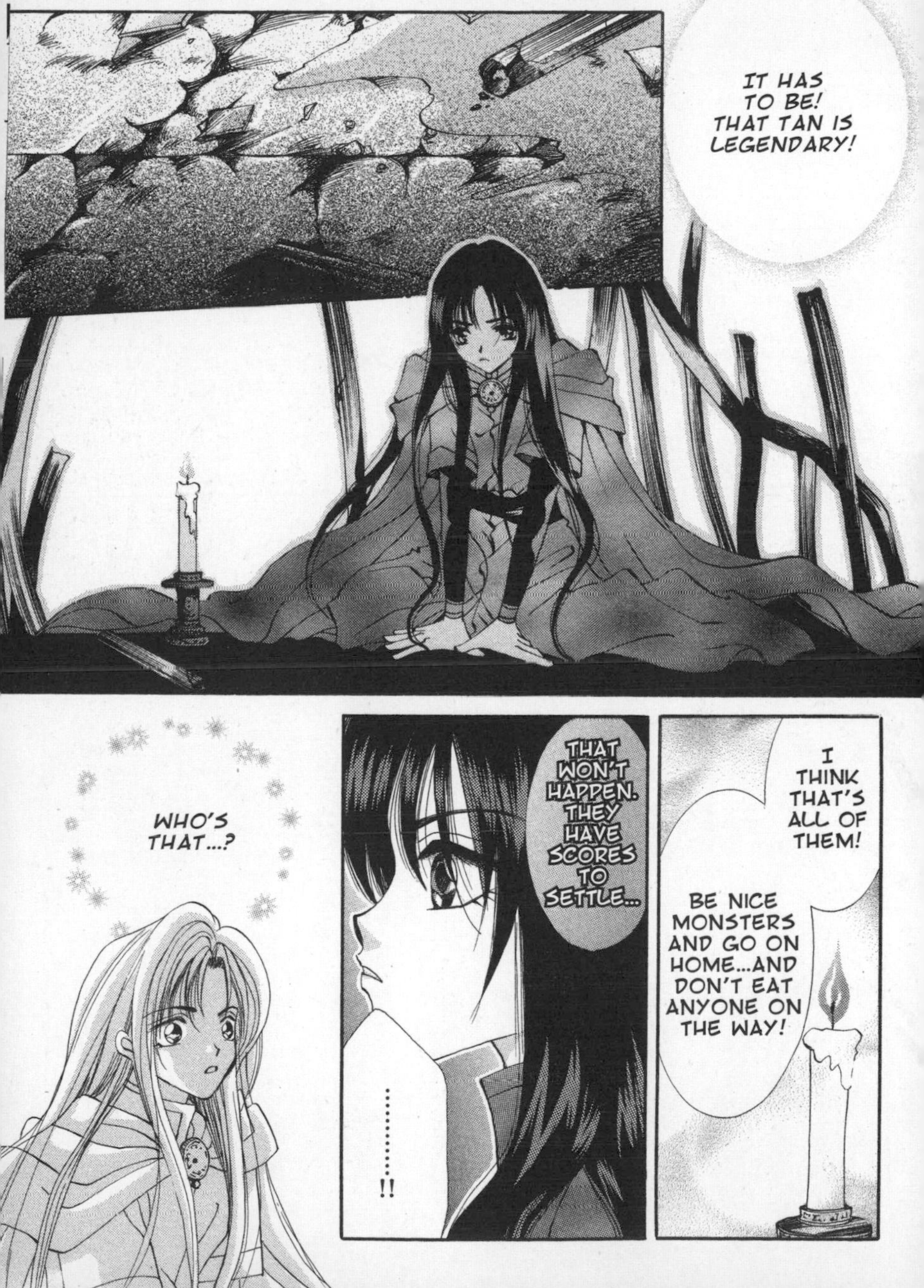
IT HAS TO BE! THAT TAN IS LEGENDARY!
I THINK THAT'S ALL OF THEM!
BE NICE MONSTERS AND GO ON HOME...AND DON'T EAT ANYONE ON THE WAY!
THAT WON'T HAPPEN. THEY HAVE SCORES TO SETTLE...
.........!!
WHO'S THAT...?

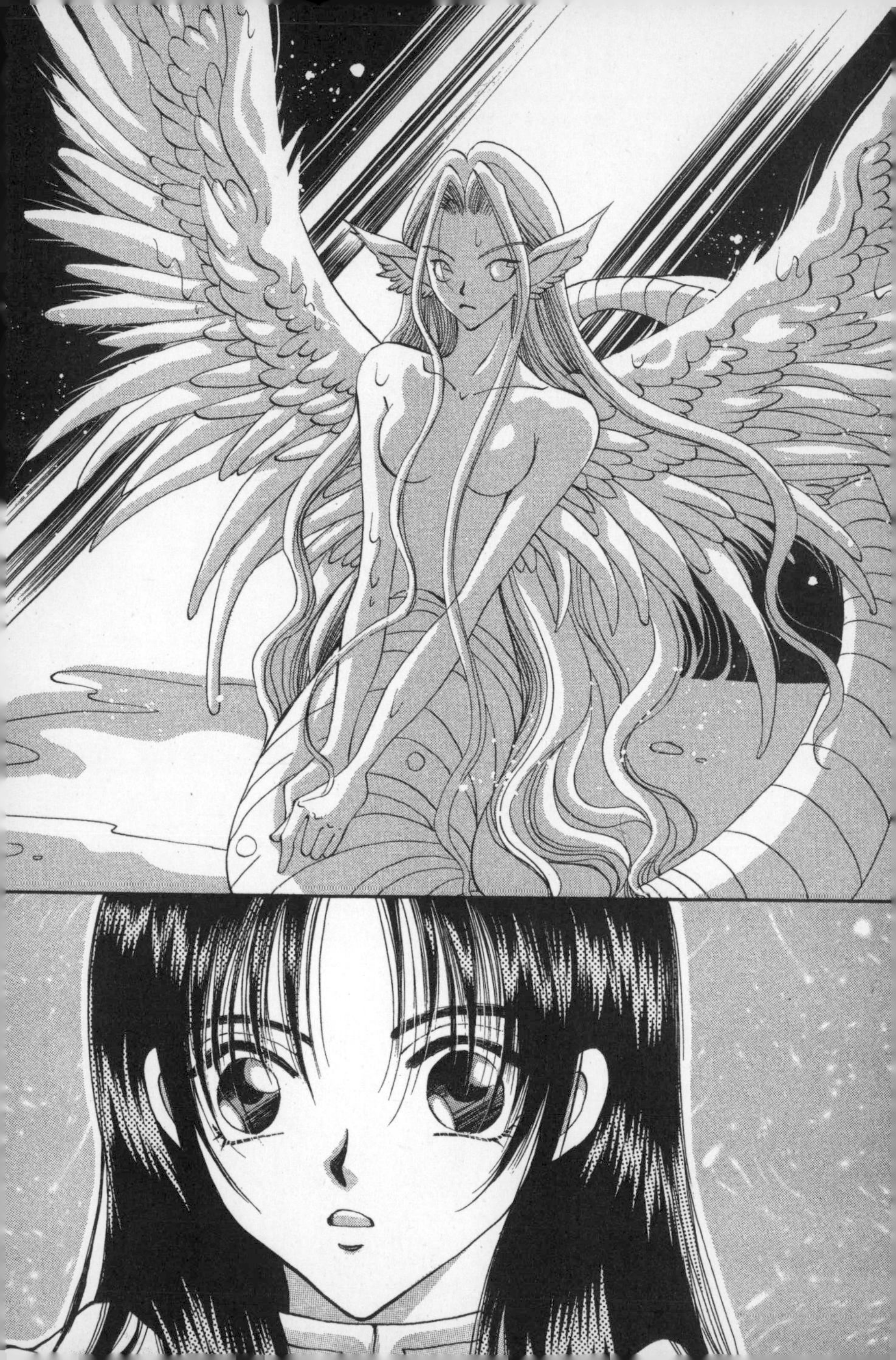

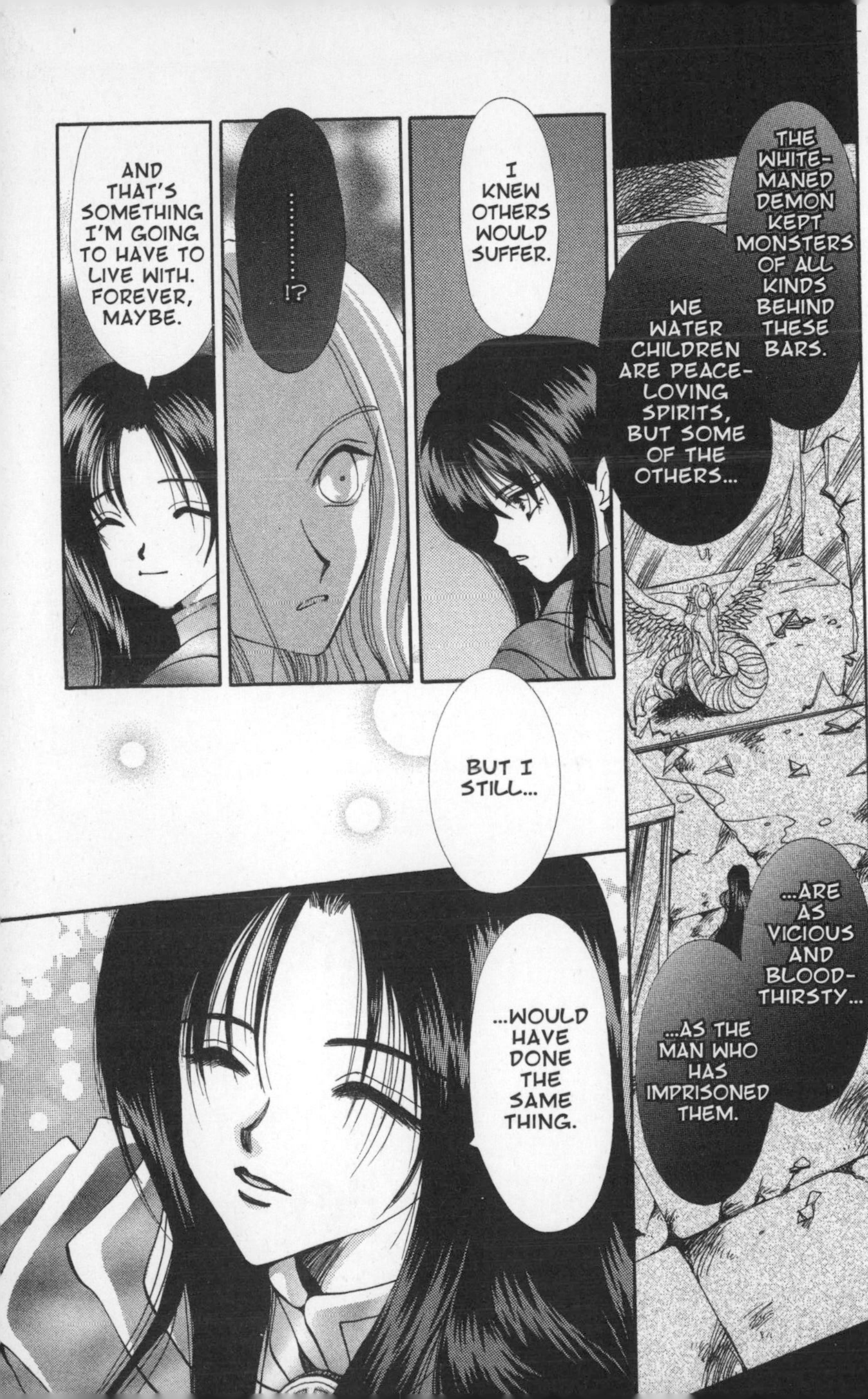
THE WHITE-MANED DEMON KEPT MONSTERS OF ALL KINDS BEHIND THESE BARS.
WE WATER CHILDREN ARE PEACE-LOVING SPIRITS, BUT SOME OF THE OTHERS...
...ARE AS VICIOUS AND BLOOD-THIRSTY...
...AS THE MAN WHO HAS IMPRISONED THEM.
I KNEW OTHERS WOULD SUFFER.
.........!?
AND THAT'S SOMETHING I'M GOING TO HAVE TO LIVE WITH. FOREVER, MAYBE.
BUT I STILL...
...WOULD HAVE DONE THE SAME THING.

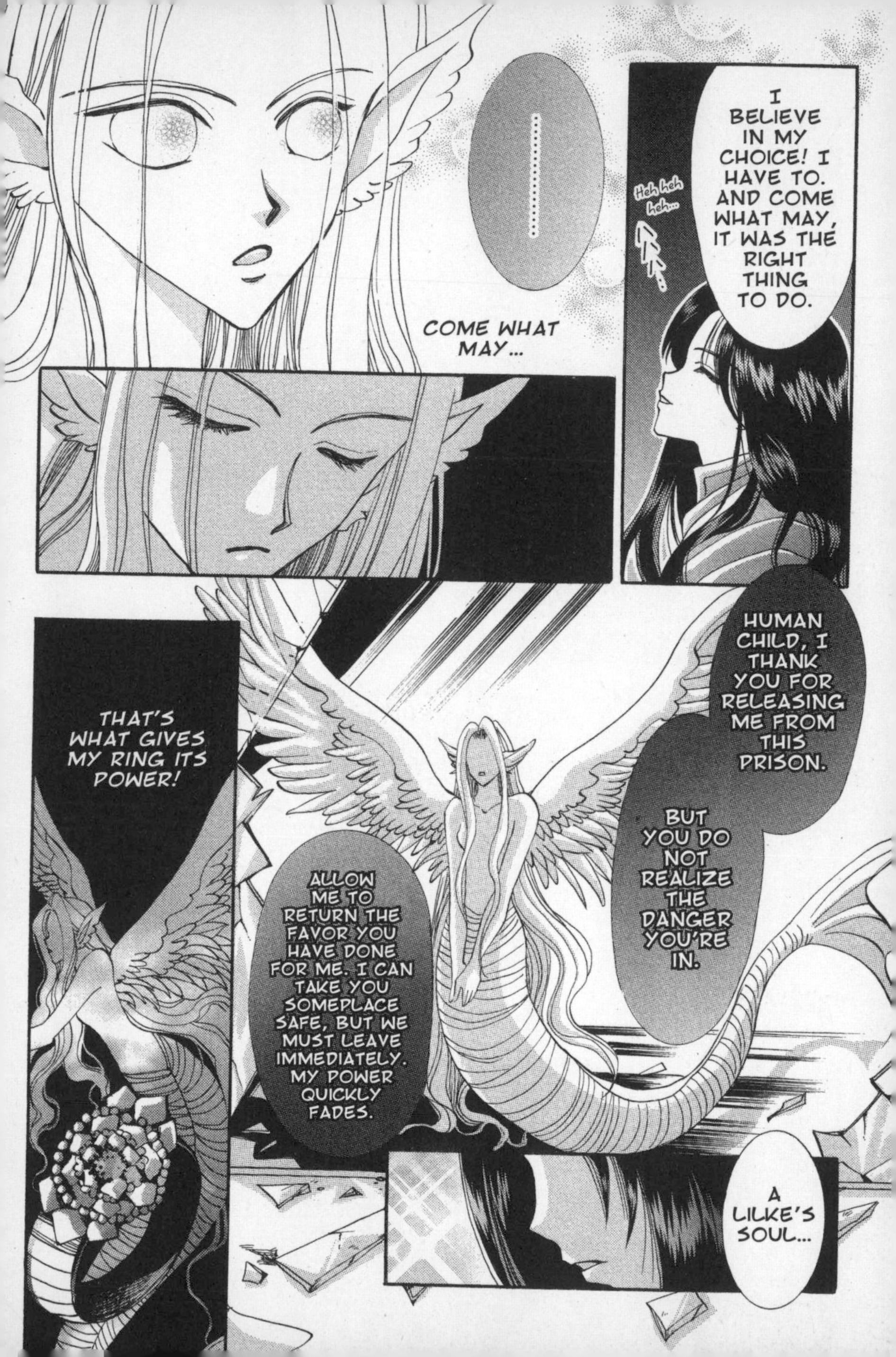
I BELIEVE IN MY CHOICE! I HAVE TO. AND COME WHAT MAY, IT WAS THE RIGHT THING TO DO.
Heh heh heh...
......
COME WHAT MAY...
HUMAN CHILD, I THANK YOU FOR RELEASING ME FROM THIS PRISON.
BUT YOU DO NOT REALIZE THE DANGER YOU'RE IN.
ALLOW ME TO RETURN THE FAVOR YOU HAVE DONE FOR ME. I CAN TAKE YOU SOMEPLACE SAFE, BUT WE MUST LEAVE IMMEDIATELY. MY POWER QUICKLY FADES.
A LILKE'S SOUL...
THAT'S WHAT GIVES MY RING ITS POWER!

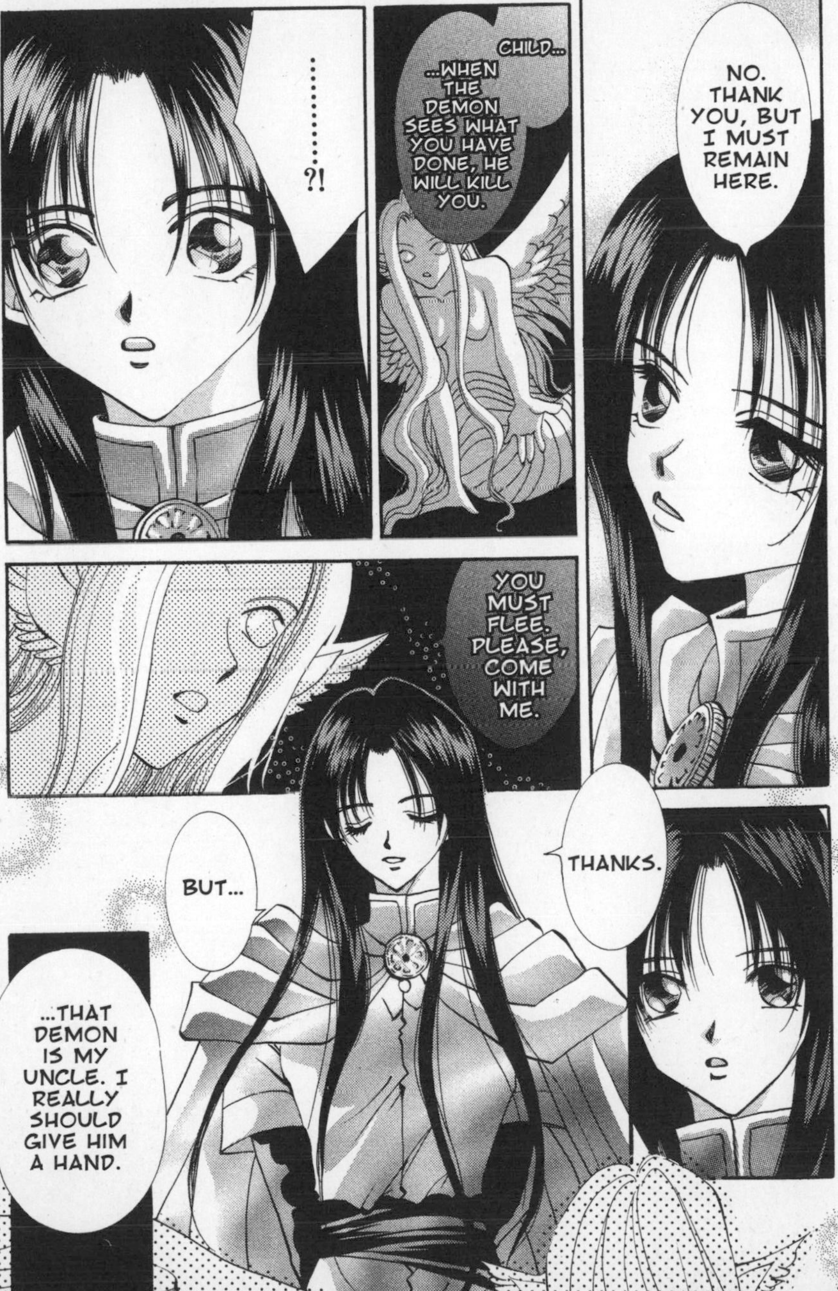
NO. THANK YOU, BUT I MUST REMAIN HERE.
CHILD... ...WHEN THE DEMON SEES WHAT YOU HAVE DONE, HE WILL KILL YOU.
......?!
YOU MUST FLEE. PLEASE, COME WITH ME.
THANKS.
BUT...
...THAT DEMON IS MY UNCLE. I REALLY SHOULD GIVE HIM A HAND.

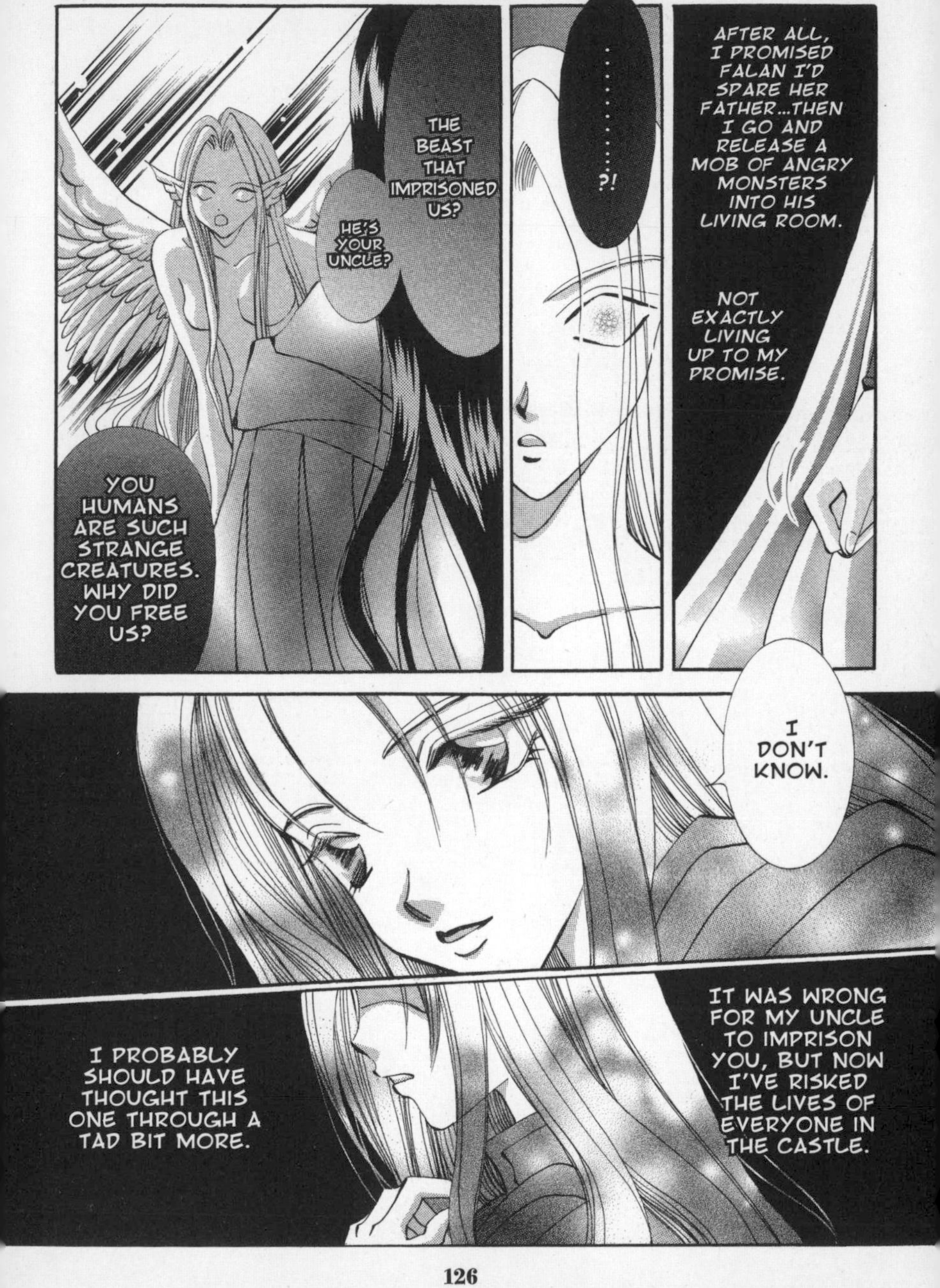
AFTER ALL, I PROMISED FALAN I'D SPARE HER FATHER...THEN I GO AND RELEASE A MOB OF ANGRY MONSTERS INTO HIS LIVING ROOM.
NOT EXACTLY LIVING UP TO MY PROMISE.
....
?!
THE BEAST THAT IMPRISONED US?
HE'S YOUR UNCLE?
YOU HUMANS ARE SUCH STRANGE CREATURES. WHY DID YOU FREE US?
I DON'T KNOW.
IT WAS WRONG FOR MY UNCLE TO IMPRISON YOU, BUT NOW I'VE RISKED THE LIVES OF EVERYONE IN THE CASTLE.
I PROBABLY SHOULD HAVE THOUGHT THIS ONE THROUGH A TAD BIT MORE.

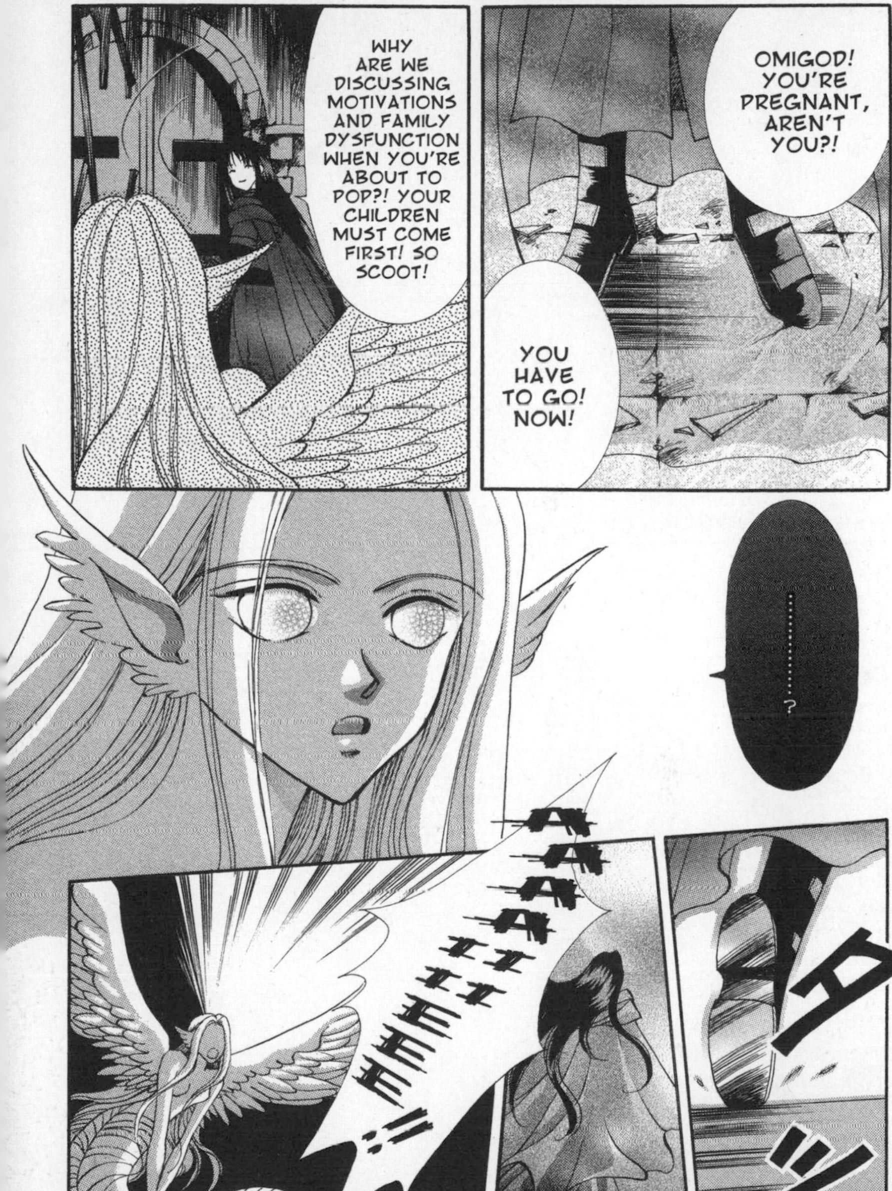
OMIGOD! YOU'RE PREGNANT, AREN'T YOU?!
YOU HAVE TO GO! NOW!
WHY ARE WE DISCUSSING MOTIVATIONS AND FAMILY DYSFUNCTION WHEN YOU'RE ABOUT TO POP?! YOUR CHILDREN MUST COME FIRST! SO SCOOT!
......?
AAAAIIIIIIEEEEE!!!

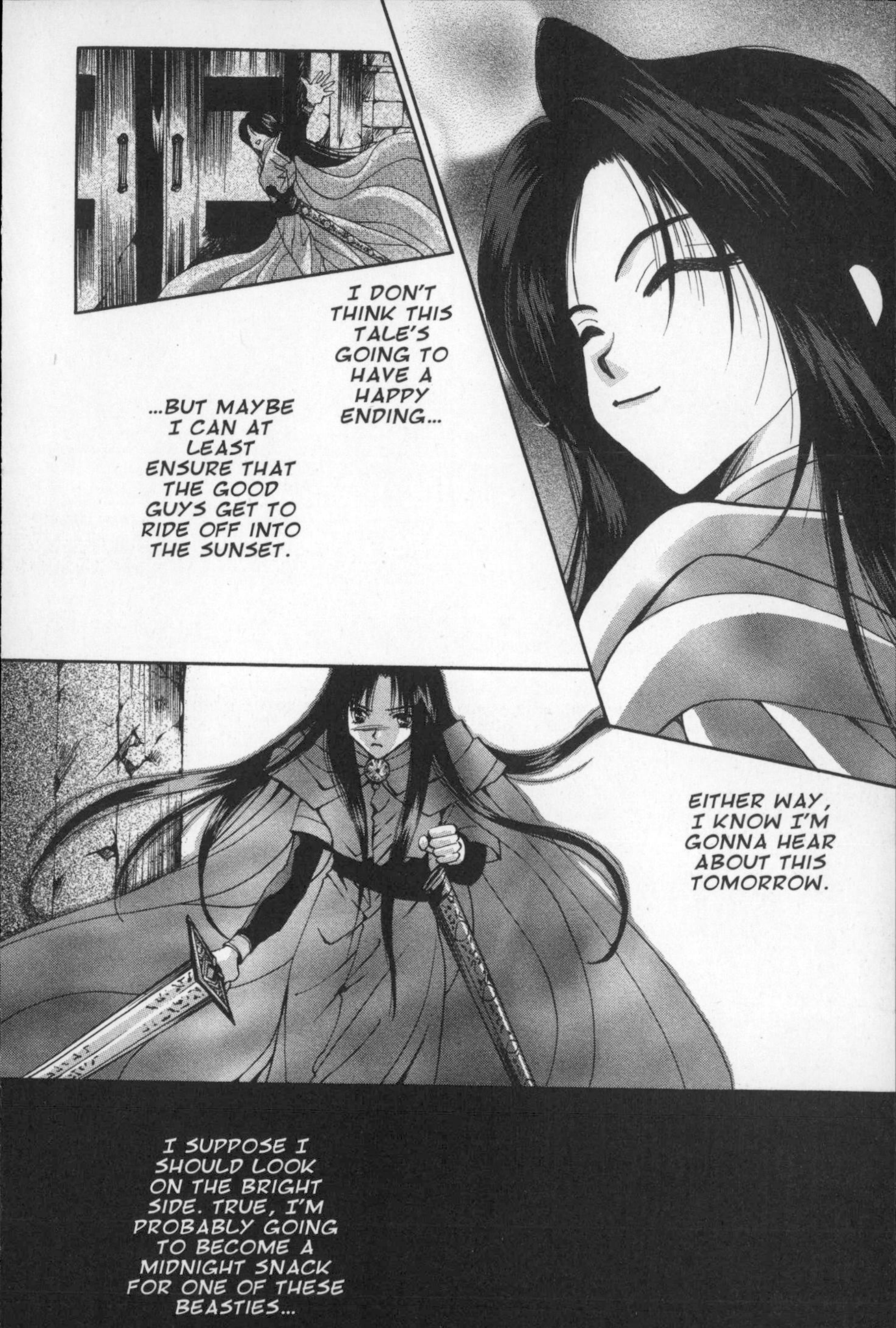
I DON'T THINK THIS TALE'S GOING TO HAVE A HAPPY ENDING...
...BUT MAYBE I CAN AT LEAST ENSURE THAT THE GOOD GUYS GET TO RIDE OFF INTO THE SUNSET.
EITHER WAY, I KNOW I'M GONNA HEAR ABOUT THIS TOMORROW.
I SUPPOSE I SHOULD LOOK ON THE BRIGHT SIDE. TRUE, I'M PROBABLY GOING TO BECOME A MIDNIGHT SNACK FOR ONE OF THESE BEASTIES...

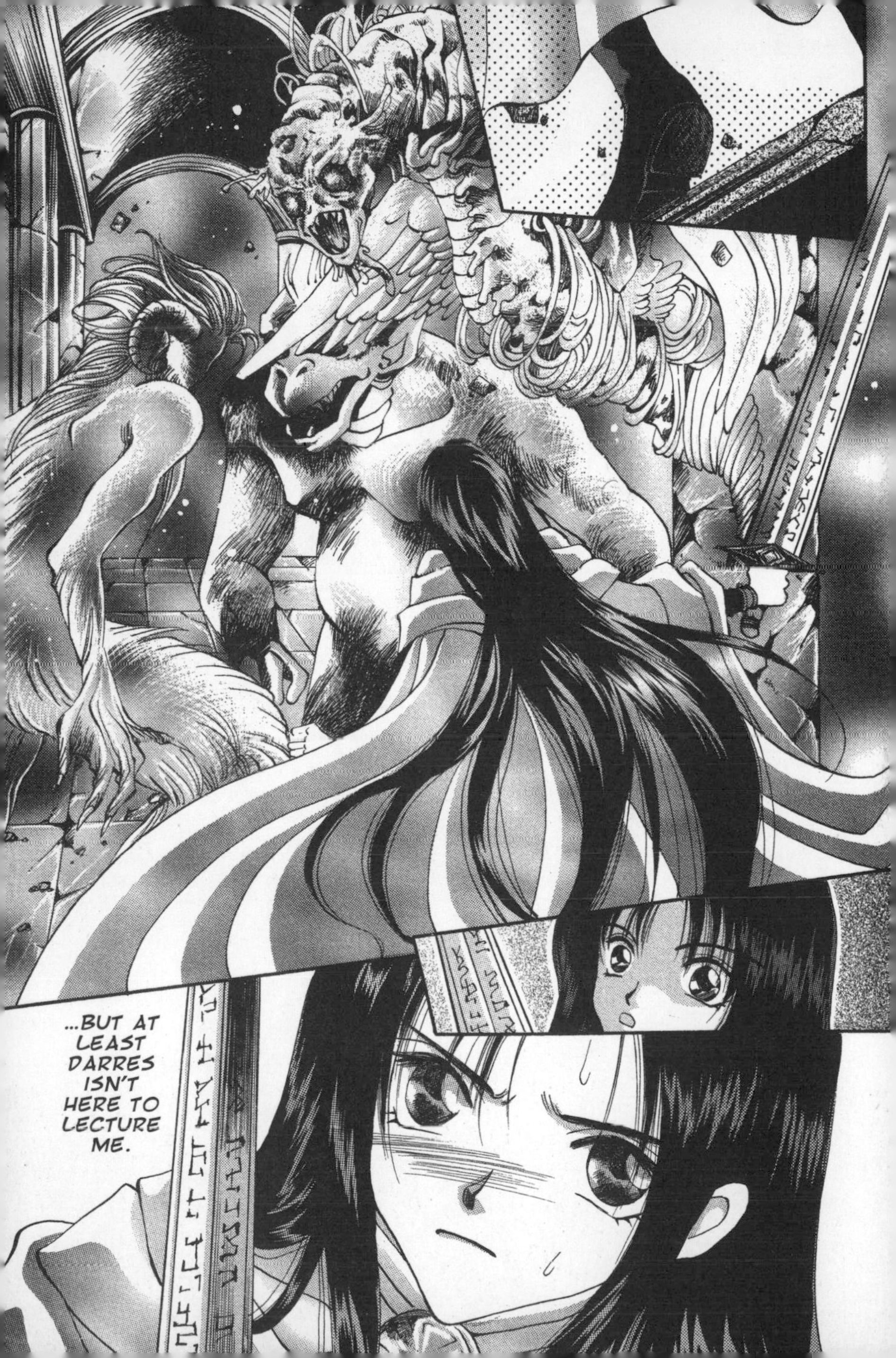
...BUT AT LEAST DARRES ISN'T HERE TO LECTURE ME.

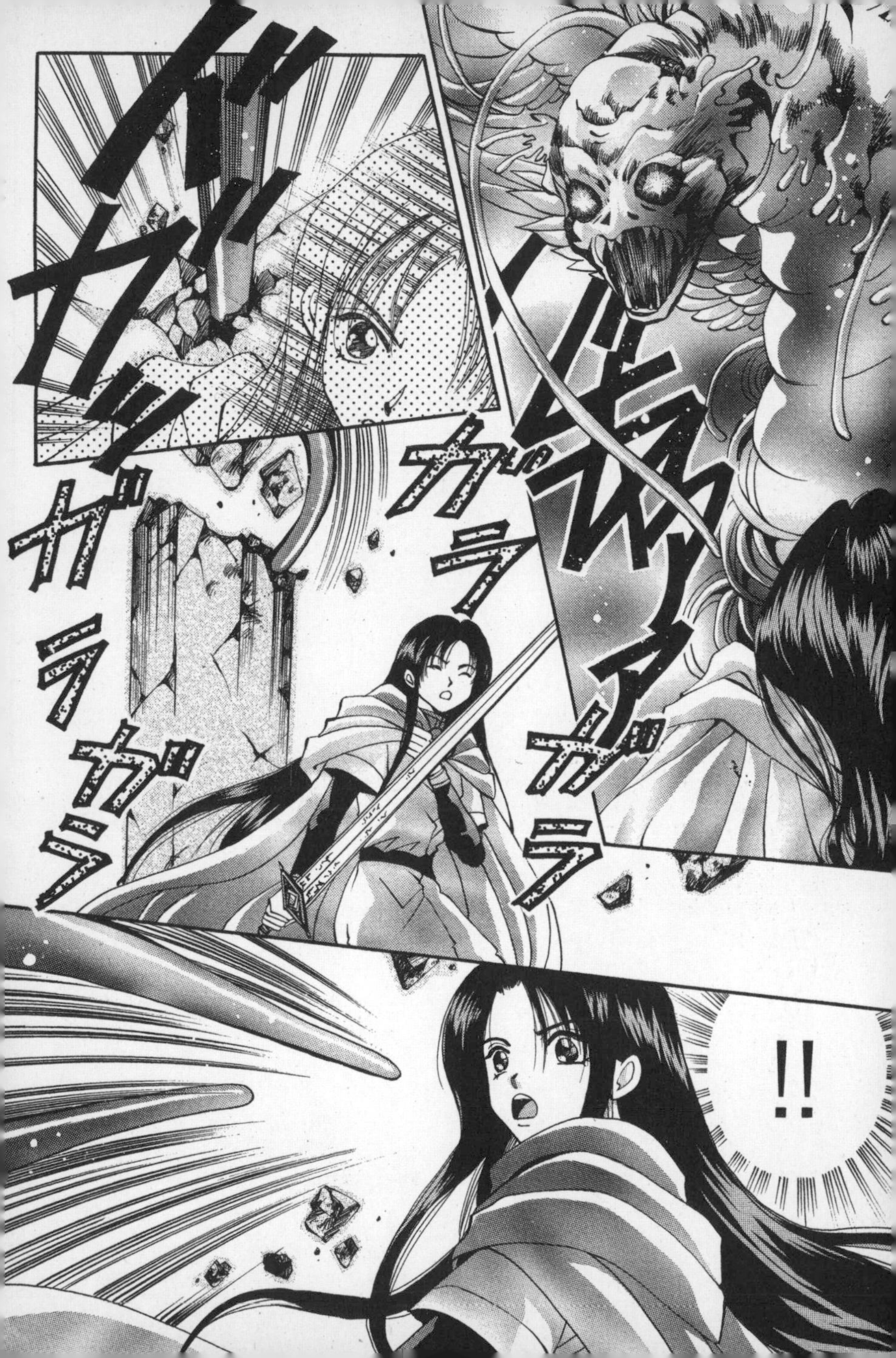
ガラ
ガラ
ガラガラ
!!

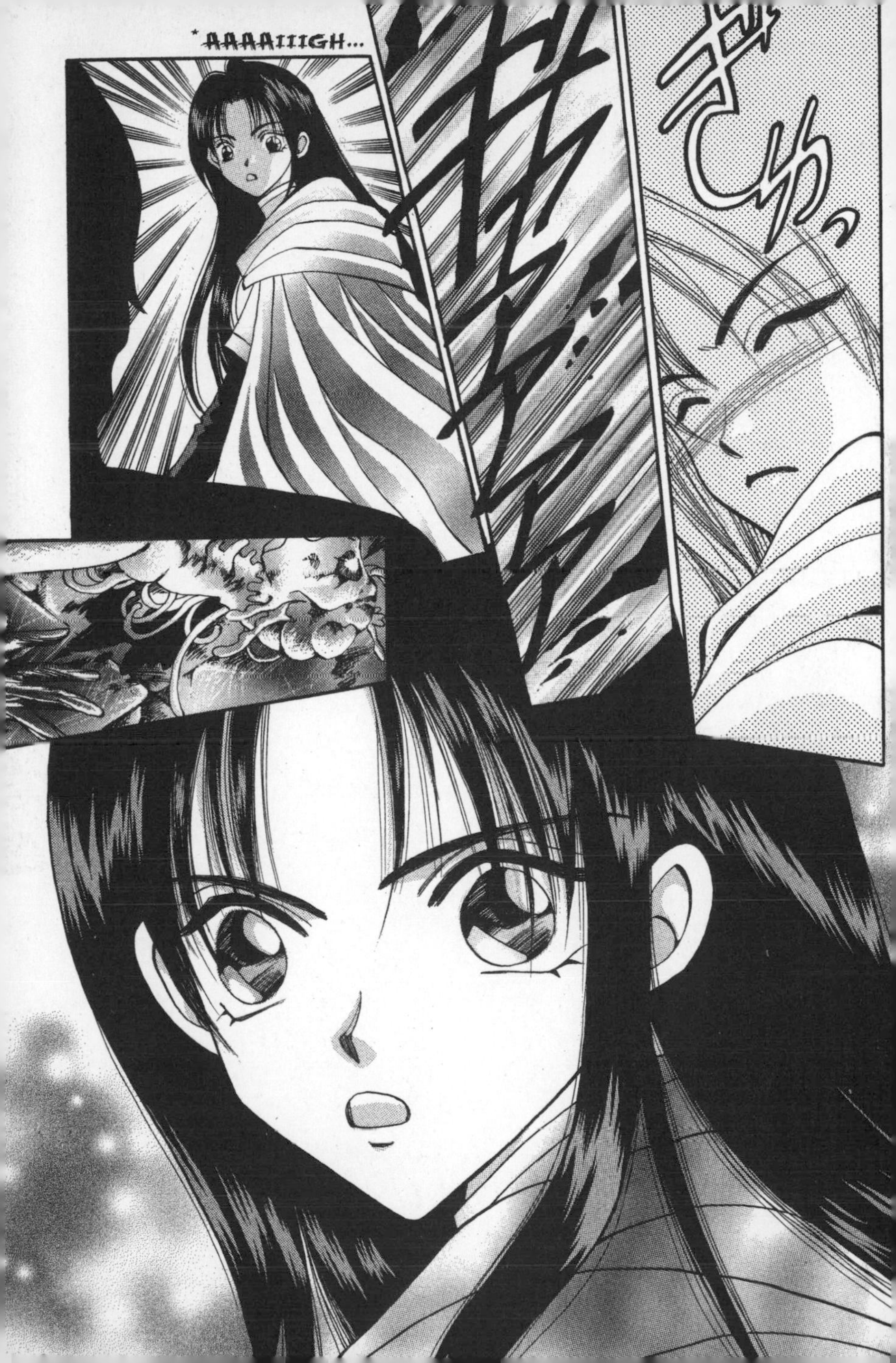
*AAAAIIIGH...

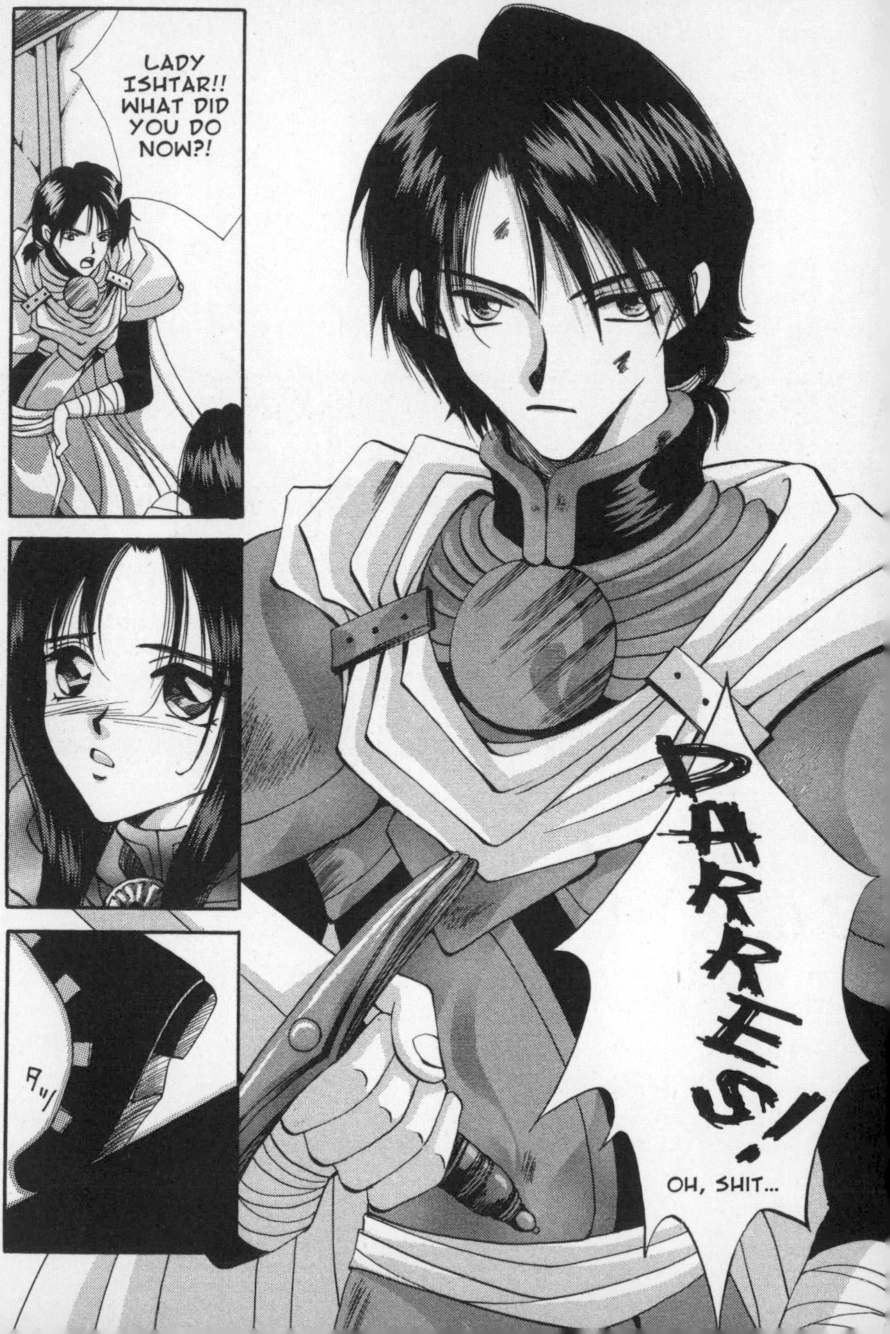
PARRES!
OH, SHIT...
LADY ISHTAR!! WHAT DID YOU DO NOW?!

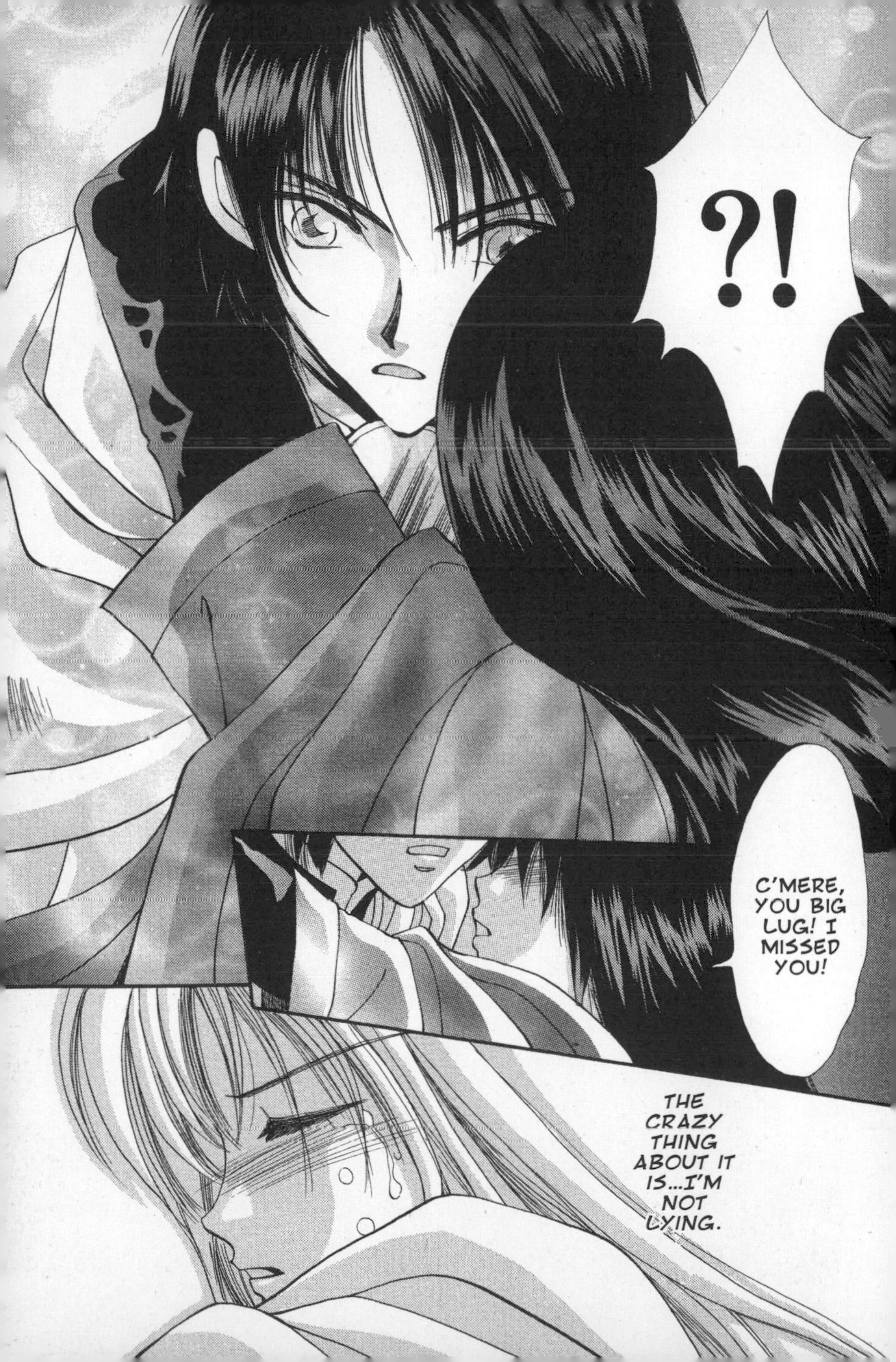
?!
C'MERE, YOU BIG LUG! I MISSED YOU!
THE CRAZY THING ABOUT IT IS...I'M NOT LYING.

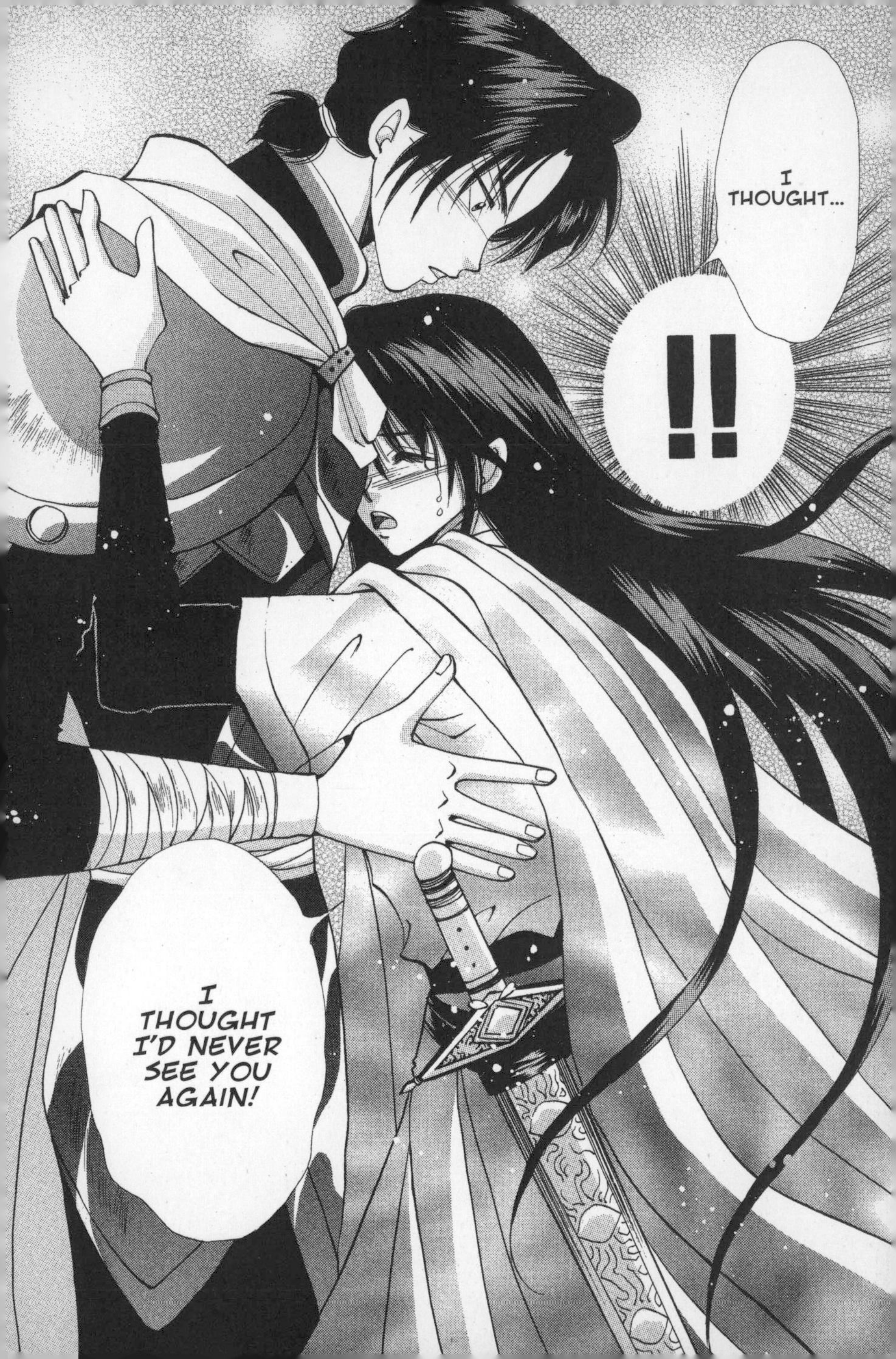
I THOUGHT...
!!
I THOUGHT I'D NEVER SEE YOU AGAIN!

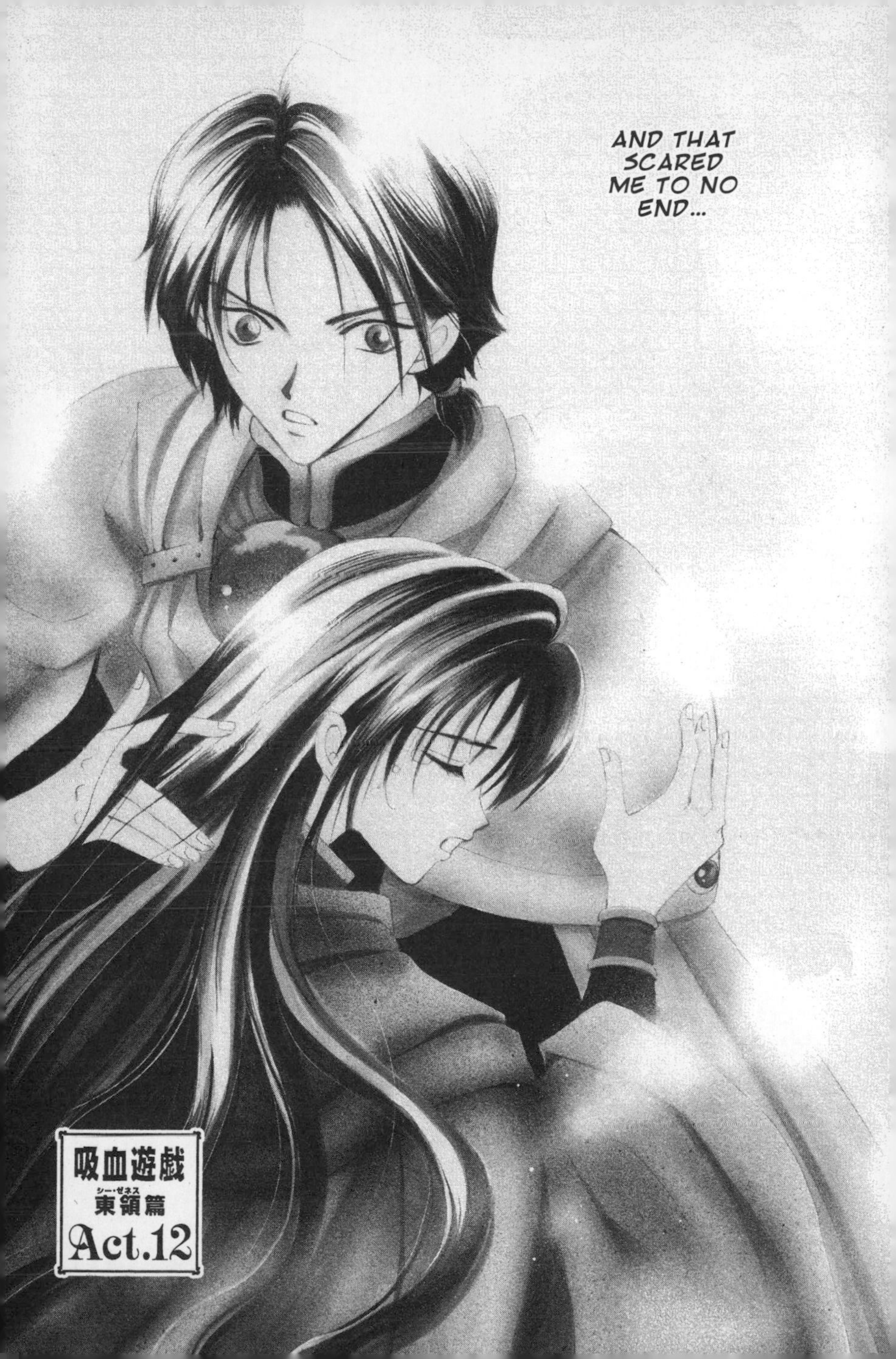
AND THAT SCARED ME TO NO END...
吸血遊戯
シー・ゼネス
東領篇
Act.12

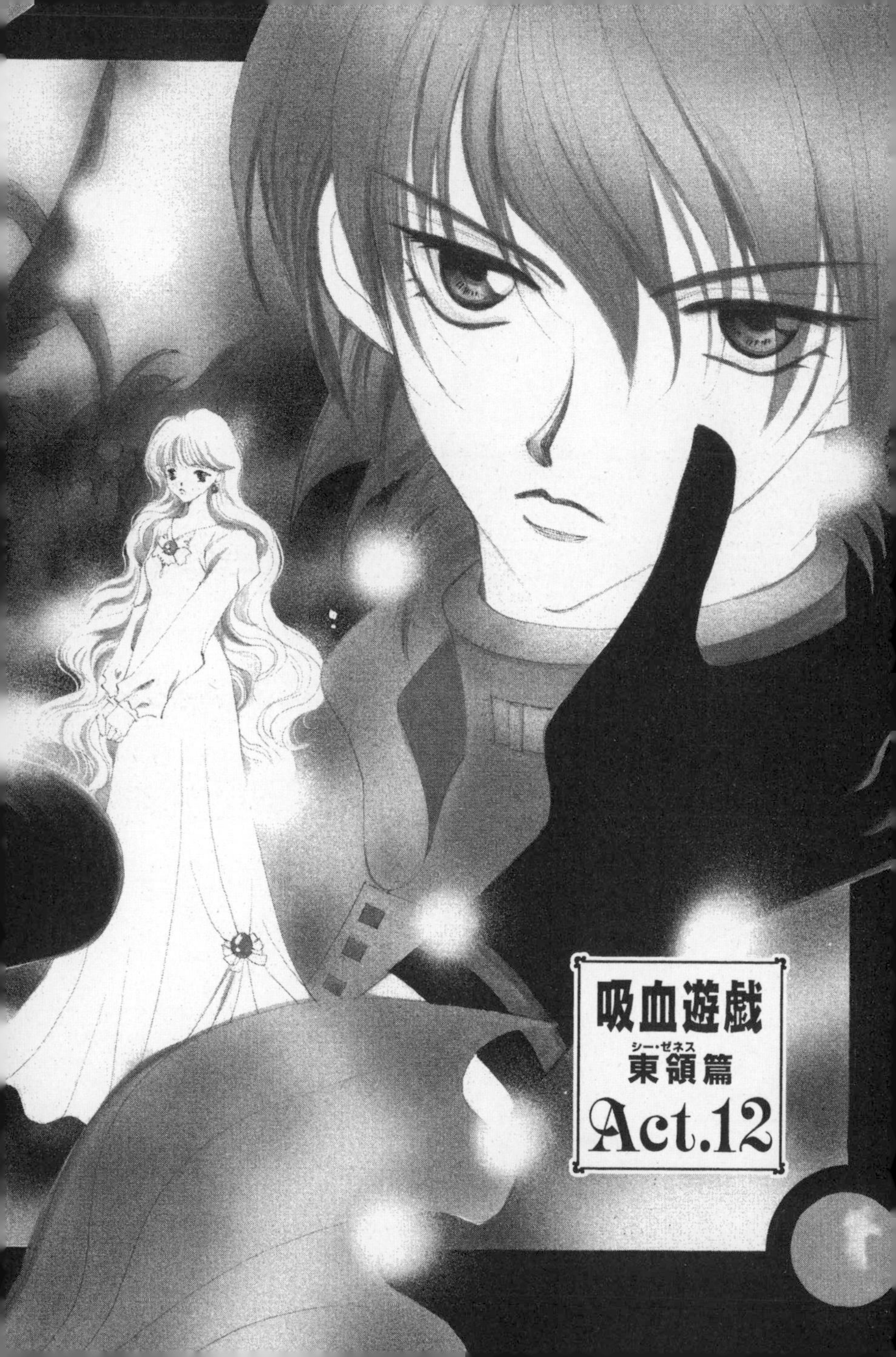

吸血遊戯
東領篇
シー・ゼネス
Act.12

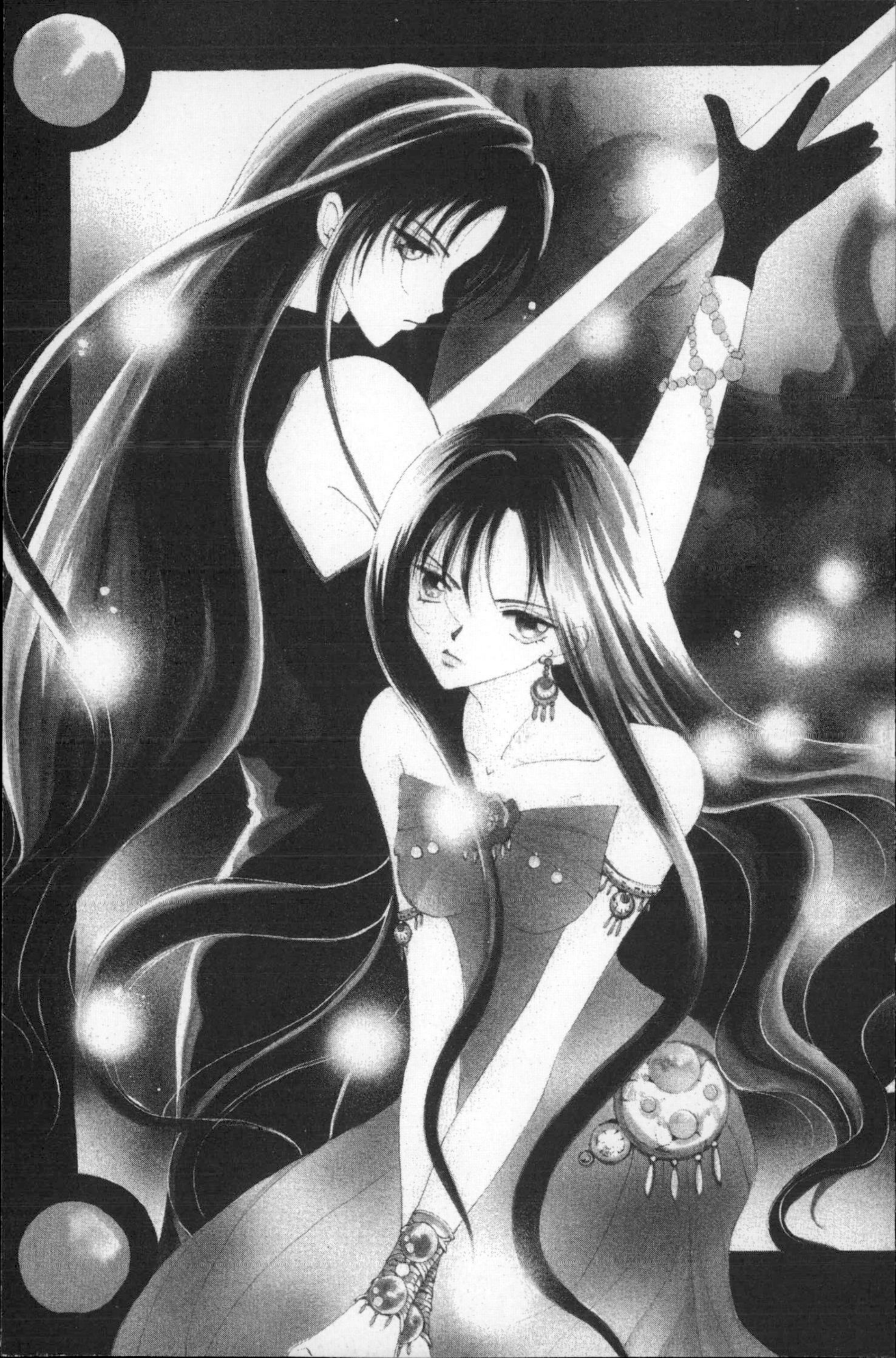

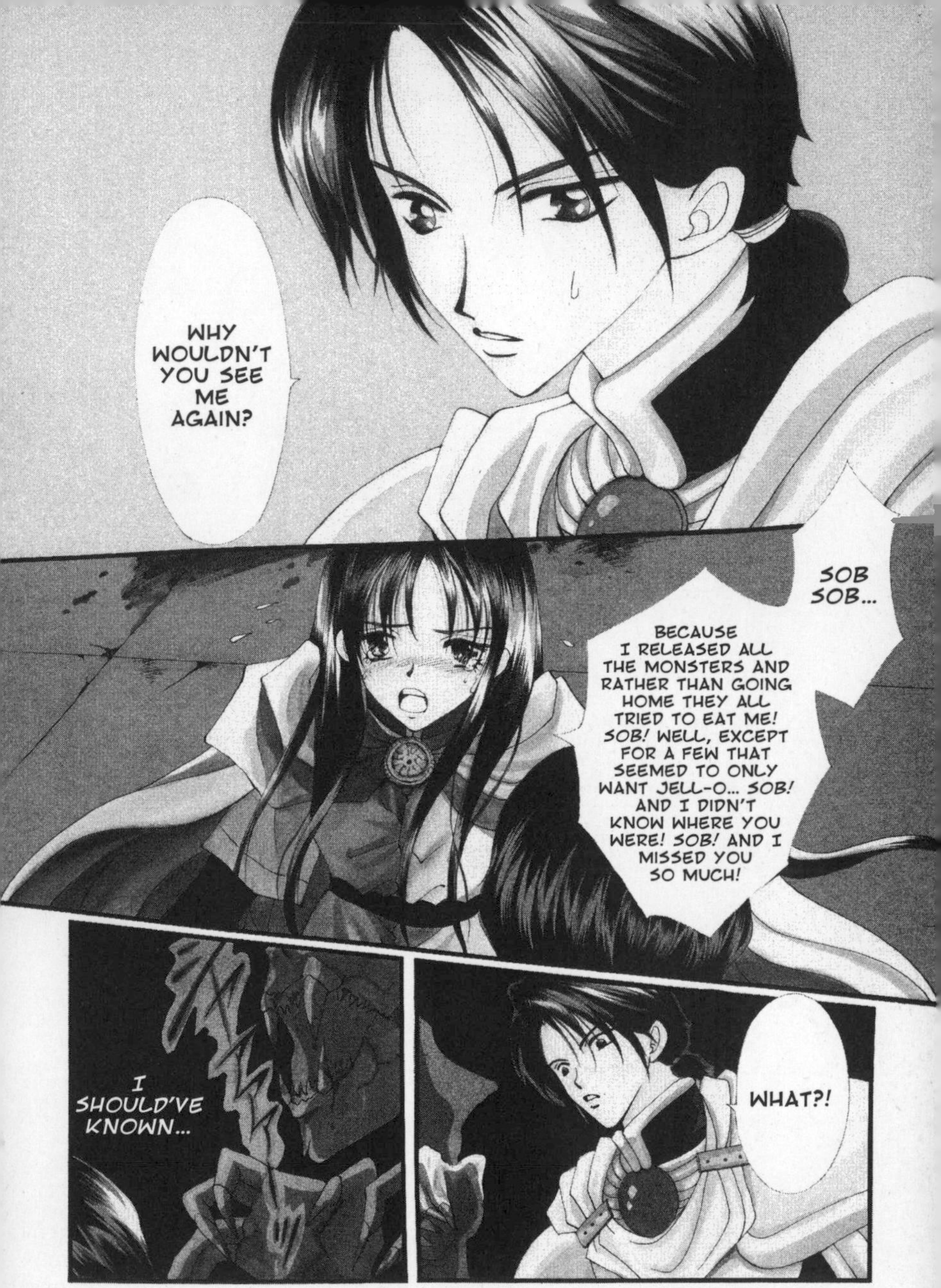
WHY WOULDN'T YOU SEE ME AGAIN?
SOB SOB...
BECAUSE I RELEASED ALL THE MONSTERS AND RATHER THAN GOING HOME THEY ALL TRIED TO EAT ME! SOB! WELL, EXCEPT FOR A FEW THAT SEEMED TO ONLY WANT JELL-O... SOB! AND I DIDN'T KNOW WHERE YOU WERE! SOB! AND I MISSED YOU SO MUCH!
WHAT?!
I SHOULD'VE KNOWN...

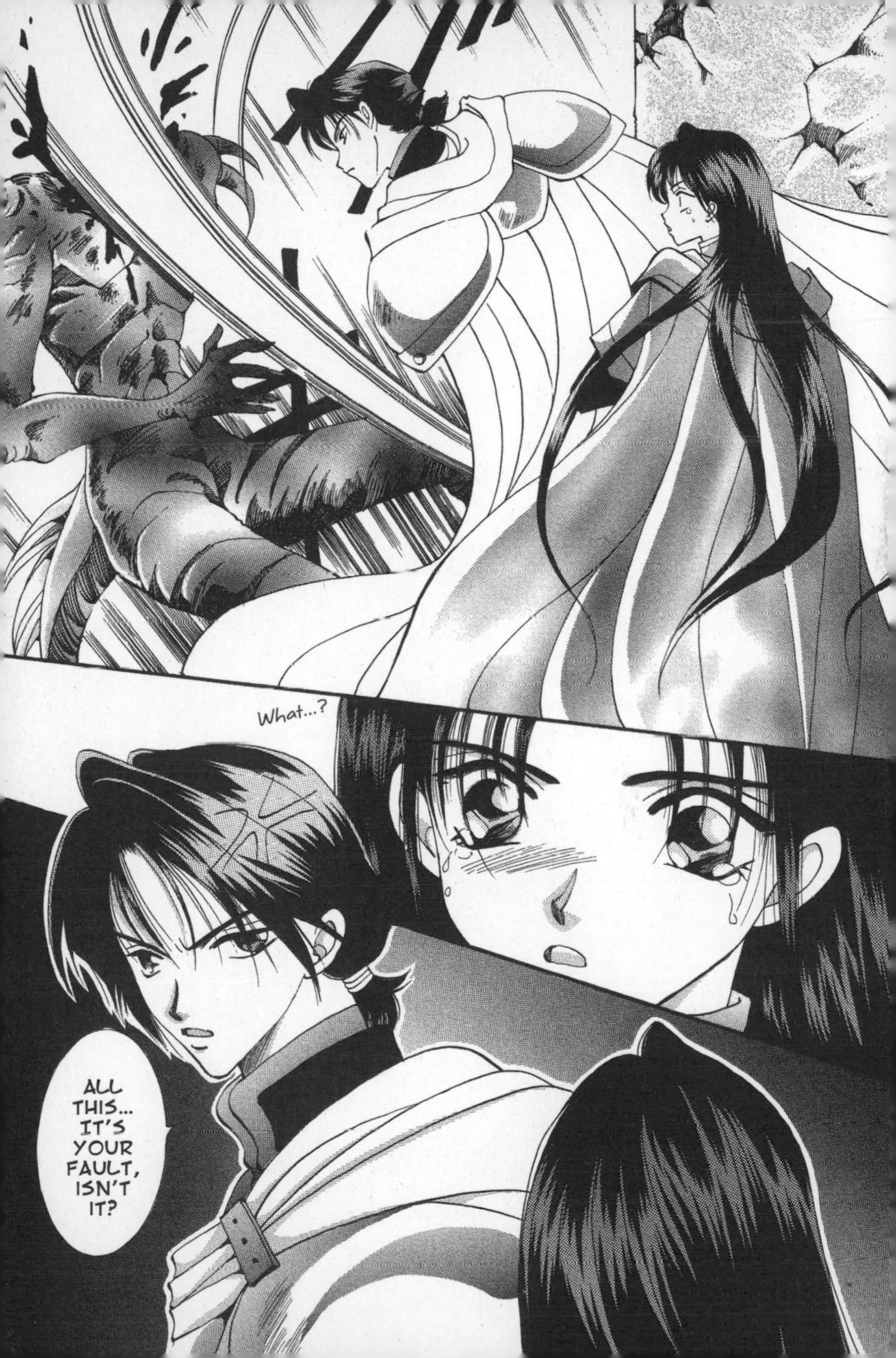
What...?
ALL THIS... IT'S YOUR FAULT, ISN'T IT?

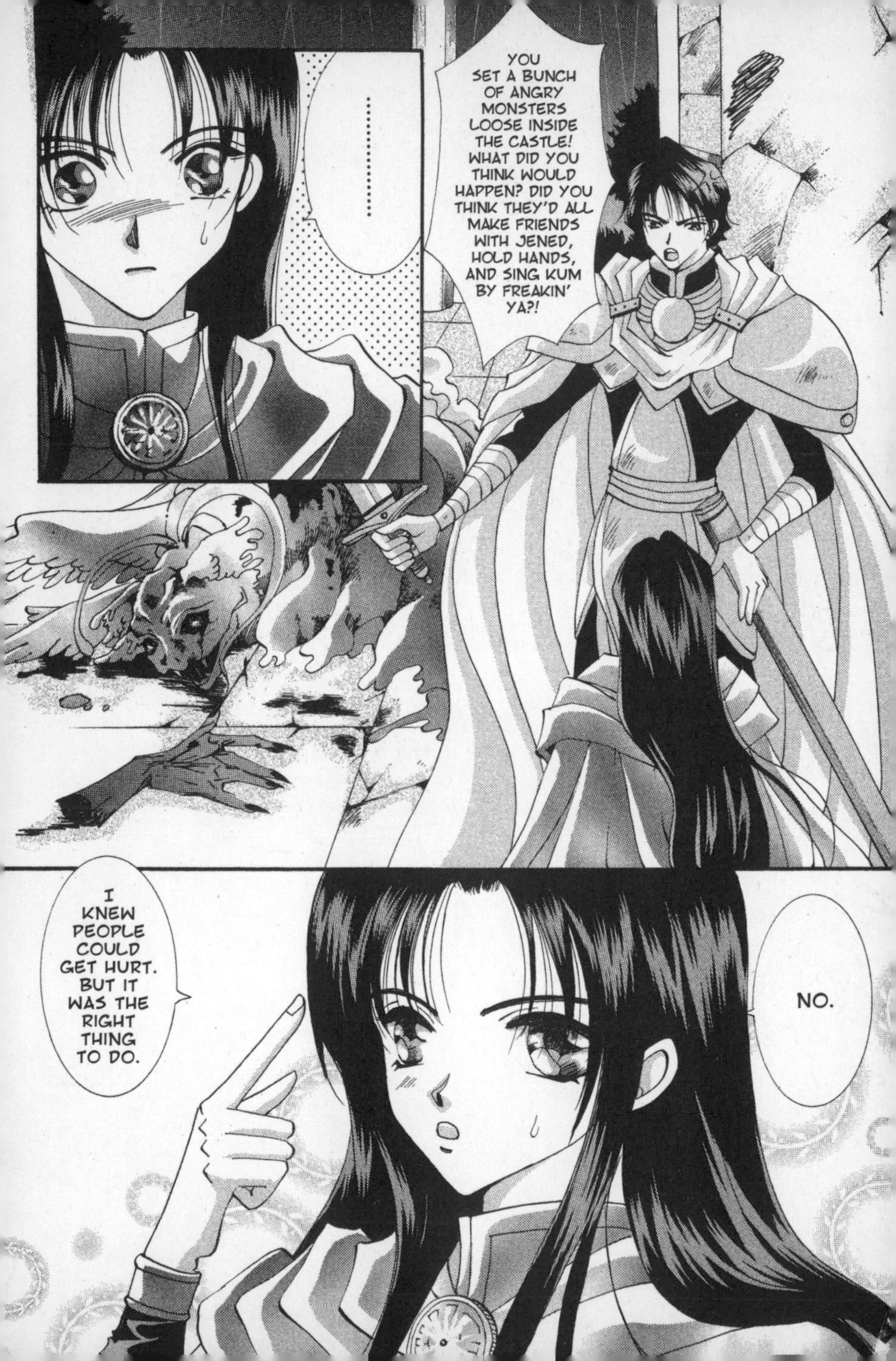
YOU SET A BUNCH OF ANGRY MONSTERS LOOSE INSIDE THE CASTLE! WHAT DID YOU THINK WOULD HAPPEN? DID YOU THINK THEY'D ALL MAKE FRIENDS WITH JENED, HOLD HANDS, AND SING KUM BY FREAKIN' YA?!
......
NO.
I KNEW PEOPLE COULD GET HURT. BUT IT WAS THE RIGHT THING TO DO.

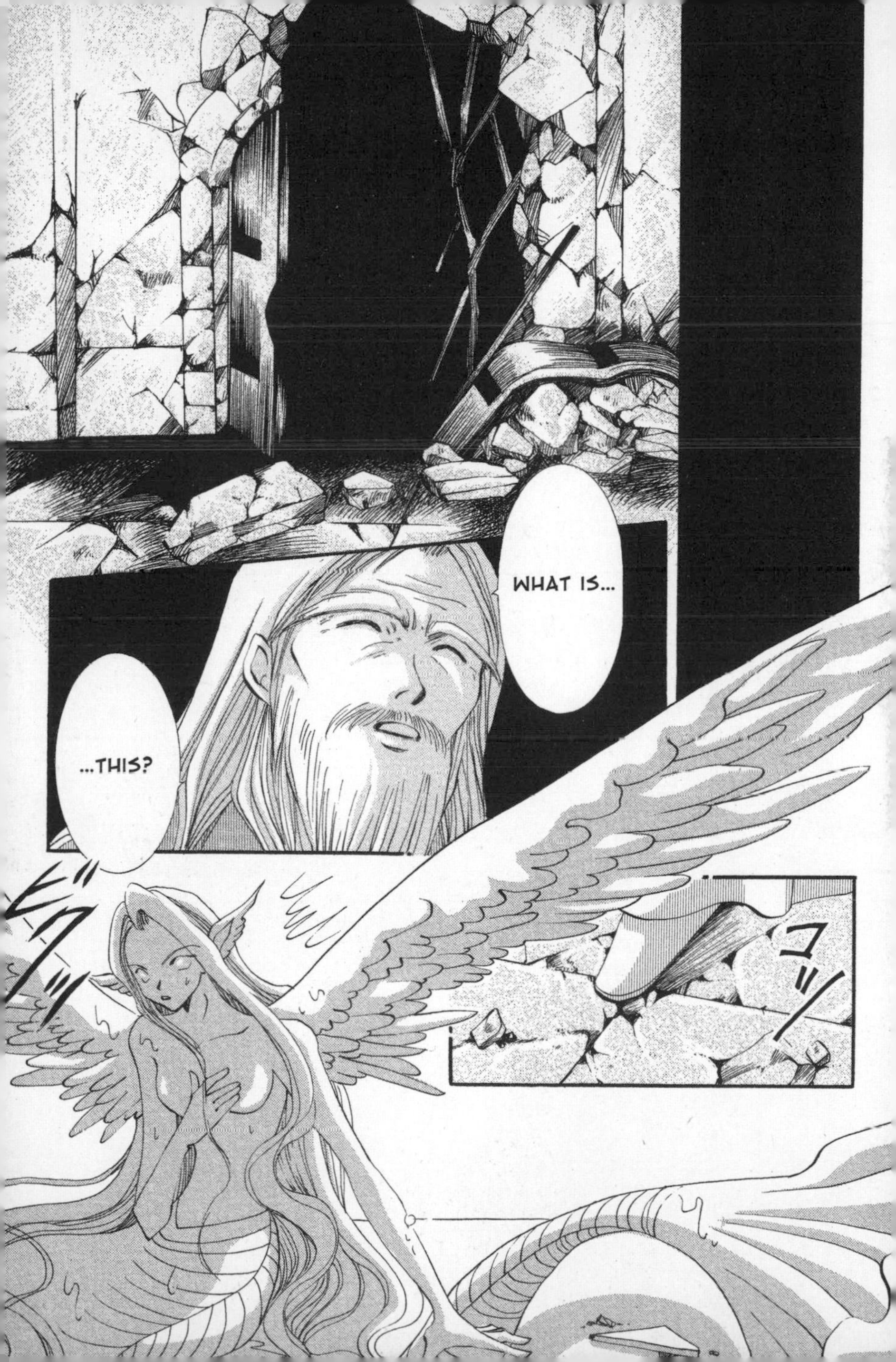
WHAT IS...
...THIS?
ビクッ

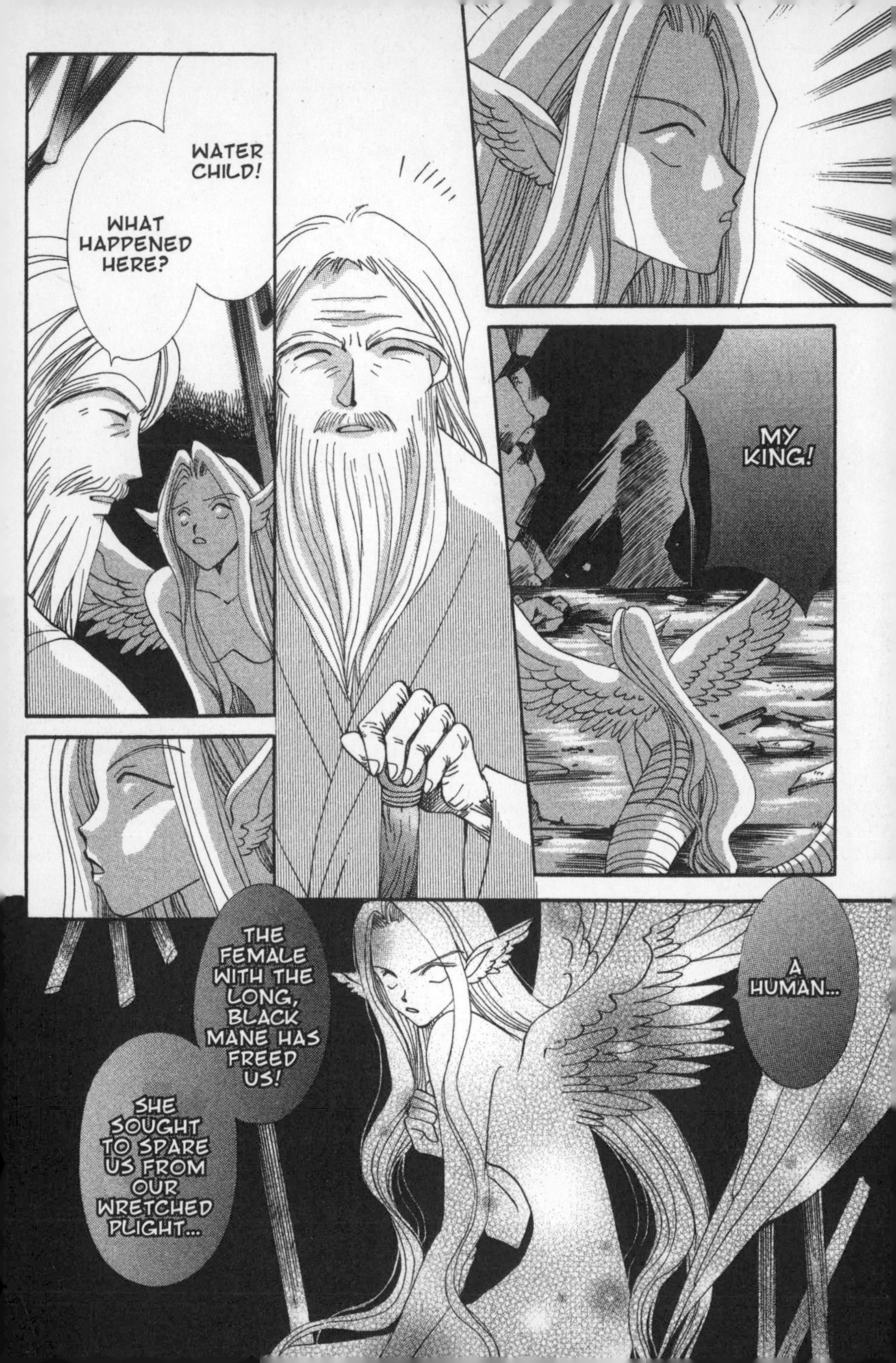
MY KING!
WATER CHILD!
WHAT HAPPENED HERE?
A HUMAN...
THE FEMALE WITH THE LONG, BLACK MANE HAS FREED US!
SHE SOUGHT TO SPARE US FROM OUR WRETCHED PLIGHT...

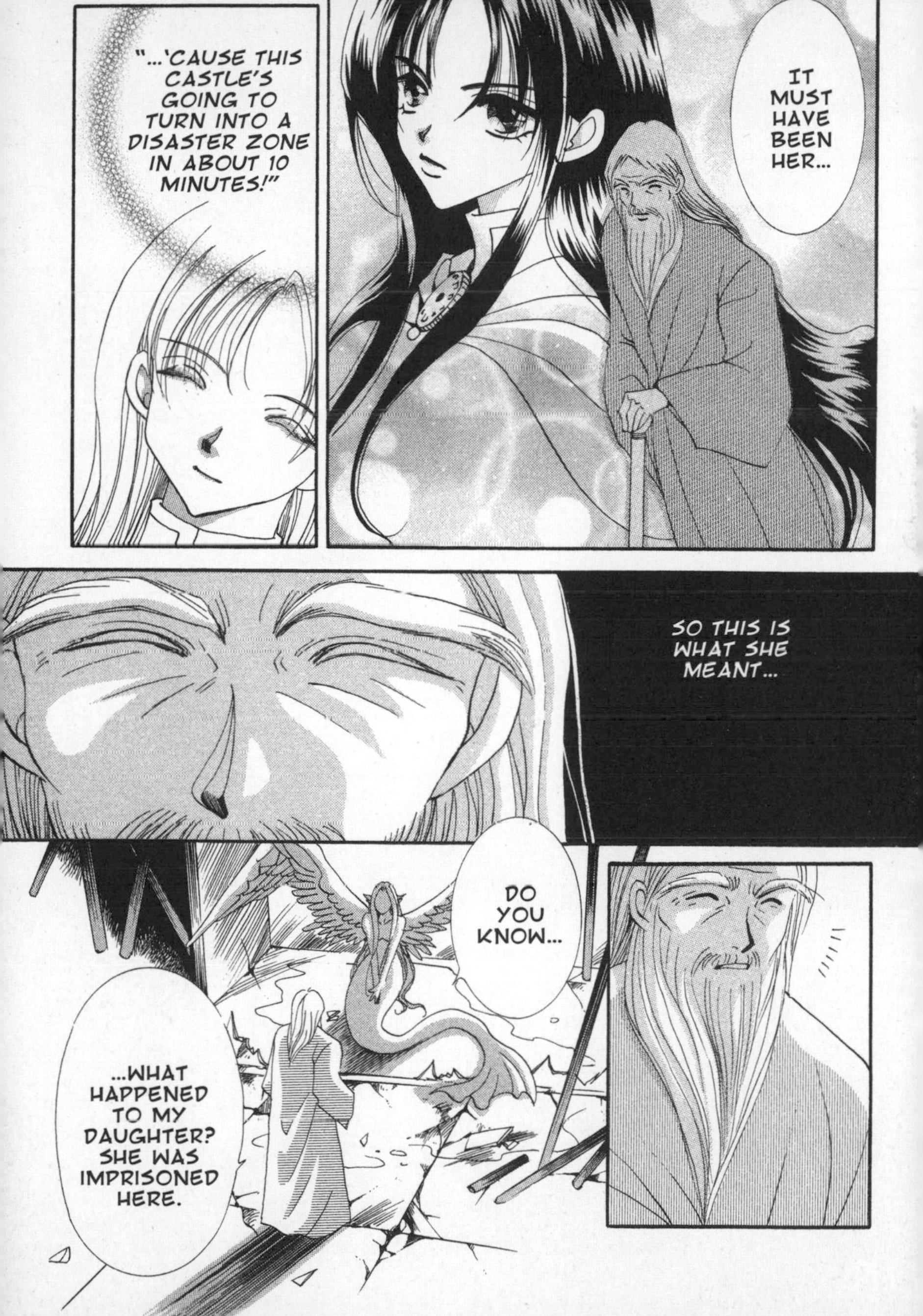
IT MUST HAVE BEEN HER...
"...'CAUSE THIS CASTLE'S GOING TO TURN INTO A DISASTER ZONE IN ABOUT 10 MINUTES!"
SO THIS IS WHAT SHE MEANT...
DO YOU KNOW...
...WHAT HAPPENED TO MY DAUGHTER? SHE WAS IMPRISONED HERE.

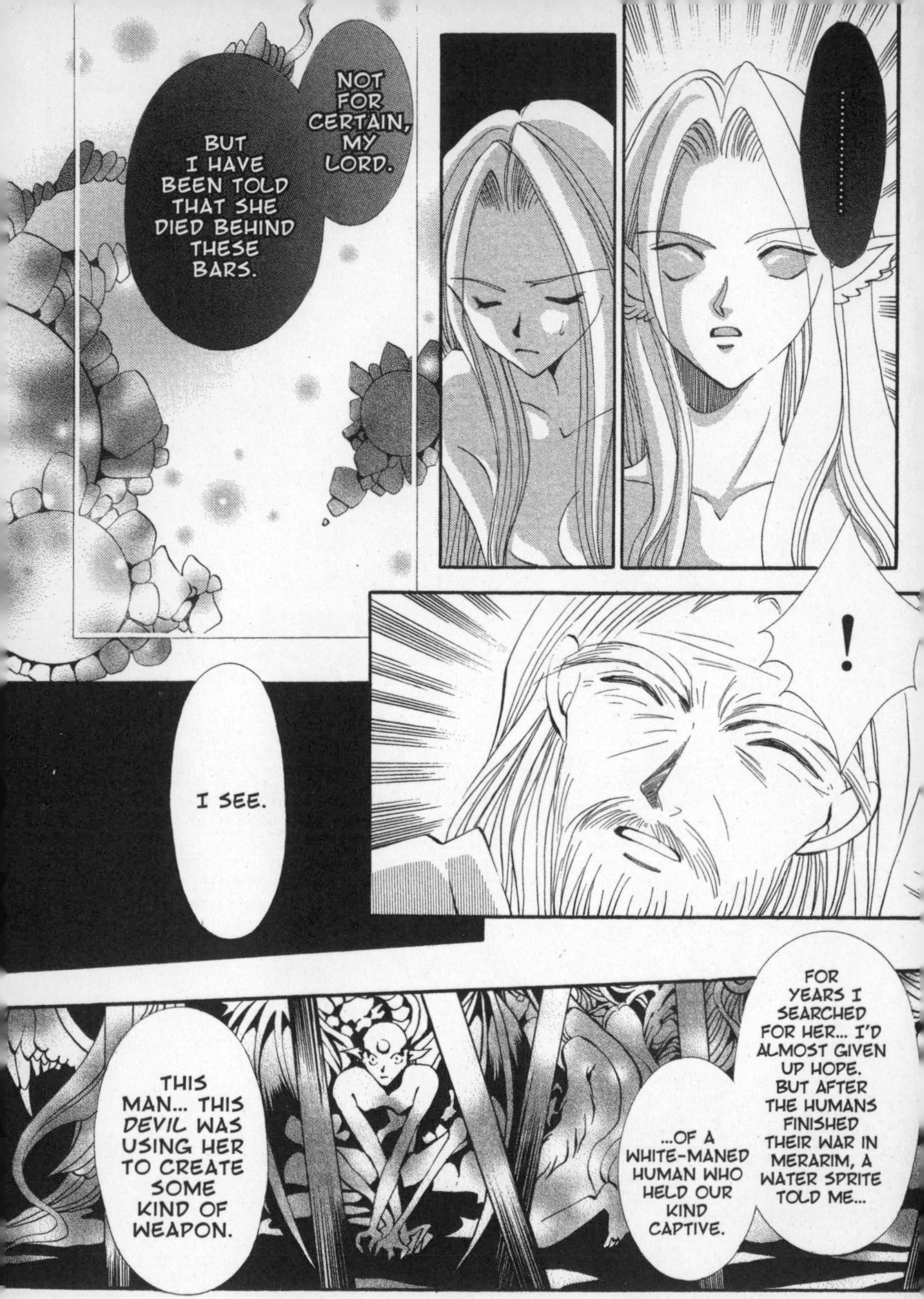
......
NOT FOR CERTAIN, MY LORD.
BUT I HAVE BEEN TOLD THAT SHE DIED BEHIND THESE BARS.
!
I SEE.
FOR YEARS I SEARCHED FOR HER... I'D ALMOST GIVEN UP HOPE. BUT AFTER THE HUMANS FINISHED THEIR WAR IN MERARIM, A WATER SPRITE TOLD ME...
...OF A WHITE-MANED HUMAN WHO HELD OUR KIND CAPTIVE.
THIS MAN... THIS *DEVIL* WAS USING HER TO CREATE SOME KIND OF WEAPON.

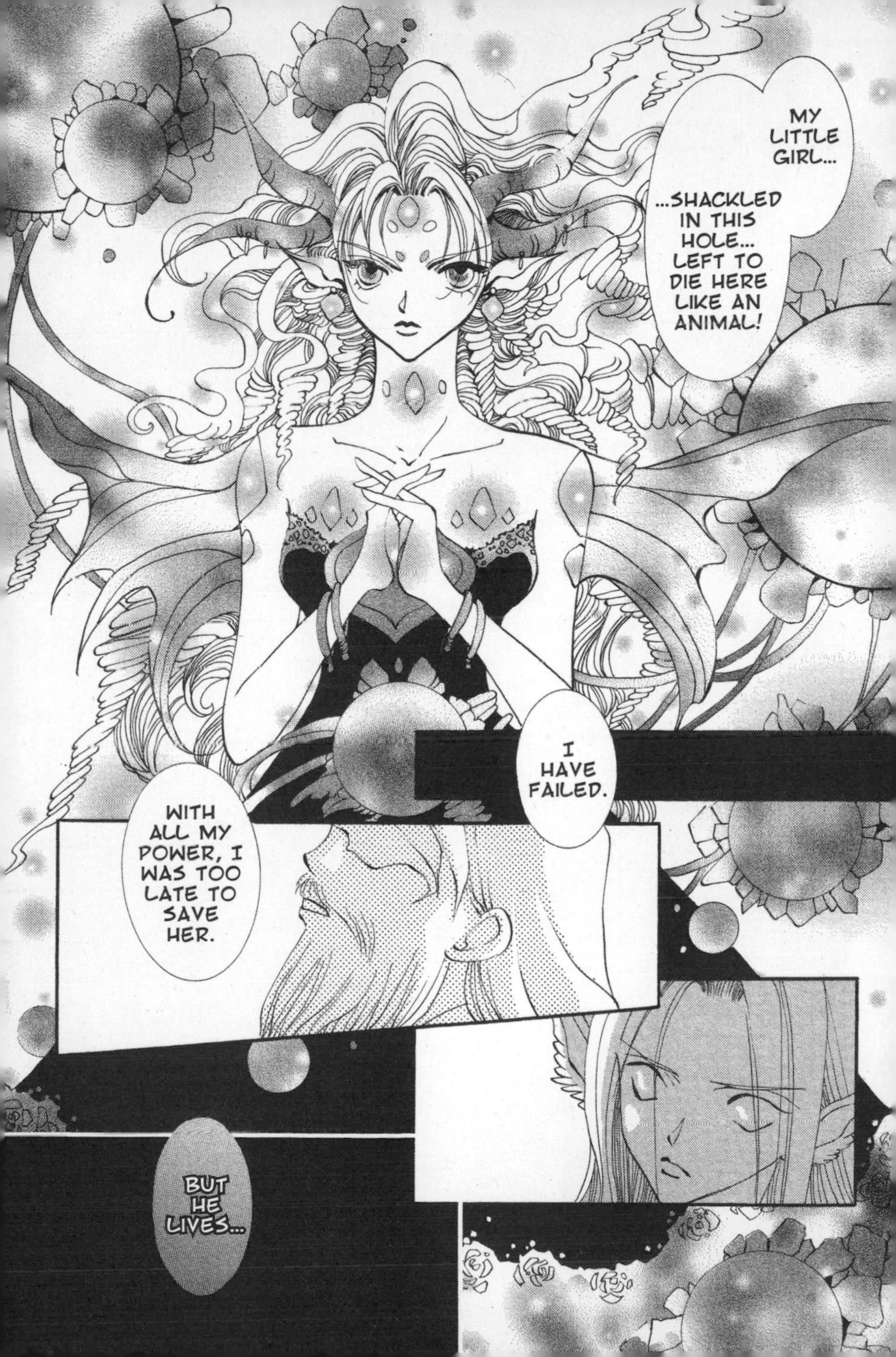
MY LITTLE GIRL...
...SHACKLED IN THIS HOLE... LEFT TO DIE HERE LIKE AN ANIMAL!
I HAVE FAILED.
WITH ALL MY POWER, I WAS TOO LATE TO SAVE HER.
BUT HE LIVES...

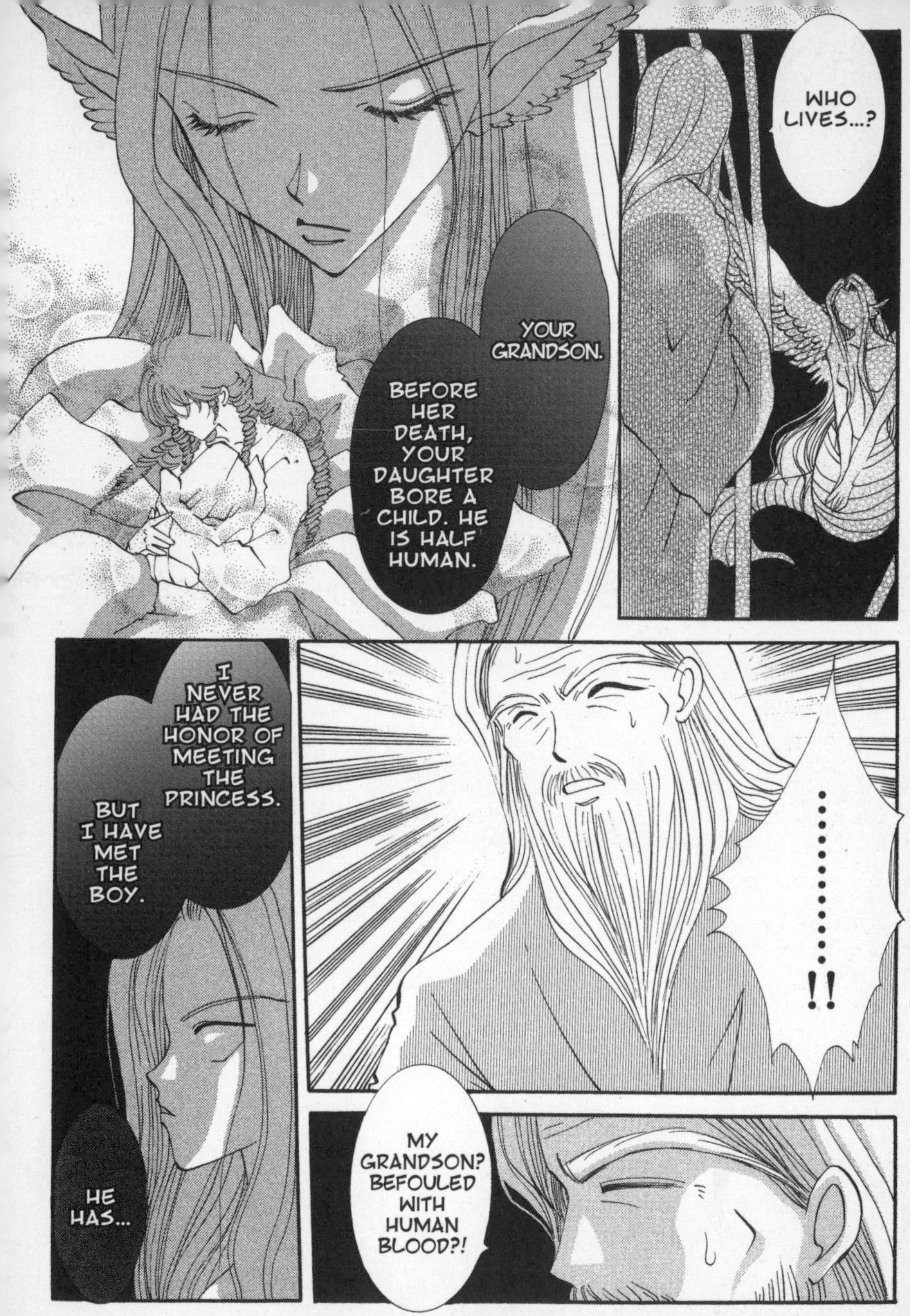
WHO LIVES...?
YOUR GRANDSON.
BEFORE HER DEATH, YOUR DAUGHTER BORE A CHILD. HE IS HALF HUMAN.
......!!
MY GRANDSON? BEFOULED WITH HUMAN BLOOD?!
I NEVER HAD THE HONOR OF MEETING THE PRINCESS.
BUT I HAVE MET THE BOY.
HE HAS...

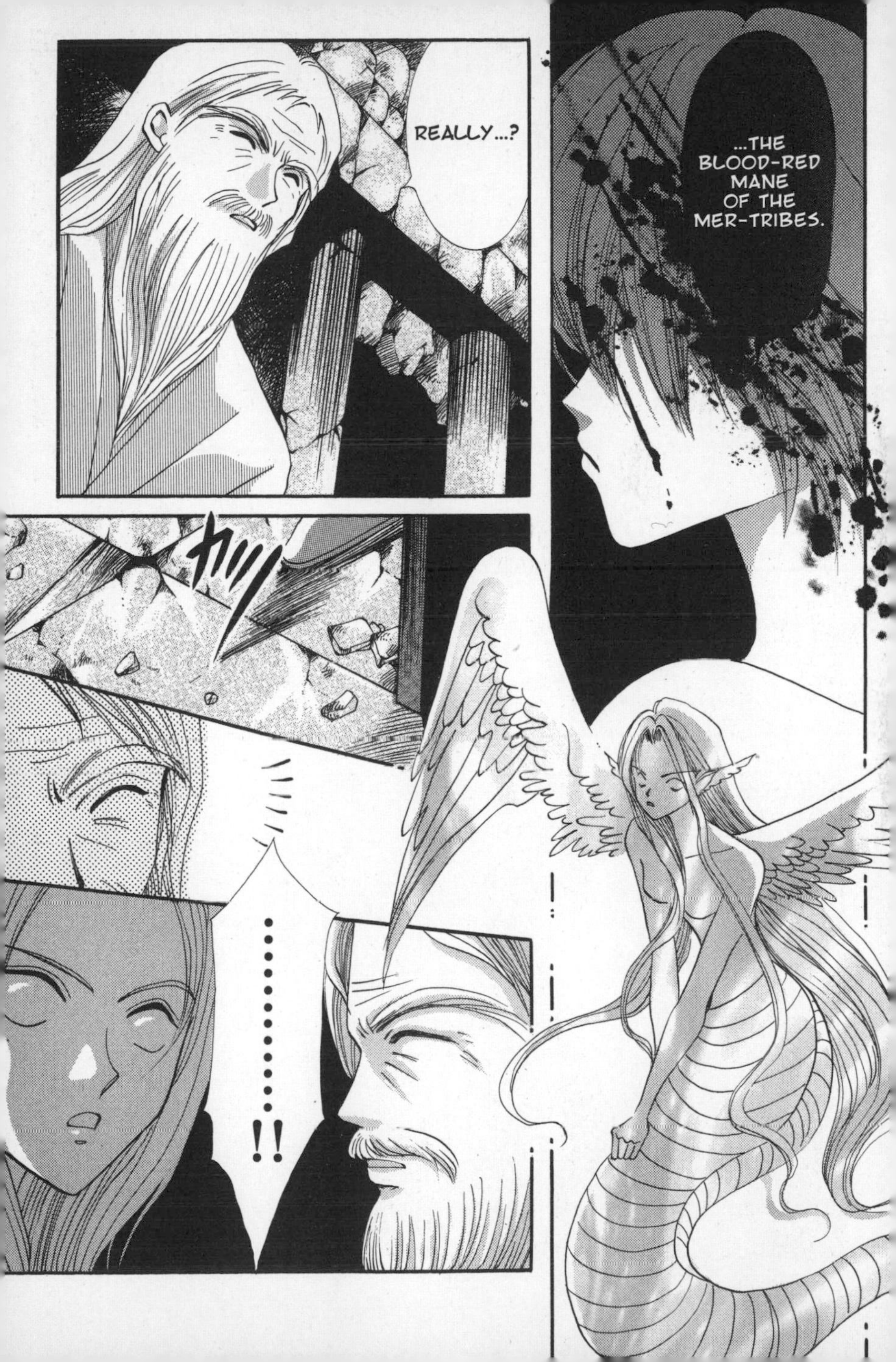
...THE BLOOD-RED MANE OF THE MER-TRIBES.
REALLY...?
カッ
........!!

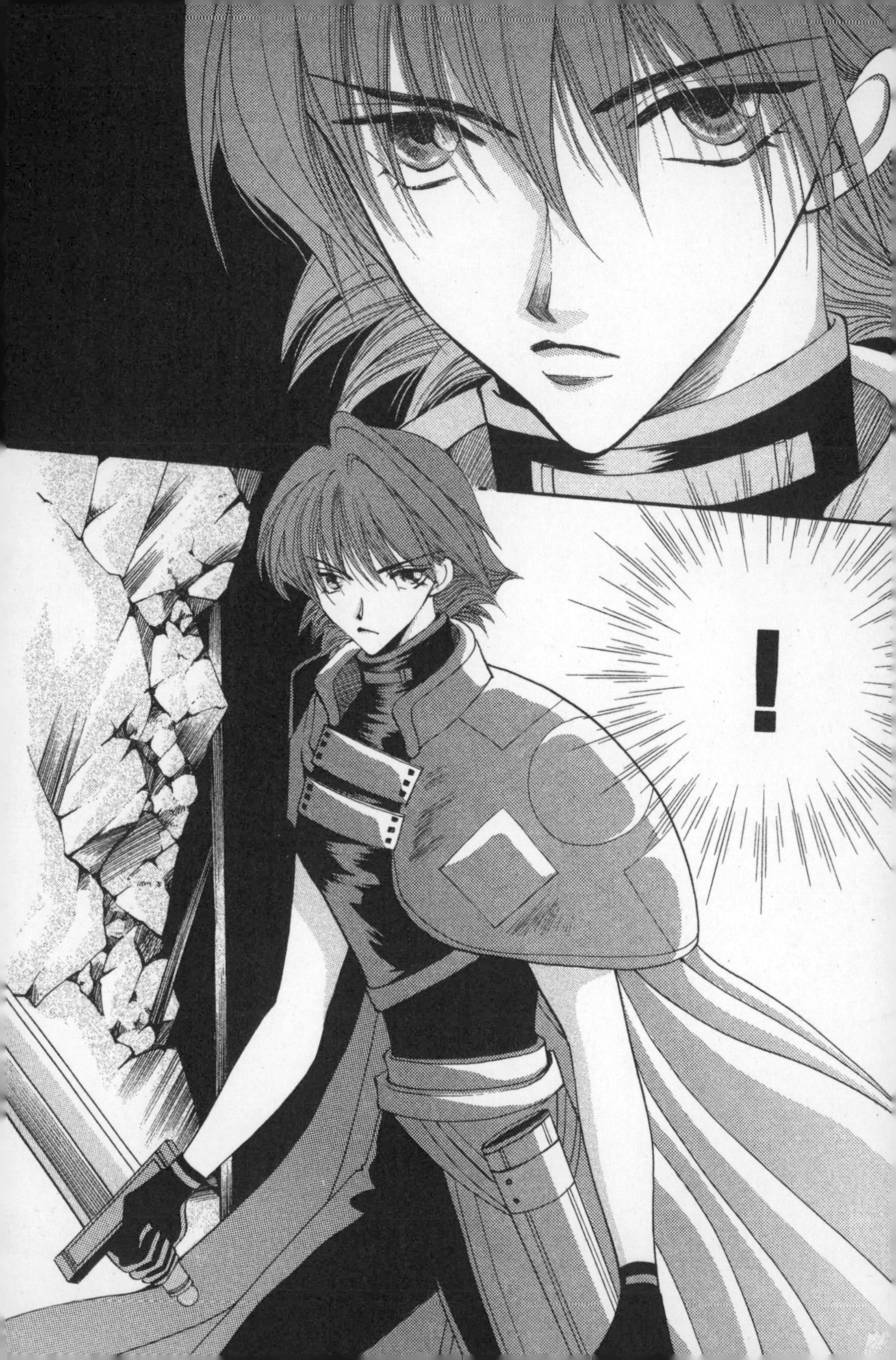
!

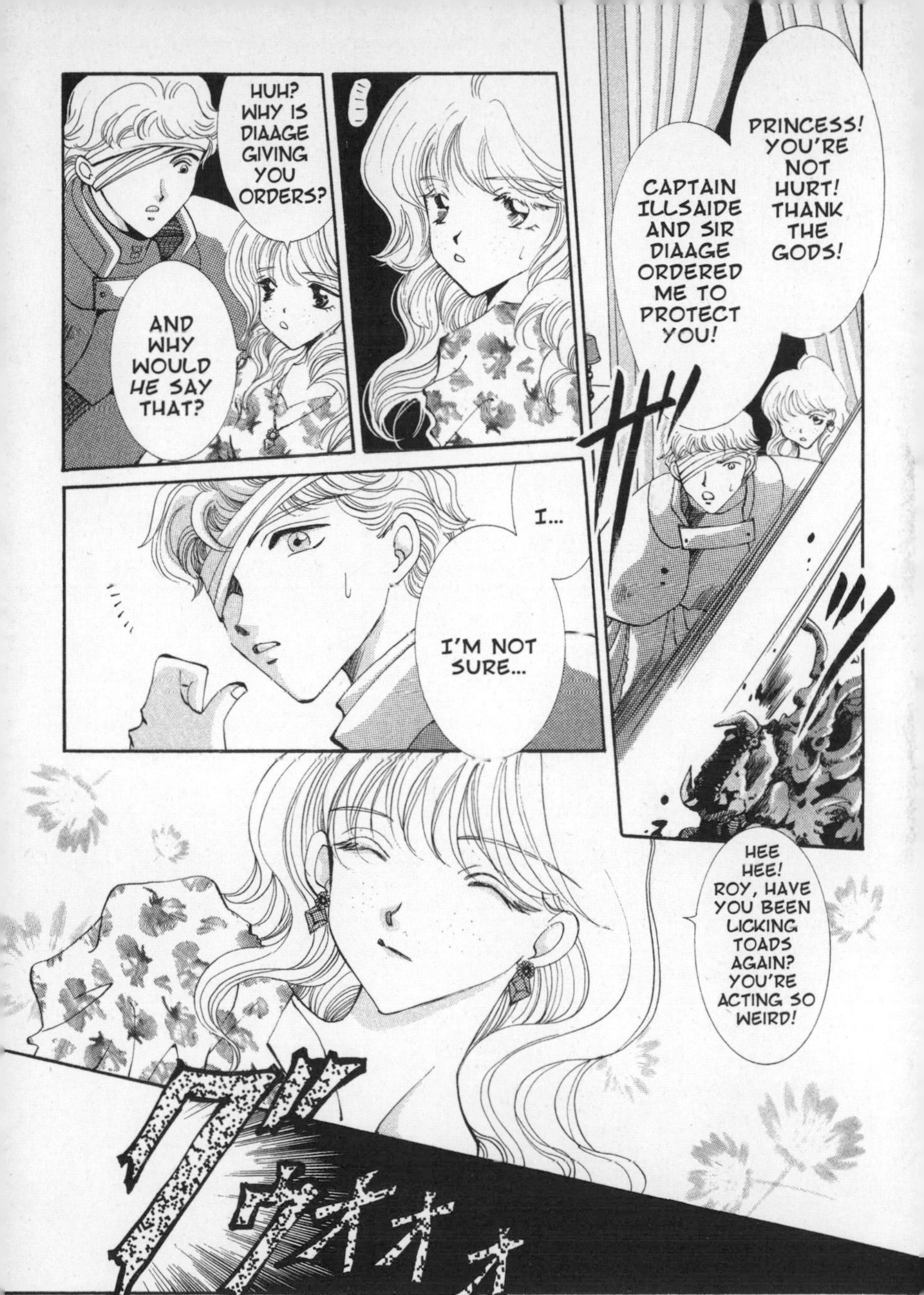
PRINCESS! YOU'RE NOT HURT! THANK THE GODS!
CAPTAIN ILLSAIDE AND SIR DIAAGE ORDERED ME TO PROTECT YOU!
!
HUH? WHY IS DIAAGE GIVING YOU ORDERS?
AND WHY WOULD HE SAY THAT?
I...
I'M NOT SURE...
HEE HEE! ROY, HAVE YOU BEEN LICKING TOADS AGAIN? YOU'RE ACTING SO WEIRD!

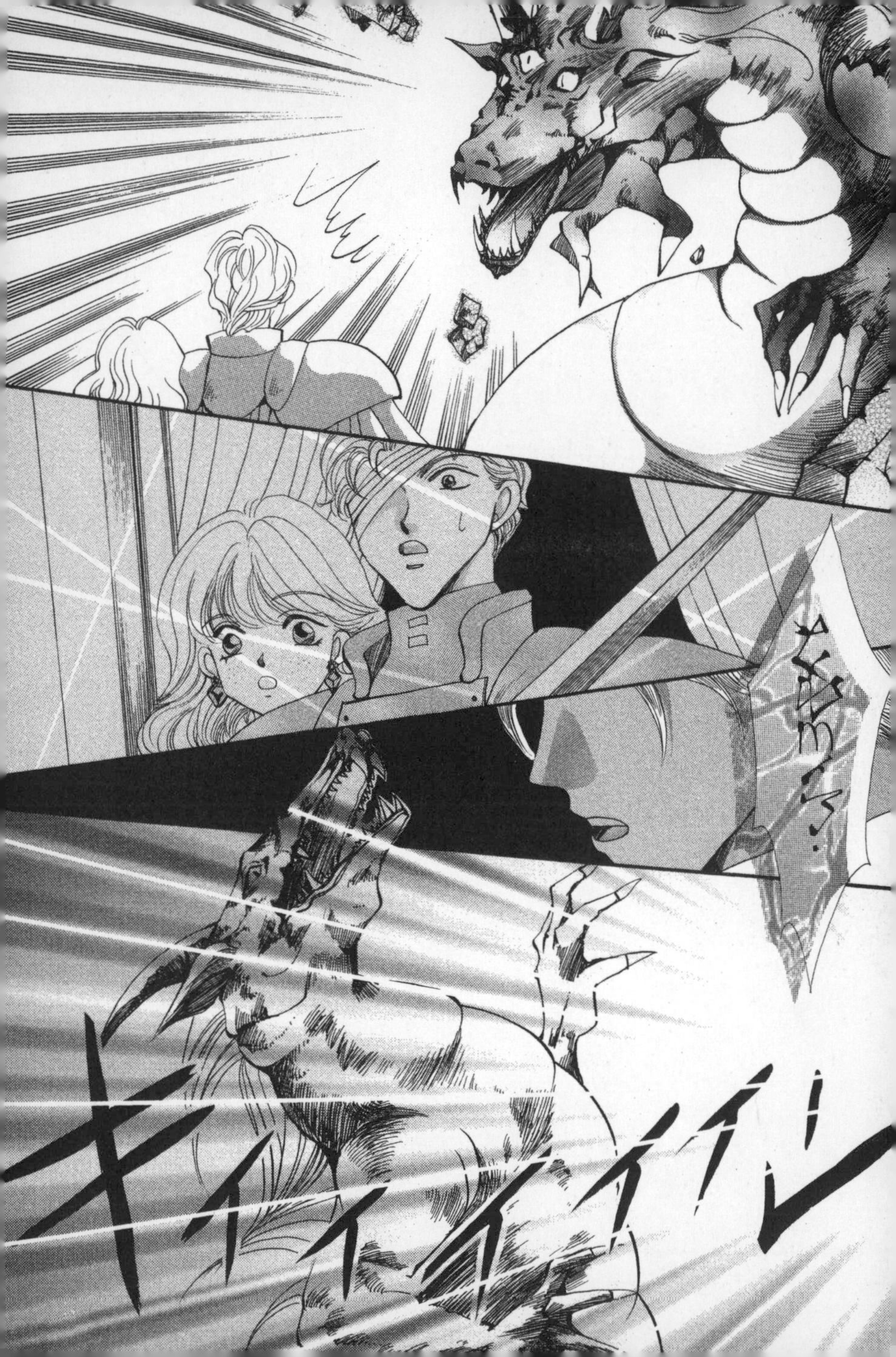
キイイイン

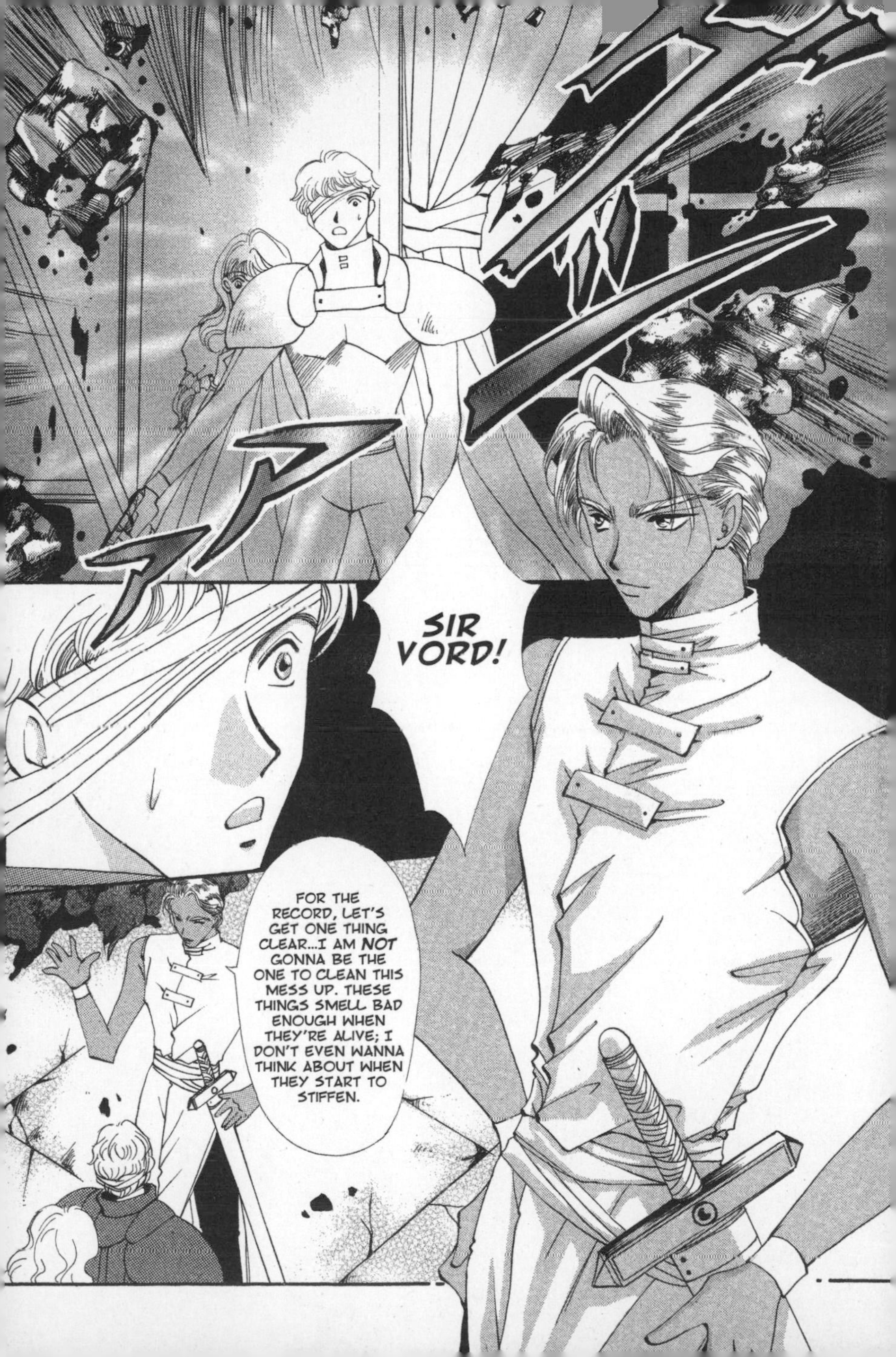
SIR VORD!
FOR THE RECORD, LET'S GET ONE THING CLEAR...I AM *NOT* GONNA BE THE ONE TO CLEAN THIS MESS UP. THESE THINGS SMELL BAD ENOUGH WHEN THEY'RE ALIVE; I DON'T EVEN WANNA THINK ABOUT WHEN THEY START TO STIFFEN.

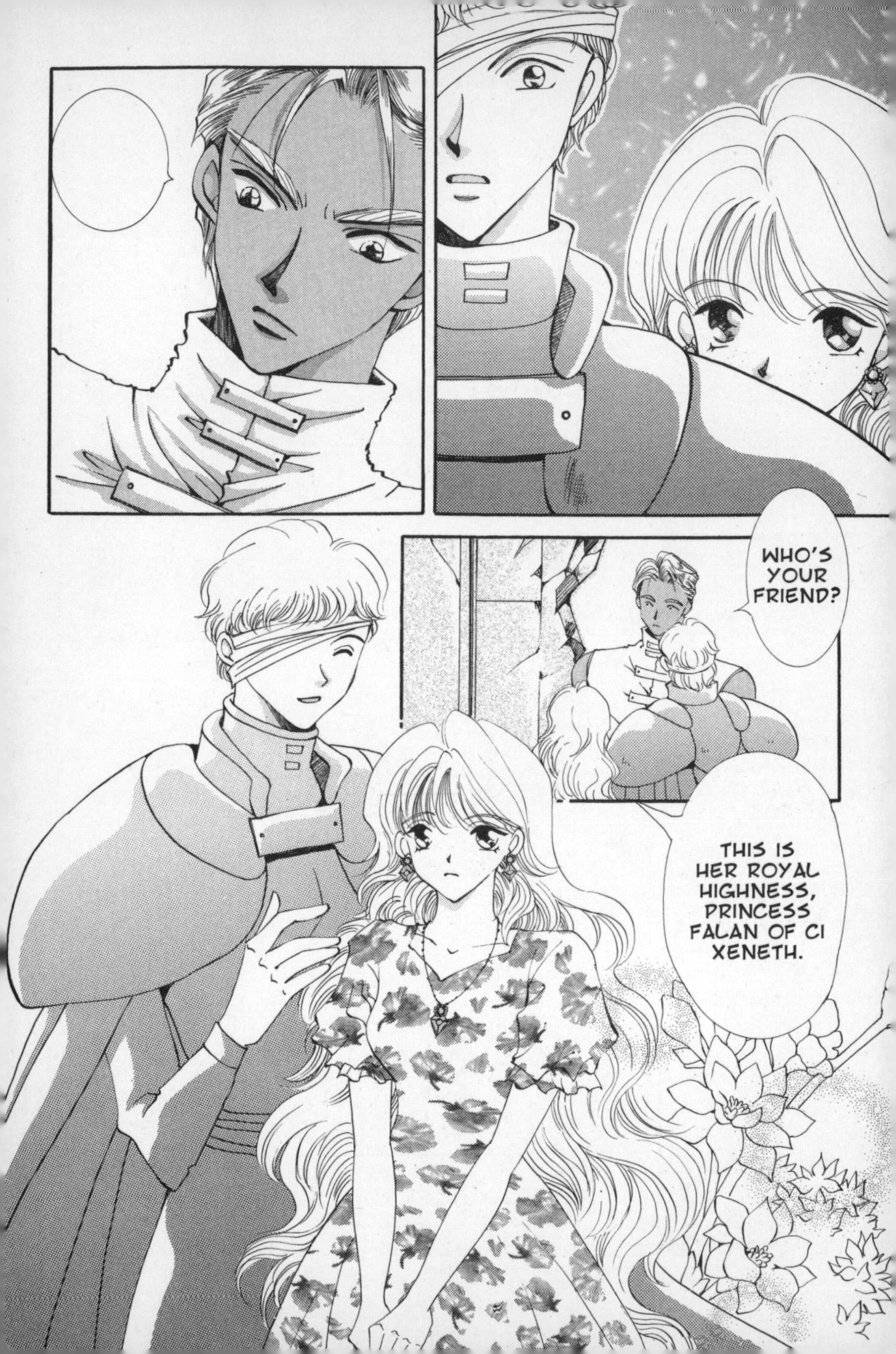
WHO'S YOUR FRIEND?
THIS IS HER ROYAL HIGHNESS, PRINCESS FALAN OF CI XENETH.

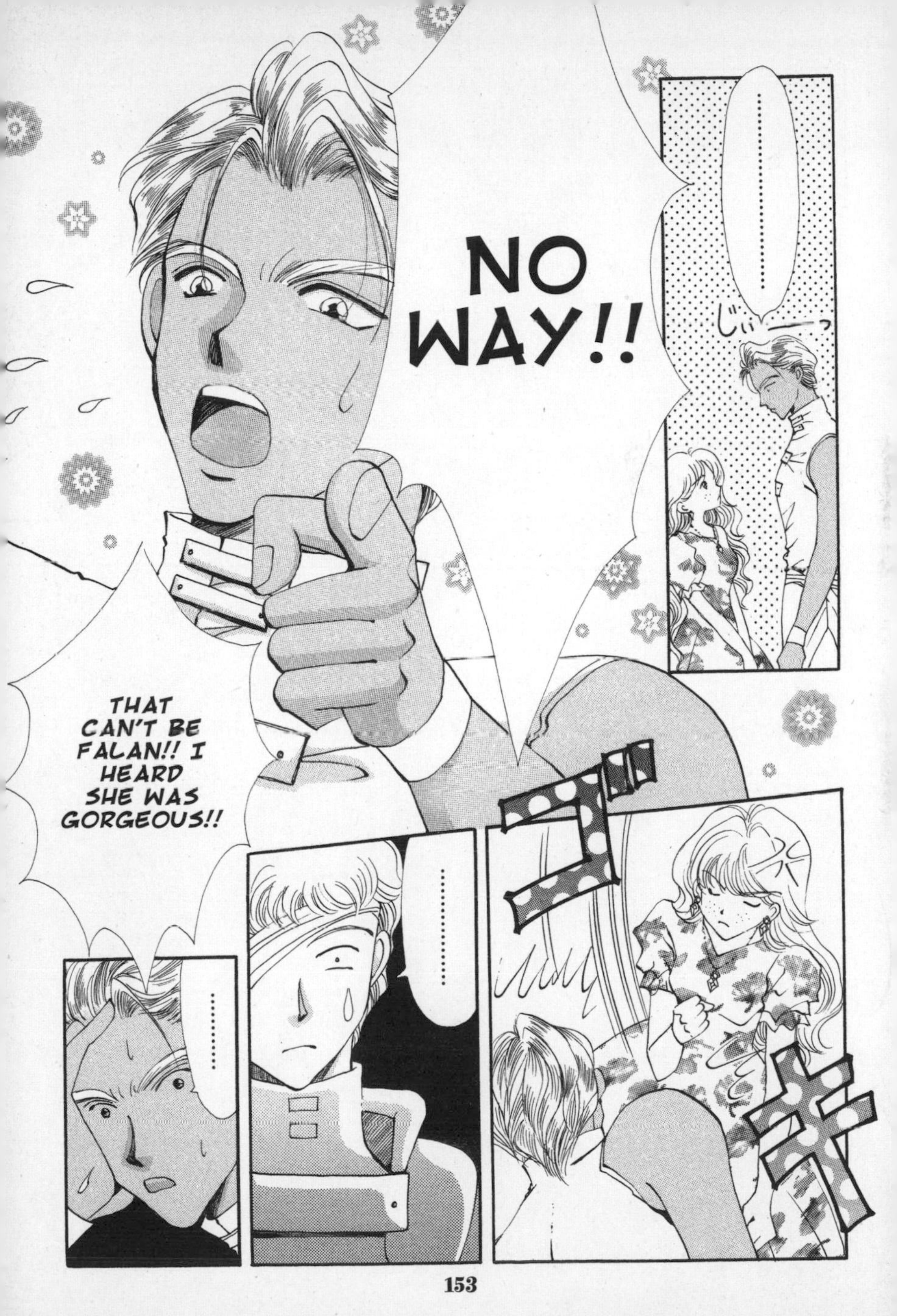
......
じぃーっ
NO WAY!!
THAT CAN'T BE FALAN!! I HEARD SHE WAS GORGEOUS!!
......
......

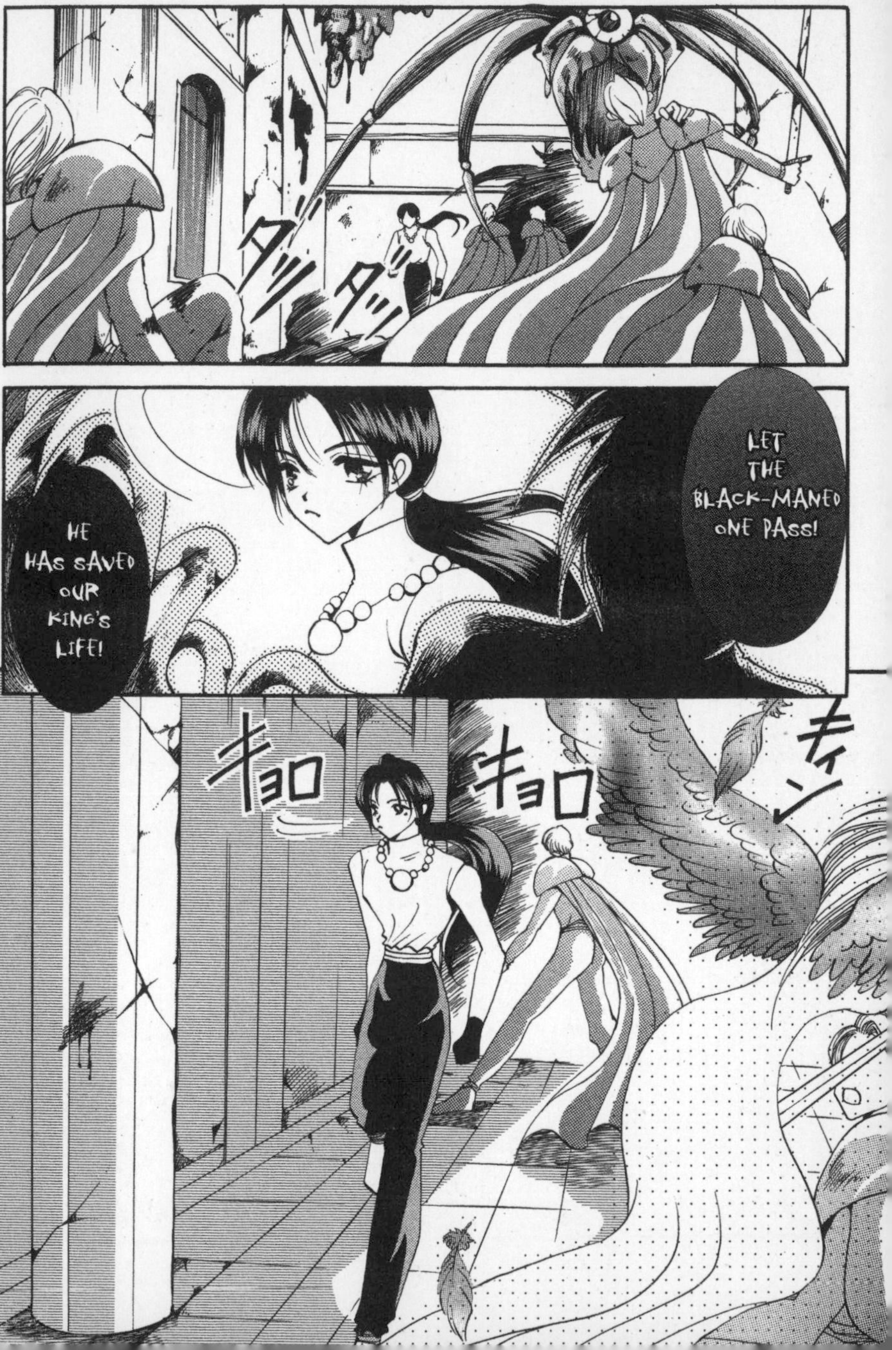
ダッ
ダッ
LET THE BLACK-MANED ONE PASS!
HE HAS SAVED OUR KING'S LIFE!
キィン
キョロ
キョロ

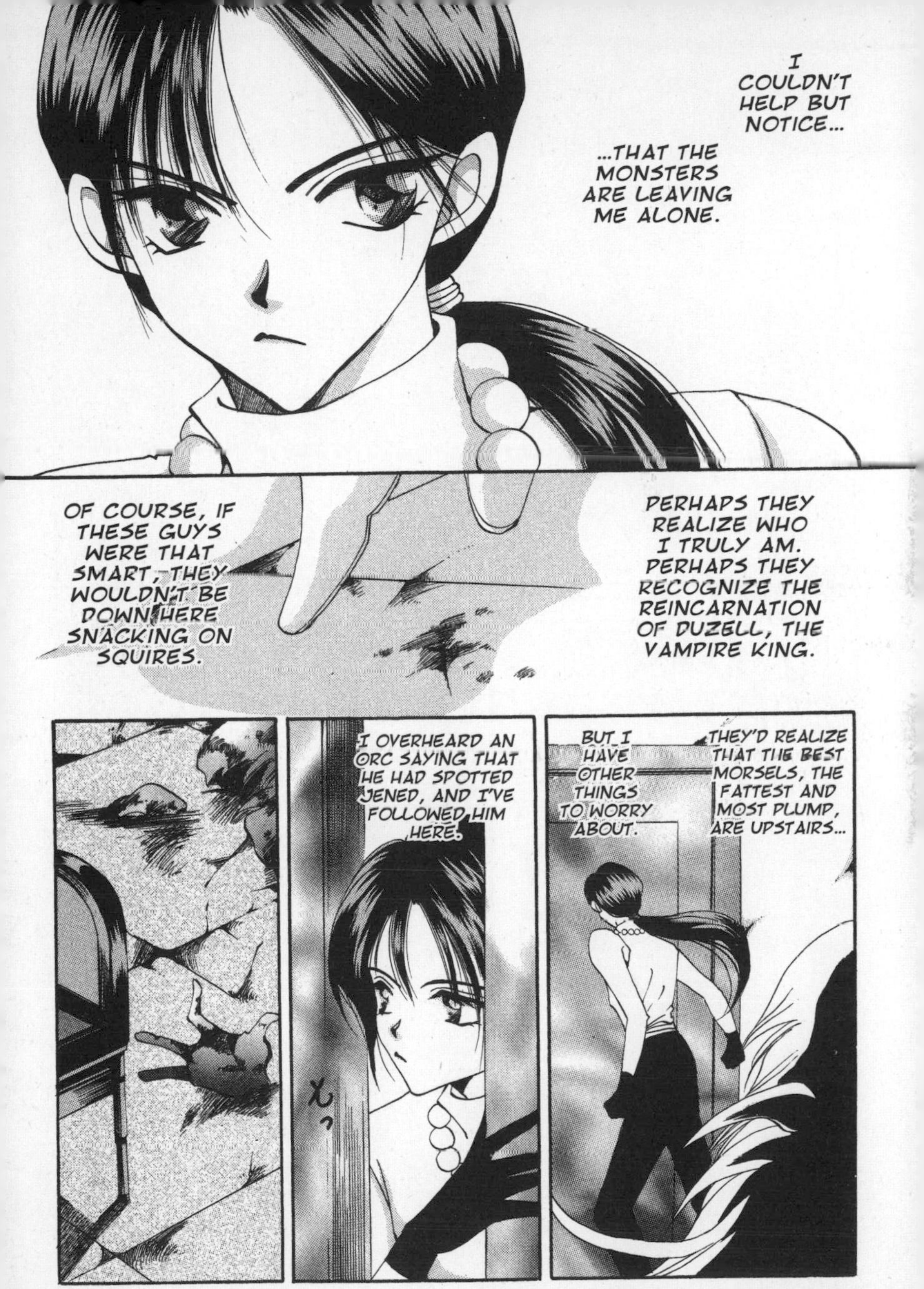
I COULDN'T HELP BUT NOTICE...
...THAT THE MONSTERS ARE LEAVING ME ALONE.
PERHAPS THEY REALIZE WHO I TRULY AM. PERHAPS THEY RECOGNIZE THE REINCARNATION OF DUZELL, THE VAMPIRE KING.
OF COURSE, IF THESE GUYS WERE THAT SMART, THEY WOULDN'T BE DOWN HERE SNACKING ON SQUIRES.
THEY'D REALIZE THAT THE BEST MORSELS, THE FATTEST AND MOST PLUMP, ARE UPSTAIRS...
BUT I HAVE OTHER THINGS TO WORRY ABOUT.
I OVERHEARD AN ORC SAYING THAT HE HAD SPOTTED JENED, AND I'VE FOLLOWED HIM HERE.

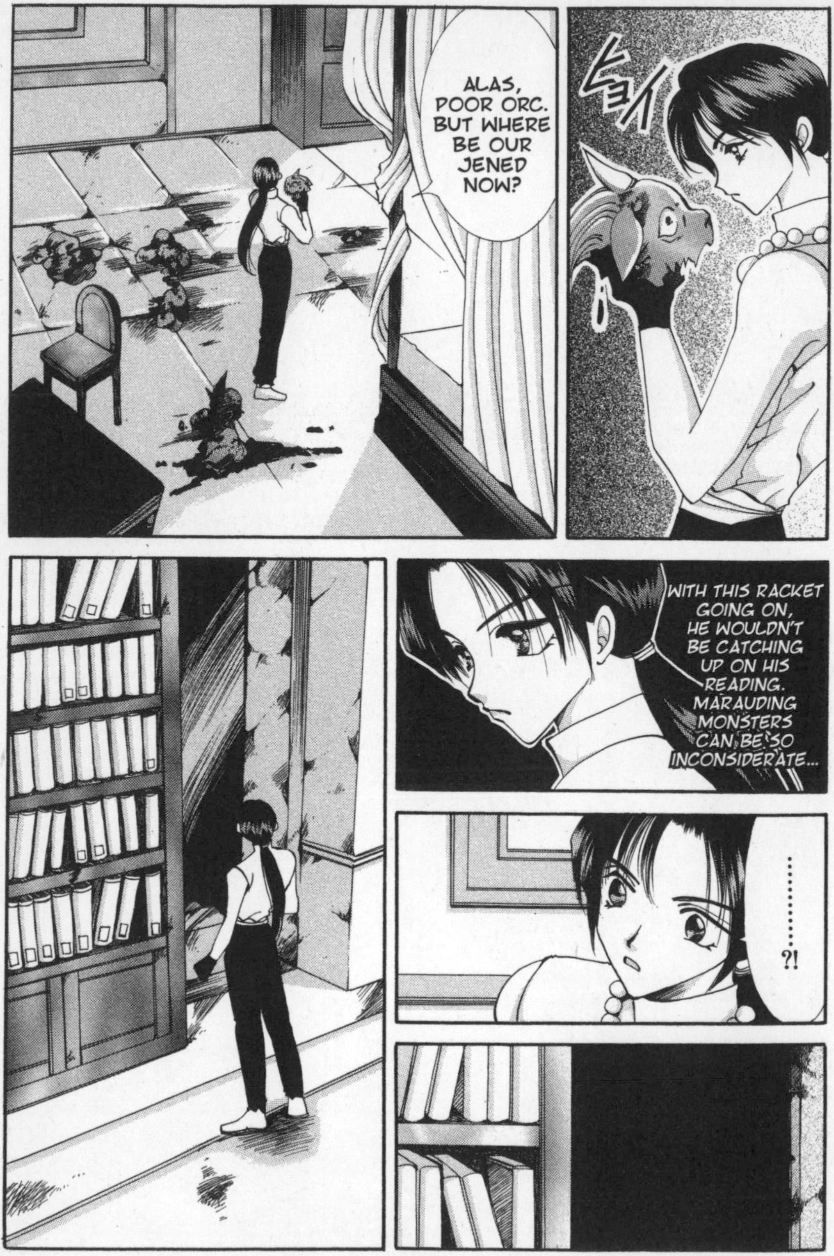
ヒョイ
ALAS, POOR ORC. BUT WHERE BE OUR JENED NOW?
WITH THIS RACKET GOING ON, HE WOULDN'T BE CATCHING UP ON HIS READING. MARAUDING MONSTERS CAN BE SO INCONSIDERATE...
......?!
.....

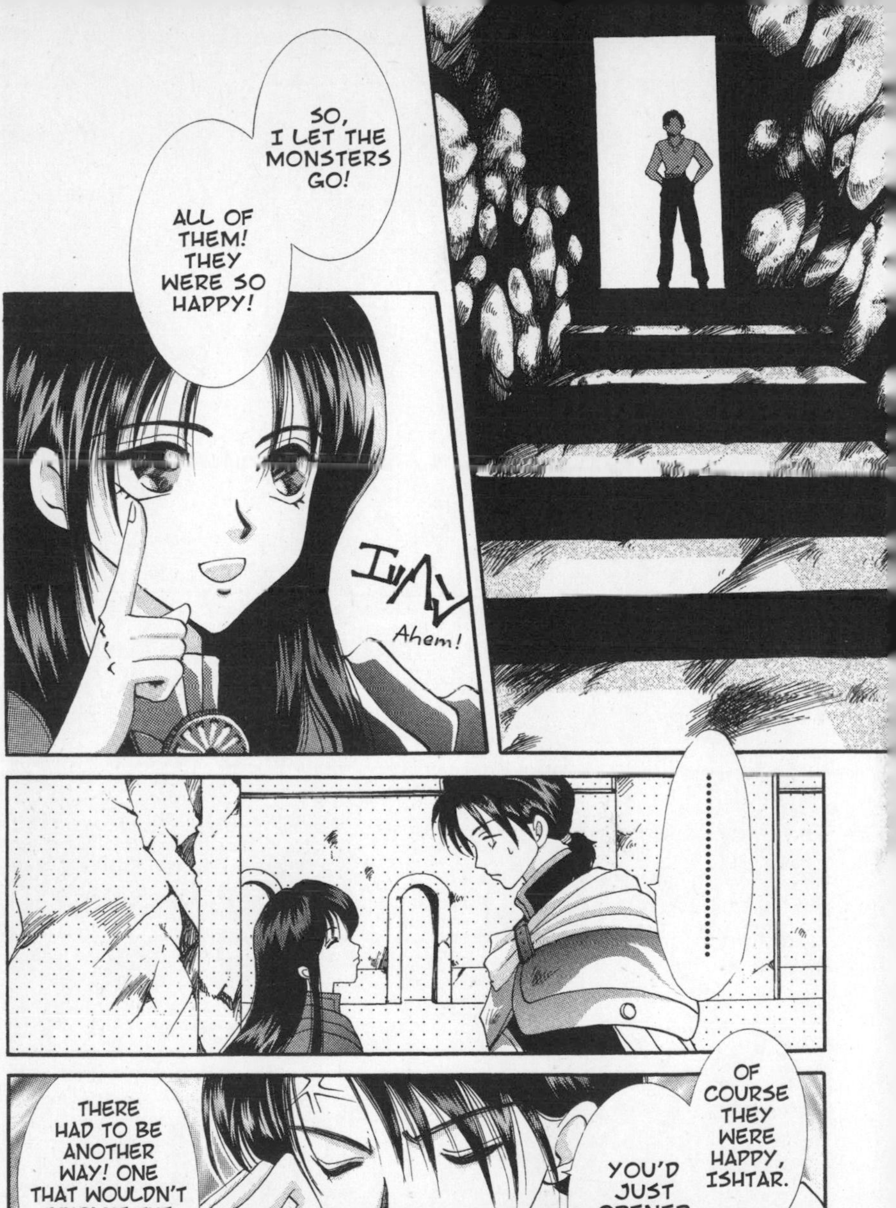
SO, I LET THE MONSTERS GO!
ALL OF THEM! THEY WERE SO HAPPY!
Ahem!
......
OF COURSE THEY WERE HAPPY, ISHTAR.
YOU'D JUST OPENED THE BUFFET!
THERE HAD TO BE ANOTHER WAY! ONE THAT WOULDN'T INVOLVE THE DESTRUCTION OF MOST OF CI XENETH!

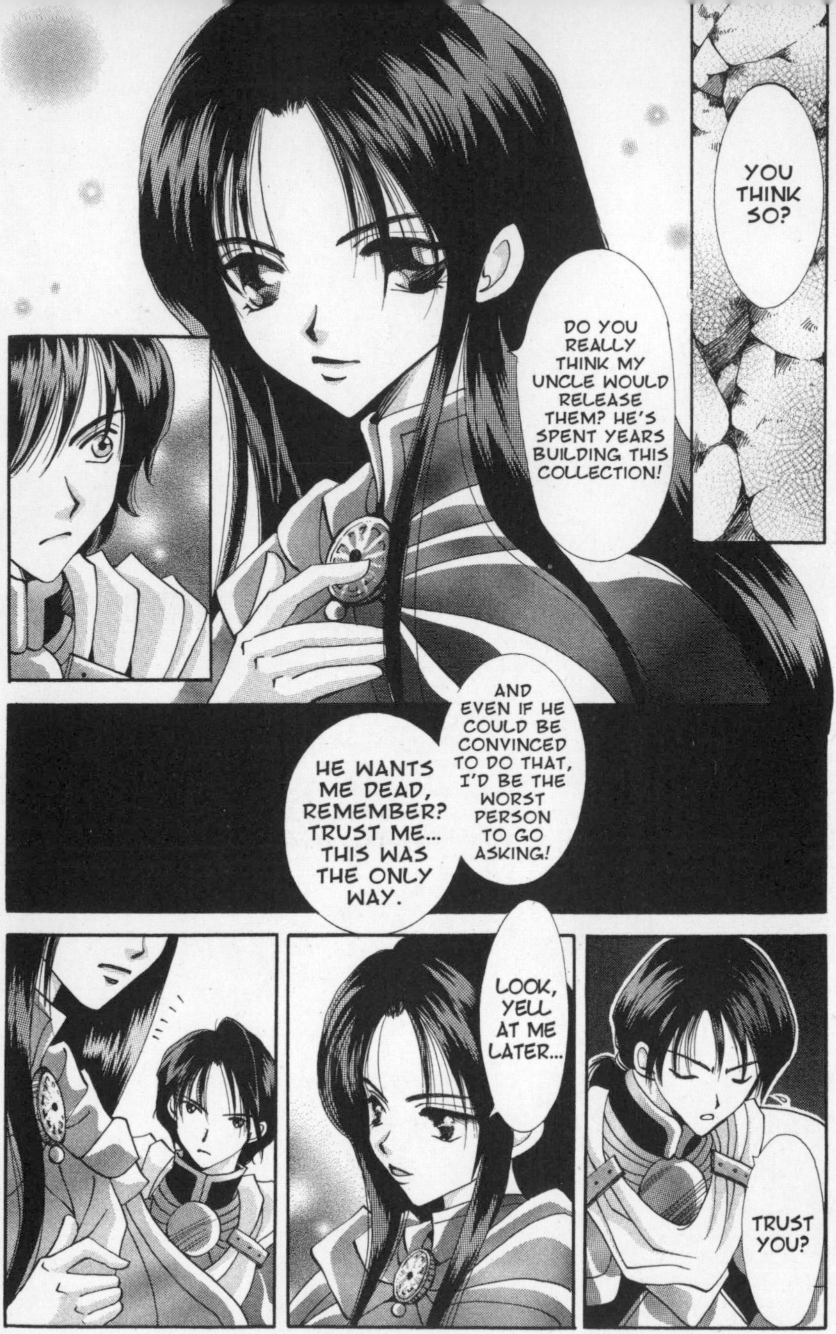
YOU THINK SO?
DO YOU REALLY THINK MY UNCLE WOULD RELEASE THEM? HE'S SPENT YEARS BUILDING THIS COLLECTION!
AND EVEN IF HE COULD BE CONVINCED TO DO THAT, I'D BE THE WORST PERSON TO GO ASKING!
HE WANTS ME DEAD, REMEMBER? TRUST ME... THIS WAS THE ONLY WAY.
TRUST YOU?
LOOK, YELL AT ME LATER...

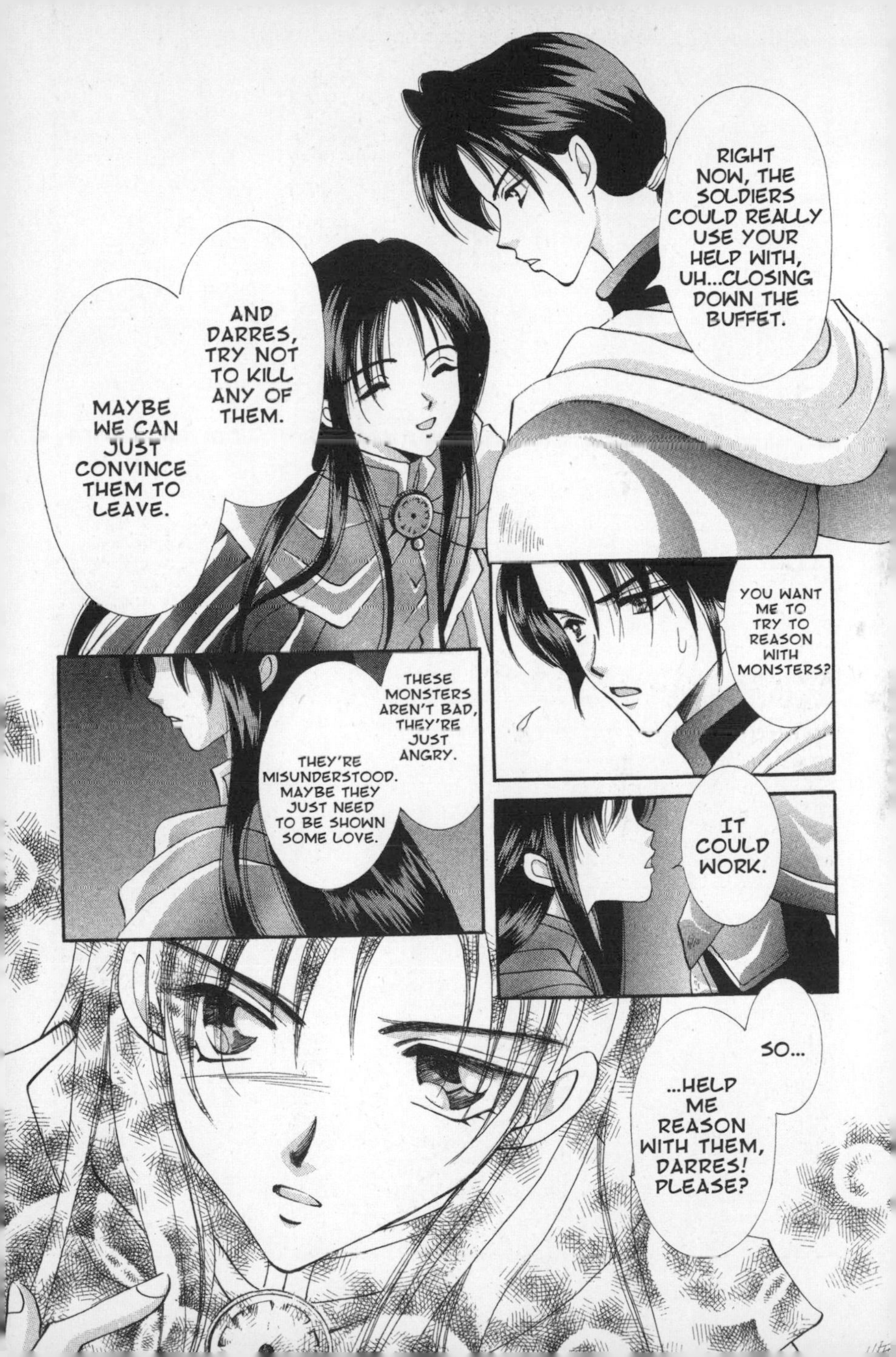
RIGHT NOW, THE SOLDIERS COULD REALLY USE YOUR HELP WITH, UH...CLOSING DOWN THE BUFFET.
AND DARRES, TRY NOT TO KILL ANY OF THEM.
MAYBE WE CAN JUST CONVINCE THEM TO LEAVE.
YOU WANT ME TO TRY TO REASON WITH MONSTERS?
IT COULD WORK.
THESE MONSTERS AREN'T BAD, THEY'RE JUST ANGRY.
THEY'RE MISUNDERSTOOD. MAYBE THEY JUST NEED TO BE SHOWN SOME LOVE.
SO...
...HELP ME REASON WITH THEM, DARRES! PLEASE?

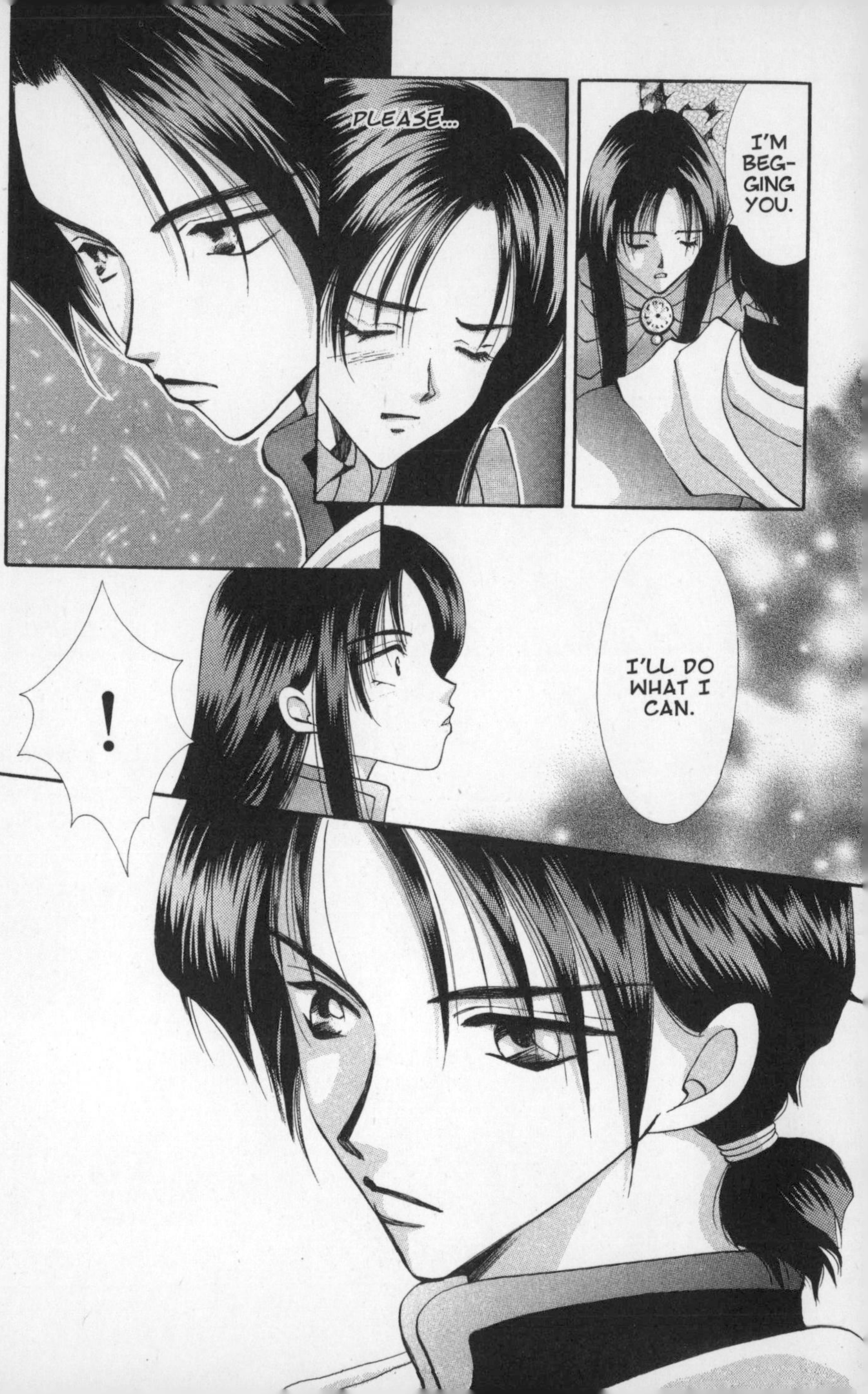
I'M BEG-GING YOU.
PLEASE...
I'LL DO WHAT I CAN.
!

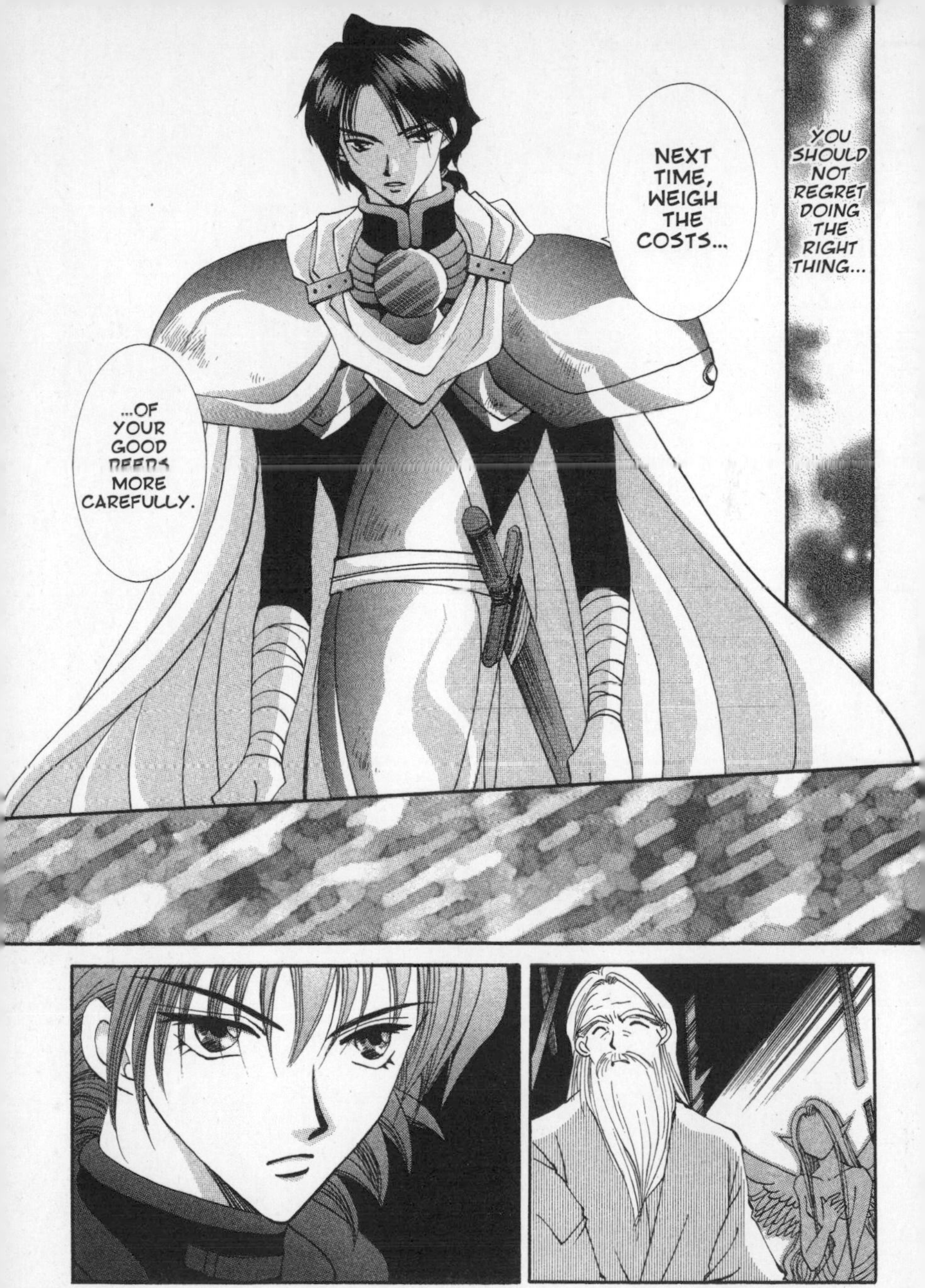
YOU SHOULD NOT REGRET DOING THE RIGHT THING...
NEXT TIME, WEIGH THE COSTS...
...OF YOUR GOOD DEEDS MORE CAREFULLY.

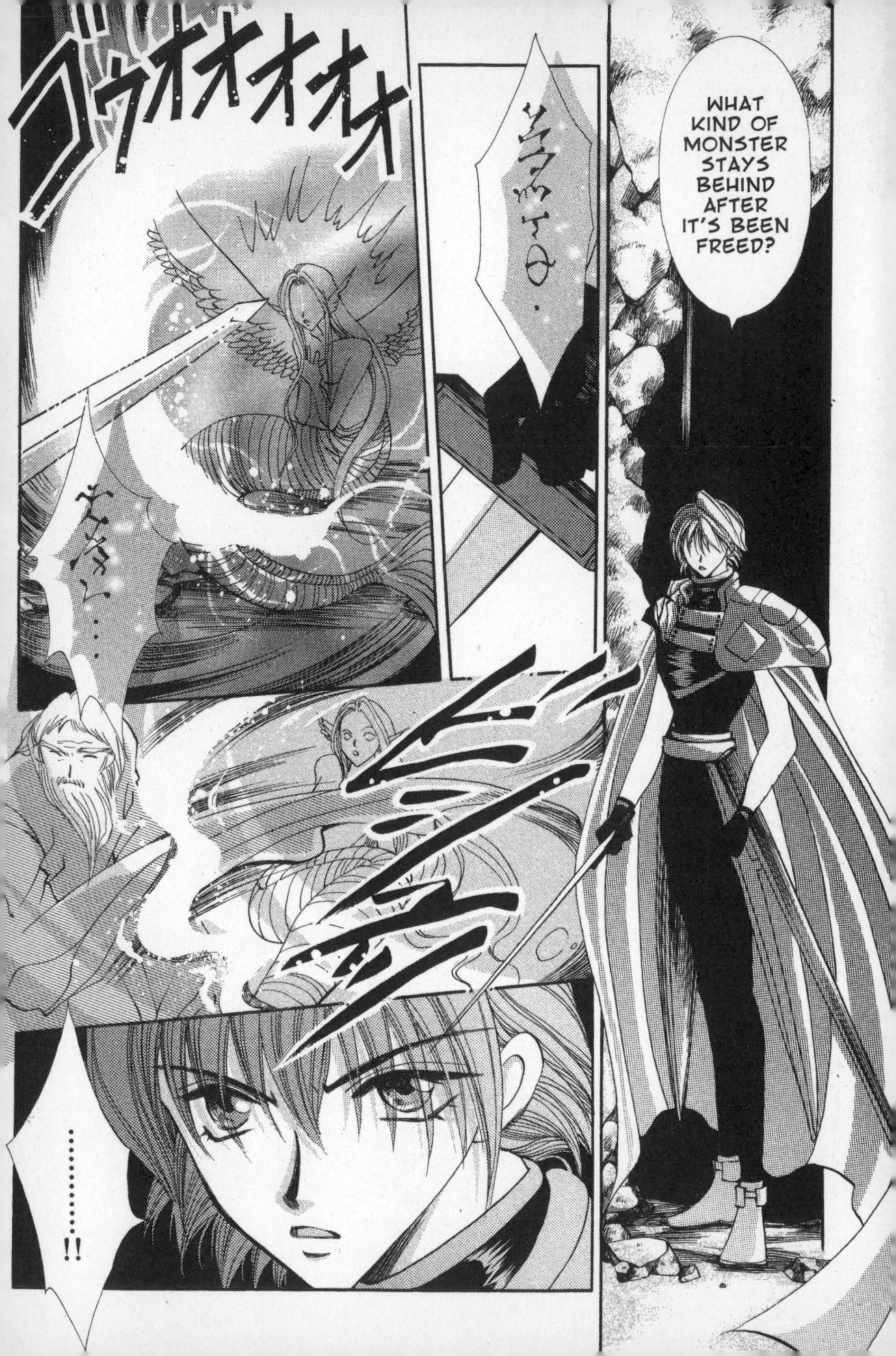
WHAT KIND OF MONSTER STAYS BEHIND AFTER IT'S BEEN FREED?
......!!

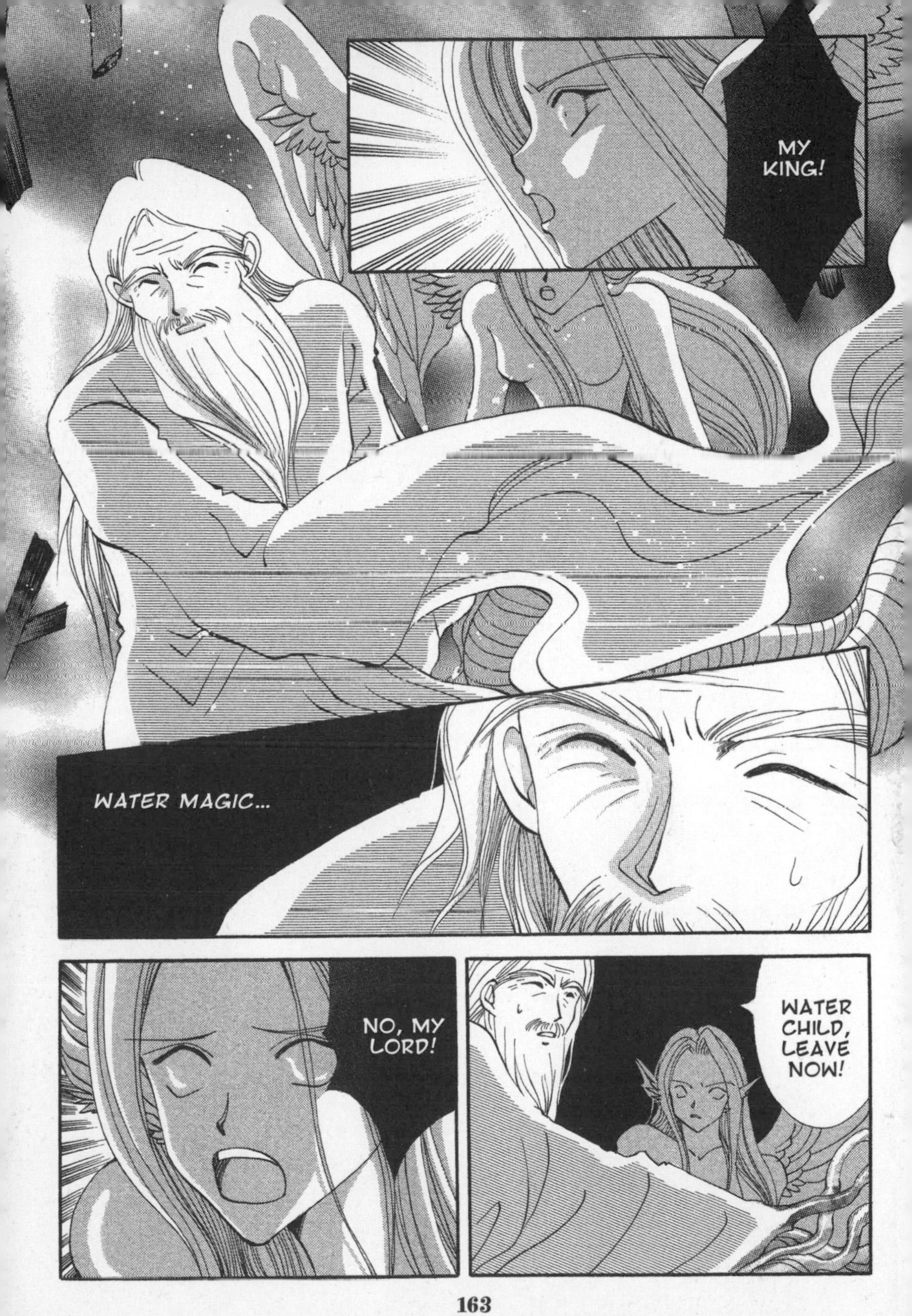
MY KING!
WATER MAGIC...
WATER CHILD, LEAVE NOW!
NO, MY LORD!

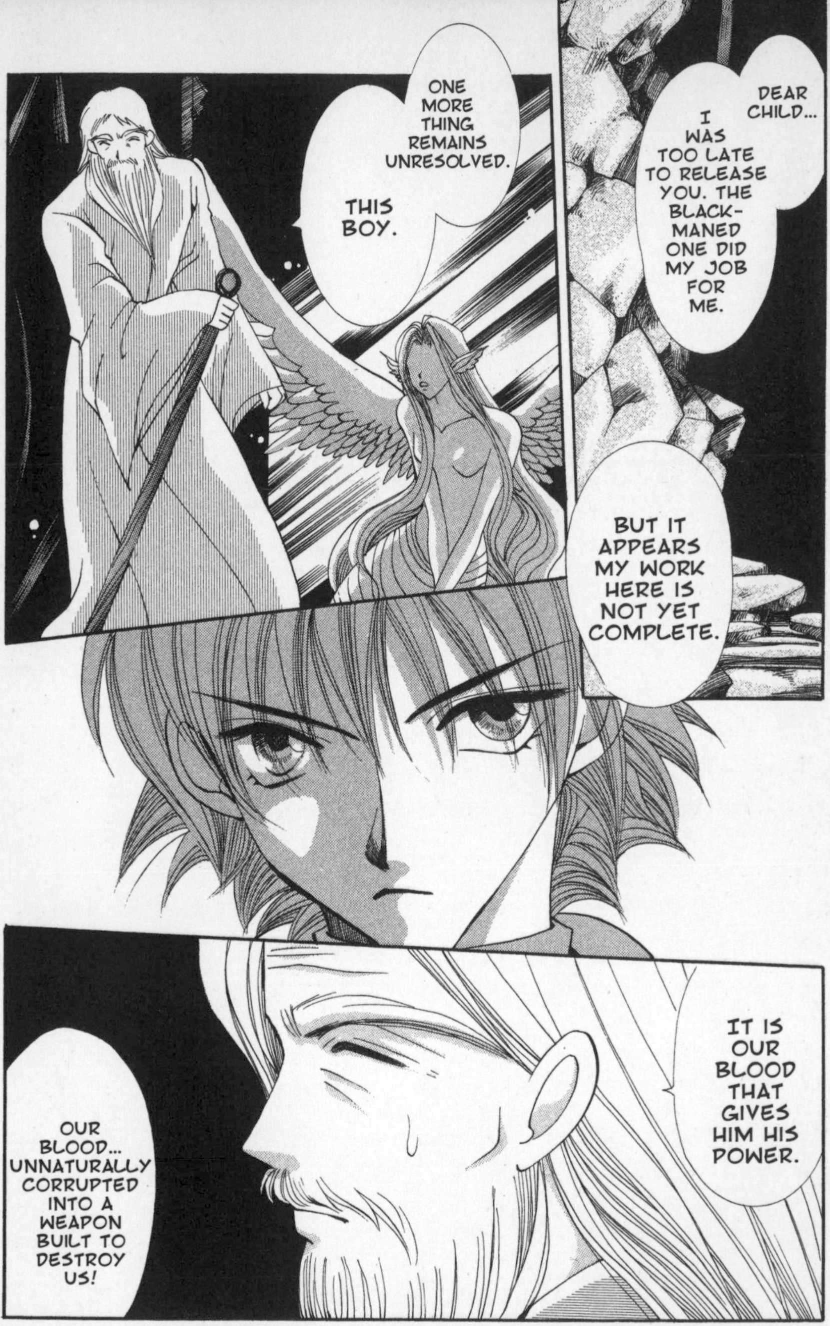
DEAR CHILD...
I WAS TOO LATE TO RELEASE YOU. THE BLACK-MANED ONE DID MY JOB FOR ME.
BUT IT APPEARS MY WORK HERE IS NOT YET COMPLETE.
ONE MORE THING REMAINS UNRESOLVED.
THIS BOY.
IT IS OUR BLOOD THAT GIVES HIM HIS POWER.
OUR BLOOD... UNNATURALLY CORRUPTED INTO A WEAPON BUILT TO DESTROY US!

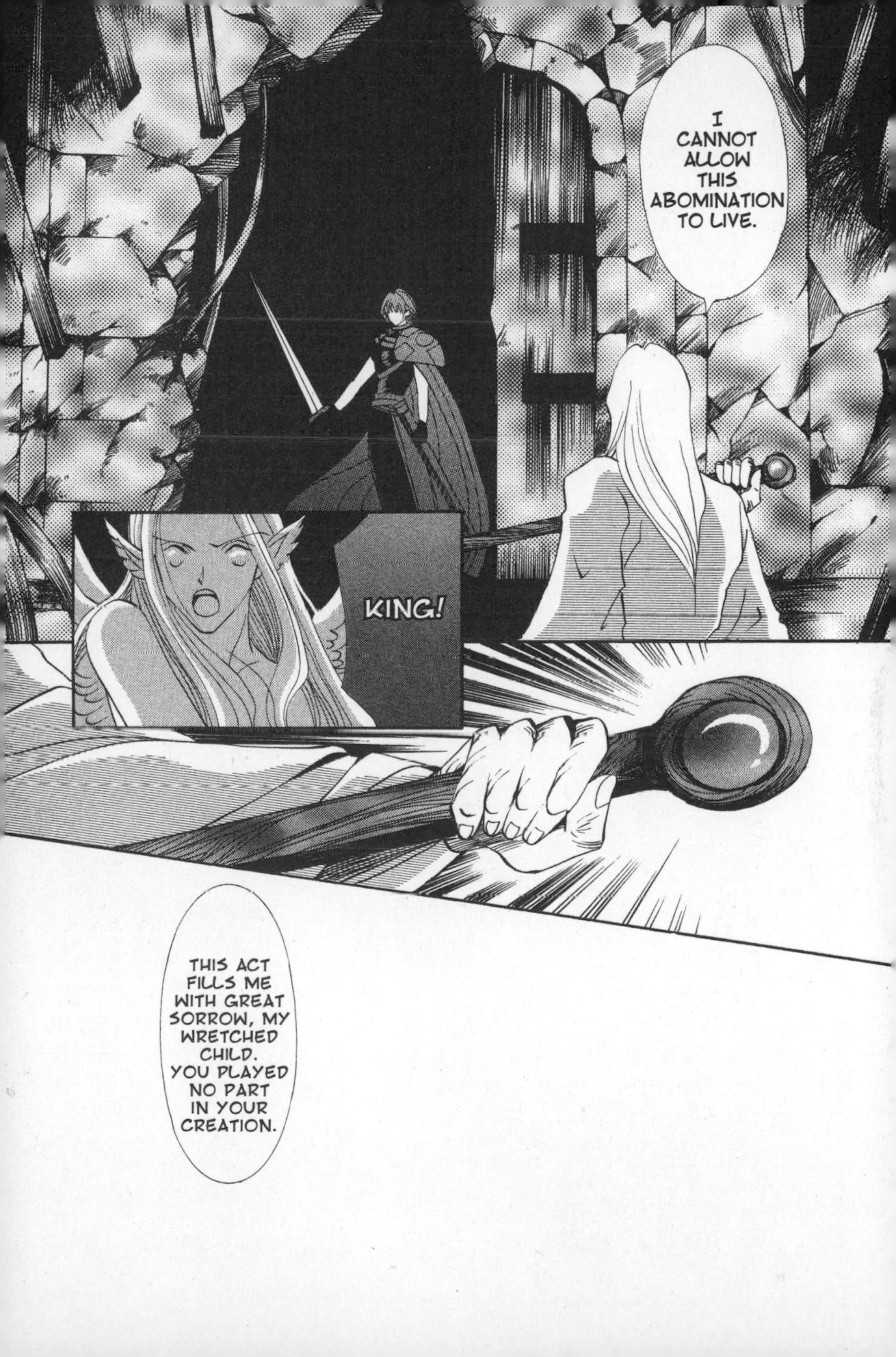
I CANNOT ALLOW THIS ABOMINATION TO LIVE.
KING!
THIS ACT FILLS ME WITH GREAT SORROW, MY WRETCHED CHILD. YOU PLAYED NO PART IN YOUR CREATION.

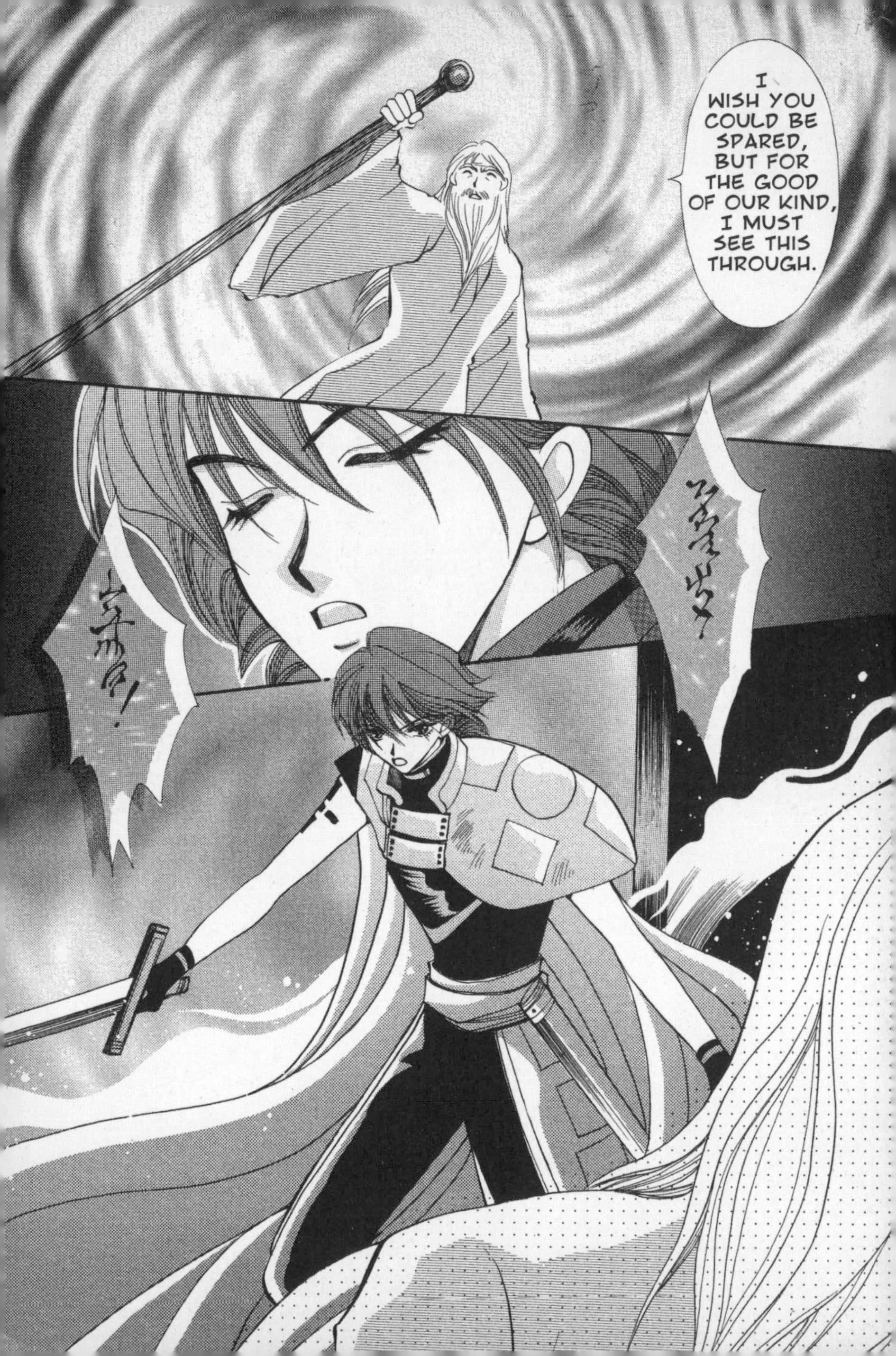
I WISH YOU COULD BE SPARED, BUT FOR THE GOOD OF OUR KIND, I MUST SEE THIS THROUGH.

吸血遊戯

東領篇（シー・ゼネス）

Act.13

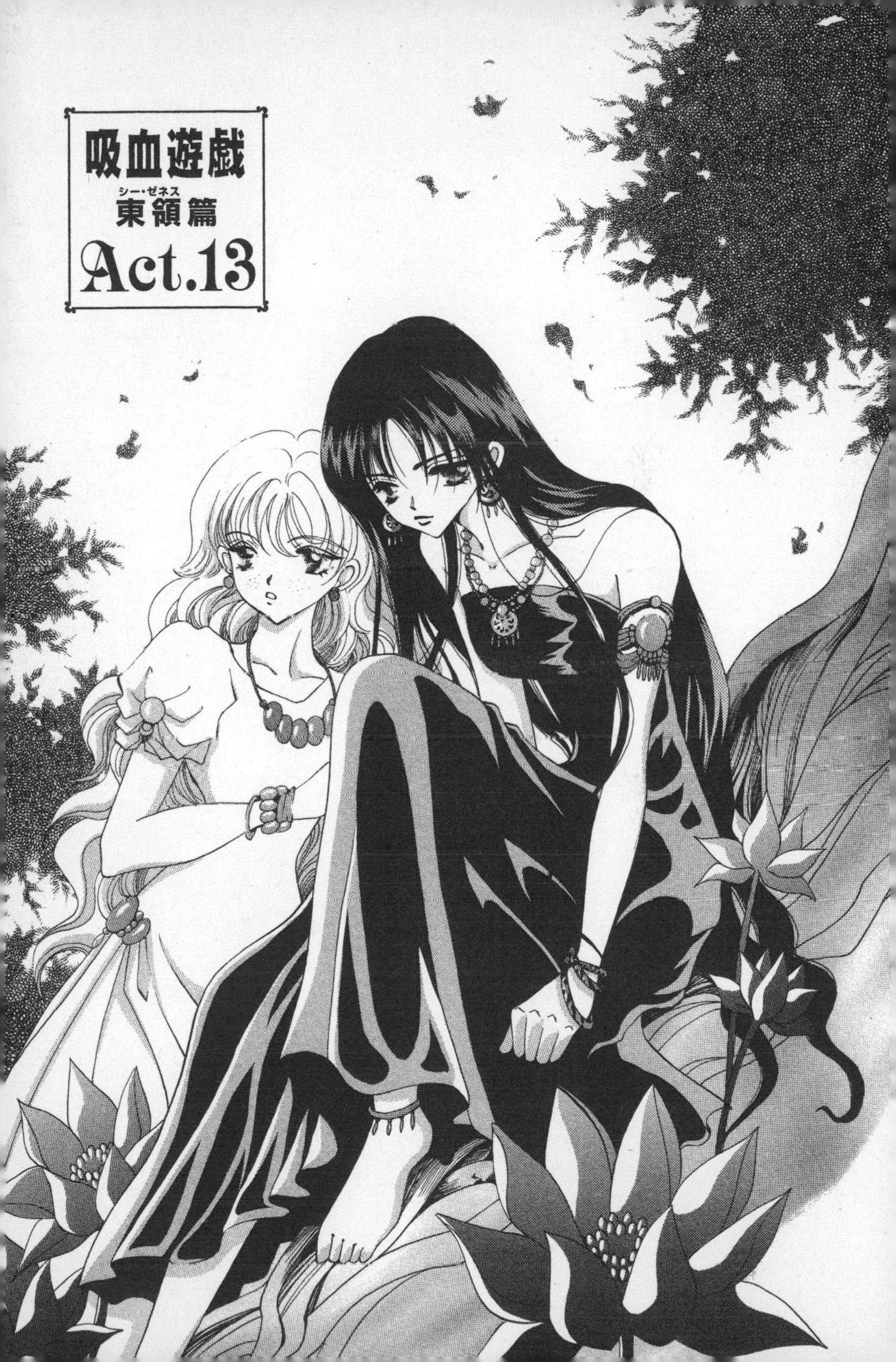

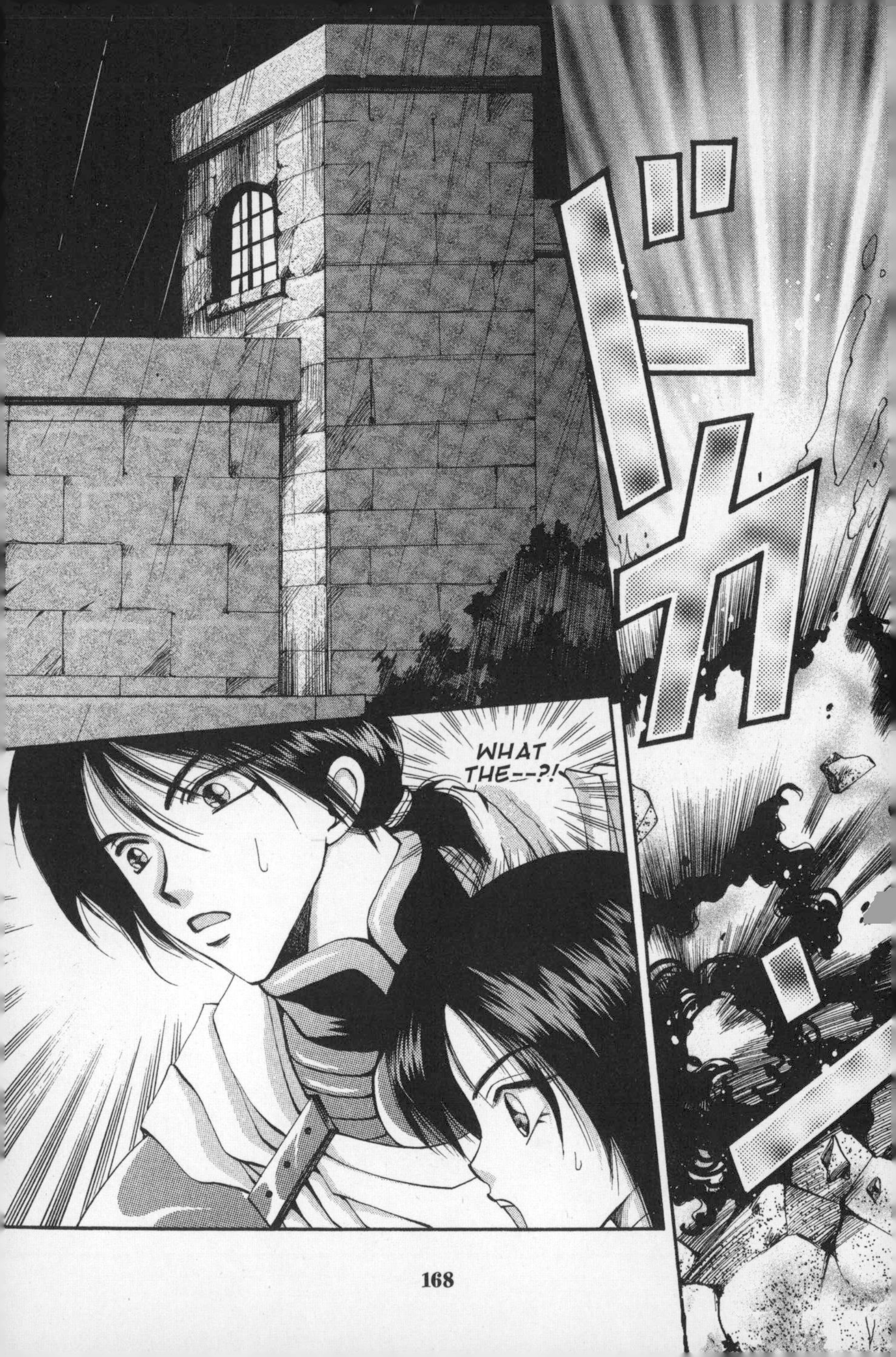
WHAT THE--?!

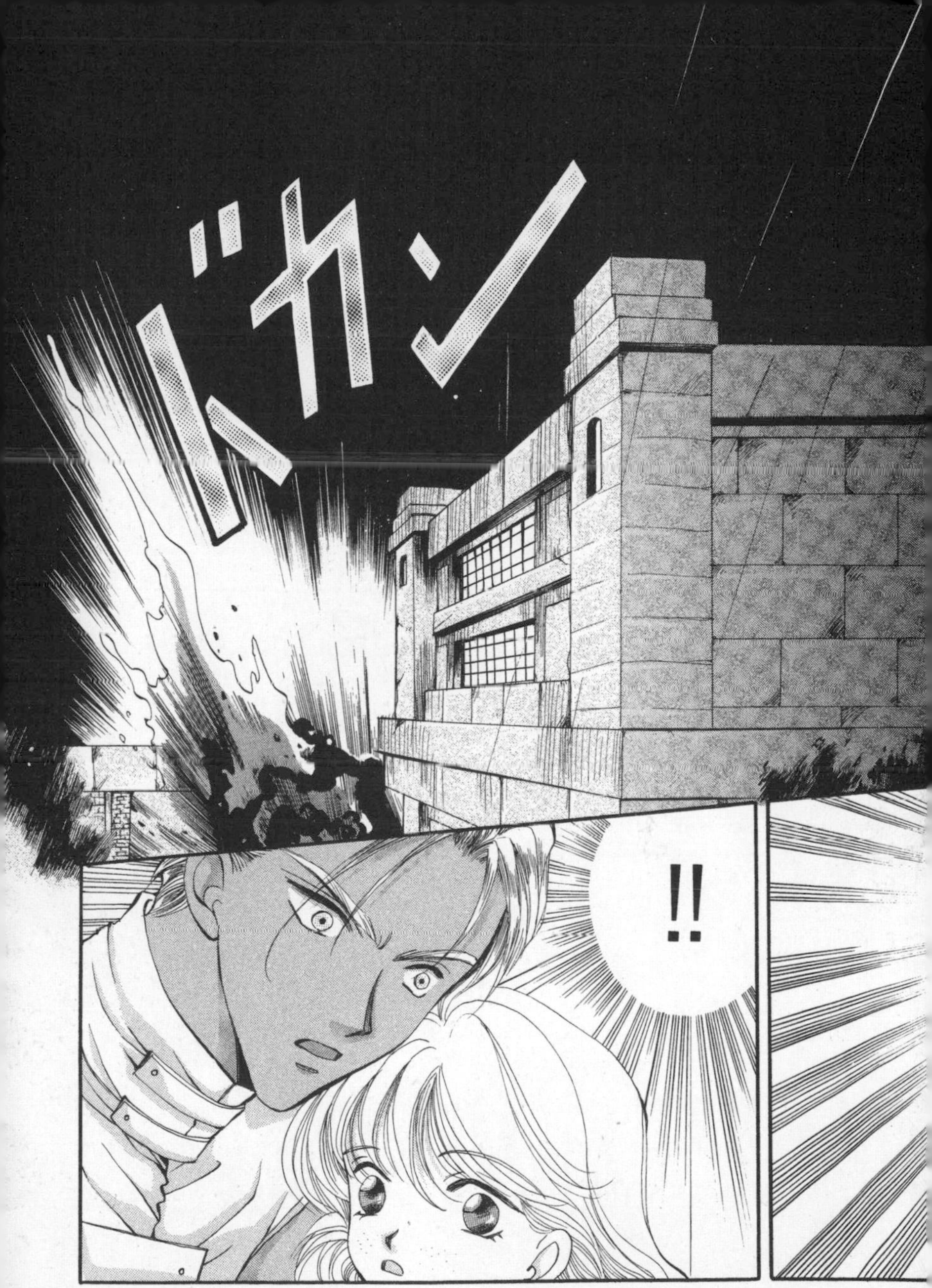
バカン
!!

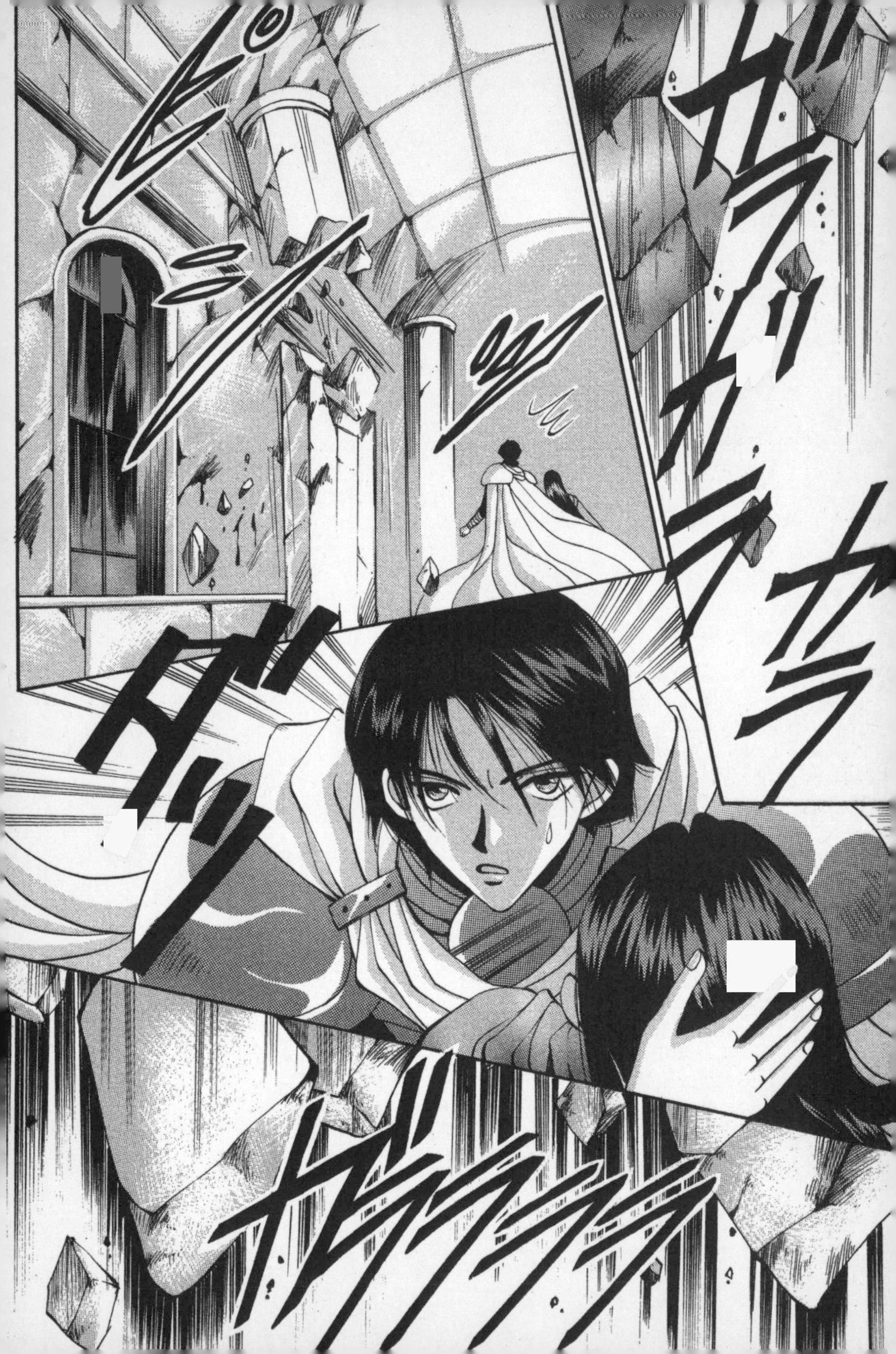
ダッ

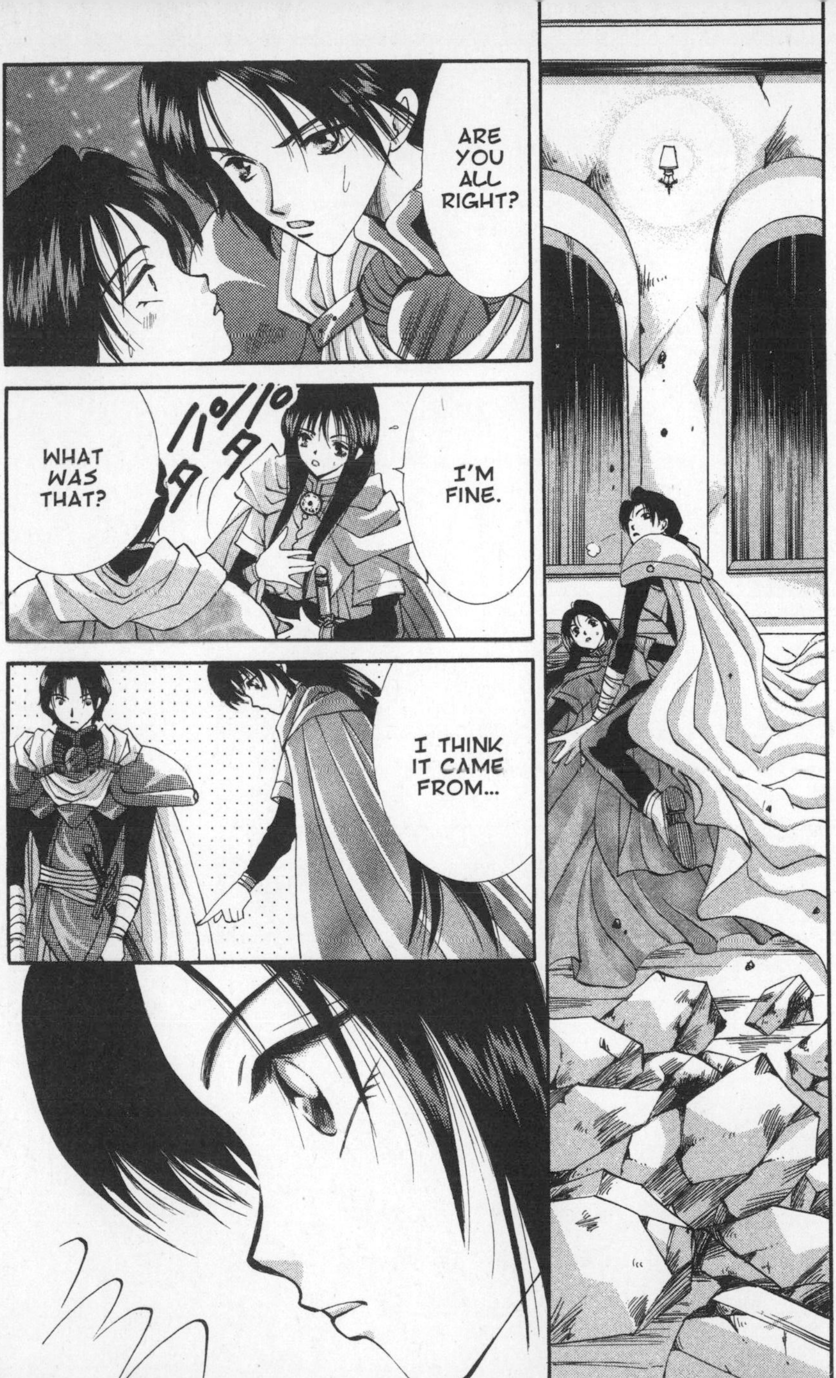
ARE YOU ALL RIGHT?
I'M FINE.
パタパタ
WHAT WAS THAT?
I THINK IT CAME FROM...

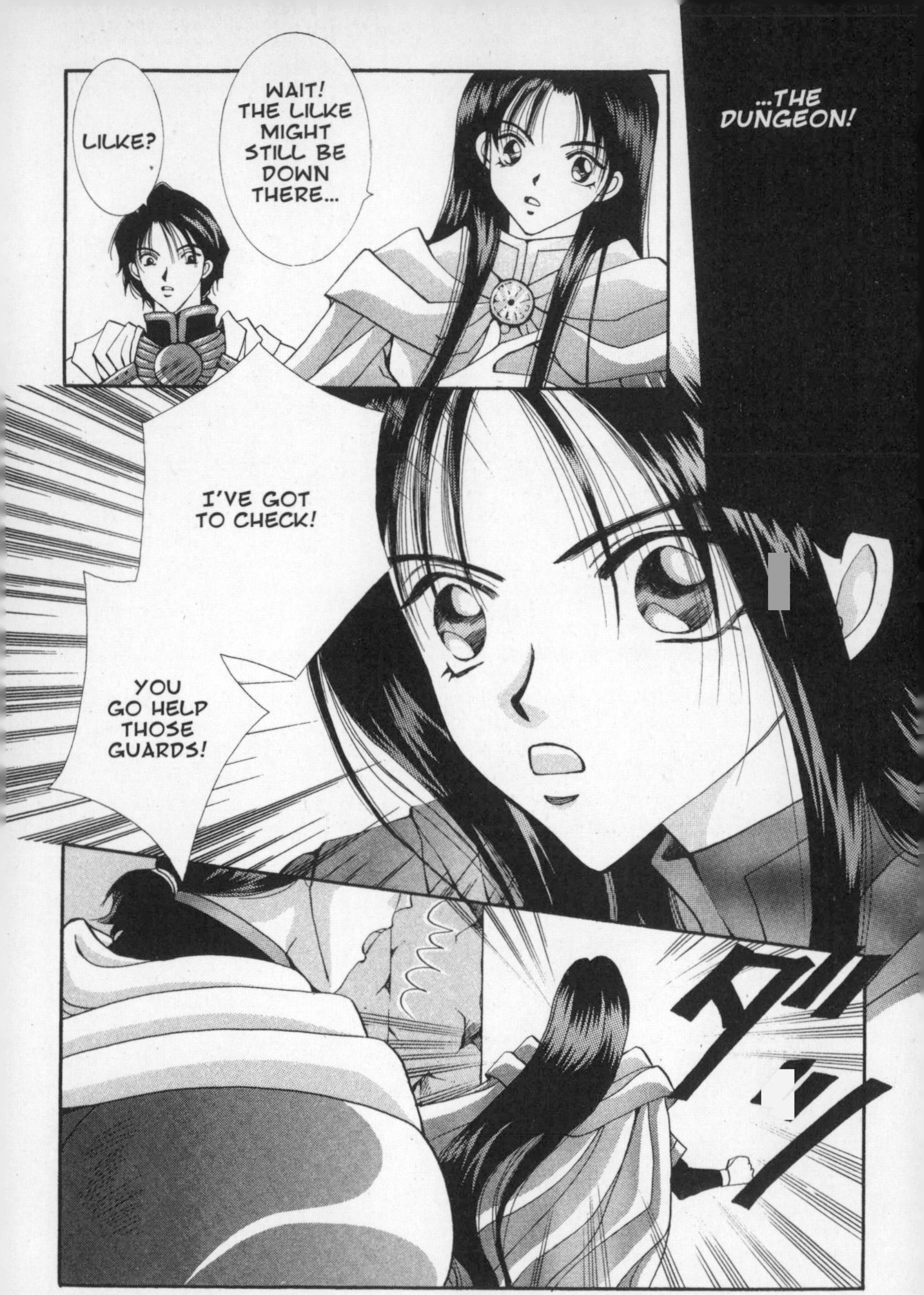
...THE DUNGEON!
WAIT! THE LILKE MIGHT STILL BE DOWN THERE...
LILKE?
I'VE GOT TO CHECK!
YOU GO HELP THOSE GUARDS!

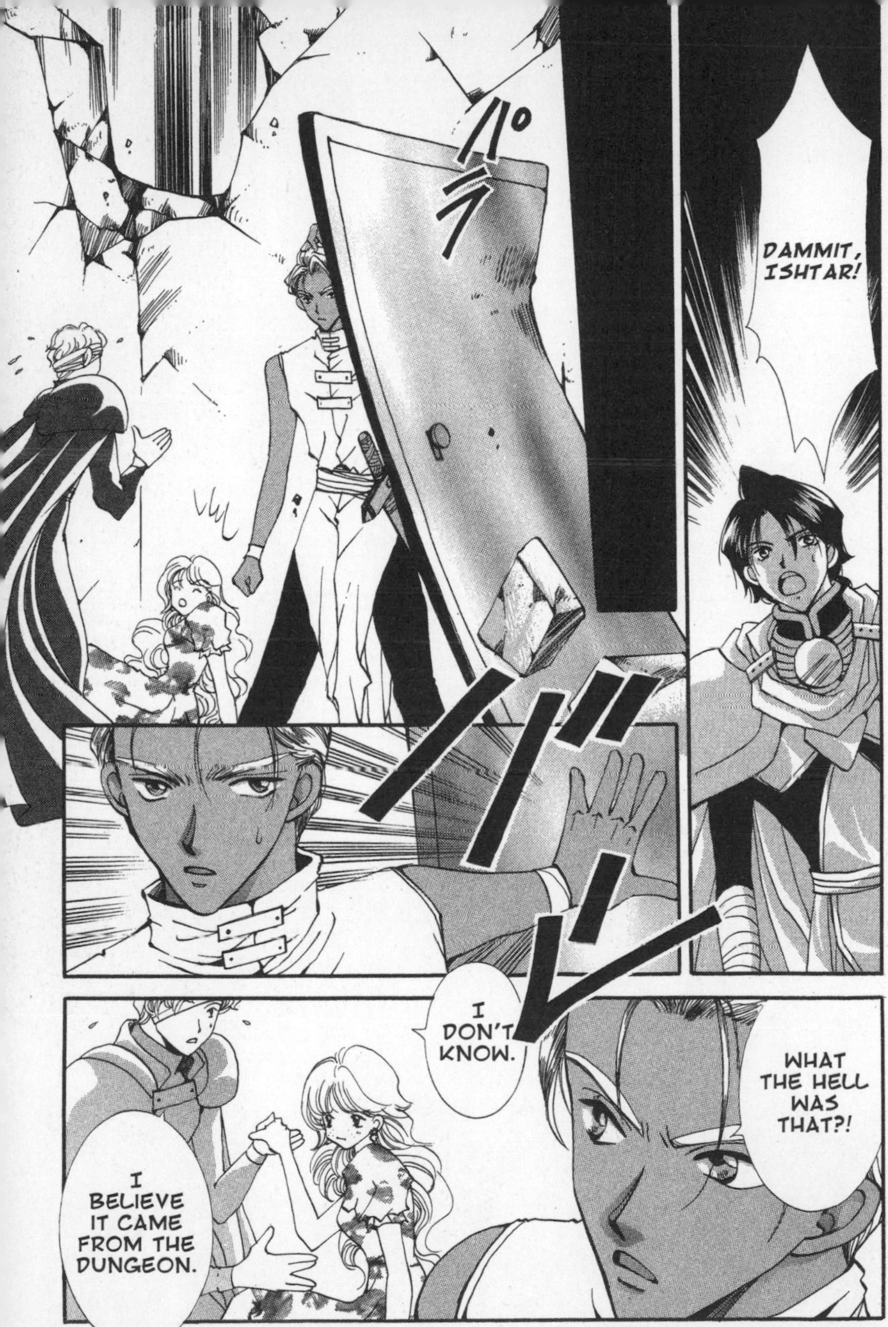
DAMMIT, ISHTAR!
パラ
バン
WHAT THE HELL WAS THAT?!
I DON'T KNOW.
I BELIEVE IT CAME FROM THE DUNGEON.

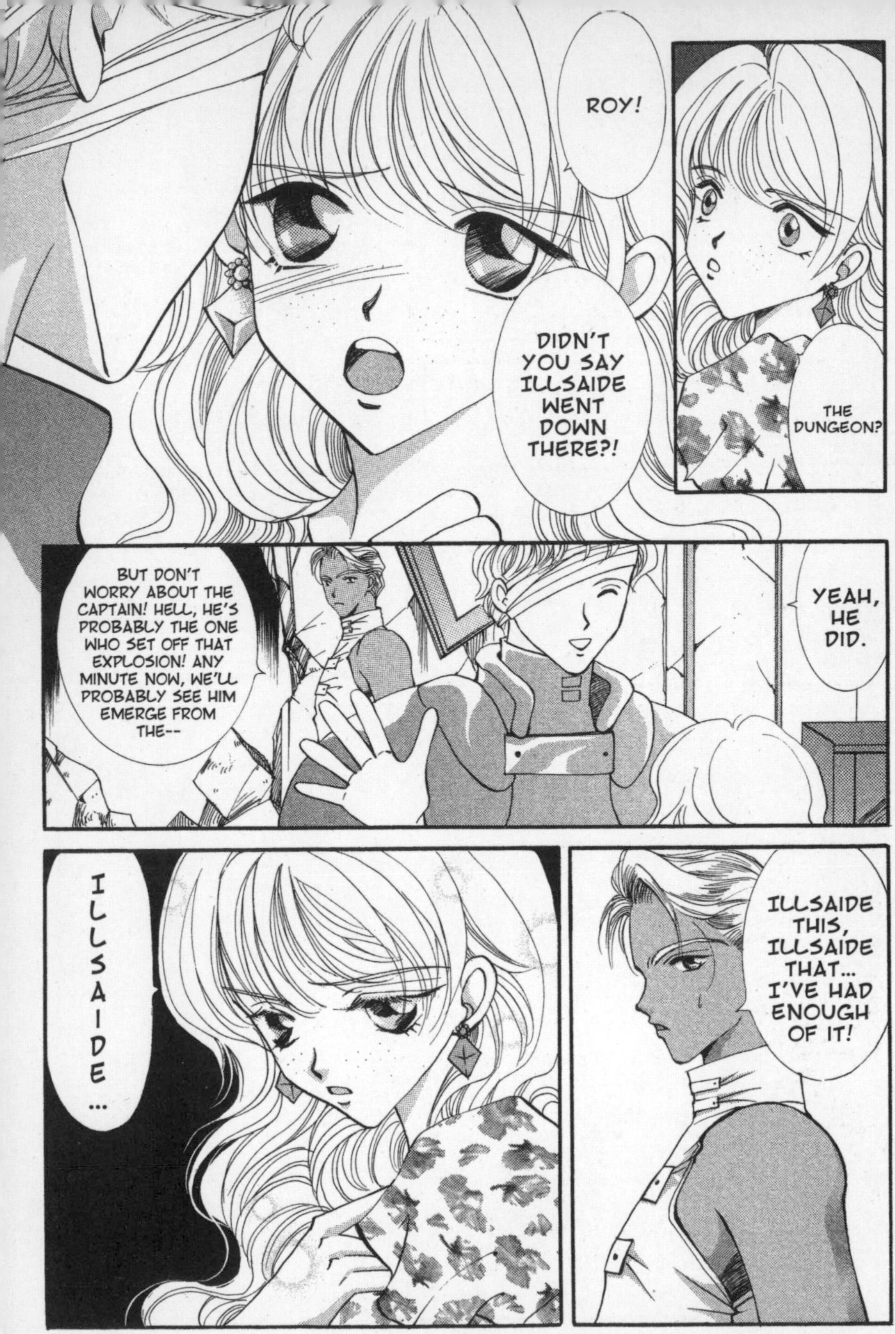
THE DUNGEON?
ROY!
DIDN'T YOU SAY ILLSAIDE WENT DOWN THERE?!
YEAH, HE DID.
BUT DON'T WORRY ABOUT THE CAPTAIN! HELL, HE'S PROBABLY THE ONE WHO SET OFF THAT EXPLOSION! ANY MINUTE NOW, WE'LL PROBABLY SEE HIM EMERGE FROM THE--
ILLSAIDE THIS, ILLSAIDE THAT... I'VE HAD ENOUGH OF IT!
ILLSAIDE...

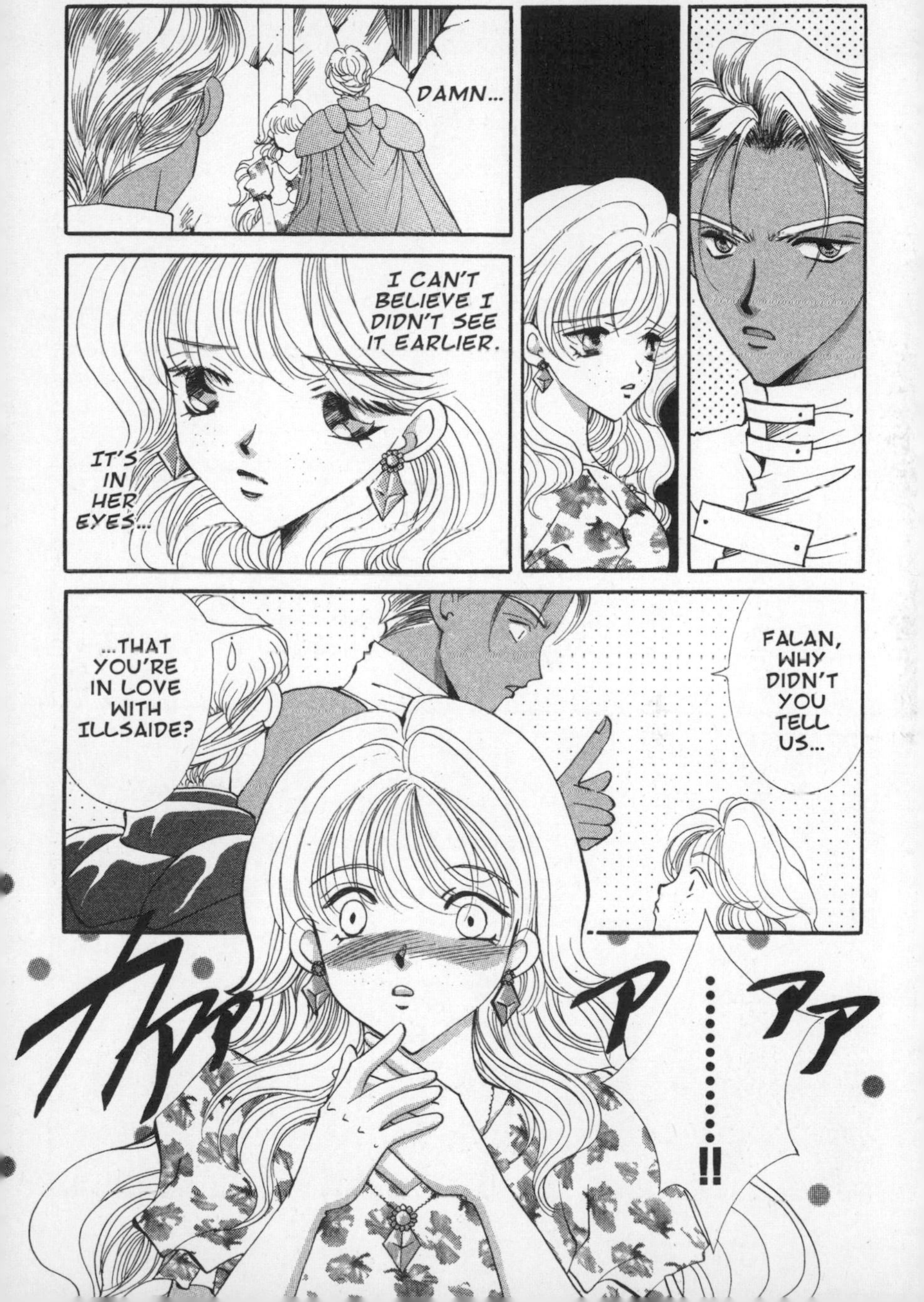
DAMN...
I CAN'T BELIEVE I DIDN'T SEE IT EARLIER.
IT'S IN HER EYES...
FALAN, WHY DIDN'T YOU TELL US...
...THAT YOU'RE IN LOVE WITH ILLSAIDE?
..........!!

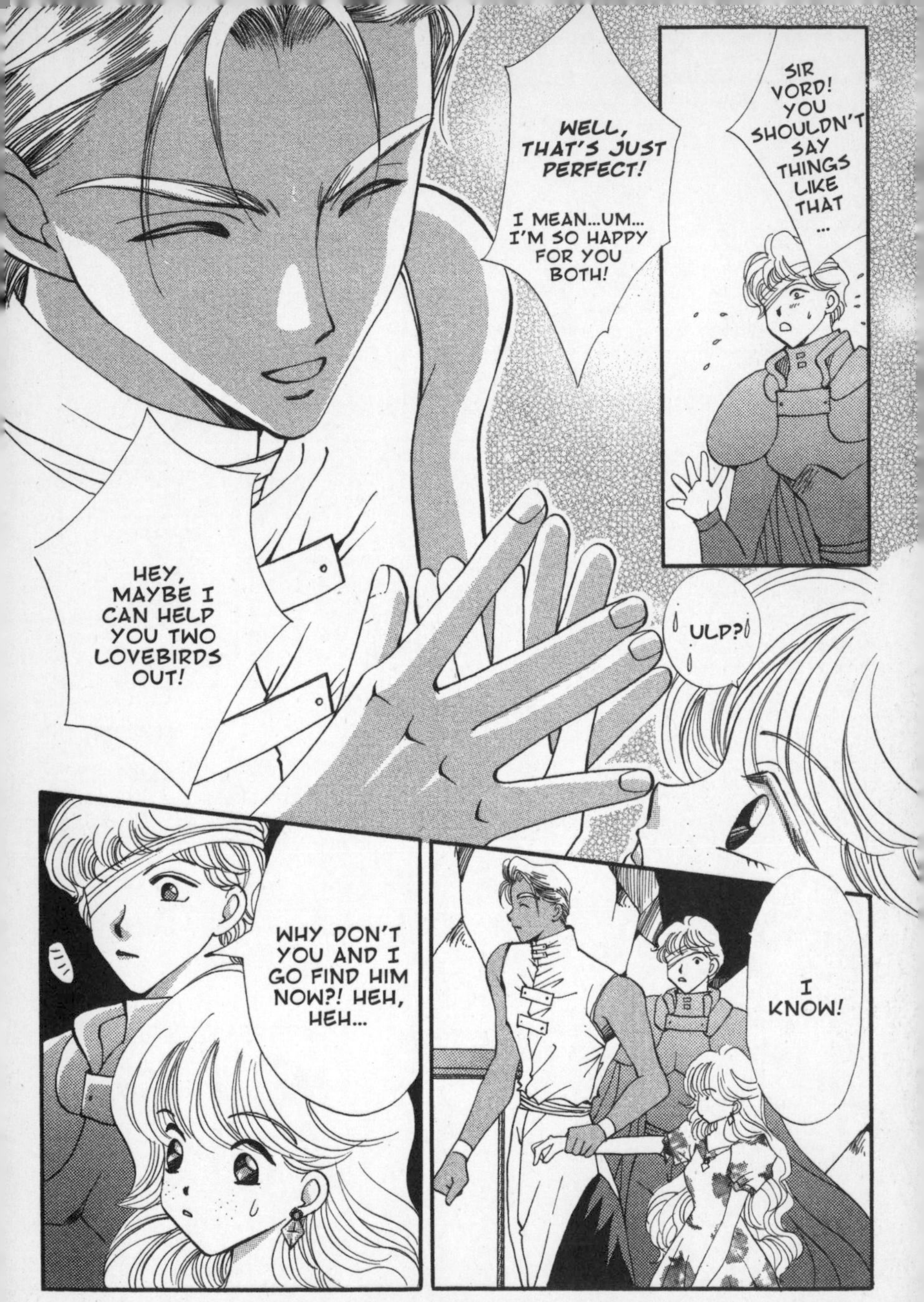
WELL, THAT'S JUST PERFECT!
I MEAN...UM... I'M SO HAPPY FOR YOU BOTH!
SIR VORD! YOU SHOULDN'T SAY THINGS LIKE THAT ...
ULP?!
HEY, MAYBE I CAN HELP YOU TWO LOVEBIRDS OUT!
I KNOW!
WHY DON'T YOU AND I GO FIND HIM NOW?! HEH, HEH...

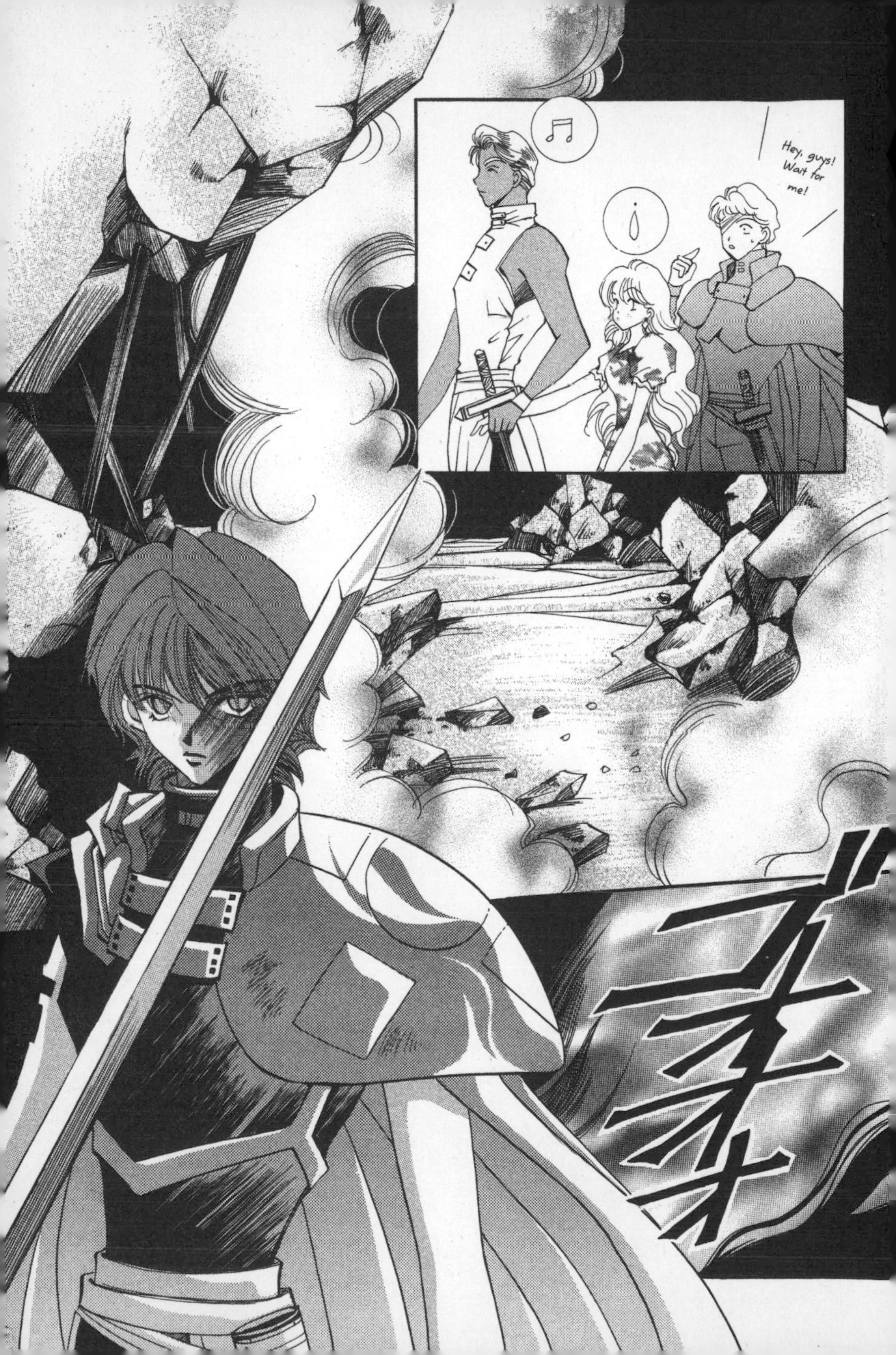
Hey, guys! Wait for me!
♫
ゴォォ

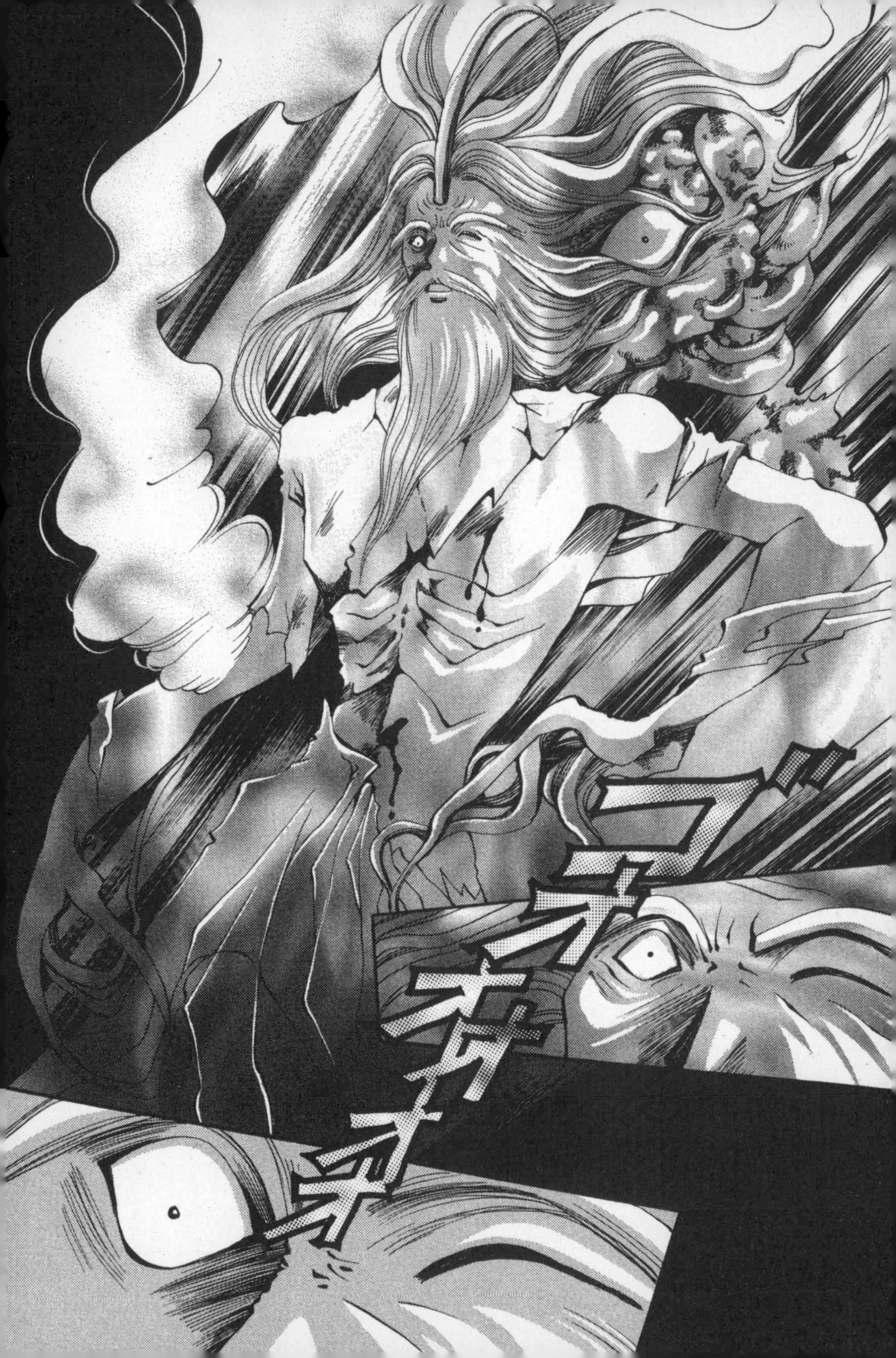
ゴオオオオオ

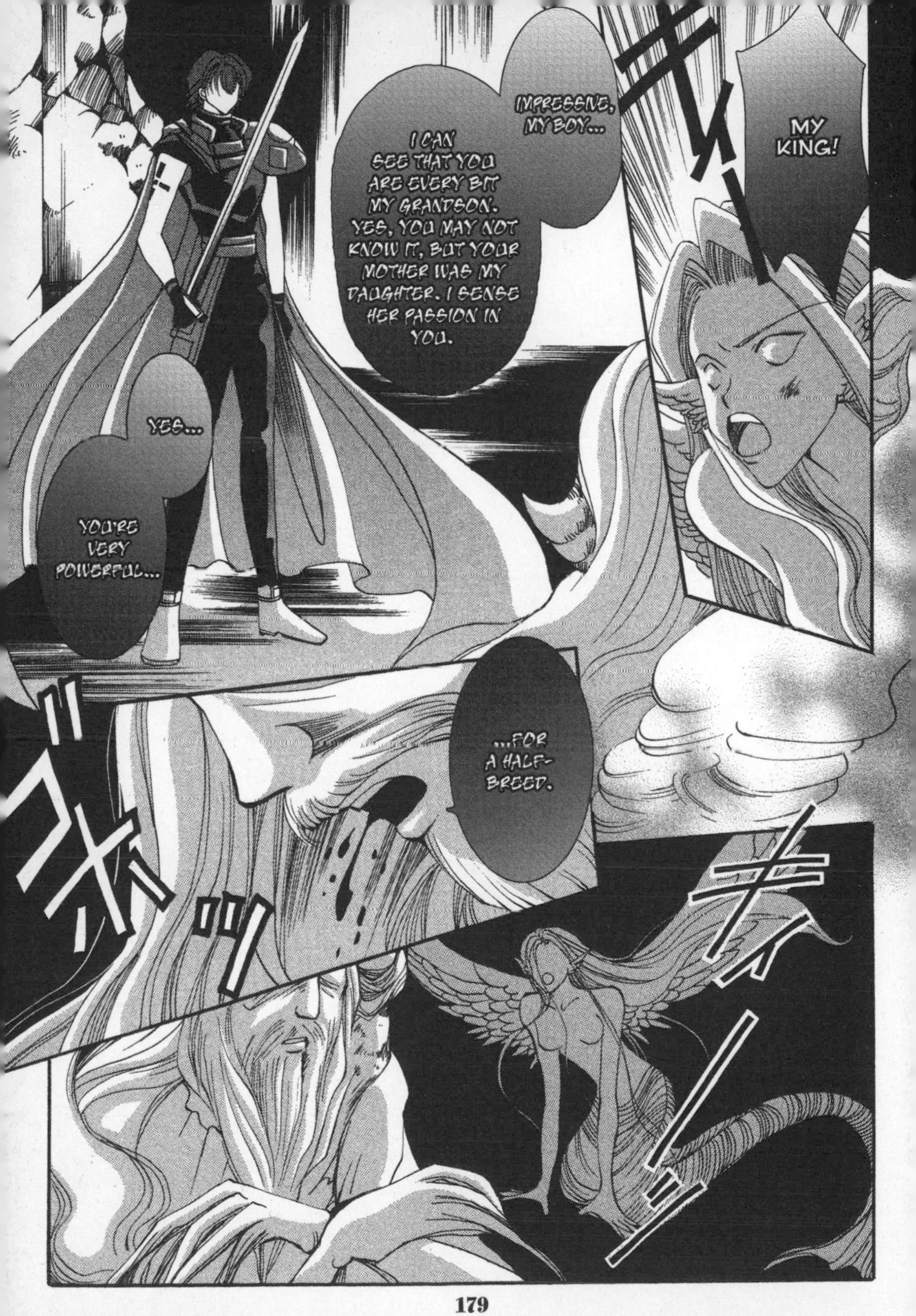
MY KING!
IMPRESSIVE, MY BOY...
I CAN SEE THAT YOU ARE EVERY BIT MY GRANDSON. YES, YOU MAY NOT KNOW IT, BUT YOUR MOTHER WAS MY DAUGHTER. I SENSE HER PASSION IN YOU.
YES...
YOU'RE VERY POWERFUL...
...FOR A HALF-BREED.

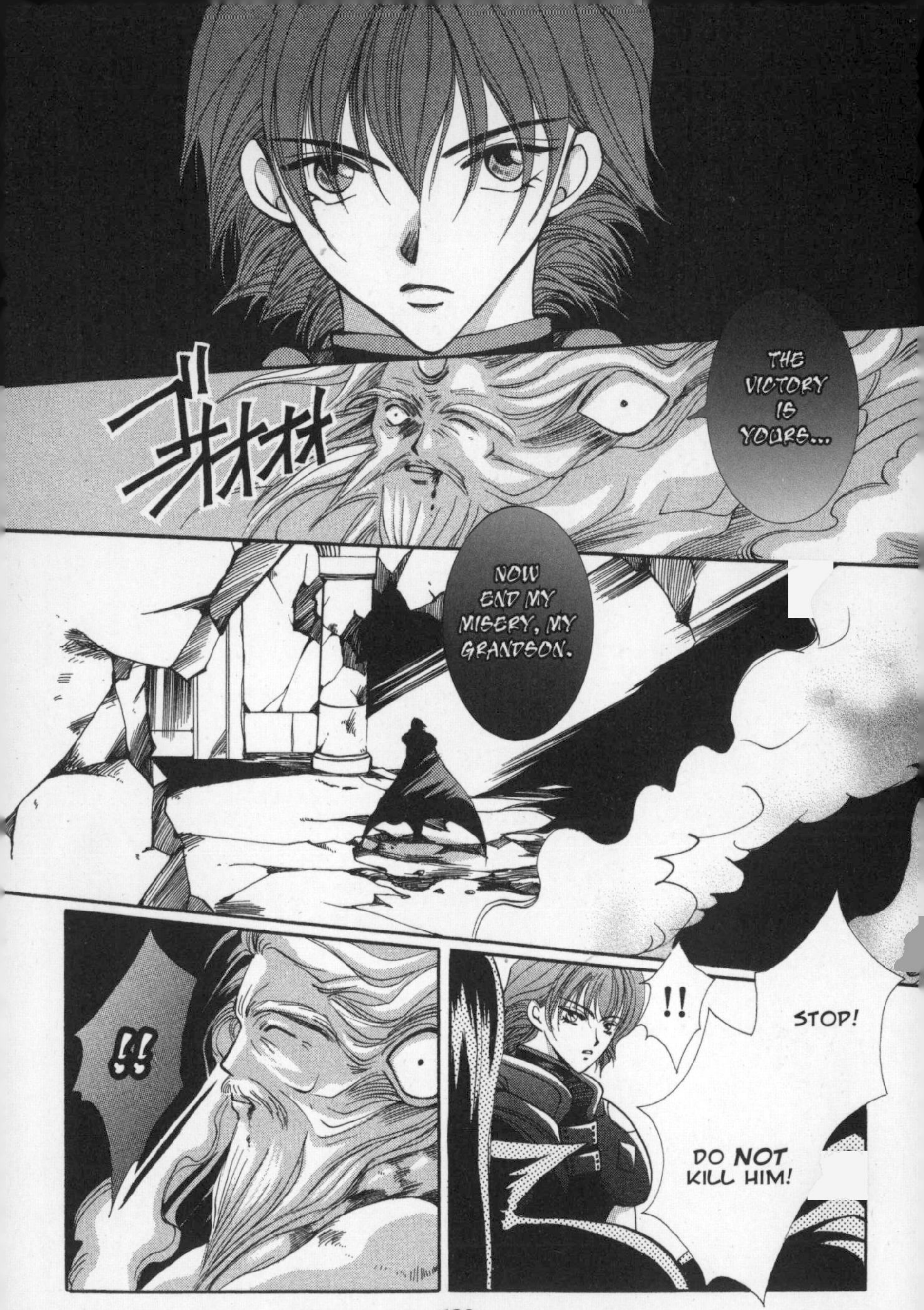
THE VICTORY IS YOURS...
ゴオオオ
NOW END MY MISERY, MY GRANDSON.
!!
STOP!
DO **NOT** KILL HIM!
!!

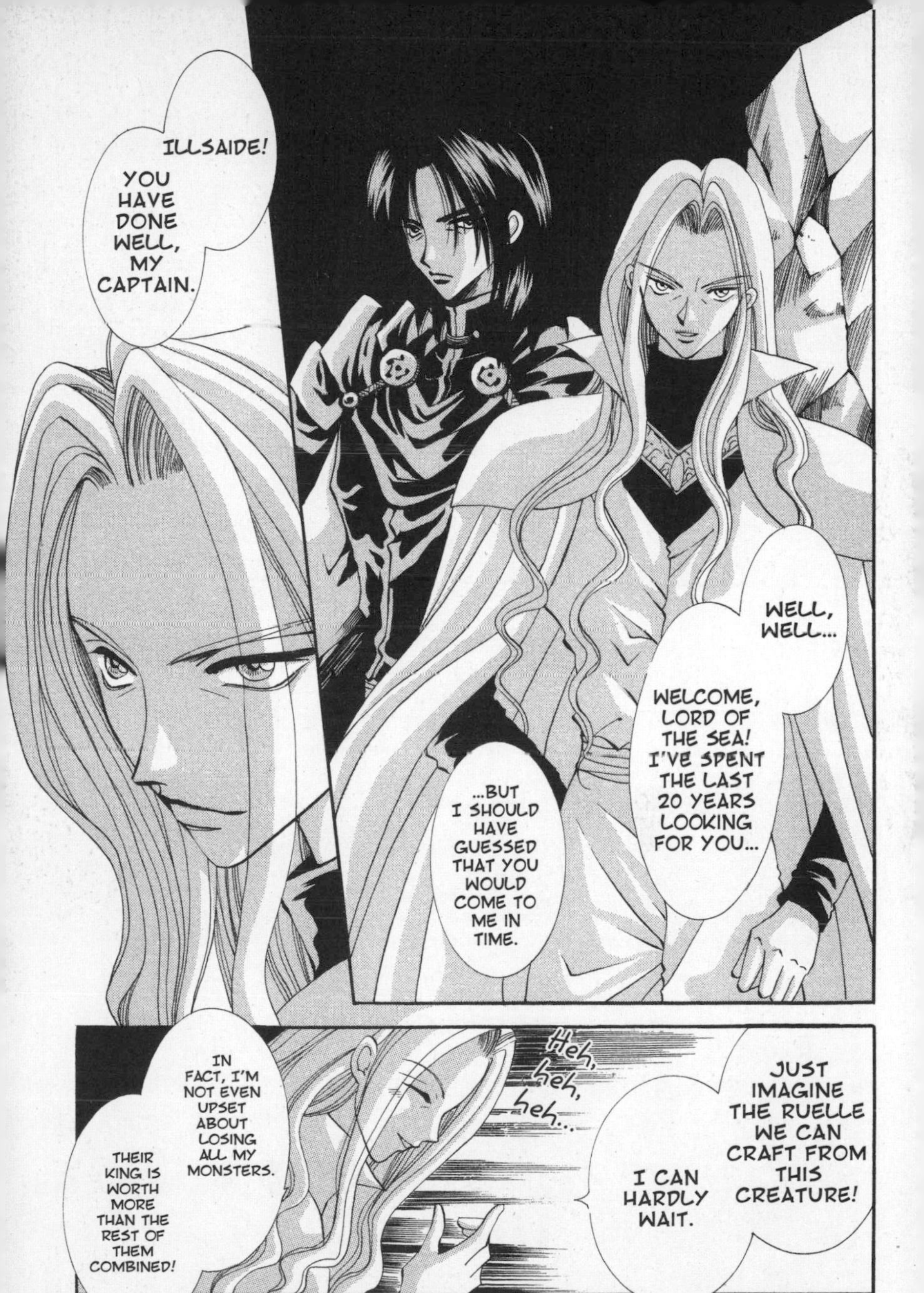
ILLSAIDE!
YOU HAVE DONE WELL, MY CAPTAIN.
WELL, WELL...
WELCOME, LORD OF THE SEA! I'VE SPENT THE LAST 20 YEARS LOOKING FOR YOU...
...BUT I SHOULD HAVE GUESSED THAT YOU WOULD COME TO ME IN TIME.
JUST IMAGINE THE RUELLE WE CAN CRAFT FROM THIS CREATURE!
I CAN HARDLY WAIT.
Heh, heh, heh...
IN FACT, I'M NOT EVEN UPSET ABOUT LOSING ALL MY MONSTERS.
THEIR KING IS WORTH MORE THAN THE REST OF THEM COMBINED!

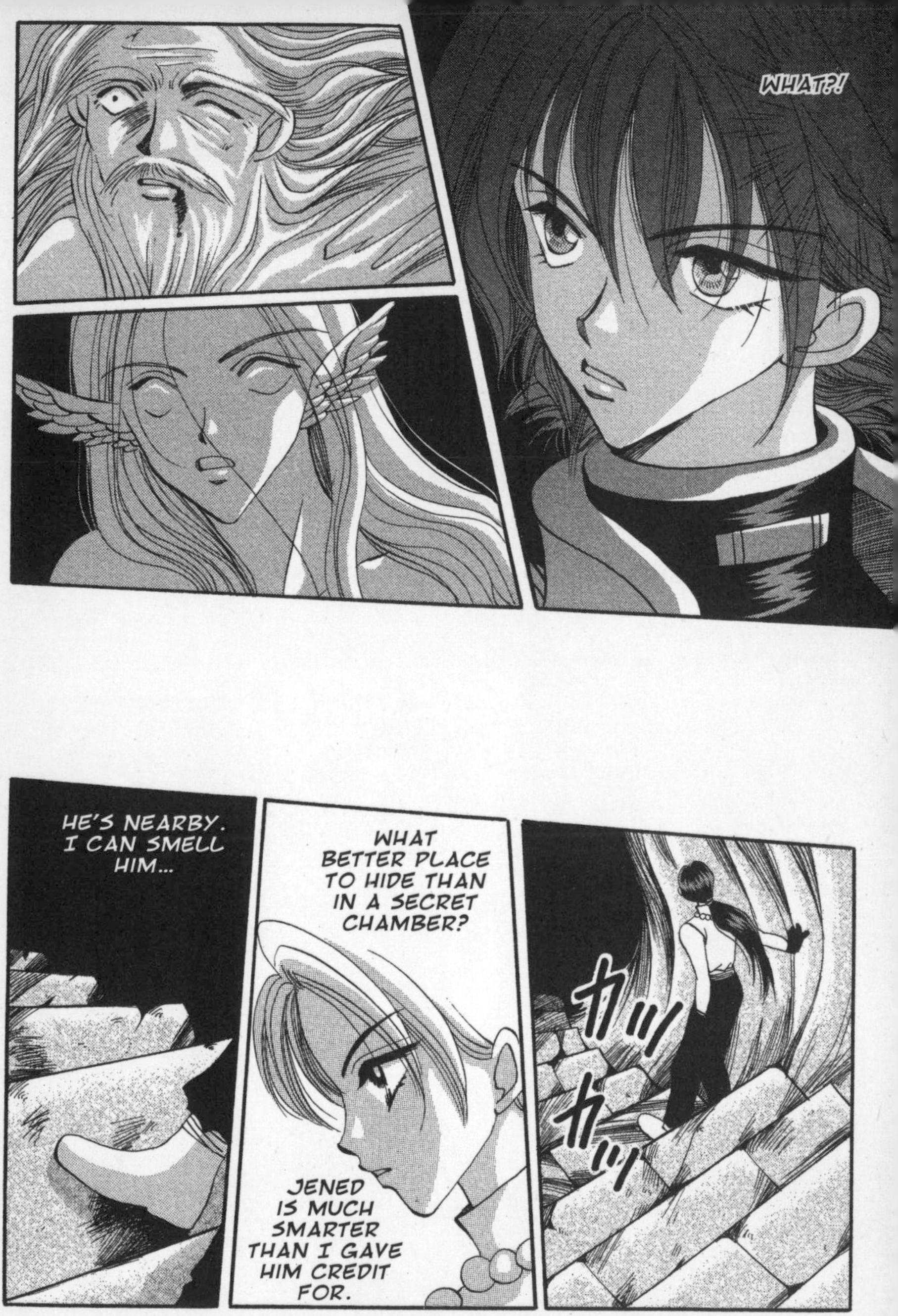
WHAT?!
カッ
カッ
WHAT BETTER PLACE TO HIDE THAN IN A SECRET CHAMBER?
JENED IS MUCH SMARTER THAN I GAVE HIM CREDIT FOR.
HE'S NEARBY. I CAN SMELL HIM...

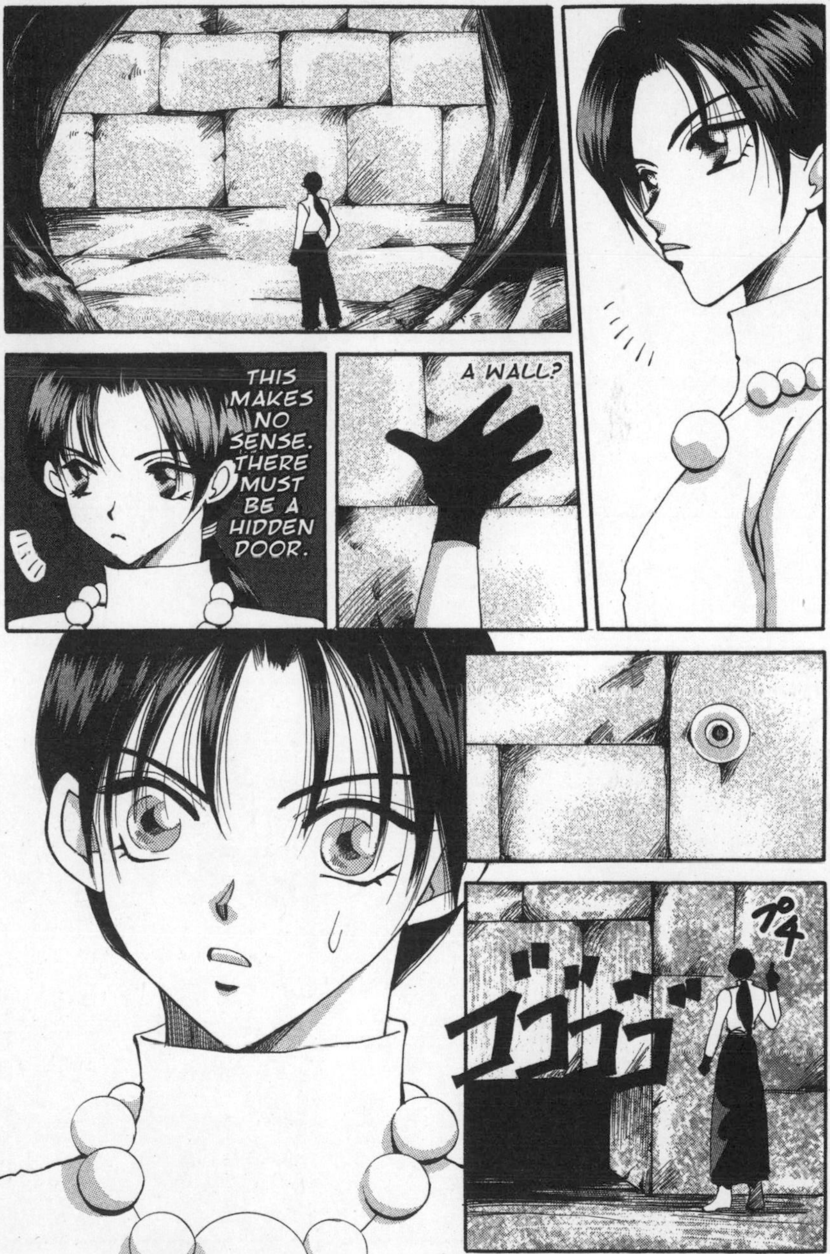
A WALL?
THIS MAKES NO SENSE. THERE MUST BE A HIDDEN DOOR.
ゴゴゴゴ

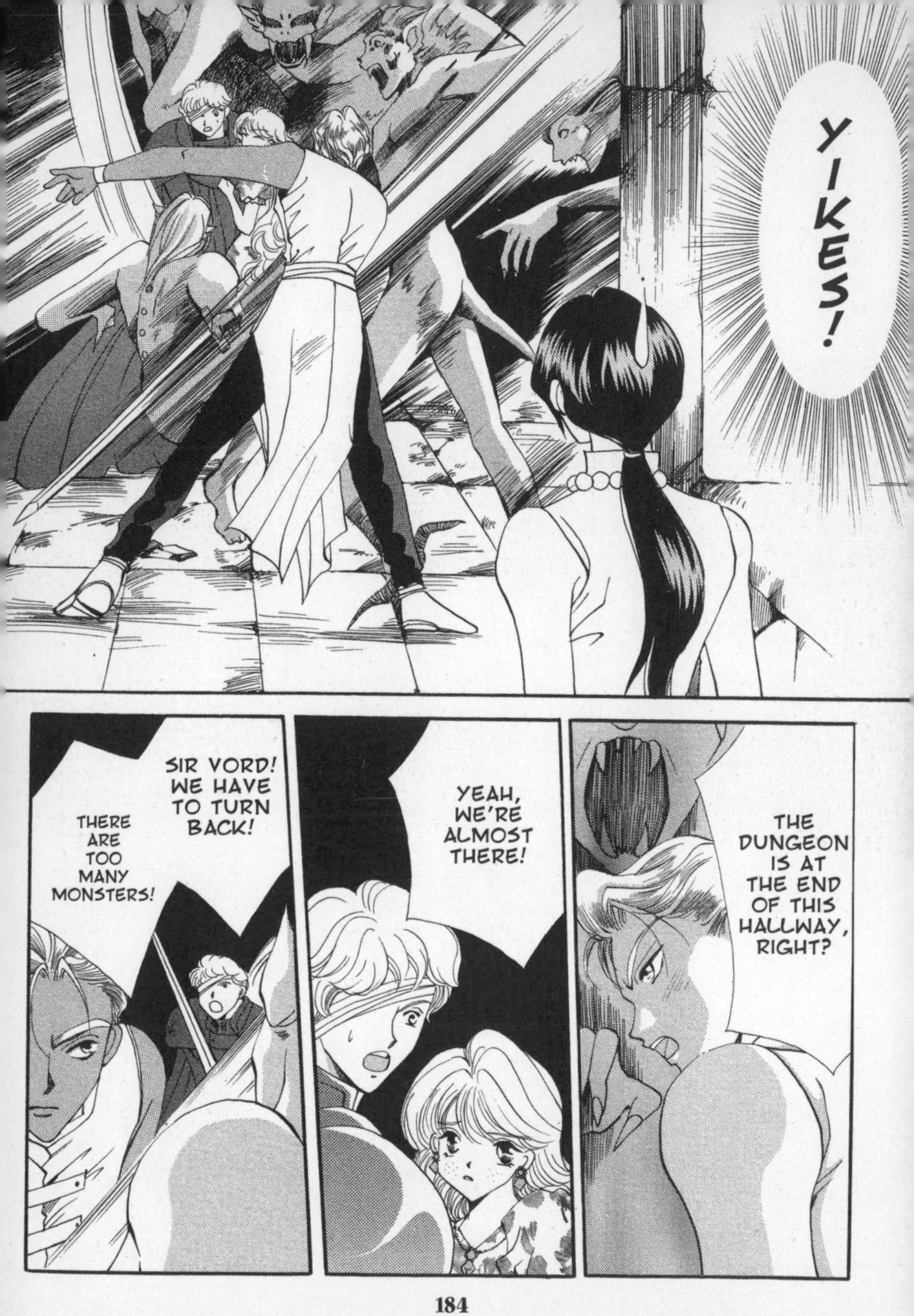
YIKES!
THE DUNGEON IS AT THE END OF THIS HALLWAY, RIGHT?
YEAH, WE'RE ALMOST THERE!
SIR VORD! WE HAVE TO TURN BACK!
THERE ARE TOO MANY MONSTERS!

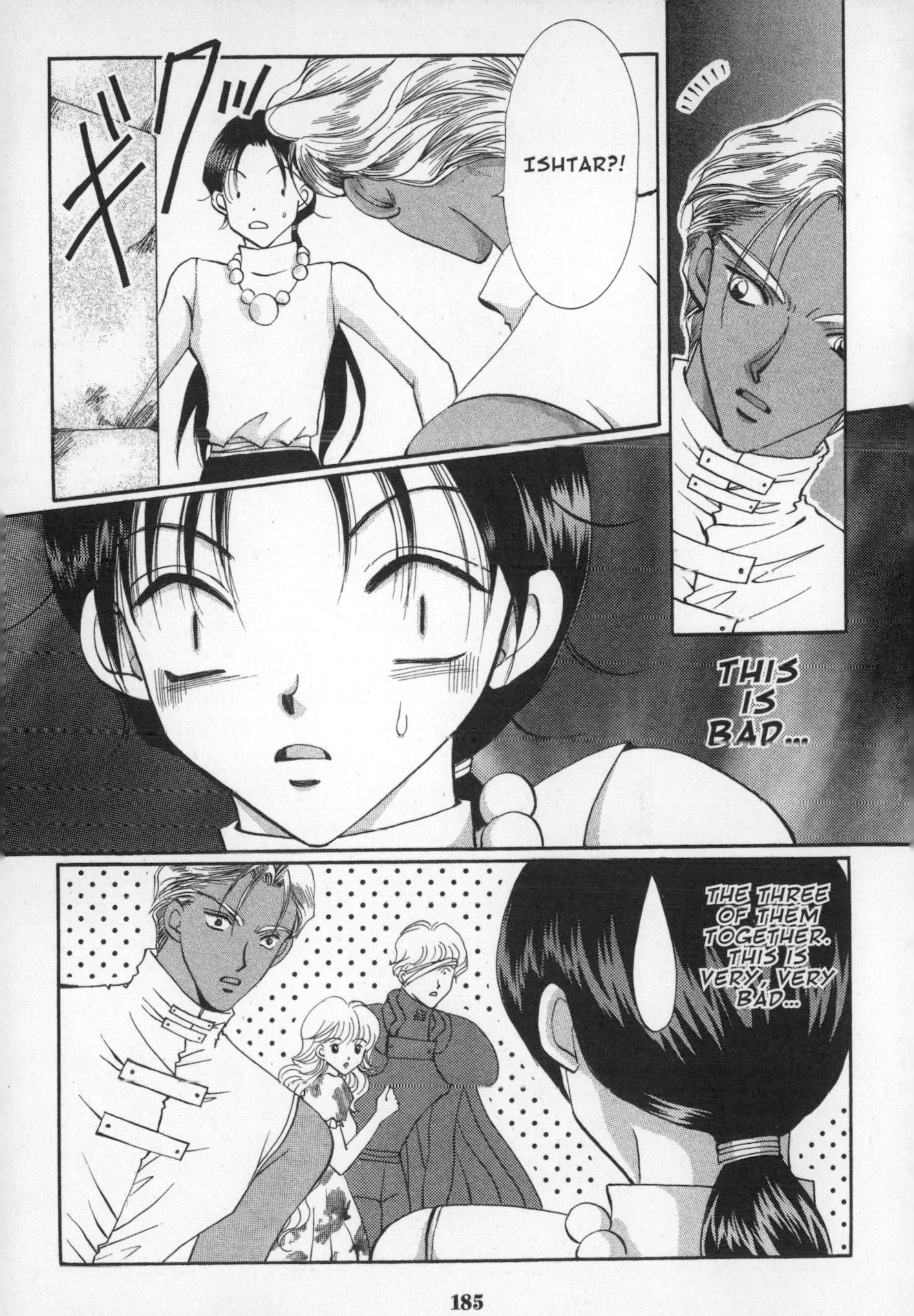
ISHTAR?!
ギクッ
THIS IS BAD...
THE THREE OF THEM TOGETHER. THIS IS VERY, VERY BAD...

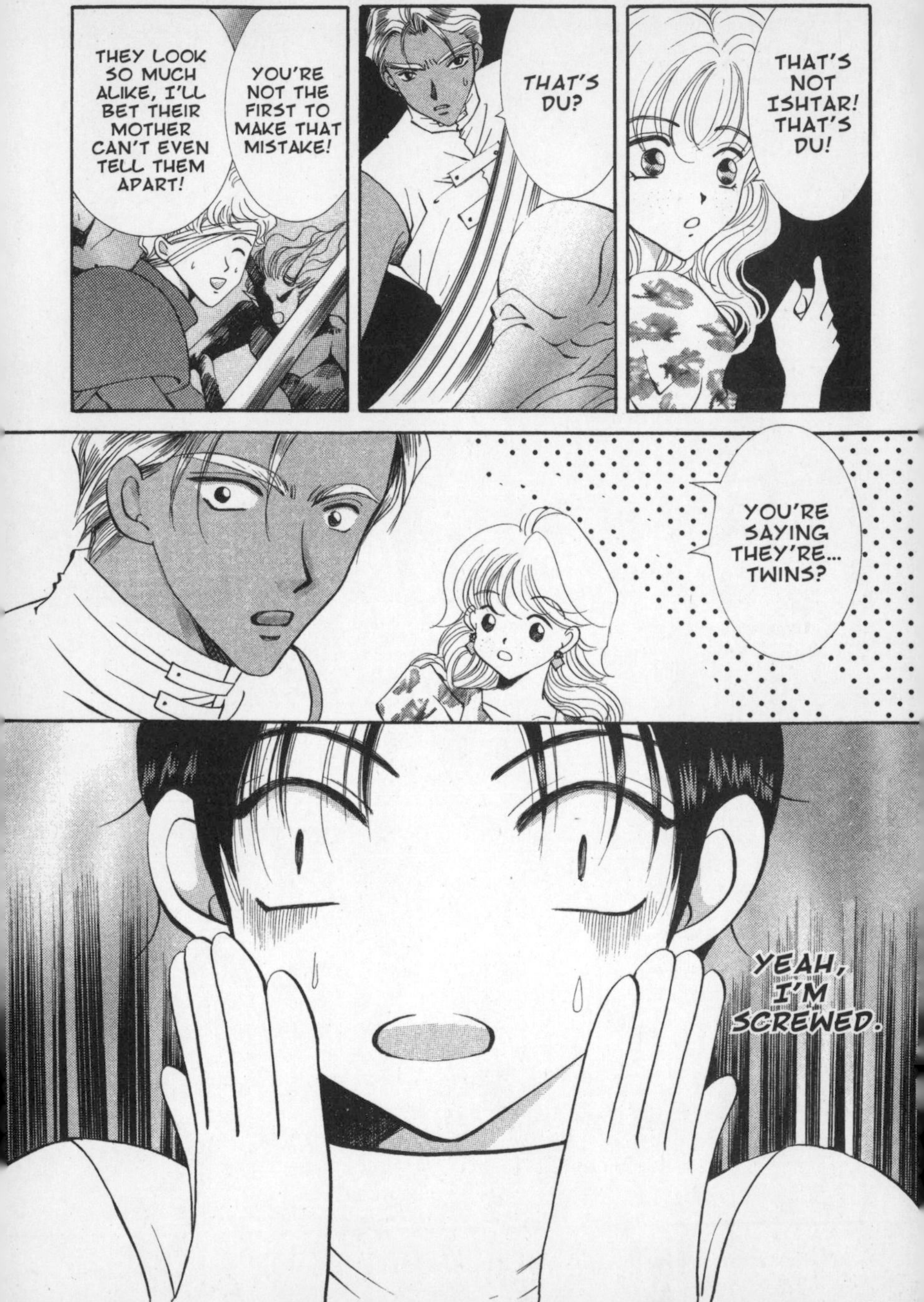
THAT'S NOT ISHTAR! THAT'S DU!
THAT'S DU?
YOU'RE NOT THE FIRST TO MAKE THAT MISTAKE!
THEY LOOK SO MUCH ALIKE, I'LL BET THEIR MOTHER CAN'T EVEN TELL THEM APART!
YOU'RE SAYING THEY'RE... TWINS?
YEAH, I'M SCREWED.

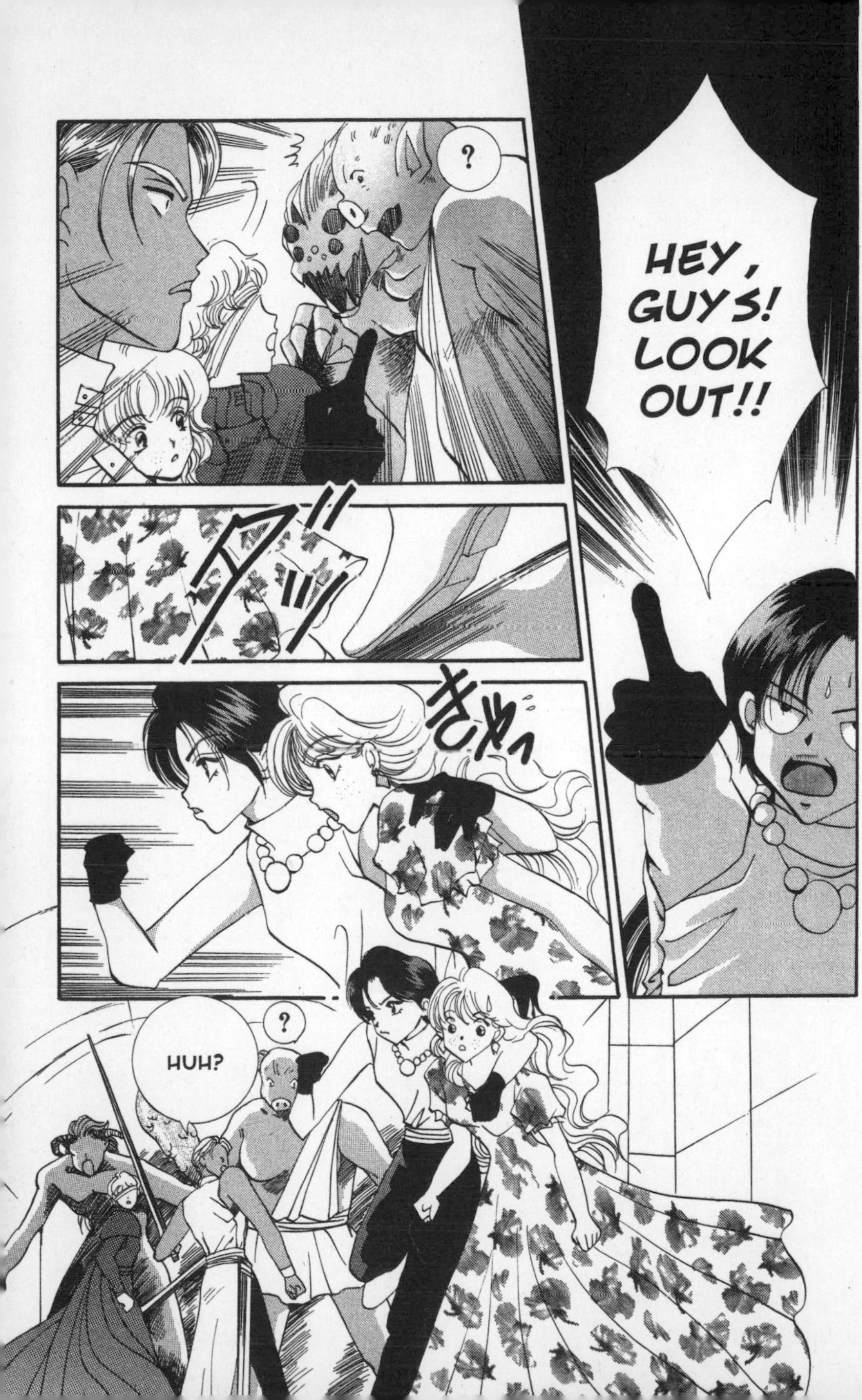
HEY, GUYS! LOOK OUT!!
?
ダッ
きゃっ
?
HUH?

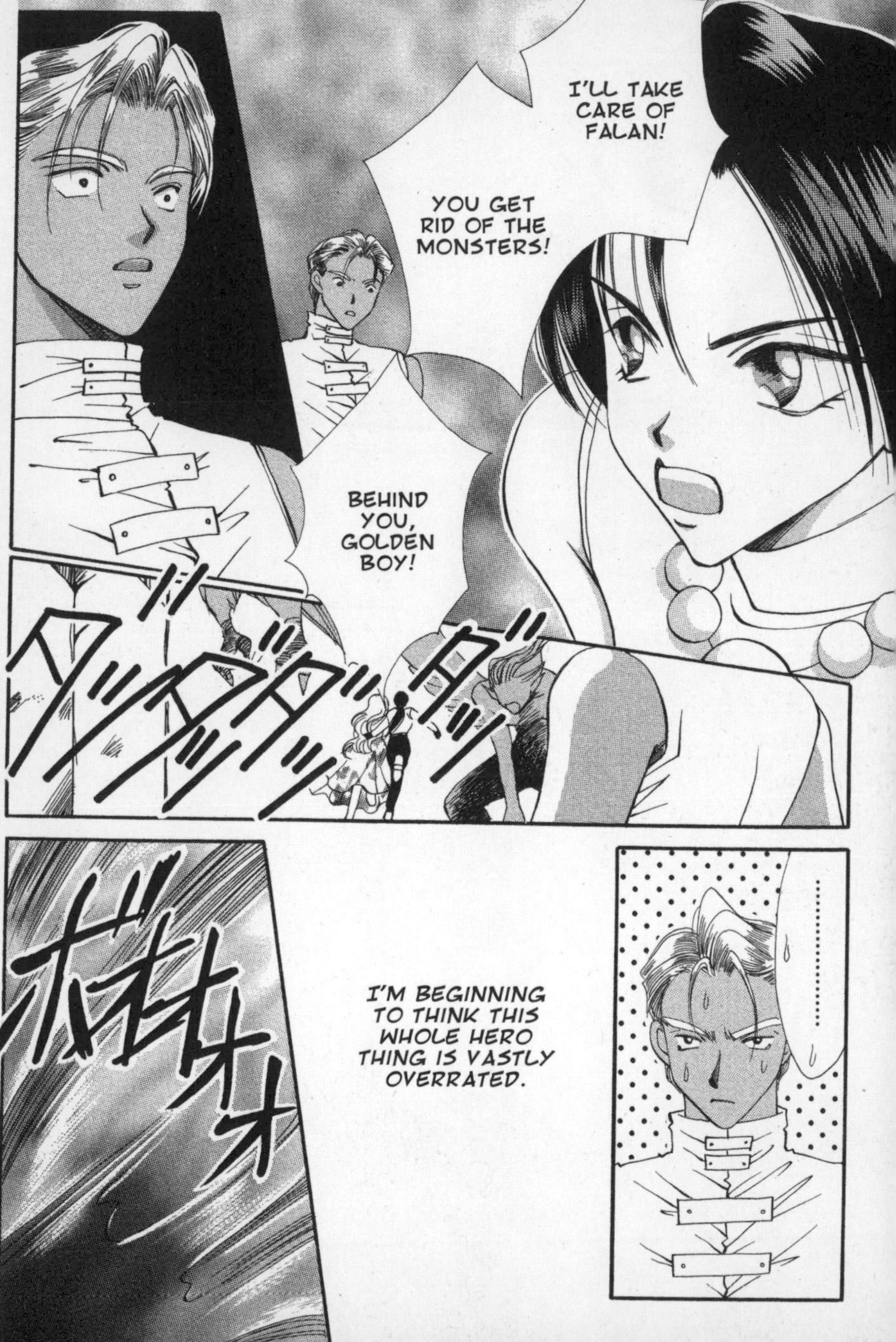
I'LL TAKE CARE OF FALAN!
YOU GET RID OF THE MONSTERS!
BEHIND YOU, GOLDEN BOY!
......
I'M BEGINNING TO THINK THIS WHOLE HERO THING IS VASTLY OVERRATED.

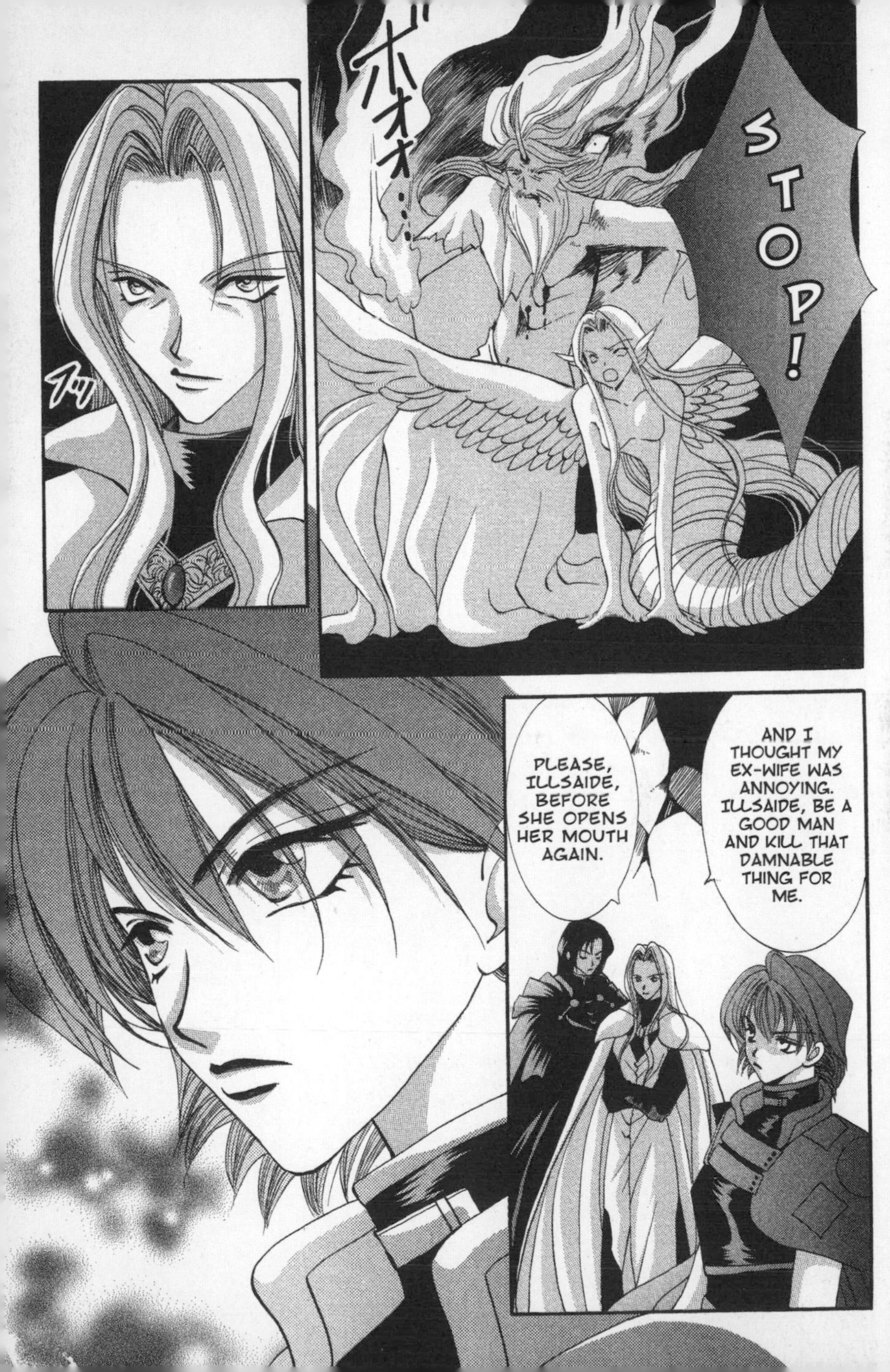
STOP!
AND I THOUGHT MY EX-WIFE WAS ANNOYING. ILLSAIDE, BE A GOOD MAN AND KILL THAT DAMNABLE THING FOR ME.
PLEASE, ILLSAIDE, BEFORE SHE OPENS HER MOUTH AGAIN.

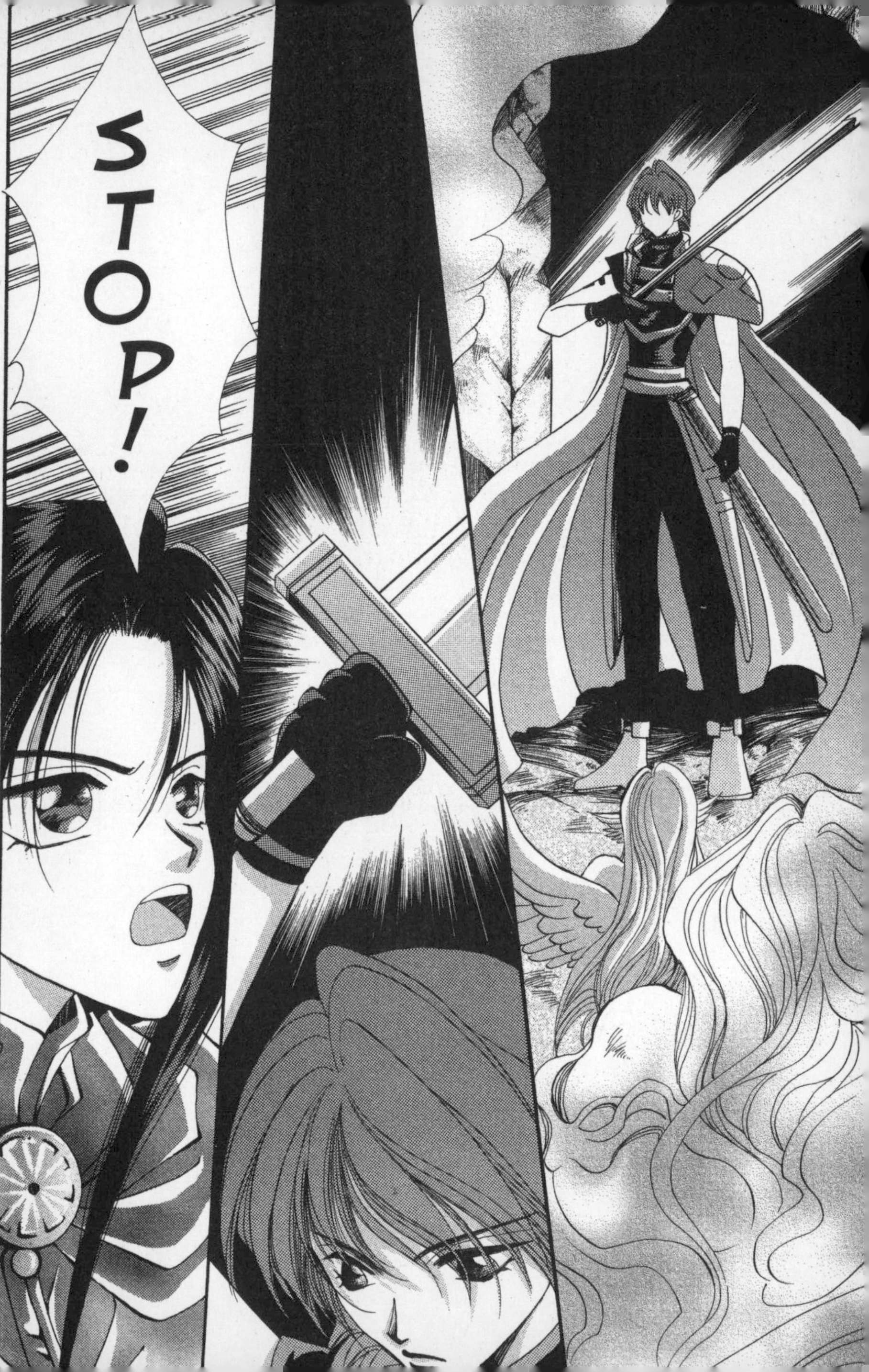
STOP!

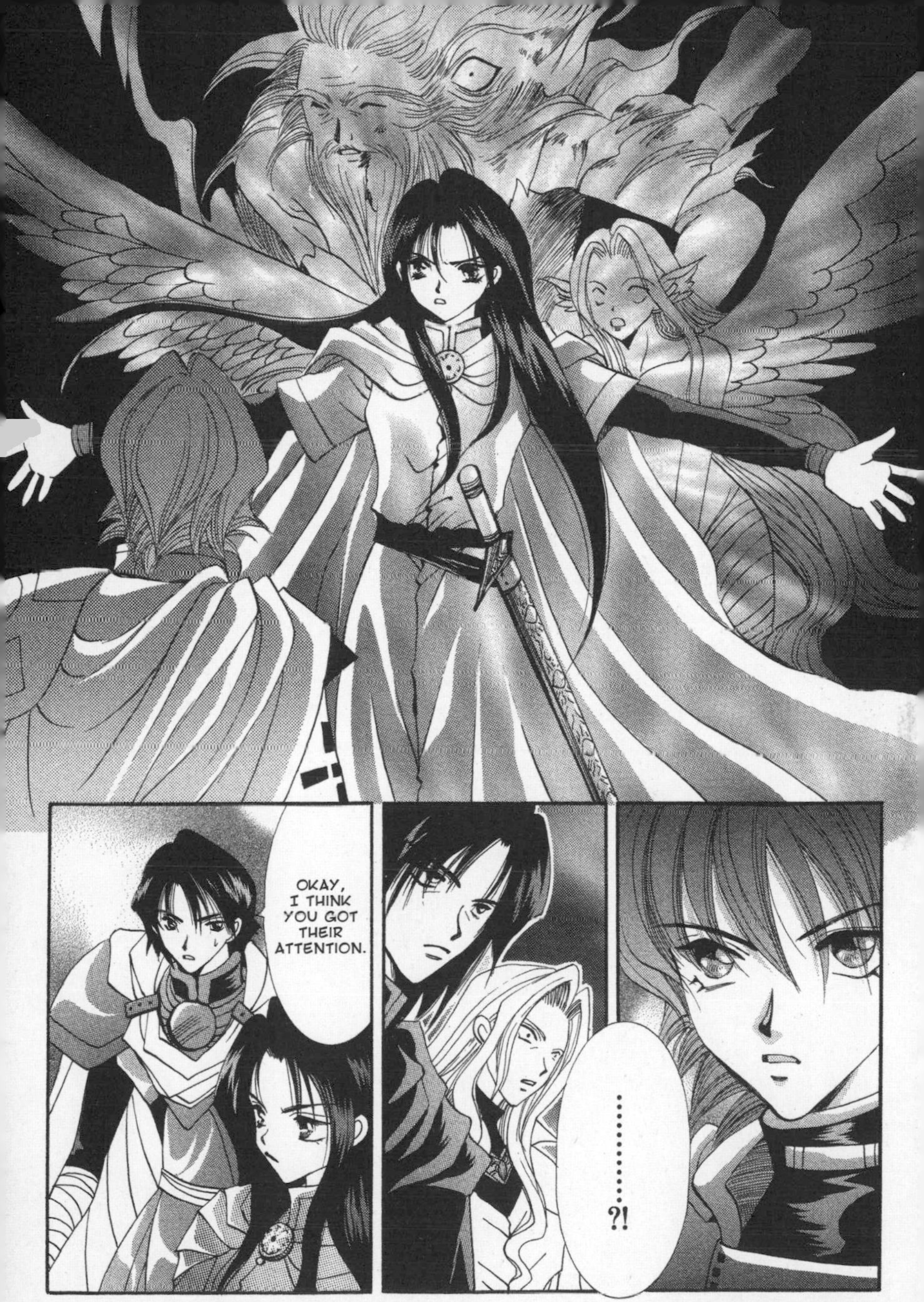

......?!
OKAY, I THINK YOU GOT THEIR ATTENTION.

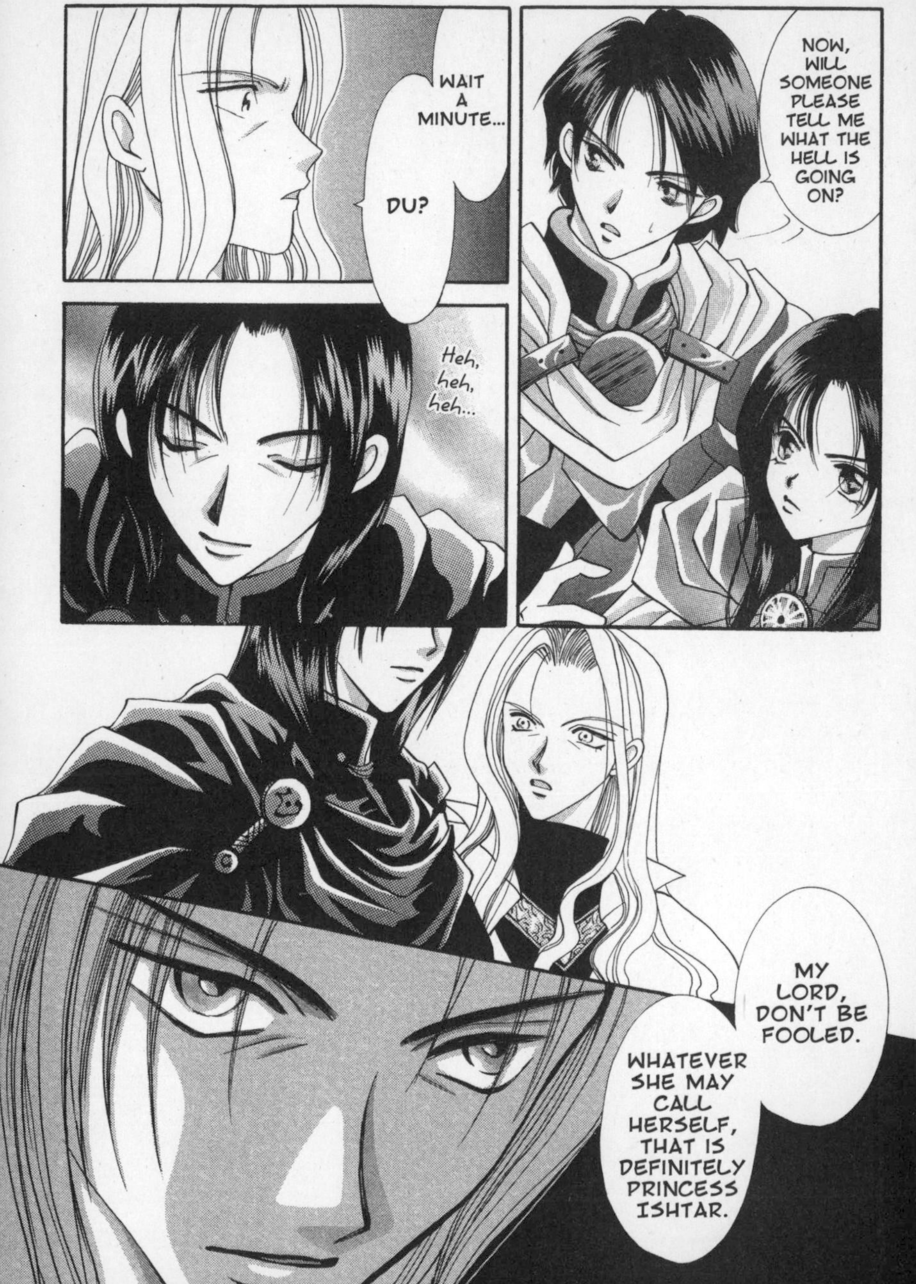
NOW, WILL SOMEONE PLEASE TELL ME WHAT THE HELL IS GOING ON?
WAIT A MINUTE...
DU?
Heh, heh, heh...
MY LORD, DON'T BE FOOLED.
WHATEVER SHE MAY CALL HERSELF, THAT IS DEFINITELY PRINCESS ISHTAR.

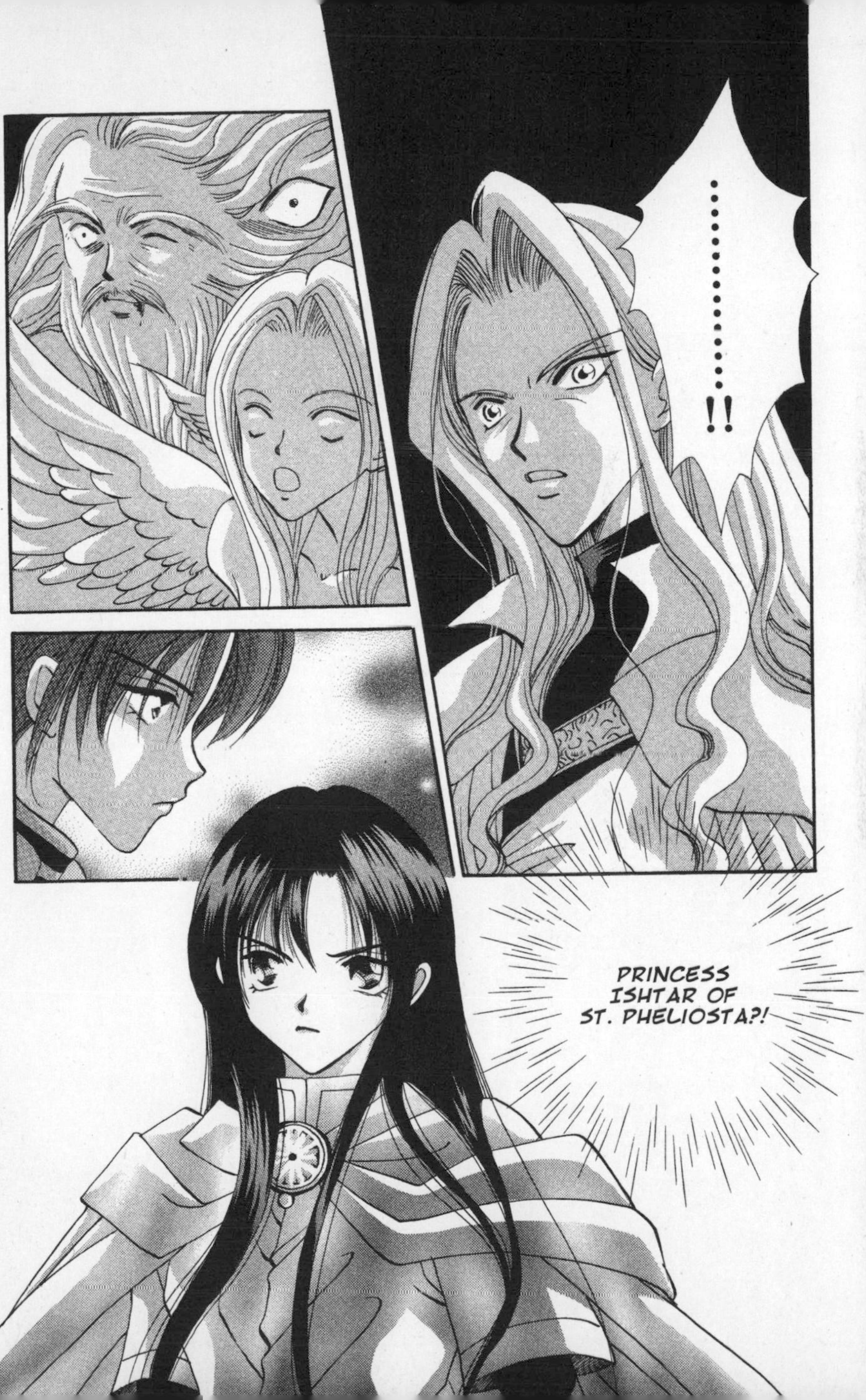
......!!
PRINCESS ISHTAR OF ST. PHELIOSTA?!

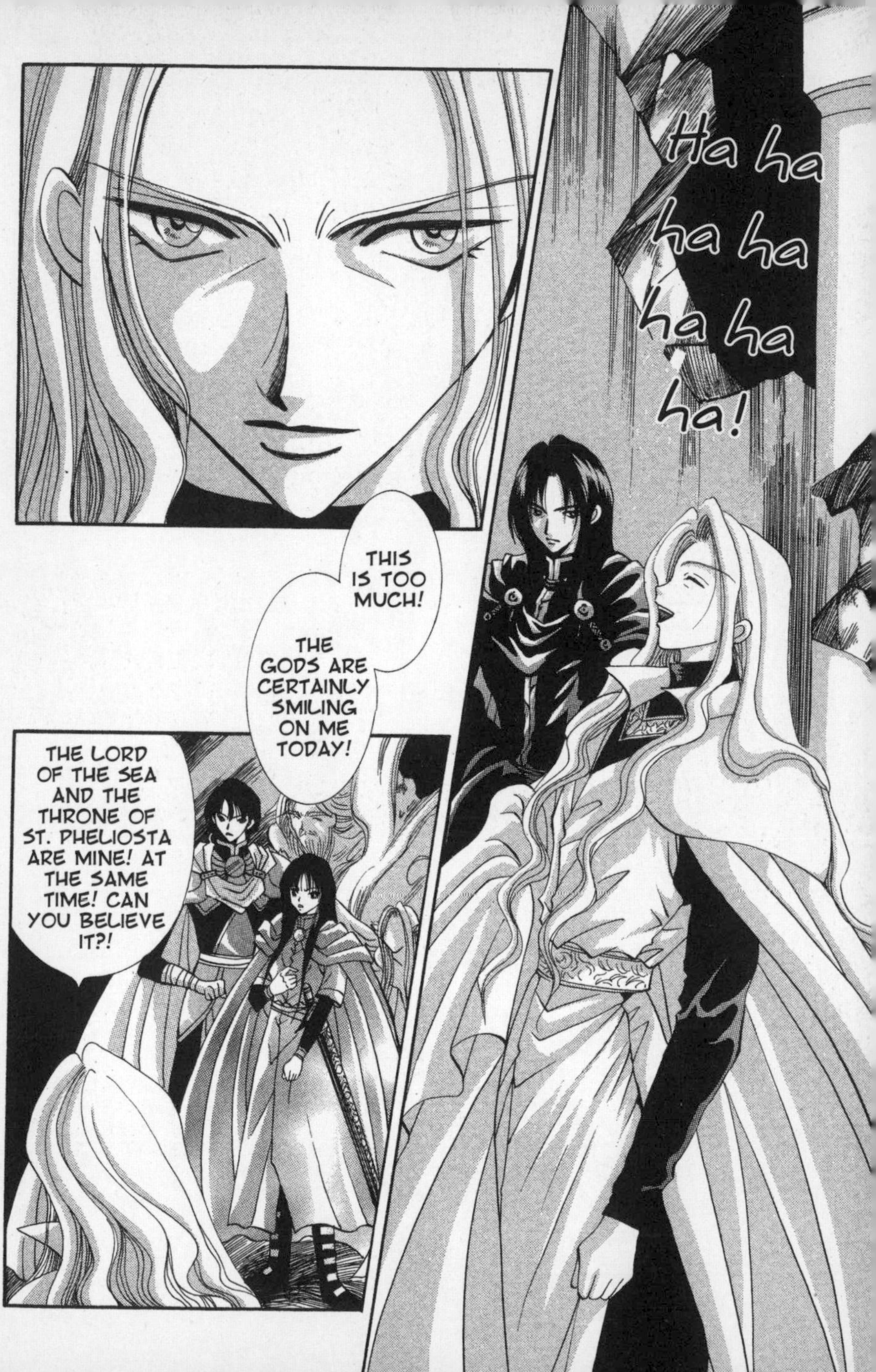
Ha ha ha ha ha ha ha!
THIS IS TOO MUCH!
THE GODS ARE CERTAINLY SMILING ON ME TODAY!
THE LORD OF THE SEA AND THE THRONE OF ST. PHELIOSTA ARE MINE! AT THE SAME TIME! CAN YOU BELIEVE IT?!

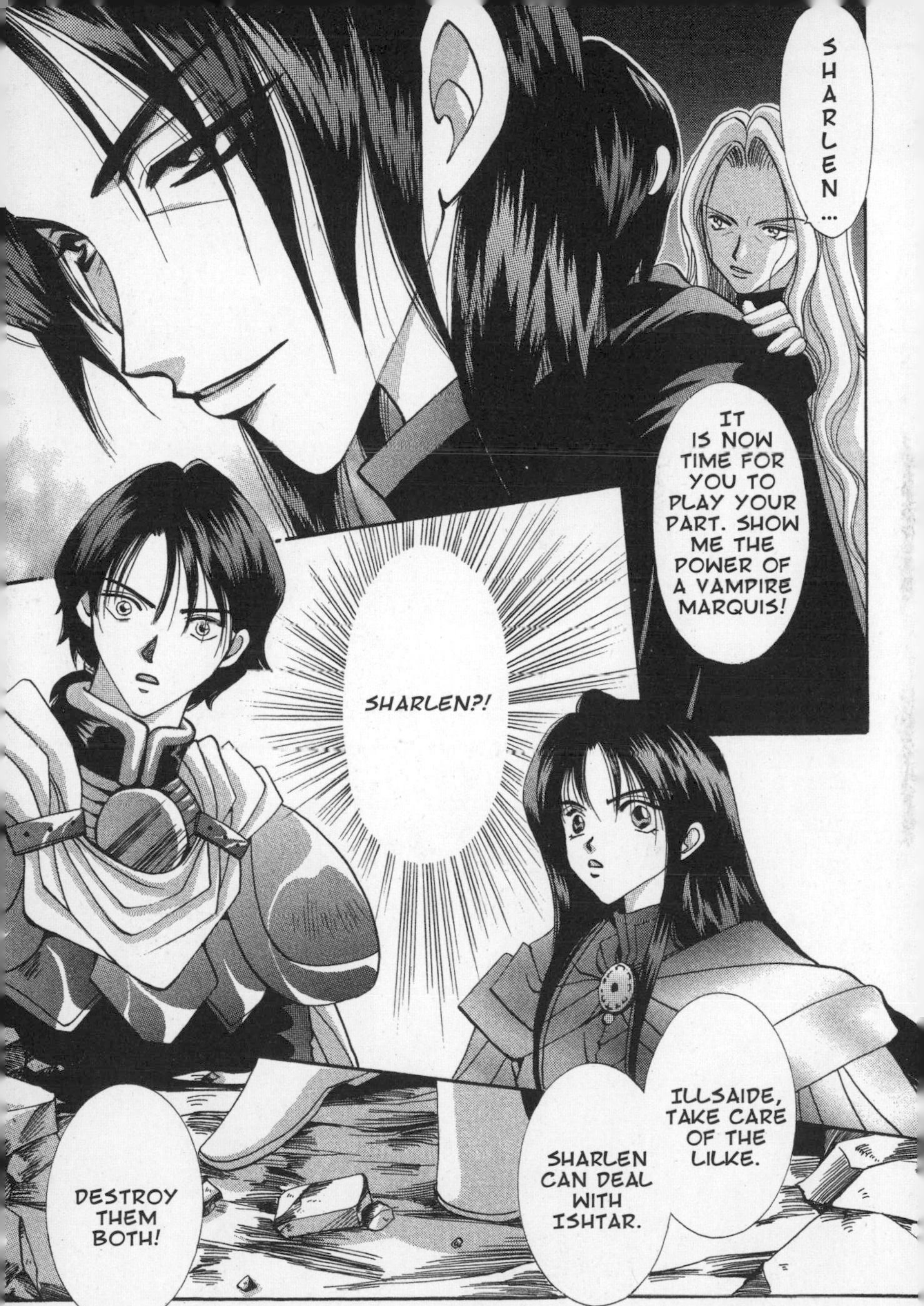
SHARLEN...
IT IS NOW TIME FOR YOU TO PLAY YOUR PART. SHOW ME THE POWER OF A VAMPIRE MARQUIS!
SHARLEN?!
ILLSAIDE, TAKE CARE OF THE LILKE.
SHARLEN CAN DEAL WITH ISHTAR.
DESTROY THEM BOTH!

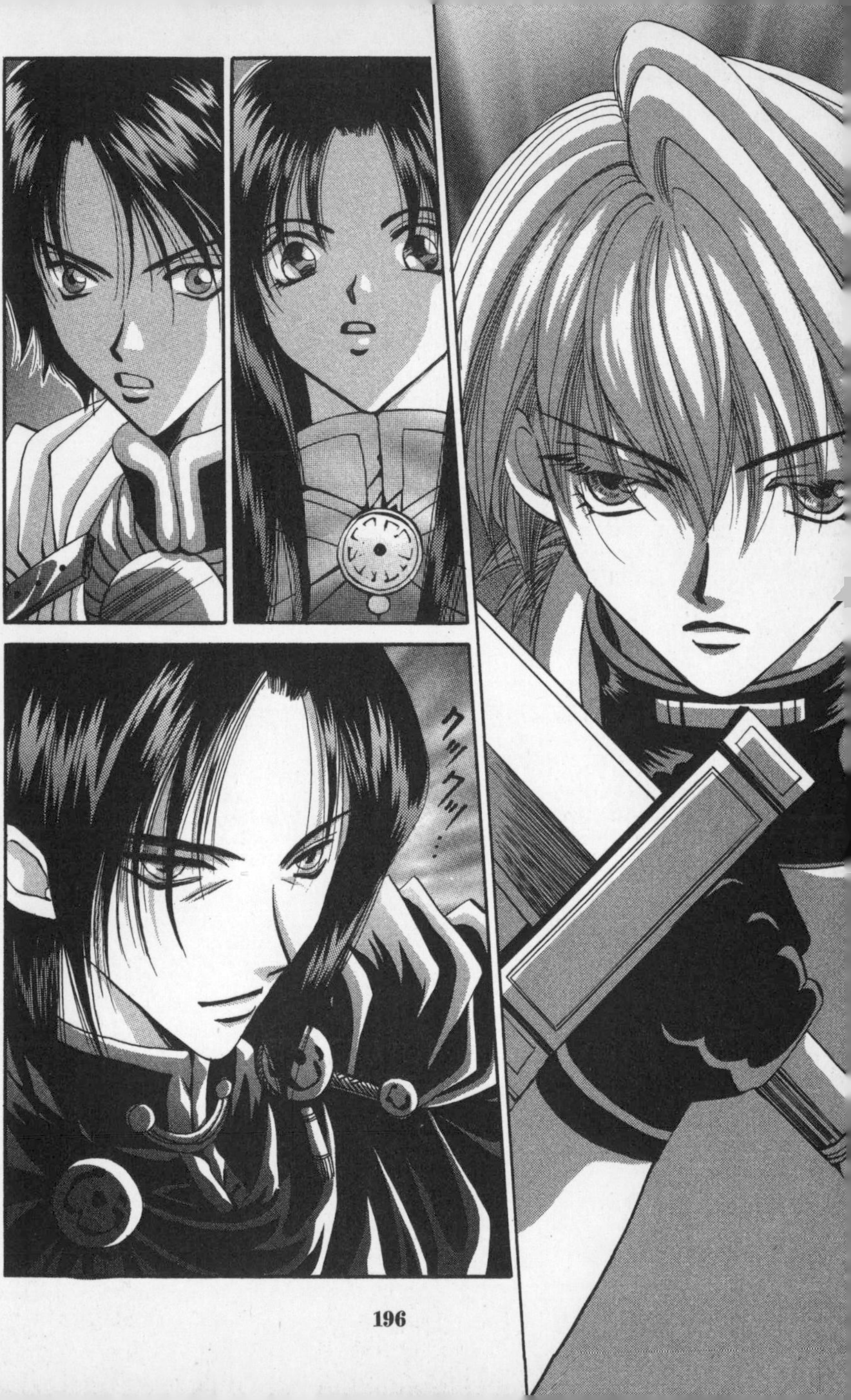
クックッ…

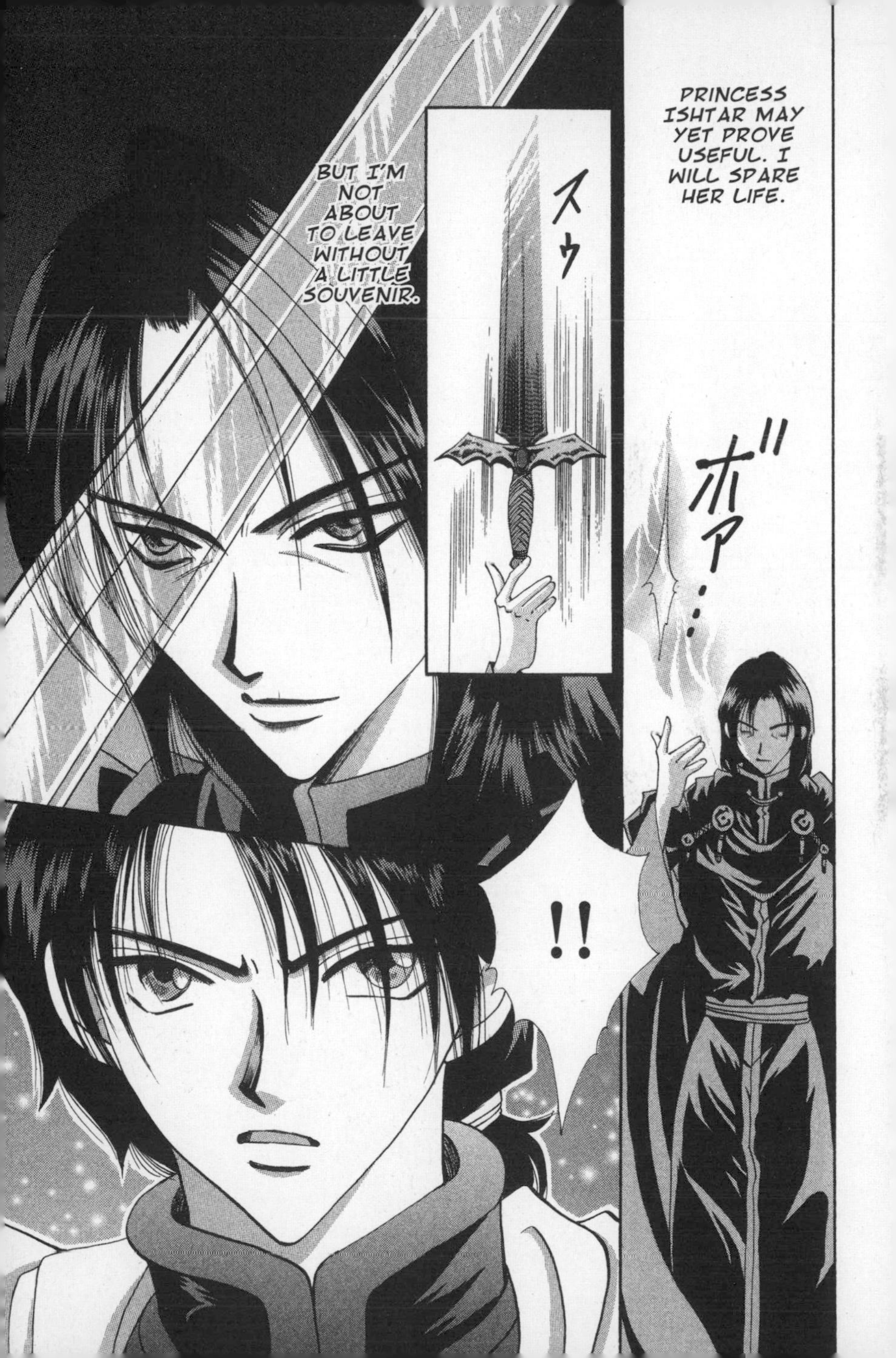
PRINCESS ISHTAR MAY YET PROVE USEFUL. I WILL SPARE HER LIFE.
ボア…
スゥ
BUT I'M NOT ABOUT TO LEAVE WITHOUT A LITTLE SOUVENIR.
!!

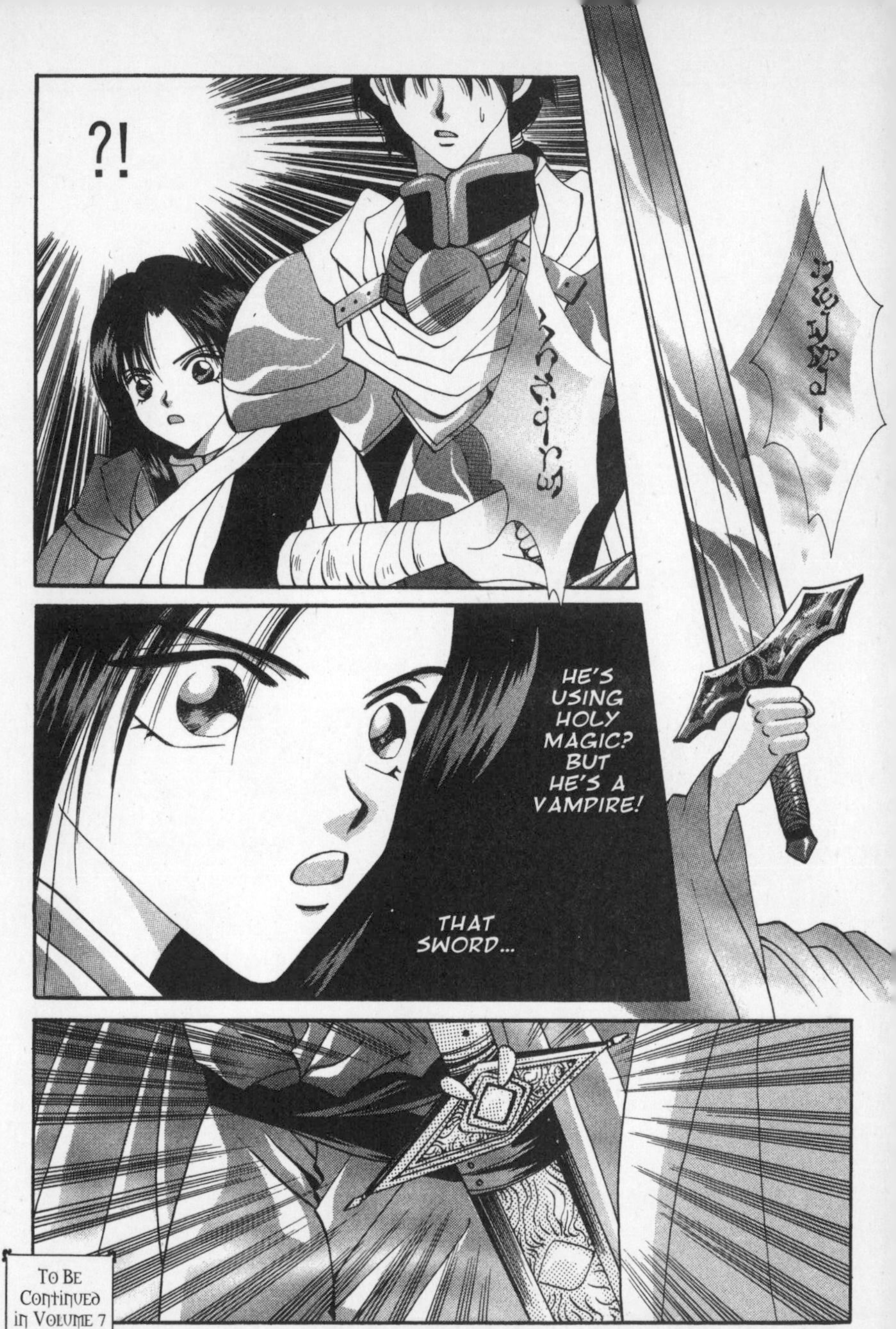
?!
HE'S USING HOLY MAGIC? BUT HE'S A VAMPIRE!
THAT SWORD...
To Be Continued in Volume 7

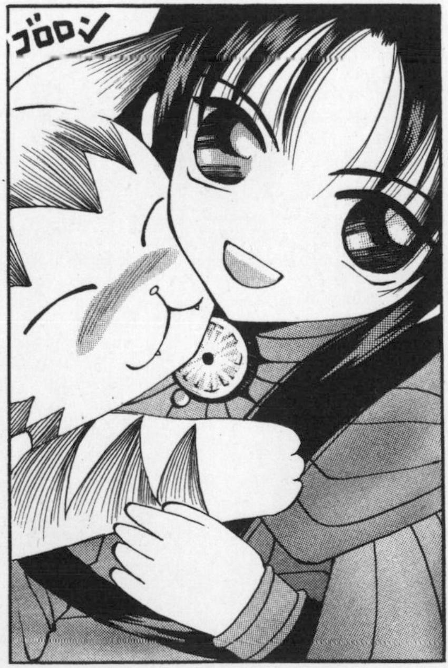
ゴロロン

Postscript

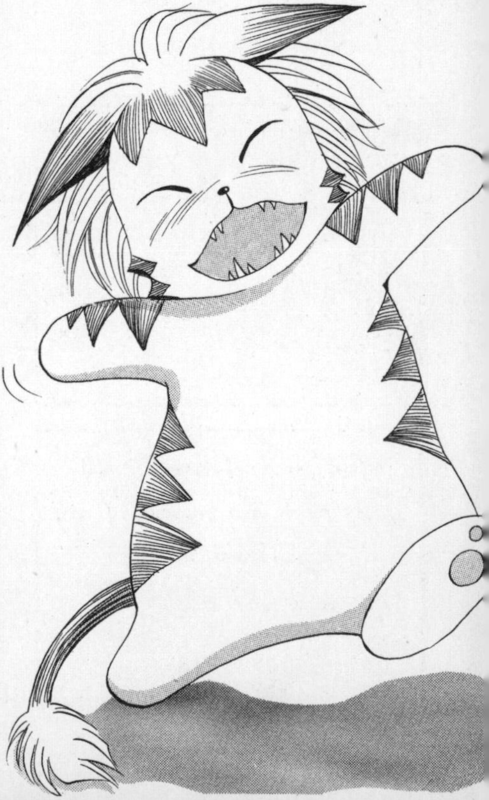

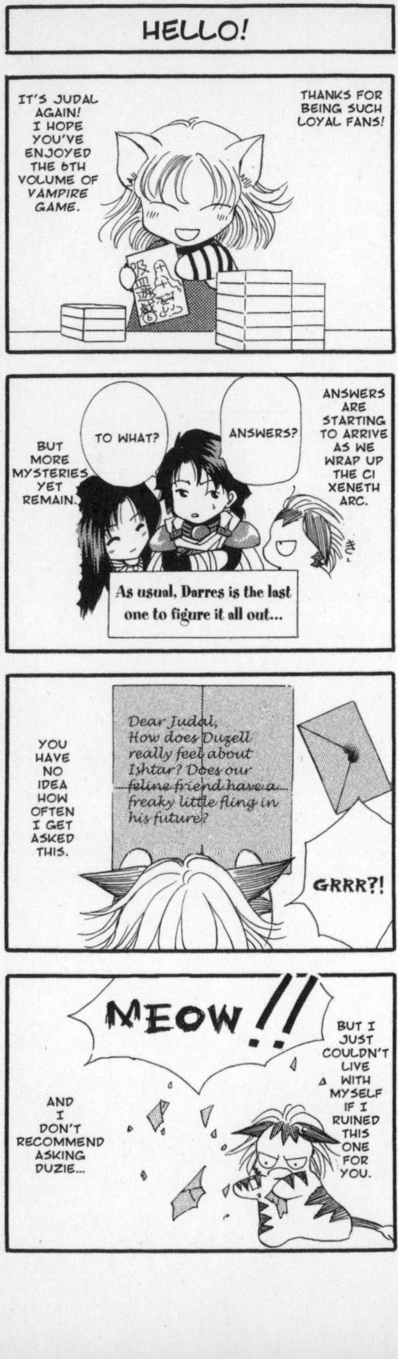
HELLO!
THANKS FOR BEING SUCH LOYAL FANS!
IT'S JUDAL AGAIN! I HOPE YOU'VE ENJOYED THE 6TH VOLUME OF VAMPIRE GAME.
ANSWERS ARE STARTING TO ARRIVE AS WE WRAP UP THE CI XENETH ARC.
ANSWERS?
TO WHAT?
BUT MORE MYSTERIES YET REMAIN.
As usual, Darres is the last one to figure it all out...
Dear Judal, How does Duzell really feel about Ishtar? Does our feline friend have a freaky little fling in his future?
YOU HAVE NO IDEA HOW OFTEN I GET ASKED THIS.
GRRR?!
MEOW!!
BUT I JUST COULDN'T LIVE WITH MYSELF IF I RUINED THIS ONE FOR YOU.
AND I DON'T RECOMMEND ASKING DUZIE...

LETTERS

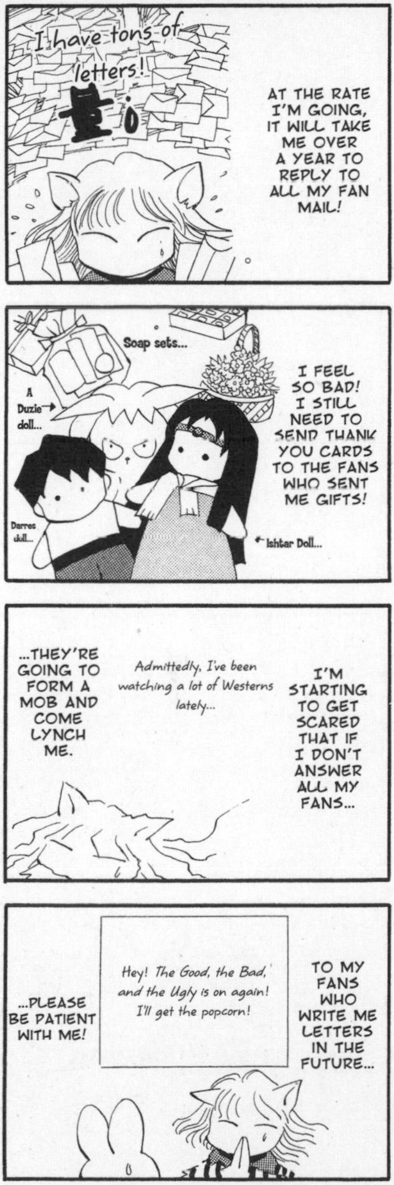

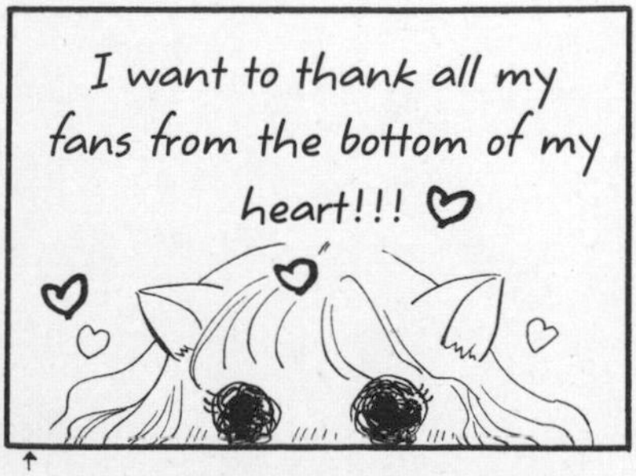

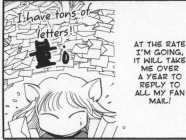

I have tons of letters!
AT THE RATE I'M GOING, IT WILL TAKE ME OVER A YEAR TO REPLY TO ALL MY FAN MAIL!
Soap sets...
A Duzie doll...
Darres doll...
Ishtar Doll...
I FEEL SO BAD! I STILL NEED TO SEND THANK YOU CARDS TO THE FANS WHO SENT ME GIFTS!
I'M STARTING TO GET SCARED THAT IF I DON'T ANSWER ALL MY FANS...
Admittedly, I've been watching a lot of Westerns lately...
...THEY'RE GOING TO FORM A MOB AND COME LYNCH ME.
TO MY FANS WHO WRITE ME LETTERS IN THE FUTURE...
Hey! The Good, the Bad, and the Ugly is on again! I'll get the popcorn!
...PLEASE BE PATIENT WITH ME!

MORE LETTERS

THE MOST POPULAR VAMPIRE GAME CHARACTERS ARE:

1. DUZELL
2. ISHTAR
3. DARRES
4. ILLSAIDE
5. VORD

ALL THE MAJOR CHARACTERS, REALLY. SEILIEZ IS PRETTY POPULAR TOO. BUT WHERE'S THE LOVE FOR KRAI?

MOST FANS WANT TO SEE THESE COUPLES GET TOGETHER:

1. ISHTAR AND DARRES
2. ISHTAR AND DUZELL
3. ILLSAIDE AND FALAN
4. ILLSAIDE AND DUZELL
5. DARRES AND YUJINN

NO ONE WANTS TO SEE JILL AND KRAI HOOK UP?

MY FAVORITE COMMENTS FROM FANS:

1. I STARTED READING VG AFTER A (FRIEND, SIBLING ETC) RECOMMENDED IT.

2. READING VG LETS ME FORGET ABOUT THE NEGATIVE THINGS IN MY LIFE. I READ VG TO RELAX. IT MAKES ME WANT TO BE A BETTER PERSON.

3. YOU'RE A VERY SEXY LITTLE CAT-GIRL THING. I'M HUNGRY. I'M GONNA MAKE A SANDWICH.

THANKS FOR THE PRAISE, GUYS. I THINK.

I want to thank all my fans from the bottom of my heart!!!

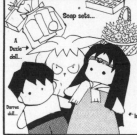

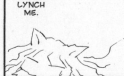

QUIZ ANSWERS

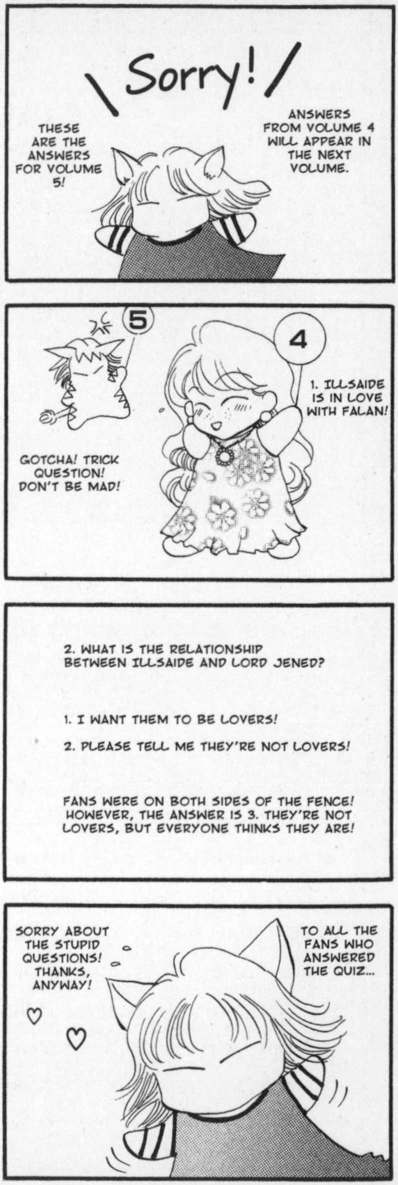
\ Sorry! /
ANSWERS FROM VOLUME 4 WILL APPEAR IN THE NEXT VOLUME.
THESE ARE THE ANSWERS FOR VOLUME 5!
4
1. ILLSAIDE IS IN LOVE WITH FALAN!
5
GOTCHA! TRICK QUESTION! DON'T BE MAD!
2. WHAT IS THE RELATIONSHIP BETWEEN ILLSAIDE AND LORD JENED?
1. I WANT THEM TO BE LOVERS!
2. PLEASE TELL ME THEY'RE NOT LOVERS!
FANS WERE ON BOTH SIDES OF THE FENCE! HOWEVER, THE ANSWER IS 3. THEY'RE NOT LOVERS, BUT EVERYONE THINKS THEY ARE!
TO ALL THE FANS WHO ANSWERED THE QUIZ...
SORRY ABOUT THE STUPID QUESTIONS! THANKS, ANYWAY!

AND FINALLY...

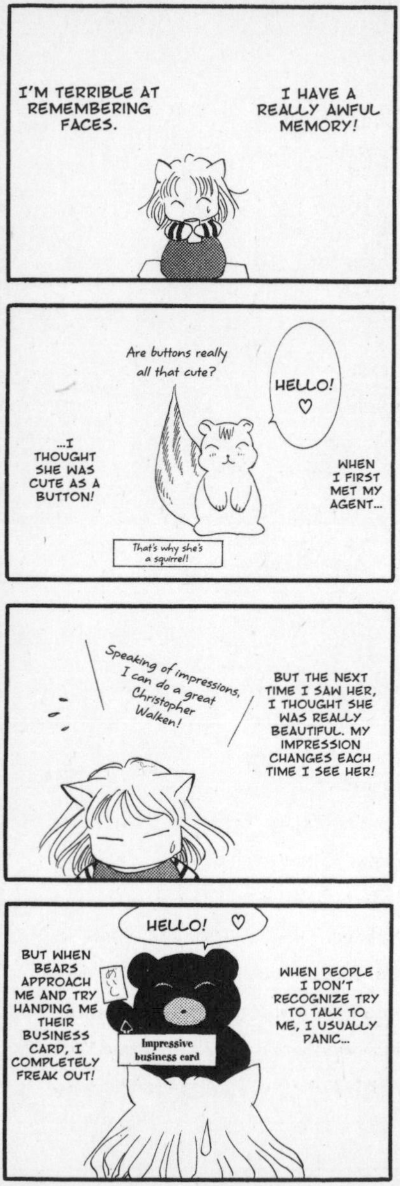
I HAVE A REALLY AWFUL MEMORY!
I'M TERRIBLE AT REMEMBERING FACES.
HELLO! ♡
Are buttons really all that cute?
WHEN I FIRST MET MY AGENT...
...I THOUGHT SHE WAS CUTE AS A BUTTON!
That's why she's a squirrel!
BUT THE NEXT TIME I SAW HER, I THOUGHT SHE WAS REALLY BEAUTIFUL. MY IMPRESSION CHANGES EACH TIME I SEE HER!
Speaking of impressions, I can do a great Christopher Walken!
HELLO! ♡
WHEN PEOPLE I DON'T RECOGNIZE TRY TO TALK TO ME, I USUALLY PANIC...
BUT WHEN BEARS APPROACH ME AND TRY HANDING ME THEIR BUSINESS CARD, I COMPLETELY FREAK OUT!
めいし
Impressive business card

VAMPIRE GAME

Next issue...

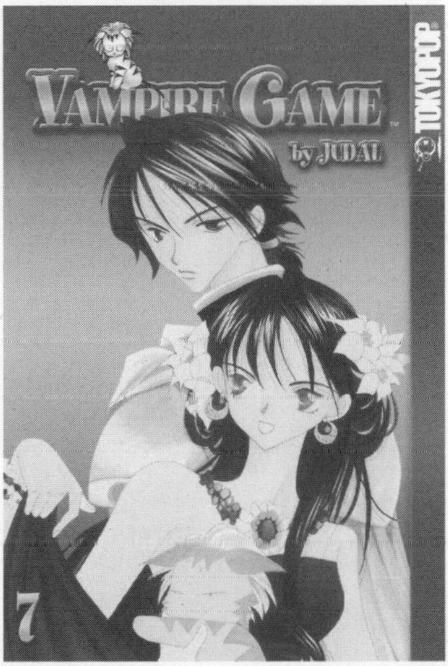
VAMPIRE GAME
by JUDAI
TOKYOPOP
7

So what's worse then finding your castle overrun by cranky monsters? Finding it overrun by cranky, hungry monsters, which is the very spot in which Jened finds himself at the start of our next volume. While the monsters run rampant, chewing everything in sight, Darres finds himself locking blades with none other than Sharlen. Severely outmatched, our hero stands little chance of defeating the Vampire Marquis on his own. Darres shouldn't take it personally. After all, with the exception of Illsaide, it's hard to imagine anyone who could. Unfortunately, Illsaide is too busy reeling in shock to be of much help to anyone. What startling event could shake the young captain to his very core? It's one of the many secrets ready to be revealed as the Ci Xeneth arc comes to its spectacular close!

ALSO AVAILABLE FROM  TOKYOPOP®

For more information visit www.TOKYOPOP.com

03.03.04T

ALSO AVAILABLE FROM TOKYOPOP®

MANGA

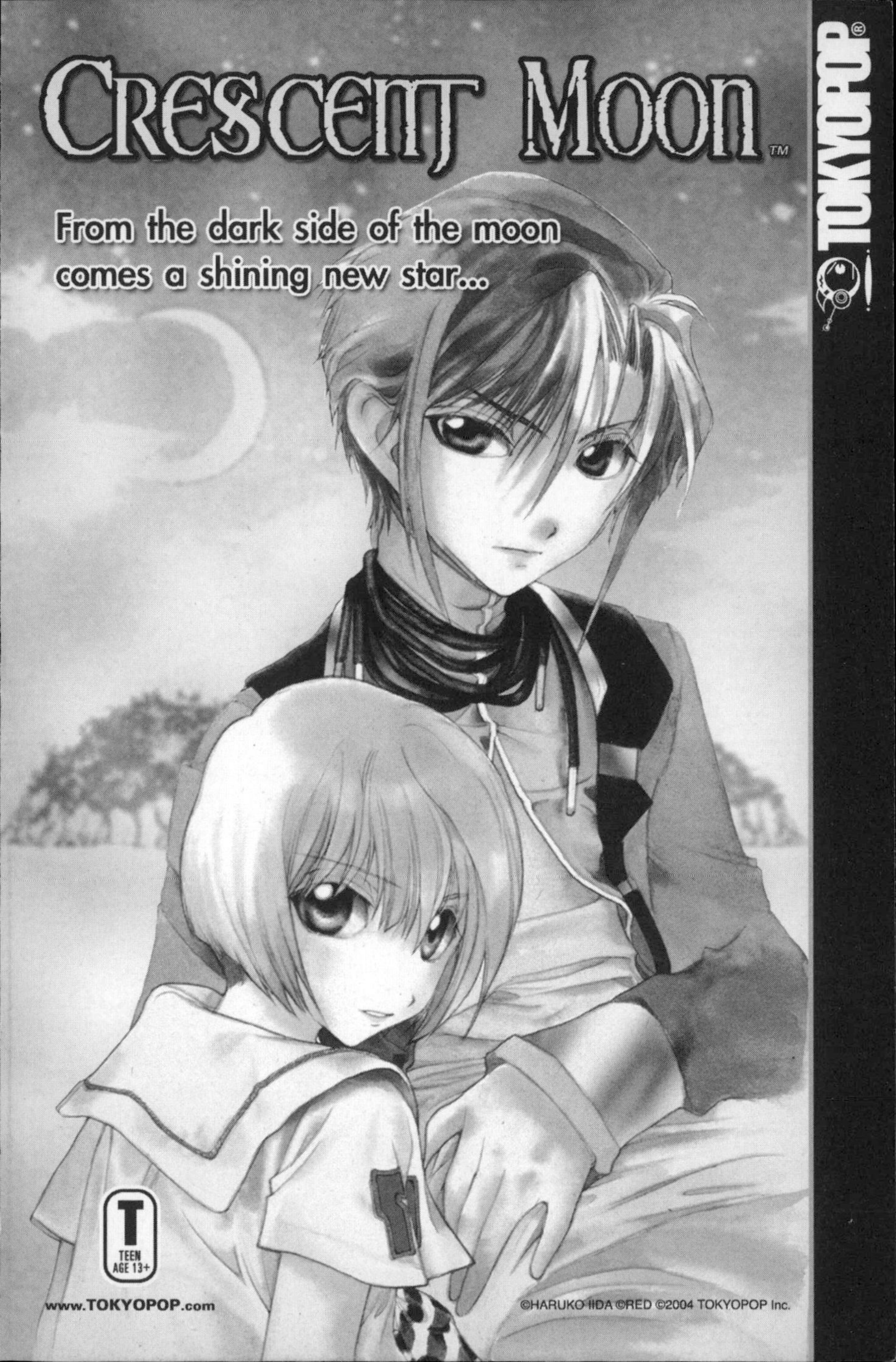
CRESCENT MOON™
From the dark side of the moon
comes a shining new star...
TOKYOPOP®
T
TEEN
AGE 13+
www.TOKYOPOP.com
©HARUKO IIDA ©RED ©2004 TOKYOPOP Inc.

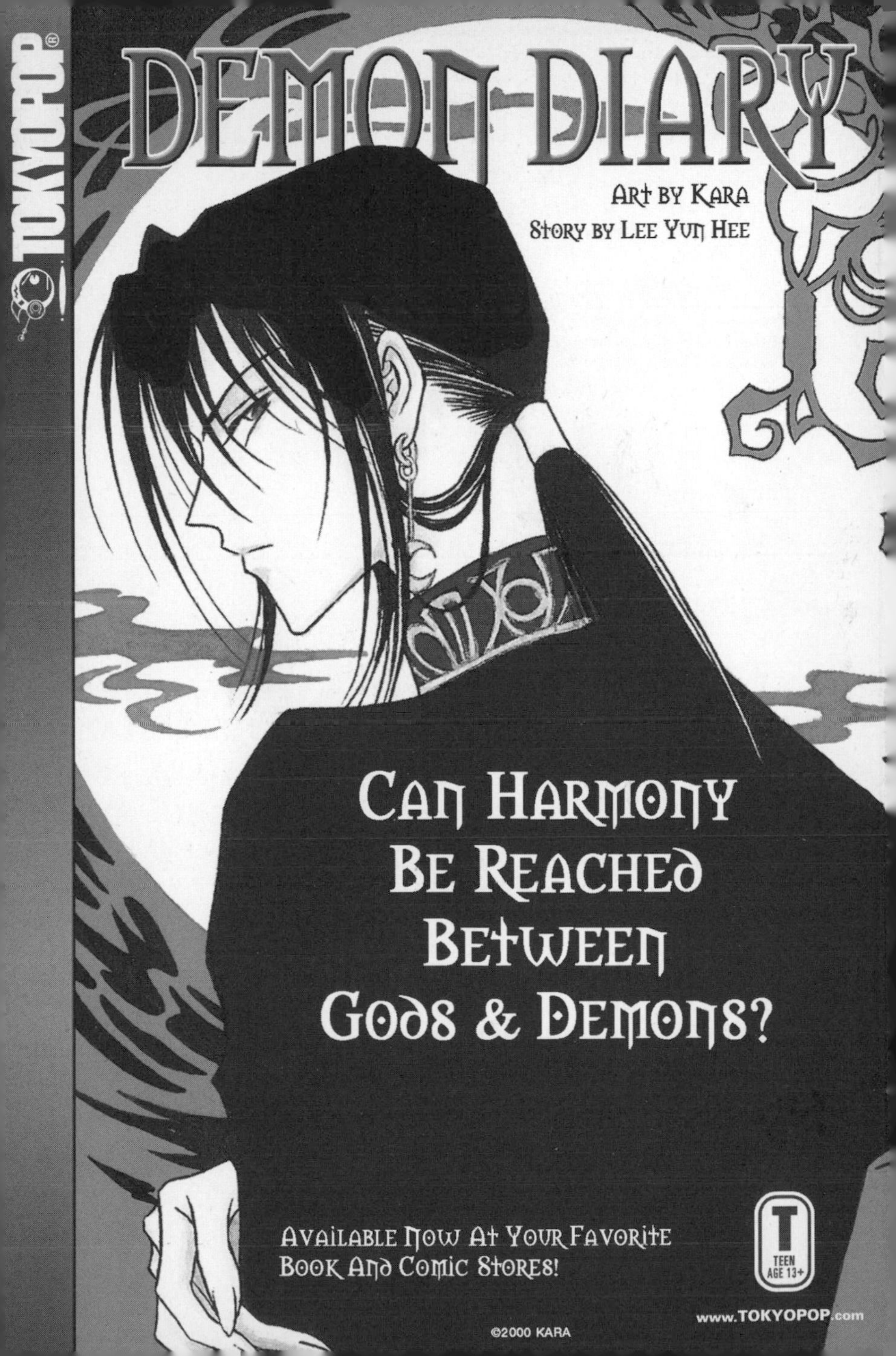
TOKYOPOP
DEMON DIARY
Art by Kara
Story by Lee Yun Hee
Can Harmony Be Reached Between Gods & Demons?
Available Now At Your Favorite Book And Comic Stores!
T TEEN AGE 13+
www.TOKYOPOP.com
©2000 KARA

STOP!

This is the back of the book.
You wouldn't want to spoil a great ending!

This book is printed "manga-style," in the authentic Japanese right-to-left format. Since none of the artwork has been flipped or altered, readers get to experience the story just as the creator intended. You've been asking for it, so TOKYOPOP® delivered: authentic, hot-off-the-press, and far more fun!

DIRECTIONS

If this is your first time reading manga-style, here's a quick guide to help you understand how it works.

It's easy... just start in the top right panel and follow the numbers. Have fun, and look for more 100% authentic manga from TOKYOPOP®!